3_

A WORLD TO THE WEST

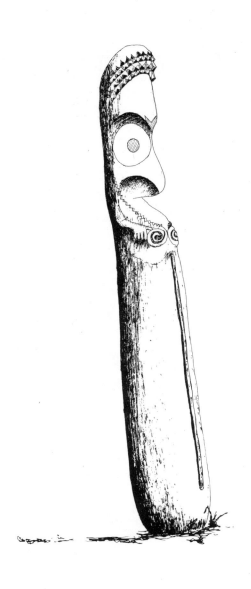

A World to the West

A Voyage Around the World

Maurice R.
Cloughley

Illustrated

David McKay Company, Inc.
New York

Library of Congress Cataloging in Publication Data
Cloughley, Maurice R.
   A world to the west.
   1. Nanook (Ketch)   2. Cloughley, Maurice R.
3. Voyages around the world—1951–   I. Title.
G420.N33C57   910'.41'0924   79-261
ISBN 0-679-51453-8

10 9 8 7 6 5 4 3 2 1

Manufactured in the United States of America

To the one who shared it all with me, the dreaming and the reality, the exhilaration, the tedium and hard work, the romance and sometimes the awful horror of it; who endured months of fear and sickness without complaint and who cheated disgracefully in the reckoning of her watches so that I might sleep all the longer.

To Katie

Contents

Track Charts

Prologue

Our first dawn of the year in Grise Fiord came on the tenth of February. Sunrise and sunset were virtually one for only the merest tip of the sun showed itself for a few moments before disappearing again behind the far distant icecaps of Devon Island.

I took my gang of Eskimo kids far up the valley that day starting off from the school in the darkness of mid-morning.

"Ilisaisi," ("teacher," for so I was known to everyone), *"Ilisaisi,* you are not Eskimo. You are *kadloona,"* they'd taunted when I expressed earlier reservations about the venture. "Maybe you nose will frozen."

So of course we went. It was 38 below but there was no wind. We scrambled from the valley floor up over the steep frontal surface of the glacier, followed it up to the high plateau lands above, and by the time we came to the edge of the mountain precipices far above the settlement the kids were strung out over a distance of a mile or more, Jopee and Kavavow in front and in possession of a pair of ptarmigan killed illegally with slingshots.

We had brought with us a supply of "school soup," a student eye-opener supplied for the breakfastless Eskimo by the Federal Government, and this was poured out of vacuum flasks and passed around, each child in turn warmed his bare hands on the cup, leaving fur mitts to dangle at the end of their shoulder harness. The laggards had to be content with lukewarm soup poured into a frozen mug.

The sun didn't fail us. At ten minutes to twelve came the dawn, earlier than down in the settlement. The noise and horseplay on the mountain's brink stopped and while Jopee quietly picked on raw frozen ptarmigan leg for dessert we gazed southward over the Devon icecap to the returning sun, bathing our dark-weary retinas in its cold brightness. The "dark period" that had begun at Hallowe'en was over at last and, whatever the calendar said, our own New Year's Day had come.

I wondered, gazing over the pale frozen sea below us, what the new year would bring for Katie and me.

Grise Fiord is a settlement of ninety Eskimos on the south coast of Ellesmere Island. No people in all the Americas live closer to the North Pole than the fifteen hunting families of Grise Fiord. I was sent in two years earlier as the teacher and administrator. It was my eleventh year in the Canadian north, Katie's sixth, and we felt that for the time being we had had enough. Much as we loved the life in the far north, we missed other things, fresh food, new faces, green trees, open water and seasons that were not winter. The time had come to indulge an old dream.

Seven years earlier I'd gone to England with the idea of buying a little sailboat and sailing her to my home in New Zealand. If only I had misspent my bachelor years to better effect, this might have worked out. As it was, I was not as rich as I imagined, and instead of leaving for New Zealand with a boat I left again for Canada with a wife.

Katie and I had met in a yacht club in Devon. Neither of us knew much more of sailing than that we wanted to sail. We were married in London, we emigrated to Canada and after our fifth year in the Canadian north we returned to England to spend the summer of 1968 searching for a long-distance cruising yacht.

We found her. *Nanook* ("polar bear" in Eskimo), or *Safari Too* as she was then called, had been built in Australia by her owner, Kurt Frost. He and his wife Pat had sailed from Sydney through Torres Strait and across the Indian Ocean to South Africa, thence via Brazil and the West Indies to England.

Safari Too was the sister ship of W.A. Robinson's *Svaap,* the ketch designed by the late John Alden that sailed the world in the early thirties. *Safari* was somewhat longer than *Svaap* for when Kurt had started building he found that the timber for the keel was longer than required and not having the heart to cut it down to size he adapted the lines to a new overall length of 34 feet. Kurt was a professional shipwright. He had built *Safari Too* for himself and his workmanship was in a class all its own.

She was built largely of Australian hardwoods, carvel planked. She was rigged as a double headsail Bermudian ketch. The accommodation was well laid out for long-distance cruising. There was headroom below for my 6 foot 2 inch frame. Quarter berths extended aft either side of the companionway. The saloon had a galley well laid out to starboard including a two-burner kerosene Primus, and a full-size chart table to port. Two stainless pipes could be set vertically through the cabin sole between these two areas and a horizontal bar set onto these to provide support at sea for the navigator or cook. A folding table of bright mahogany stood between settees that could convert, if needed, to Pullman berths. Behind these were clothes lockers and ample book shelves. The fo'c'sle contained a chain locker, room for rope and sail stowage, and a head.

A 40-gallon water tank extended underneath one of the quarter berths and a 30-gallon fuel tank was fitted at the end of the other. This supplied the 4½ horsepower Yanmar diesel engine that was installed beneath the companionway.

The cockpit was self-draining. It was also snug and comfortable. A hatch fitted into the after-deck gave access to the lazarette, a large space at the stern for the stowing of fenders, paint tins, jerry cans and other bulky items. The deck itself was attractively laid with planks of Australian white beech and it was ample enough to walk on easily from stem to stern without crowding against rigging, coachroof and guardrails. It was a deck meant for sunbathing under sunny skies or for sleeping on at night in the tropics.

Our whole summer that year had been spent clambering through a bewildering variety of hundreds of yachts all on the second-hand market. Each one seemed to have something, or several things, wrong with it and we were about to give up the search and return to Canada when *Safari Too* came sailing in from the Azores and put onto the market. No boat in the world could have suited us better. The price was right and without even taking her out for a trial sail (for we had neither the doubt implicit in trials, nor the time) we bought her, left her in the Hamble River and returned to Canada for one more winter in Grise Fiord.

By early April our daylight had increased so much that even at midnight it was not really dark. It was still very cold throughout those sunny days, between 20 and 40 below, but our winter lethargy was shaken. It was fun to be out and we were envious of nobody.

From then on I began to have plenty of empty desks in the classroom as first the boys and later their sisters joined in the long hunting journeys of their parents. The time had come for the annual polar bear hunt. Across the Arctic the bear population had dwindled seriously with over-hunting and new regulations had been imposed that year limiting the number of bears to be taken by each Eskimo community, a restriction that the hunters accepted as sensible and necessary. When the quota of twenty-seven bears was filled and creamy white polar bear skins hung on every clothes line, it was time for the families to travel overland through the mountains to the fishing lakes away to the north where Arctic char could be speared through holes in the ice. Early in May the seals began to climb out of their *agloos* or breathing holes onto the top of the ice to bask in the sunshine, so seal stalking was then in vogue with the boys.

Two of my older boys were gone on a dog-team patrol undertaken by the Mountie, Dick Vitt. Dick, who was in charge of the northernmost detachment of the R.C.M.P. and who was more storekeeper, welfare officer and dispenser of medicine than policeman to the Grise Fiord people, had received orders to destroy the police dog team in the spring so he made one final patrol in the old style travelling across Devon Island and as far west as Resolute Bay on Cornwallis Island before returning. This 740-mile round trip took six weeks, and the rifle shots echoing off the mountains several days after he returned brought the end to the last police dog team in the Arctic and to a long romantic era.

One winter on Baffin Island Katie and I had ourselves logged a total of 800 miles by dog team, travelling with local hunters and sleeping overnight in igloos. But in Grise Fiord by this time all the men were using snowmobiles. A few huskies were still kept by the hunters on long chains of the sea ice, more from force of habit than anything for they were unused except by the schoolboys in the springtime. However we were visited in May by a group of Greenlanders who had travelled 600 miles by dog team from their home settlement to pay a social visit to Grise Fiord, and when these people left Katie and I and some local hunters travelled with them some fifty miles to the floe edge to join in a walrus hunt which would supply meat for their teams on the long homeward journey. At the end of this gory hunt one of the men, Markusie, after whittling away at the fatty flesh adhering to a long bone solemnly presented the bone to Katie as a souvenir of the hunt. It was the bacculum or penis bone of the male walrus. It was almost the size and shape of an ax handle with a thickish knob at one end and a nice natural hand grip at the other. Markusie knew that we had a sailboat and he had once seen a movie about pirates.

"Ilisaisi," he said, "the world, I hear, is full of bad people. When you go to Elisapeenuna" (Elizabeth's Land as the Eskimos called England) "and you sail your boat far over the sea where many thieves live, maybe you will need this."

It was certainly a fine weapon, I reflected. And no doubt the poor walrus had thought so too.

"It's funny that the male walruses have these bones," I commented to Markusie. "We don't. I wonder why they need them."

"Ilisaisi," he exclaimed with withering forebearance, "don't you know that the water is very cold? Of course they need those bones. You just jump into that water and see if you can manage to do what they do without one."

The remaining weeks of spring went all too quickly. Manuals of celestial navigation were re-read, trunks were packed and consigned to England and instructions left for the person replacing me. Those children still in the settlement played outside all through the sunlit hours of night. Some came to school after having had no sleep at all and I let them sleep on the carpet. But when those eyes that were still awake looked longingly out the window to the skeins of snowgeese flying north against the blue sky, I closed school and with a picnic lunch on our backs we went climbing the mountains and hunting Arctic hares across the disappearing snowfields in the valleys. Nothing can quite compare to this arrival of spring in the high latitudes when the grip of the long winter is loosened at last and the streams gush everywhere over the bright land and out onto the sea ice.

At the end of June we said goodbye to everyone in Grise Fiord, climbed onto the little plane that stood on the winter runway on the sea ice and left it all behind us. I wondered gazing down at the vast ice-torn land if we would ever return.

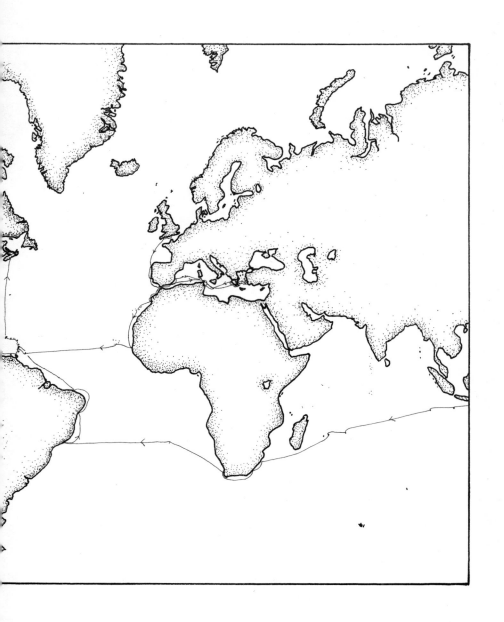

I

England to the Aegean

All July, Katie and I worked hard to prepare ourselves and our boat for sea. *Nanook* lay quietly at her berth in the Port Hamble marina. She looked smart in her fresh coat of white and blue paint and her new stainless steel rigging, almost as glossy as her big expensive glass-plastic neighbors but she lay more deeply in the water than they did with a year's stores stowed below, the fuel and water tanks filled and two large trunks of personal gear from Canada swallowed up by the generous lockers. She seemed somnolent and content, seemingly unaware that she was about to begin a long-dreamed-of voyage. Yard officials had come to wish us well, friends and relatives had completed their farewells and there remained nothing further to do except to go. It was a cool dull day with an unpleasant wind blowing down the river and I would have procrastinated for an hour or a day if any excuse had presented itself, but none did. I felt apprehensive and suddenly reluctant, but since we hoped to reach Greece before winter, the first of August (saving a gale), had been our avowed date of departure, and go we must.

"Just let go the forward warp when I say," I called to Katie. "I'll slip the stern warp and then we'll back out under power. Nothing to it." I started the diesel, brought the stern warp aboard and nodded to Katie, "Okay, let go."

I shoved the gear lever into reverse and held the tiller well over to bring the stern round to the shore, the bow towards the river exit. Slowly we gathered way. Clear of the jetty the wind gripped our bow and helped swing us down. "Funny," I thought, "we're not turning." I accelerated the engine, but the wind had taken a grip on the bow and we were swinging the wrong way, bow in to the shore. The space between the two jetties was too narrow to let us motor forward in a semi-circle and we lay helpless, racing in reverse gear but still drifting down onto the smart set

1

on the next jetty. Our reverse, I learned later, was quite ineffectual unless we ran it at slow speed when it would take a slight grip on the water, but even then there was no authority in it.

Shouts of advice came from several directions. "Honey, what are you *doing*?" Katie cried agonizingly. There was nothing I could do except prepare to fend off from the fancy gin palaces downwind whose owners stared at us with annoyance and distaste. I should have held on to our bow line or raised and backed the jib, but it was now too late; we ground against one of the jetty piles, the stern swung around against glossy plastic topsides and the bowsprit entangled itself in someone else's rigging. Several helpful souls came to fend us off and struggled to swing our bows around to point us in the direction where we could do the least harm to anyone else, toward the river. The only damage in fact was to our dignity and with red faces we moved into forward gear and motored downriver, our world voyage thus begun.

That occasion was the very first time we had taken *Nanook* anywhere. She had not even left the river since the Frosts had first brought her in. This seems strange to me only in retrospect; I thought nothing of it at the time. All July we had busied ourselves with endless lists of things to be bought, fitted, fixed or done.

"Swing the compass," went the list. "Order new CQR anchor and chain; find a kerosene iron; pick up charts and pilots; have sextant checked over in So'ton; get boarding ladder; write to Customs, Falmouth re bonded booze; order chronometer watch; do we need vacuum cleaner? test bilge pumps; ask X if Seafix RDF radios are any good; what kind of liferaft?" The lists went on and on, and far from getting shorter as July wore on, they seemed to grow longer all the time. At any rate they had kept us holed up in the Hamble all month and not until now had we taken the time to try out our new yacht.

We had timed our departure so that we could sail west through the Solent and carry a favourable tide under us as we went out past the Needles into the Channel. Despite our qualms and jitters all seemed to go well. The diesel behaved perfectly, the sails slid smoothly up without jamming, we weren't run down by a Hovercraft in Southampton Water, the north wind didn't turn itself into a westerly gale. Even the steering vane, that simple and supremely important gadget that controlled the rudder by means of an underwater trim tab and held the yacht's course at a given angle to the wind, any angle of our own choosing, even it worked perfectly as we romped along on a reach past Beaulieu and Lymington. How happy we felt to leave the crowded Solent behind us, and how pleased we were with our little ketch as we drank cups of tea in the cockpit and steered manually out the narrow passage past the Needles, the tide spewing us forward into the open Channel.

"This is the life," I declared. "There really isn't anything to it."

Away to starboard there appeared an awesome line of white breaking water where the ebbing stream thrashed over the shallow Brambles Bank. Several other vessels were passing through the Needles Channel at the time. I passed the tiller to Katie.

"Just keep an eye on that ship ahead," I said. "Let her pass on the port side. I'll clear up below." I was gone for just a moment when on glancing out again I noticed that the white water over the Brambles was a great deal closer.

"My God," I cried, "steer out to port quickly. The tide's carrying us down onto the Brambles." Katie had been too intent on avoiding the ship to notice anything else and meanwhile the wind had suddenly fallen light in the lee of the land leaving us to drift rapidly onto the bank. I leaped below and swung the diesel handle over. The little engine thumped into life and by the time I was back into the cockpit and had the lever rammed into forward gear, *Nanook* was already rising and falling heavily on the first swells at the edge of the bank. The sound and sight of crashing water all along our starboard side filled us with horror. Frantically I trimmed sheets and pushed the throttle to its extreme limit. Slowly *Nanook* worked across the line of breakers, edging gradually away upstream of them. We stared back at the cheated white crests, our hearts pounding, Katie in tears and the little engine racing. A few moments later we were free of the tide's grip and clear of the last buoy. With a sigh of relief I turned the engine off. Never after did I ask so much of it as on that first day.

I had so wanted this first cruise to be a pleasant and reassuring one for Katie who was almost a complete novice to sailing, not much given to any romantic ideas of the sea, very disposed to seasickness and a nonswimmer to boot. I was learning, certainly, but it still seemed an inauspicious start.

A favouring wind from east of north settled in to fill the main, and as we were anxious to make our westing down-Channel at least as far as some Devonshire haven we continued on all night. Katie was quite unable yet to face the galley, so while she sat determinedly cheerful in the cockpit until evening, dry-mouthed from the effect of anti-seasickness tablets and eyes glued to the horizon as if to cling to that one thing in her horrid new world that didn't heave up and down, I went below to do what I could on the stove. It wasn't much. I found myself scarcely less susceptible than Katie when once below, and before I got through my sorry little effort of boiled potatoes and a tin of luncheon meat I felt thoroughly sick. We sat and ate in the cockpit in silence while *Nanook* steered herself west past St. Alban's Head. The wind eased and we rolled in the Channel swell. Katie went below to her bunk having only pecked at her plate. I'd managed two small potatoes and it seemed to me that the tin of meat must be justified. I boldly lopped a large piece off with my fork but before this could be dispatched my mouth swam, salivating with nausea, and I lurched to the guardrails, vomiting wretchedly.

The wind died away late in the evening and the sky darkened with humid black clouds charged with electricity. It looked thoroughly unpleasant and we wished we were in some cosy port where we could ignore the ominous rumble of thunder and the flashes that lit the oily black rain-pocked swell. I took the sails down rather than leave them slatting uselessly in the rain. We were well beyond Portland Bill and well inside the shipping lanes so we kept our watches from the shelter under the hatch.

A breeze and a blue sky returned with the dawn, as did our spirits. All night I had suffered violently from seasickness, which surprised me for I had always thought myself more or less immune to it. My watches had been spent quietly agonizing over what we had undertaken. I felt depressed at the thought that we had probably bitten off more than we could chew, and that in reality we were entirely unsuited to the kind of thing we were now embarked upon.

But things looked differently in the morning sunshine. The motion no longer affected me and I felt confident that I could work in the bilge in a near gale, hung-over, without any further problems with *mal de mer,* and indeed from then on seasickness never bothered me. Or if really pressed I would still claim like the captain of the *Pinafore,* "Well, *hardly* ever." For Katie it was to be a different matter.

With the light wind we resumed our course slowly across Lyme Bay. Towards evening the high green coast of Devon appeared ahead. *Nanook* sailed in past the grand old guardian towers of Dartmouth and we christened the brand new CQR anchor in the mud at the bottom of the Dart.

The next ten days were spent cruising slowly down the West Country. We tried to forget the long distance to Greece and the lateness of the season, as it seemed to us. We felt content just to idle along westwards and to absorb to the full this mellow land of sailors, green fields, soft rains and cream teas. After rounding Start Point we made a sentimental visit to Salcombe where Katie and I had first met and our dreams of distant voyages together were born. For the payment of a few pence in dues to the harbourmaster we anchored overnight between rolling pastures, amongst bright little dinghies aswarm on the sunny flood stream, and rowed ashore to follow the trails around the coast and munch our Cornish pasties on the high headlands.

We reached past Plymouth to Cawsand and on to Fowey, the "little gray sea town that clings along one side of the harbour" as Kenneth Graham's Sea Rat described it . Fowey was my favourite; I liked its hilly narrow twisted little one-way streets and the long woodsy rambles from Polruan over on the river's steep east bank.

The late Peter Pye's famous old gaff cutter, *Moonraker,* was there hauled up on the bank looking neglected and mournful under the trees like an old dog that has lost its master, as indeed *Moonraker* had. Just around the bend, freighters were taking on cargos of kaolin, china clay. A hundred thousand tons of the stuff is exported there annually, leaving behind a coating of white dust on buildings, grass and trees along the river bank upstream. On the horizon to the north, great pyramids of waste, the "Cornish Alps," could be seen around the kaolin pits.

A short sail brought us to the once-charming little fishing port of Mevagissey which is now, at least in August, all glitter and honky-tonk, swarming with tourists and campers. From there we sailed on round Dodman Point, Gull Rock and the Bizzies, catching mackerel with a feather all the way along, and explored the tranquil forested arms of the Helford River for a day before going north to the fine old port of Falmouth and finally across to St. Mawes in the Fal estuary where we lay at anchor for a week. There were still various things not yet crossed off our lists and we spent several days commuting on the ferry across the harbour to Falmouth to shop for supplies; kerosene, anoraks, fresh food, a life raft, a case each of duty free rum and Scotch.

For the last few days we were joined at St. Mawes by Katie's parents. They had come down from London to say good-bye to us. We knew how they were feeling; it was hard enough to be saying good-bye again for so many years, but for us to be going off across the world like this in such a little boat? Still they put a brave face on their misgivings and never once expressed what even I had been suspecting—that we were undertaking much more than we could handle.

Though a few minor things on our lists remained undone, we at last felt more or less ready and it seems that on a yacht nobody can be readier than that, except those who never leave port. The four of us spent a final day ashore together, rambling through cow pastures and hamlets and picking blackberries for a farewell feast. In the evening we were visited by a single-hander who had anchored close by us, a Canadian from Winnipeg, white haired and soft spoken. John Struchinsky was planning to sail his handsome little Vertue sloop *Bonaventure de Lys* across to the West Indies and Canada, "but not yet, not this year. One more winter I think in England." He had already spent one winter living on his little yacht at Yarmouth and we wondered how he could face a second English winter with such equanimity.

The next morning, 19th August, we rowed ashore and completed our farewells, and in another half hour with the dinghy stowed over the coachroof we lifted our two anchors and hoisted sail to the land breeze. *Nanook* glided quietly past St. Anthony's light and swept south with a pleasant easy motion past the Helford River and the Lizard. The fair wind held, the glass was steady, and we set course to clear well to the west of Ushant and on across Biscay to Vigo. *Nanook* lifted her graceful backside to the long Atlantic swell and settled down to follow the sun south, Spain many miles beyond the bowsprit and "Old England on the lee."

Normally a yacht bound westwards around the world would cruise south down the Atlantic till encountering the trade winds west of the African coast, and follow those winds west. Our own plan was to go first into the Mediterranean and winter there, preferably in some quiet corner as far east as the Aegean before turning west to the open ocean the next season. This plan, I thought, would not only give us the chance to absorb some ancient history but would at the same time provide us with a gentle introduction to the seafaring life. In the latter instance I was quite wrong, but fortunately we didn't yet know it.

As the last of England slipped slowly under the horizon, we settled down to a routine which was simple and easy but which seemed to preclude the wasted effort of worry. We broke the Customs seals on the cupboard doors and unpacked our new radio receiver, a battery tape recorder and my new Accutron chronometer-watch all bought out of bond. Katie packed away the two cases of liquor and played tapes in the cockpit. I began recording readings on the barometer, marked up our dead reckoning on the chart and practised sun sights with the sextant, putting into practice at last all the theory I had learned during those long Arctic winters. And meanwhile, at the urging of the northwest wind, *Nanook* steadily ticked off the miles on her Sumlog dial at the side of the chart table.

We stayed well out to the west of Ushant, the rugged island at

On a quiet day at sea, the Skipper uses his old brass sextant to shoot another position line.

Brittany's farthest Atlantic end, so as to be well clear of the busy Channel-to-Finisterre shipping lane across Biscay. This and the steering vane enabled us to take life easy at nights instead of sitting constantly in the cockpit steering manually and vacantly watching for ships. We simply stuck our heads out the hatch periodically to scan the horizon and check the course on the compass, and not until we were closing the Spanish coast five days later did we encounter any shipping. The northwest wind held throughout most of the voyage, too strong at times so that I twice took the main off for the sake of a few hours of peace, a timid indulgence that would have been scorned by the hairshirts of ocean racing, for the weather was not really too bad for such a place as Biscay.

All this time, Katie had battled uncomplainingly with the curse of seasickness. The tablets didn't help much and she spent her days and nights alternating between sitting in the cockpit and lying prostrate on her bunk, the only two situations she could tolerate. Of necessity the galley continued to be my territory.

Off Finisterre on Spain's northwest shoulder, the wind had become a warm quartering northerly that drove us merrily down the lovely high coast. We were sorry not to be visiting all the enticing *rias* or deep inlets for this is good cruising and the people of Galicia are a friendly and hospitable lot who understand *marineros* and the vagaries of the sea. But the thought of all the miles ahead prevented us from doing more than make a brief visit to Vigo and the surrounding area. We entered the *ria* by passing through the northern approach channel inside the Islas Cies, a group of islands lying across the mouth of the *ria*. Many fishing boats were at work near the islands, their filthy exhausts belching black fumes over the water. One of these we thought to be on fire and altered course towards it before we realized the real cause of all that smoke.

The warm dry afternoon wind whipped down off the hills heeling *Nanook* well over as we sailed up the *ria* towards the city. We knew Vigo had a yacht club, but seeing no sign of it after a couple of tacks along the waterfront we crossed over to the sheltered weather shore and anchored for the night close in off the attractive little town of Cangas. It was a Sunday evening and everyone was out in Sunday best promenading the waterfront, seeing and being seen. We happily absorbed every detail as we sat in the cockpit drinking a pre-supper sundowner. The air was filled with the gay noises of gossip, laughter and car horns and the sound of such things was music to our ears.

Motoring back to the Vigo shore in the morning we followed the directions of fishermen and discovered the little yacht basin just beyond the commercial docks. The basin was narrow and crowded and we had to be content with tying up on the outside of four other cruising yachts, American, Portuguese and British. Across this obstacle course the customs officials stumbled to give us a polite and painless entry and then with thoughts of fresh food ashore we in turn stumbled back across the line of yachts to place our feet on land again. We felt the curious sensation of the land itself pitching and heaving like the sea. But this may have been partly the result of our having to run the gauntlet of those other yachts, the owners of each one insisting that we stop by for a glass of wine, brandy or whatever else they were drinking at that early mid-morning hour.

On the dock a young man stood watching our approach. A Canadian himself he was curious to see the maple leaf flying on our mizzen mast. We chatted together for a short time and discovered to our delight that we had a mutual friend in Bob Christie, a geologist whom we'd so recently left in Grise Fiord. The stranger offered to show us the sights.

Vigo at the time was enjoying a fiesta. Processions filled the streets and the place had an air of gaiety and bustle. We stayed there enjoying ourselves for two days and then sailed out to explore the near-empty beaches we had seen on the north side of the *ria* and to escape the noisy fireworks that peppered the air over Vigo each afternoon.

In the little bay of Limens where a valley flanked by piney hills came down to the sea, we dropped anchor and rowed ashore to the white empty beach. The place seemed sleepy and forgotten, just as we hoped. Two women busied themselves at a stream washing clothes on a cement slab, a man stood gazing at us nearby and a donkey cropped at the dry summer grass. We sat down on the sand to admire the view so recently enhanced (or so we reckoned) by the arrival of our little ketch. Meanwhile the man approached and Katie exhausted her Spanish by wishing *"Buenas dias"* on him.

"Good morning," replied the native. "Would you like to come to my house? Would you like a wheesky?"

It was only half past nine and my corn flakes had scarcely yet digested. I wondered if it might be a national failing this drinking at all hours. But "When in Rome . . ." goes the old proverb which generally serves to encourage foreign weaknesses rather than foreign virtues.

"Why yes," I replied, "we'd be very happy to."

Luis Bastida Gonzalez was a shoe salesman from Vigo who with his wife, his young family and several friends was enjoying his annual holiday in the tranquility of Limens. Luis had a small vine-covered villa set back in a grove of pines and bamboo, and to this cheerful den we now retired. Every year at this time the Gonzalez family came to Limens to escape the heat, noise and bustle of Vigo, but it seemed to me that they brought some of it with them in the form of their friends, two other couples and their various children. (They said, by way of explaining the exploding population, that they always "make their children here each summer.") Drinks were pressed into our hands and conversation flowed back and forth for an hour through Luis the interpreter while we explained where we came from and where bound, where they lived, whether they liked their wives, how many children they had and how many more they were going to have.

Appointments were made for us to return for lunch at one and dinner at nine, and for part of the day we escaped from all this attention, to wander on our own up the peaceful valley following a Roman road and crossing a small Roman bridge that was still in use after two thousand years. Later, Katie gathered soap and a pile of laundry and joined the black-skirted gathering around the laundry pool at the stream. She tried as well as she could to keep up with the old lady next to her whose vigorous attacks on the linen seemed to threaten at least the fabric if not the little cement platform itself. The old lady halted her private little war to gaze in dismay at Katie's ineffectual sloshing. She lit in with a cascade of Spanish and, more to the point, a practical demonstration of how it should be done. Katie smiled profusely, nodded her head, said *"Sí, sí,"* and redoubled her efforts. The lady was not impressed. She glanced around at me with a look of sorrow and reproach that young men should be so blind as not to foresee what they must live with. Another and longer lesson followed. Her own work neglected, the ancient señora took our bunk sheets and demonstrated the finer points of rubbing between the hands, pounding on the platform, rinsing in the stream, all accompanied so that this time there would be no misunderstanding by the young foreigner, in special Spanish, a little slower and a lot louder. I thought Katie's performance then improved quite a lot but the good lady of Linens didn't. She abruptly cut short Katie's efforts, took the sheets and did them all herself.

Back at the Gonzalez villa lunch consisted of the finest Spanish omelet that I or anyone else has ever tasted, and the evening consisted of small mountains of food, followed by wine and music under the pine trees, folk songs, Spanish dances and the merry whine of the bagpipes of Galicia.

As we sat under the trees in the darkness, Antonio the piper produced a large skillet and poured into it half a bottle of Scotch whisky. A large heap of sugar was added to one side of this pool and the whole lot was then set on fire. It burned with a high blue flame while the sugar was gradually stirred in with a ladle. After the whisky had been burning for some time, a great slug of wine was added. More stirring followed, more wine and more stirring while all eyes followed the ladle on the burning surface of liquid. Finally with a hefty puff Antonio blew out the flames and ladled long portions of the nightcap into all the glasses. It was warm, pungent and sweet.

"We have this drink every night here," they said. "That's why we have so many children."

In return for all this hospitality we undertook to take this roisterous party the next morning for a cruise out to the Islas Cíes. Sure enough, there they were at dawn on the beach with their picnic hampers, children and bagpipes, and they scrambled one after another into *Nanuapik*, our little plywood dinghy (the name means polar bear cub), with a cheerful disregard for the low freeboard and heavy surf.

The Cíes islands are high, bold and beautiful, covered in tall grass, scrub and forest. The seaward coast has been eroded by the Atlantic into a wilderness of rock and cliff but pleasant beaches, lagoons and anchorages lay on the east side. In their heyday, the Vikings occupied these islands and used them as a base from which to harry coastal settlements and to rest on the long voyages to the Mediterranean. Even now only a handful of people live there and upon landing we supposed we had found a spot quite unspoiled, remote and free of any tourists other than ourselves. But soon a ferry pulled into a jetty and a great crowd disgorged for a day's picnic on the island.

"Locals," I said reassuringly to Katie. "At least no foreigners ever get this far." But the ferry continued spilling its human cargo onto the beach. Fat mamas staked out sections of sand with blankets and baskets. The younger set carried tents and rucksacks towards the forest and one old man wheeled ashore a mobile ice cream stall.

A family parked themselves beside us, giving us a glance as if to say, "Would you mind moving your dinghy across off our place?" When they did speak, Mum, Dad and kids, it was in English with a Midlands accent. The children changed into bathing suits with Mum's help and ran squealing into the waves. Mum stretched her legs in the sunshine, lifted her skirts above her white knees and sat happily watching her brood. Dad rolled his pants up close to his knees, placed his sandals neatly on the sand beside him and settled down to read his way through the "Daily Express."

We longed to stay on these pleasant shores but time was short if we were to reach Greece before the gales of early winter, and we allowed ourselves only one other indulgence. Every place has its "must" and this locality had Bayona, a town overlooking a small bay just to the south of the *ria*, an hour's sail from Limens. So the day after delivering our friends back home through the surf to the accompaniment of inebriated bagpipes, we sailed off and put our anchor down below the castellated ramparts of Bayona and rowed ashore to the place where the crew of Columbus's *Pinta* landed after the first voyage to the New World. What a lovely place to return to. Bayona's twisted little streets were a delight and the people were friendly and helpful, even, in the case of shopkeepers, to going out and doing our shopping for us when they didn't have what we wanted.

But the Portuguese Trades were blowing strong and steady out of the north. A fair wind is not to be wasted so after only a few hours in Bayona we went back aboard, stowed the dinghy and by 1700 we were reaching past the lighthouse out to sea.

We were bound for Cascais, the seaside town to the west of Lisbon, outside the Tagus estuary. As the sun dropped and the wind picked up, *Nanook* roared on southwards through the seas and poor Katie was again in distress from seasickness and again my indifferent cuisine had to serve us both. But progress was good. With a double-reefed main we sailed along at times at eight knots. The rigging seemed taut as a violin and down below chaos reigned as tins and saucepans clinked and crashed in their cupboards. The crest of a wave came through the open hatch and cascaded onto the cabin sole. Katie struggled to mop up the mess in between throes of being sick. We covered 143 miles in the first 24 hours and the anchor was down in the bay of Cascais only 45 hours out of Bayona despite our having motored for the final five hours with no wind.

It seemed strange to lie in the anchorage off Cascais with the open ocean to the southwest and nothing but water between *Nanook* and South America. We had a long sleep and found a light south wind blowing onshore next morning, but it gradually fell away so after laying out the kedge just to make sure of our holding we rowed ashore, left *Nanuapik* upside down on the beach amongst the fishing boats, and caught the suburban train into Lisbon for our first look at the interesting old city.

The following morning we went ashore again to pursue bread, vegetables and meat at the Cascais market, and after exhausting what little Portuguese money we had left we collected our passports from the customs office and carried the light wind out to sea. *Nanook* quietly swept south at 5½ knots with scarcely any motion while for lunch Katie cooked up a fine Vigo omelet accompanied by wine, salad, bread rolls and grapes. Life at sea is not always an intolerable hardship. All afternoon we sailed on in perfect conditions over the smooth sea, sunbathing naked on the deck and reading novels while the wind vane held our course for Cape St. Vincent.

We were close to the shipping lanes so we kept watches of three hours each throughout the night and the boredom was relieved by the porpoises that puffed around the hull from time to time. On the second day out we came across a small open boat with four men in it about ten miles offshore. They were busy fishing with lines and baited hooks and one of them waved us over. As we sailed close in to them they called cheerfully to us in Portuguese and threw two enormous fish into our cockpit. I made signs that we had only two mouths on board to feed and we only needed one fish, so I threw the bigger one back whereupon a third fish, much bigger even than the first two was flung over the lifelines and the men signalled to us not to argue the point and wished us a good voyage. I hurried below while Katie prepared to make another tack past them and came up with a bottle of Scotch which I tossed into their fish tub, hoping it might cheer their hearts on the way home. Later in the day we gybed to the port tack under the lee of Cape St. Vincent where we had to keep a careful watch, for the waters around the high headland were aswarm with ships.

Two days later, Katie sighted the coast of Morocco to the south and in a few more hours we had closed the Straits of Gibraltar. While *Nanook* ran in with a westerly under her skirts we happily turned our backs on the Atlantic and our faces towards the great blue sea of Poseidon himself.

Porpoises frolicked along with us as we crossed from near the African shore towards Tarifa, the southernmost tip of continental Europe, and on into the bay of Algeciras. The Rock loomed ahead of us to the northeast. Britain's nearest colony was then becoming her biggest headache as Spanish hostility increased, and the town at the bottom of the Rock seemed to be staring out across the bay to Algeciras where the last links between Spain and the colony had recently been cut. Outside the harbour a police launch came out to meet us and directed us to the small yacht anchorage beside the airport. On the way in an R.A.F. helicopter buzzed us three times. Each time it flew lower over the masts, blasting us with air and noise in a stupid game of chicken. I could have sworn that it missed the burgee on our mainmast by inches.

We rather enjoyed our brief stay at Gibraltar. *Nanook* was left at her anchor while we climbed to the top of the Rock and took note of the caves and the apes and the duty-free "bargains" on the main street. The Rock is a unique and interesting place but we felt it would pall after a few weeks and we wondered at some of our fellow yachtsmen in the marina who could face with enthusiasm the prospect of wintering there.

Pitching into a steep swell, we headed out of the bay on the morning of 7th September, and once around Europa Point we set a course eastwards into this blue sea of our dreams. For years we had read, planned and dreamed of this moment, bound east, the great "river of sea" behind us and sun-baked islands, civilization's cradle and the wine-dark seas of Odysseus far ahead. By midday the westerly wind was up to Force 5 and rising, so that by early afternoon we abandoned our intention of going in to Adra or Motril on Spain's southern coast and raced onwards instead at 5½ knots under bare poles in half a gale that blew the rest of the day and the following night, lifting the incoming Atlantic current into steep crashing banks of water.

The next morning the wind had eased somewhat and with the little staysail up and the wind on the port quarter I set a new course for Almeria. Still the wind went down and up went the mainsail. An hour later I set the mizzen and soon after that the genoa, and before long we lay becalmed in a blue swell with all five sails slatting uselessly. The Sierra Nevada range was visible in the haze to the north. We had ten miles to cover to Almeria and I had to start the diesel to get there before nightfall. Gale and calm. It was a pattern that was to become all too familiar before we were done with this sea of our dreams.

For two days *Nanook* lay quietly at anchor in the commercial harbour while Katie and I enjoyed ourselves ashore, prowling the streets of Almeria and the high citadel. It was sunny of course and much too hot but the beer was cold and cheap and the harbour was fit for swimming in and given these conditions much heat can be endured. Still we kept glancing fretfully back at the chart table and measuring off the distances yet to go.

Wet decks and big seas. *Nanook* fairly flies under reduced sail at the tail end of a violent storm.

Katie ponders the setting sun as a gentle breeze scarcely ripples the wide, flat sea.

How nice, we thought, if only we were already in Malta. With this thought nagging at us we stocked the galley with fresh food, muscatel, cheap grapes and beer, and promising ourselves another visit to Almeria the next year we motored out to face the 900 miles to Malta. It seemed an appalling distance, but we determined to get it behind us in one long hop.

Our first two days out were slow with very light winds, and the diesel, noisy and hot as it was, helped to relieve the boredom that sets in when progress drags. But two hundred miles out the barometer dropped noticeably and a sudden change took place. My log records for 1615, 12th September, "Under power. No wind. Log 190 miles." Two hours later it reads, "Shut off engine and still doing 6½ knots," and an hour later, "All sails off. Wind is away up. We are running before." A gale was upon us, Force 7 in the evening and up to 8 in the night. Katie was violently ill and we were both apprehensive, but again it was going our way and I was happy enough to let *Nanook* steer herself before the gathering seas which she did quite well with the steering vane engaged. We were close to the North African shipping lane so we had to keep scanning the horizon for ships that might be on a collision course with us. But except for these regular glances around into the wild inky scene outside, we both stayed below with the companionway hatch tightly closed, lying on our bunks and listening to the shrieking outside. We hardly slept at all.

By morning the gale was much worse, Force 9 by my estimate and gusting often well into Force 10. The air was filled with spray and as I came out the hatch it slapped into my face like handfuls of gravel. Wavecrests were slamming hard onto the hull and we surged down the face of the waves at a frightening speed. The grey seas were tremendously long and streaked with spume, with yawning great valleys between them that seemed about to engulf us in a watery void. But *Nanook* gallantly lifted her stern high up each awesome onrushing grey wall towards the next tumbling crest and, slipping backwards up the advancing slope yet still rushing forwards through the water she would rise again and slide without effort over the top.

Katie lay below all this time. She was afraid and thoroughly sick. Since our first night in the English Channel I'd had no further problems with seasickness and even now I felt well enough in that respect, but every journey into the cockpit, where I sat wide-eyed and white-knuckled with my safety harness clipped to the shrouds, left me dry-mouthed with fear and wishing both of us to hell and gone back on dry land a thousand miles from salt water. As Gonzalo said, "The wills above be done, but I would fain die a dry death."

Nanook steered herself over the roaring slopes, but as the grey day wore on so the seas increased, and every now and then along would come some especially inspired sea streaked with driving spindrift, rearing up behind us higher than its neighbours and topped with a fearsome crashing white crest. When one of these arrived we surged up to eight or nine knots. Several times the rushing crests threw the stern over and *Nanook* broached, beam on to the seas, burying her lee deck in the turbulent foam. I then had to scramble carefully aft over the slippery deck, disconnect the wind vane, return to the cockpit and hold the tiller hard up to weather until *Nanook* slowly turned downwind again. I'd never experienced anything like this before but I felt we were going too fast and that it was time to carry out what the textbooks suggested which was to trail a long warp astern in a loop with one end secured on each quarter. The resultant drag would slow the boat and hold the stern more firmly to the seas. I accordingly struggled aft out of the fo'c'sle with thirty heavy fathoms of 1½ inch diameter hemp and soon had this bent onto the massive stanchions on the after deck. *Nanook* steadied and the helm felt more responsive. The loop was sometimes lifted and thrown forwards on the advancing crests and at those times its grip on the water was slackened. We were still doing about four knots so I streamed two shorter warps in addition to the first which helped distribute the changing strains between each other. As one rope slackened another took up. All this drag made *Nanook* much less maneuverable in the event of a threatened collision but we appeared to be well clear of the east-west shipping lanes and the two of us, our stomachs tight with nervous tension, lay below most of the time staring up at the leaky decks over our bunks and wishing fervently for the wind to ease.

Another long night came upon us with no apparent change in sight. We swallowed an unappetizing meal and lay below, prepared for another sleepless night. There was nothing to do except keep a look-out for ships, the signalling lamp at the ready, and watch our course which still carried us on to the east.

Long hour followed long hour. By 0300 of the 14th the howling outside seemed to have lost some of its insane quality and by dawn, though the seas reared behind us as high as ever, the crests all passed under us without their vindictive smashing. The wind was down to Force 6 and with a belly full of porridge I scrambled into the cockpit and began the long chore of recovering the three warps which by then had become thoroughly tangled with each other. It took me two hours to separate them.

With sail again raised we ploughed on to the east and held the wind for another night and day until off Cap Bon on the Tunisian corner where no swell was left and the wind was a mere whisper. Then came a long tedious battle with light head winds past the Italian island of Pantellaria and from there we motored in a sweaty haze all the way across a flat blue mirror to the sunny ridges of Malta.

We were ten days out of Almeria and the Sumlog read exactly 999.9 miles when we thankfully dropped the anchor with a crash into the harbour of Marsaxlok at the south end of the island. The clanking chain scared off two little pilot fish that had stayed with us at the bows for the last hundred miles. The crowded town of yellow stone buildings massed along one corner of the harbour where a swarm of gaily painted fishing boats bobbed at their moorings. We flew the yellow quarantine flag for the benefit of the officials ashore, but there was no response. We'd been advised in England to go first to Marsaxlok but I found on going ashore and phoning Customs that we were breaking the law by entering anywhere except Valetta. However we were allowed to stay there the night and we enjoyed the luxury of eating at the table and turning in to sleep peacefully from suppertime until dawn.

At 0530 a sudden northeasterly gust struck at us across the harbour and I awoke with a start, struggled to the hatch, took a glance outside and settled back to doze for another half hour. But the holding ground was poor and when more gusts hammered at us about 0600 I had the good fortune to glance out just in time to find us dragging into shallow rocky ground. I rushed below, called to Katie and swung hard on the diesel starting handle. As the little one cylinder thumped into life I hurried back on deck, pyjamas flailing in the rising wind, and began hauling in the chain. By that time Katie was in the cockpit still groggy from a heavy sleep, but she had the engine in gear and we were on our way out of the place.

The hard slog upwind through a steep chop to the entrance to Valetta harbour took most of our morning. Sea and sky were grey and it had begun to rain. On the way up the coast we passed a 20,000 ton tanker called the *Angel Gabriel*. She lay at anchor waiting for wharf space inside the main harbour. Some of the crew gazed down at us and waved as we beat past under the bows. We smiled a bit at the ship's name and wondered if her namesake helped stand watches from aloft in times of stress. We were soon to know the answer to that one.

We motored into the big yacht marina in Lazaretto Creek and moored stern-to with a long bow line out to a buoy and two lines from the stern onto shore bollards. Many other yachts and charter cruisers shared the quayside on each side of us. The mooring procedure was accompanied by a great deal of nail chewing for it was our first attempt at a "Mediterranean moor" and not only did it require a reverse gear which, virtually, we just didn't have, but it was performed under the critical eyes of sundry other yachtsmen, waiting Customs officers and the ever-curious public strolling the waterfront and pausing in their hundreds (or so it seemed to us) to observe our incompetence.

In fact we never again moored in the Mediterranean or anywhere else in this manner. Instead when a "Med moor" was required, we always dropped the kedge on a warp over the stern and motored bow in to the quay. Mooring bow-in had many advantages. We were able to use the bowsprit as a gangplank rather than have to carry one, we had more privacy in our cabin from the public gaze, our deepest draught was always farthest from the quayside, damage to the steering vane was avoided, and by hauling out on the kedge warp when leaving we eliminated the need for a reverse gear. The two of us eventually became quite competent at this revised procedure and soon overcame the jittery feeling of "harbouritis" that is familiar to so many sailors.

It was well that we had entered Lazaretto Creek when we did. The northeasterly wind had been considerate enough to ease a little while we made our entry to Valetta but by evening it had resumed its threatening tone and we lay awake for much of the night listening to the incessant blattering in the rigging and feeling the growing swell bending in from the entrance.

By 0600 there was no doubt about it. We had to get out of bed and tend our lines and fenders for the fury of a full gale, an out-of-season *gregale,* was unleashed upon the islands. How *Nanook* heaved and snubbed in the wind as water whipped over her bows from sharp little waves that arose over the narrow fetch of the creek. How violently the gale tore at us as we scurried up and down the deck in horror moving our fenders and carrying extra lines ashore. I started the diesel and for two hours kept it running in forward gear to help overcome the force of the wind on the bow for I had a mere half-inch nylon line out to the buoy, an old line at that, and I worried that it wouldn't hold.

"No rain here since April," we'd been told the day before by the Customs men. But now it fell in white blinding horizontal torrents. Behind us, in the park across the road, trees crashed to the ground and all up and down the quayside yacht owners and crews dashed about in the rainy chaos doing whatever they could think of to hold their boats off. By 0930 all the chandleries had sold out their stocks of heavy rope. By the afternoon 7½ inches of rain had fallen over Valetta and by evening up in St. Paul's Bay (where Paul himself was shipwrecked in just such a *gregale)* twelve small craft were driven ashore and sunk, some of them total losses, while down the coast in the other direction the *Angel Gabriel* had also dragged. Some of her crew (perhaps, we thought, some who waved at us) were lost overboard in the turbulent foam on the coast and the ship herself lay an abject wreck, broken in half on the rocks.

The gale had eased somewhat by the following day, though the seas remained fearful, smashing themselves violently on the yellow coast and rolling round the corners of the harbour into Lazaretto Creek. But when it was all over and the yachties gathered again in the Britannia Bar to talk about the storm and catch up on harbour gossip, still the wind held in the northeast, blowing day after day from the same quarter, and still Greece lay upwind, a long hard slog unless the wind changed.

While we were thus windbound, Katie and I filled our days in by working on the boat and touring about the island. Malta at the time was *en fete.* First there was the fifth anniversary of independence to celebrate, then came a succession of religious days with first one church and then another parading statues through the streets and peppering the night air with explosive fireworks. Malta is a devoutly Catholic place. The skyline abounds with churches and cathedrals that vie with each other for architectural dominance and splendour, while street crowds are well sprinkled with the solemn habits of various religious orders. Street signs near the marina reminded the foreigners not to appear in public indecently clad in bikinis, and the bored-looking young sailors on shore leave from the Sixth Fleet had to content themselves with bars and bus rides. There seemed to me no need for Ma back home in the States to worry about what sort of trouble her little boy gets into in Valetta.

A large number of more-or-less retired British people have chosen Malta as their permanent home in the sun. We met many of them, people of all ages, some left over from military or colonial postings there, others more recently arrived who just wanted to get away from the English climate and avoid punitive British taxes on their invested earnings. We felt surprised that so many could be content to remain within the confines of what seemed to us a rather dull little group of islands. What on earth, we wondered, did they do with themselves? Endless rounds of cocktail parties perhaps; boating, bridge, a little mild wife-swapping. Personally I'd prefer to pay my taxes and remain in merry old England.

The northeast wind continued and October had arrived. Katie and I looked gloomily at each other and finally said, "Well, let's give it a try anyway. At the worst we can always come back here for the winter."

Departures from port never seem to be much fun. Katie would promptly get seasick after a few days in port and my own specialty was a morbid yearning for the land and a feeling of depression at having to commit ourselves again to the uncertain sea. Plenty of other yachtsmen have the same problem. But at no time did I ever feel as depressed as on this occasion. Greece seemed as enticing as ever, but it still lay a long way off, the season seemed to be advancing quickly and the alternative of wintering in Malta seemed thoroughly unthinkable. I suppose the vagaries of the Mediterranean were beginning to tell.

By dawn of the next day all these troubles were forgotten, as they usually are when land is at last out of sight, and to my delight I found the wind slowly backing until I was able to lay our course for Cape Malea, the southernmost tip of the Peloponnesus. However our friendly northerly faded after a few hours, and dropped away to nothing. The seas settled to a gentle swell and then to nothing at all but a flat sheen of glass under a cloudless breathless sky. The sails hung limp in the sunshine. The booms jerked idly to the ends of their sheets as *Nanook* gently wallowed and finally even her gentle rolling ceased altogether and the masts pointed straight up as if we lay at anchor in a land-locked creek. The sun wheeling across the sky was the only thing that moved, and the horizon was almost invisible so perfectly did the mirror reflect the blue dome overhead. The world seemed to have stopped.

For four days we alternately slept, lay panting naked in a sweaty daze on the deck (cooling ourselves periodically with buckets of sea water) or motored on until we grew sick of the noise and heat below. There was nothing to do and not much more to see. We motored past a little fish lying motionless in the shade of a large floating leaf. A few migrating swallows stopped from time to time, refusing our proffered bread and water, and a hoopoe on its way back to North Africa for the winter spent a night on the guard rails. Its amusing appearance so reminded us of a friend in Canada that we named it "David" after him.

By this time Katie, who has a voracious appetite for books and never lost an opportunity to swap paperbacks with other yachts, had consumed every interesting novel on our shelves and was reduced to whodunnits. As she resignedly opened an Agatha Christie she told me to guess who the culprit would prove to be.

"The doctor," I replied without thinking.

"Oh," she said five minutes later. "You may be right. There is a doctor in it."

Three hours later she threw the book onto the swaps shelf and said, "That's funny. You were absolutely right. It was the doctor."

On the fourth night of this calm a thin veil of cirrus slipped in under the stars. A change was coming. The following day brought with it a few catspaws over the surface that filled the sails and brought to our ears the welcome music of waves chuckling along the bows. The Sumlog needle quivered and jumped slightly away from the end of the scale. One knot, one and a half and before long we were doing six. The afternoon brought with it a great gathering of dramatic cauliflowers of cumulus and a hardening of the sky that turned our blue Mediterranean into a steely chop. Thunderclouds rolled aloft, astern and to the north and finally all around us. Later in the afternoon we were treated to the grisly sight of waterspouts. From the dark lowering clouds blackish trunks of whirling vapour pointed downwards, growing menacingly until they embraced the sea surface itself. The lower end of each spout then became white as the spinning air tore salt spray off the surface. Four or five of these waterspouts were visible in various directions at once, and as one weakened and receded into the clouds another developed somewhere else. What the wind speed inside these twisting monsters could have been I don't know. They were an awesome sight and I was chilled at the possibility of our being engulfed by one of them, but like us they kept their distance and by evening they had all dissolved into the gathering gloom.

We were by then getting close to the west coast of Greece. I had intended to sail clear around the jagged southern fingers of the Peloponnesus and to make our official entry at Nauplion in the Gulf of Argolis. But with the weather worsening we felt anxious to make port as soon as possible so I set a new course for Pylos on the southwest coast, a course I held until the wind veered and forced us to sail north on the other tack. The night was squally and black. Lightning flickered and flashed around us nearly all night long with an accompanying chorus of crashing thunder to keep our nerves on edge. In the middle of the night we crossed the busy shipping lane leading from Cape Malea to the west and I spent a wet and nervous hour signalling angrily at ships' bridges with our R.A.F. war-surplus signalling lamp. We also had our radar reflector mounted high on the mizzen and we wondered if either of these aids ever brought us to the attention of the watch on the bridge. Probably not. We always took our own avoiding action well in advance and the ships swept past us, never deigning so far as we could tell to pay the slightest attention to such flotsam as ourselves.

With dawn, the clouds and the unstable charged air were rolled back by a northwesterly that sent *Nanook* ploughing happily eastwards until the coast of Greece appeared far ahead. By midday, sun out and wind gone, we had closed the coast and motored in through the entrance to Navarino Bay. A rambling Venetian fortress guarded the dry limestone heights to starboard, and to port the even more dramatic ramparts all along the eastern side of the island of Sphacteria towered high over the bay. The sweet resinous scent of forest-after-rain greeted us within the headlands. The land closed behind us shutting off the sea to the west. We were in Greece at last.

By this time our bad habit of entering a new country on Sunday was well established so we were not surprised at the throngs of well-dressed strollers who paused on the quayside to gaze at our approach. Every Greek port had its small contingent of white-uniformed sailors, teen-aged conscripts mostly, who hung about in barracks at the harbour-master's office. Two of these youths directed us to a reserved part of the quay, helped us secure, and then took us to the customs office across the road. The official there backed us each into an armchair, produced cigarettes and sent out to the *cafenion* around the corner for thick Turkish coffee for three. Meanwhile we learned our first three or four Greek words and completed various declarations on our official cruising log, a document we would have to present at every port while in Greek waters.

During our sojourn in the Arctic, Katie and I had thoroughly studied from books the problem of wintering in Greece and even then we had decided on going to the wooded little island of Spetsai close against the Peloponnesus on its eastern side. For the yacht, Spetsai offered a harbour that was clean and safe in all weather conditions, and with a local population of three thousand the place would be big enough to provide a few basic amenities and small enough to be peaceful and intimate. So at any rate we hoped, and now that we were only 160 sea miles from Spetsai we wanted to cover the distance as soon as possible and settle down for a time to a peaceful harbour-bound existence.

However constant gale warnings kept us at Pylos for the next three days so we cooled our heels by prowling the food stalls in the main square, dining out at tables on the waterfront and absorbing a little local history, of which there is ample. Where in Greece is there not? It was here, in the spacious waters of Navarino Bay that Greek independence from despotic centuries-old Turkish rule was born. In 1827 Admiral Codrington entered the bay in the command of twenty-seven allied British, French and Russian men-o-war. Already at anchor in the bay were 82 warships of the occupying Turkish-Egyptian forces. Some trigger-happy Turk opened up on boats of the allied fleet and this sparked off a monumental battle that lasted many hours and destroyed nearly all the Turkish fleet. They still lie there on the bottom of the bay, but as with so many other historical sites in Greece have long since been plundered by treasure and curio seekers. Then going back a bit there is another medieval fortress at Paleokastro (Greek for "ancient castle") at the north end of the bay. And further back still there is King Nestor's palace of 1200 B.C. lying unearthed, or at least its foundations are, and more ancient still presumably is the bat-infested cave near Paleokastro where the precocious infant Hermes hid away the sacred cattle after stealing them from Apollo.

At last with a forecast of variable Force 3 winds and a sunny blue sky, *Nanook's* moorings were slipped and we caught a light breeze to carry us down the coast to Methoni, then with a left turn past the deserted islands of Sapienza and Venetico we sailed out over a gentle sea across the Gulf of Kalamata. Progress was slow across the gulf most of the day which meant that it was dark well before we had raised the light of Cape Matapan at the extreme southern tip of the middle finger of the Peloponnesus. Four miles round the cape on the east side was the sheltered little bay of Port Kaio where I had meant to anchor for the night. But there was no chance of that now. The night was black and a rising north-easter was heaping steep seas onto our bow.

"Don't worry, we'll make for Kapsali on the south end of Kithera," I assured Katie who was depressed and frightened, and once again very sick. "Kapsali will give us much better shelter in this wind. Just this one more night at sea. . . ." By dawn we were off the high Kithera coast under very reduced canvas and a full gale was once more upon us, hurling itself down on our little yacht and hammering at our sails as we tried to beat up towards the harbour. Every foot to windward was a tormenting struggle. After several hours of this we came at last close in to the precipitous southern coast. I had hoped for a degree of shelter under the lee of such high rugged bluffs but instead the wind ripped down off the heights and tore even more furiously at the sea surface than it did out in the open as if angry at having been forced to rise up over the land. Just out from the supposed shelter of Kapsali's harbour, about half a mile from the entrance, we found the wind blowing at a maniac rate, tearing white sheets of water off the surface and screaming through the rigging with the fury of fifty witches. The lee rail was buried in froth. Down below, the motion as well as the noise of the wind, the thundering sails and the labouring engine was altogether more than our frayed nerves could stand. "Let's forget about Kithera," Katie called at me in anguish. "Can't we just lie ahull?" I couldn't have agreed more. I clawed forward over the deck to the mainmast, clipping my safety harness to lifelines and shrouds as I went, and dowsed the reefed main and staysail, (all that was left still up), lashed the tiller down, and shut off the engine. Suddenly all became peaceful again. The gale was firmly shut outside the companionway hatch. *Nanook* ceased her belaboured punching and lay with a gentle lifting and falling, beam on to the seas. She occasionally threw her capping rail down into the brine as a steep sea struck her weather side but she rolled gently back each time with a sea-kindly motion that was a great relief after the torment of the previous hours. "Blow winds and crack your cheeks," she seemed to say to the din in her rigging.

Except for the cooking of meals and the occasional glance out for shipping, we lay strapped in our bunks for the rest of the day, the following night and the day after. All this time I tuned in regularly to the Athens radio for the shipping forecasts in the Greek language, which with the knowledge of a dozen or so words could be more or less understandable. One thing though puzzled me; every bulletin seemed to contain some reference to "October 4" and almost a week had passed since that date. I soon realised that they were forecasting winds "Okto Beaufort" or Force 8.

That was small comfort to us as we lay listening to the incessant din outside. We reassured ourselves with promises that we would move ashore into a little Greek villa as soon as we arrived in Spetsai, that we would never again choose to stay out at night when a port offered itself, and that in fact we would give up the idea of sailing around the world altogether, since we were so obviously unsuited to it, and hurry back to the Arctic where we belonged. But "vows made in storms are forgotten in calms," and these were no exception.

There was no let-up in the wind and no improvement seemed imminent so we decided to retreat back to Pylos and with the stout little staysail up I set a course to the northwest.

But in the middle of the night the wind seemed at last to be easing so again we turned onto the other tack and tried for Kithera arriving close in to the coast towards midday, and again we were driven off by the relentless gale. This time we made for the shelter of Port Kaio near Cape

Matapan, arriving there late in the afternoon, and there at last, under the blank eyes of a deserted monastery, we dropped the anchor.

We were both greatly relieved to lie peacefully in the little anchorage but we couldn't enjoy it for long. Our anchorage was sheltered from all winds except the cursed *meltemi,* the north-easter we had been enduring, and though it had eased a lot during the afternoon, it was forecast to return during the night and I much preferred to face it again at sea rather than in the bay, so we resolved to clear out after a brief rest. But even the hope of that rest was illusory. Having foolishly allowed the main and staysail to develop long tears along the luff I now had to set to work to repair the damage, a chore that took me three hours. By that time it was dark again and with a decent meal inside us we felt our way out and put to sea to try our luck again, this time with the Elephonisos Channel north of Kithera. A night of tacking well up into the gulf in a Force 4 to 5 wind still out of the north-east brought us within the channel, and early in the fresh clear dawn we sailed close-hauled past the northern coast of Kithera to starboard, and to port the two-thousand-foot frown of Cape Malea. "Round Malea and forget your native land." So said the sailors of Ancient Greece bound for the raw untutored lands of the west. But the words might just as well have served for us bound east, for here at last we entered the fabled Aegean.

We sailed eastward on the port tack far enough to lay a course on the other tack to Spetsai, but as the bright sunny morning wore on, the wind that had so opposed our entry into the Aegean fell away to a light air.

By early afternoon we abandoned all pretence of sailing and began motoring the final fifty miles north with sails furled for the last time that year. After lying off half the night waiting for the day light near Spetsepoula, Spetsai's little neighbour and the private island retreat of Stavros Niarchos, we motored the final few miles in the morning into the snug and pleasant little harbour that was to be *Nanook's* home for the winter. With a long stern anchor warp across the creek *Nanook* nosed her way in amongst the local *caiques,* the wooden trading and fishing boats characteristic of the Greek islands, and she was secured to two of the old cannons that had once defended the island and that now stood upright in a line along the quayside.

This last passage from Pylos had taken us five days and nights and according to the Sumlog we had sailed 358 miles in that time to make good a good distance of 160 miles. From Gibraltar on, light airs, gales and flat calms had been our portion and we had had a total of only thirty six hours of reasonable sailing ever since entering the Straits. We were now beginning to realise what an unpredictable and difficult place the Mediterranean is for a boat under sail. The Odyssey could only have happened there. We went ashore to the little waterside restaurant run by Xaralambos and sat down in the sunshine on the vine-covered terrace and

began to celebrate our arrival. We felt inordinately pleased with ourselves.

Having resolutely secured *Nanook* for the winter to the mud and
cannons of Spetsai, we now relaxed into a pleasant routine of idling and
eating of the lotus. We wandered around the waterfront each morning to
the town a mile distant to buy bread straight from the baker's oven and
pick up a few vegetables and fruit from the *caique* that brought them from
the mainland. We kept the *galloni* topped up with retsina wine for our
own consumption as well as for the entertainment of a succession of
visitors. ("This resinated wine from the Peloponnesus is anathema to
Western palates," the guidebooks warned us. We didn't find it so.) We
went hiking along the roads, giving way only to horse-drawn carriages for
the islanders had banished motorcars to the mainland. We went swimming
on the newly deserted beaches and climbing in the warm pine forests.

Shipboard chores had to be faced from time to time. Sails had to be
sewn, the stove now on a steady diet of dirty kerosene had to be
frequently cleaned, letters written, bilges pumped. But nothing was
incapable of waiting until the next day. Imperative tasks were delayed for
weeks until a moment of boredom allowed us to attend to them. For the

The little inlet on the island of Spetsai where *Nanook* spent her first
winter.

time being we'd had enough of the daily struggle and we allowed nothing to upset our avowed intention of enjoying ourselves.

To help us out in that respect we had the good fortune to be joined later in October by *Thistle,* a black Scottish fishing boat which nosed in alongside us in a gap vacated by one of the local *caiques.* Aboard *Thistle* Tony Powell and his wife Si with their three children had taken a year off and cruised from their home in England down through the French canals and via the French and Italian islands to Greece. Their cheerful company and in particular Tony's salacious wit helped enliven many a winter's night. Also amongst the many white-washed houses that crowded the side of the harbour was the hospitable home of another English couple, Richard and Erica Clarke. We all have our weaknesses, and Richard's was an enthusiasm for snakes and lizards. He was something of an amateur expert on the subject of reptiles. He kept cages of them around the house and in endless pursuit of them he and Erica had made expeditions far and wide through Greece and the Middle East.

It happened that I had bought in England a small Seagull outboard for mounting on the tender and by the time we reached Greece I realized that I much preferred to row the little dinghy however far the distance, quite apart from my dislike of having petrol aboard. Richard, ever hopeful of finding a new sub-species, badly wanted to investigate the reptile life on the many uninhabited islands in the area near Spetsai. He already had a dinghy. So we exchanged the Seagull for two months' rent of a small villa adjoining his house and Katie and I moved ourselves ashore in anticipation of colder weather.

In fact high pressure prevailed all over Europe that autumn and we enjoyed many weeks of sunshine and light breezes long after the *siroccos* or southerly gales should have set in. For "The Thistles" this pleasant circumstance was spoiled a little by the annoying daily assurance from the BBC that England was enjoying a hot and unprecedentedly sunny autumn.

At this time Richard's days were filled with enthusiastic jaunts in his dinghy out to the islands in search of lizards. Undaunted by distance he puttered his way over the glassy blue sea to examine islets and rocks in an ever-widening radius. Tony and I were a bit dumbfounded. The dinghy was a flimsy affair of thin plywood and as short trips turned into voyages Tony felt constrained to ask Erica, who encouraged Richard in all this, whether or not she was trying to bump him off. Erica just laughed and said, "Oh, he can do as he likes. If he sinks so much the worse for him." In fact Richard did get caught in the sort of sudden blow that the Aegean so well knows how to serve up without warning, and having been almost pooped before regaining the mainland, he took the hint and abandoned for that year any further quest for reptiles.

But before Christmas arrived the winter season had come to stay. Occasional southerly gales sent caiques scurrying for the shelter of the creek. Sweaters abloom with mould were dragged out of our lockers to counter the chill, donkey loads of firewood came down out of the pine forest to be sold at the little houses of the *Spetsaiotes,* and not even Spetsai's small but eccentric foreign colony any longer indulged in masochistic daily swims.

With the last of the tourists long gone the little town relapsed into a comfortable routine of somnolence and gentle ease. A little bit of work at times, when the mood was on, and a lot of times spent playing cards and drinking retsina at the *cafenion.*

Occasionally on a Saturday night or on somebody's "Saint's Day," Xaralambos's restaurant would explode in a frenzy of good cheer. Tables groaned with delectable mutton stews, *calamaris* or *oktopodi,* mousaka and chips, salads of tomato, onion, *feta* cheese and olive oil, while every remaining chink of table cloth was crowded with glasses and carafes of wine. The tables of Xaralambos were no place for cosy *tête-à-têtes.* If you weren't joining in the fun somebody across the room would order a plate of chips for your table or a bottle of retsina. Someone, usually Yolanda the tomboy, would seize a plate (or even a heap of them) and hurl it to the floor to punctuate an excited tirade, or to defy a recent ban on plate smashing pronounced by the puritanical junta in Athens. Xaralambos, quite unruffled, just added the plates to the bill and swept the pieces away before the police came.

Lines of men inspired by the peculiarly Greek 1–2–3, 1–2, rhythms blaring out of the jukebox danced together with arms across each other's shoulders in the fascinating styles of older days. Dancing is a predominantly masculine art in Greece and one is reminded of the showy strutting cockerel when someone like Andreou, slim, lithe and graceful, takes to the floor. Dark Andreou, the builder of caiques, after dancing alone for a few minutes, stops, seizes the back of his wooden chair in his teeth, and with arms outstretched and neck muscles straining, raises it up over his head and continues his elegant solo ballet till the record runs out.

II

A Winter Interlude

With the Suez Canal closed, the Mediterranean at that time was a backwater to ocean voyagers and we faced the prospect of doubling back on our wake through the Straits of Gibraltar a year later which seemed a pity. But one of our ideas in going to Greece was to trace a journey far south into Africa during the idle winter months when Aegean cruising is out of the question and the cool dry season comes to the lands of Africa north of the equator. Our plan was to travel overland through the countries of the Nile living cheaply and using whatever local transportation was available. Tony and the crew of *Thistle* undertook to keep a close eye on *Nanook* and on New Year's Day we left on the ferry to Piraeus.

A two-day voyage by ship brought us south out of the winter and into the warm sunshine of Alexandria. We found that we had the company of a number of other young Western people on the ship, all bound like us down through Africa and we had the luck to share the company of some of them for much of our journey. We checked into the Alexandria Youth Hostel in the company of two Americans, Harry Gerhart and Brian Kelly and a young Australian couple. After a brief stay at the hostel where we removed the undeclared dollar bills from the linings of our clothes and converted them to piastres at the street rate, the six of us rode the train across the delta to Cairo. Here Katie and I parted company from our friends for the time being. For one thing the youth hostel where they stayed would not accept either our membership, or adding insult to injury, our qualification to the category of "youth." For another, we had already "done" the tourist things years before on our honeymoon. So after a quick gallop on horseback out in the desert to "Sahara City" for a cold beer, Katie and I continued south up the long green valley by train, travelling third class with the hordes.

The journey was interesting but it wasn't easy. The train was full at the Cairo station, but a crowded land knows no state of absolute fullness and as the day wore on every station along the way added more and more to the scrambling shouting masses, black-robed women, boys in pyjamas, old men in cast-off clothing scrambling in through the windows and scruffy soldiers going home on free passes, conscripts mostly, dressed in scratchy looking unpressed khaki uniforms that terminated in greasy hats at one end and worn-out sneakers at the other.

We however were the real freaks of the carriage. Two green apples in a basket of sticky dates. All day while the ageless Egyptian panorama slipped by the window we were inundated with well-meaning attention. Why did we come to Egypt? they asked over and over. What did we think of the regime in Cairo? Did we like the Israelis? How much money did we make in Canada? Were we married? For how long? Did we have any children? Then, (great consternation) *Why not?* Meanwhile those who spoke no English plied us instead with sweet cakes, hunks of sugar cane, glasses of sweet black tea and oranges.

Luxor with its incredible array of tombs and temples kept us occupied for several days until our friends joined us from Cairo. Most of our time had been spent with a certain Hasaan and his donkeys that had carried us into the mountains and the royal burial valleys to the west.

"What have you two been doing here all this time?" Harry wanted to know.

"Oh tramping around old temples over the other side," said Katie, "and climbing in and out of tombs. But mostly just sitting on our asses."

Twice every week at the Aswan High Dam a group of elderly barges secured together with wire rope cast off from their dock and headed up Lake Nasser to the Sudanese border. Having to keep an appointment with one of these, we jostled our way back onto a train and waded through all the usual third class litter of papers, fruit rind and spat-out sugar cane fibre till we found a seat beside a pleasant old Nubian man called Mahmoud who chatted to us in English about his years working with the British army, and about the state of affairs in Egypt and the world.

"All we want," he said, "is to have our land back and to live in peace like brothers. We're not a warrior people. We are a nation of farmers and most of us are sick of war."

Leaving behind the High Dam with its protective crop of barrage balloons we entered on an artificial lake so wide in places that the shore disappeared beyond the horizon and so long that it took us until morning of the third day to reach the Sudanese border. Beneath those waters lie the drowned lands and villages of Nubia and except for the relocated temples of Abu Simbel nothing remains to be seen in any direction but the contradictions of desert and fresh water.

Khartoum lay 26 hours away from the railhead at the end of the lake. Katie and I and our four friends found ourselves an empty compartment on the train. As the first few miles rolled by, the first grey fingers of dust smeared the window, got into our eyes and destroyed the enchantment of the desert sunset glowing red on the stark mesas to the east. We dined on dry bread and jam and hard-boiled eggs, and washed this down with sweet water from a long earthenware pitcher at the end of the carriage.

It was, as the Beatles would say, "a hard day's night." Three of us curled up on the dusty wooden floor, two more on the seats and one in the luggage rack. The train took the desert shortcut across the Nile's great S bend and by morning we had rejoined the river where it boils northwards at the fifth cataract. We were filthy. The dust was in our eyes and nostrils. It crunched between our teeth and with a light beating it flew in clouds from our clothes. Our hair was grey and sticky from grit. The land was flat, empty and featureless right to the horizon, worse than the Canadian prairies.

But eventually we came to the town of Atbara where the river of that name, the Nile's final tributary, brings down its seasonal flood from Ethiopia. We refreshed ourselves with cups of sweet tea and rejoined the train for the tedium of the long ride to the river town of Shendi, a name evocative of great markets where ivory, camels and fun-loving Galla girls from Ethiopia were bought and sold not so long ago as time is measured on the Nile. The camels at least are still items of commerce. Our train was delayed here three hours waiting for another train to pass. Every wagon was full of camels and there must have been fifty wagons.

"Camel train," Katie mumbled.

Khartoum at the confluence of the two Niles demanded several days of our time if only to extract from the Ministry of the Interior permission to go on any further. We established ourselves at the youth hostel, a place run with benign neglect that allowed us to come and go at all hours and all six of us to share a room without having to worry about the nonsense of segregating the sexes.

The Australian couple decided to travel south by steamer up the White Nile. Katie and I had that trip in mind for the return journey and decided with the Americans, Harry and Brian, to go east from Khartoum into Ethiopia. So the four of us set off together by bus across an appalling plain of grey dust to the green irrigated lands of the Atbara and the town of Kassala close against the Ethiopian foothills.

The border lands were aswarm with *shifta* (bandits) and we noticed that all the tough-looking fuzzy-haired tribesmen who came riding into town on their camels had swords strapped to their sides. The four of us flew across this no-man's-land and up to the town of Asmara, 8000 feet up at the edge of the Ethiopian highlands, and after wishing Brian and Harry luck on their journey to Addis, Katie and I diverted from the steep escarpment lands to the fierce heat of Massawa on the Red Sea, where we relaxed for a few days on the beaches of deserted offshore islands.

Back in Asmara we joined a shrill quarrelsome mob of local people for the journey by bus to Addis. It promised to be a long test of endurance. We travelled only by day as all traffic had to be off the highways at night because of the *shifta*. The road reared and plunged the first day into the rugged wilderness of the Simien Mountains and the scenery became more astonishing at every bend. The bus whined up and down and around all day in low gear and it had barely extricated itself from the yawning gorge of the Takkaze River before the sky turned dark and we pulled into the primitive little town of Addi Arkai, where in the usual absence of anything else we dined on the ubiquitous national dish of *wat* a fiery red meat and gristle stew, and a sour grey fermented bread called *injera,* a strange damp flabby substance like grey foam rubber. Katie quickly came to dislike the stuff but I always managed to shove a yard or two of the flat mess down before giving up. At least it was a good vehicle for conveying *wat* to the mouth in the prevailing absence of cutlery.

We retired to a cheap little hostelry with instructions that we were to be called at four to catch the bus. It was well that the night ended as soon as it did. Before leaving I checked on the sheets for I felt itchy. I counted fully four varieties of insects there, and of all these the bed bugs had a working majority. Back on the bus I counted 41 bites on one leg alone. I itched maddeningly for the next three days. Yet Katie came through the night unscathed.

Another day followed through a land yellowed by the dry season till we arrived at the outlet to Lake Tana, the source of the Blue Nile.

Here Katie and I decided on a diversion and let the bus continue without us. The Tesissat Falls on the Blue Nile are several miles below the outlet. In the dry season they are a long series of thundering cataracts interrupted by outcrops of rocks and trees at the edge of the precipice. They are very attractive but not especially awesome on the scale of the Victoria or Murchison Falls. They are, as Dr. Johnson said of the Giant's Causeway, "worth seeing, yes, but not worth going to see."

We were to regret losing our bus connection. The next bus going to Addis was big and modern to the extent at least that it had a radio at the dashboard and three loudspeakers over the aisle. No sooner were we on the road to Addis after the usual delays than we were subjected to a steady diet of caterwauling Ethiopian music turned up to a screeching full volume. I like to think my tastes in music are reasonably catholic. I can enjoy an Eskimo dirge or the songs of Greece with their five or seven beats to the bar, Arab music is hauntingly attractive in modest doses, evocative of veiled women, mosques, markets and camel dung. Even a few lines of atonal wailing of the Indian sitar can be tolerated without great effort. But I positively draw the line at the hideous high pitched repetitive yowling of those highlanders. It went on and on for hours on end without pause killing conversation and destroying our enjoyment of the passing scene. We tried cotton wool in our ears, then chewing gum, but the electronic screeching seemed to enter through the skull itself vibrating the very juices of the brain.

We stopped for the night in a dull little village and found for ourselves an insect-free bed. Katie had been less able to endure the exquisite torture of that bus than I and now dissolved in tears. She was reduced to a nervous jelly, she said, and she swore she could not endure another day of it, much as we wanted to reach Addis and be done with the open road.

Later when all seemed quiet I groped around in my rucksack for a knife and strode nonchalantly toward the bus intending to unscrew the speakers and sabotage the wiring but alas some people were on board sleeping. I prepared to go ahead anyway and carry the thing through with stealth. But the sleepers stirred and mumbled and looked at me. I gave them five minutes to settle down again and began turning the screws when a robed figure sat up sharply and began accusing me in loud tones, waking the others and stirring up a hornet's nest from which I quickly retreated, hoping at least that I'd ruined a night's sleep for the wretch.

We returned aboard next morning with misgivings and for most of that day we were served up with the same entertainment. But at least progress was better. The long ear-popping descent into the canyon of the Blue Nile was followed by flatter plateau lands and by late afternoon we were striding happily through the streets of lively Addis Ababa, where to our delight we discovered Brian and Harry in a little Italian restaurant. It was nice to be with friends again but it was not for long. They were off next morning on a plane to Nairobi. We ourselves were soon bound west on a side journey to Gambela in the remote province of Illubabor, a most unEthiopan place where big game inhabit a hot jungled land of rivers flowing to the White Nile. In this unlikely corner of a Caucasoid land the people are Negro tribesmen related to those living in the southern Sudan and indeed many were refugees of the nasty little Sudanese war downriver. They were a friendly and interesting people, given to tribal cicatrices, beads, ivory arm bands and as little clothing as decently possible, that depending on whether in town or out.

We found lodgings in a tin shanty that called itself a hotel and excepting for the heat and insects we rather enjoyed the funny little place. Like so many backward communities around the globe, Gambela had in addition to its other insoluble problems a number of American missionaries and some Peace Corps volunteers. The latter were a cheerful little group who didn't take themselves too seriously and consequently were on good terms with the local people. Just a month previously one of their number while bathing in the Baro River had been taken by a crocodile. He had waded out waist deep when he was suddenly snatched under. The water thrashed white for a few moments and then he was gone. The river was sealed off up and downstream and after a long patient hunt a huge crocodile was discovered and killed and the body removed from the gory stomach, the only recognizable piece being part of a leg.

Each day around noon I went down to the Baro to cool off in the water but with this story in mind as well as my concern for the danger of bilharzia I was a lot more circumspect than I otherwise would have been in such tormenting heat.

I was sitting on a stone once with feet and ankles in the water when another naked bather, a tribesman from downriver, came to borrow my soap. He'd learned English at a mission school in the Sudan. As he waded out he asked me why I didn't venture into the river myself and my explanation set him chortling with glee. "*Firange* (foreigners) no more swim," he giggled.

When he rejoined me at the edge he settled himself on another stone and recounted tales of the troubles in the Sudan between government troops and tribesmen and of how he had managed to escape into Ethiopia.

I had a beer beside me and offered him a drink, but no thanks, he couldn't drink beer, he was a Moslem. I remarked that it must be hard to follow Islam in such a thirsty land, but he would have none of that. He had tried both and it was harder, he assured me, to be a Christian. He complained that Christianity placed unreasonable strictures on his love life and if he had to do without something he preferred the don'ts of Islam to the don'ts of Christianity.

> Thou shalt have one god only. Who
> Would be at the expense of two?

There was only one way south out of Ethiopia and that was by air. Returning to Addis, we flew from there to Nairobi and after a few days of civilization and game parks we hitch-hiked into pre-Amin Uganda and continued by air from Entebbe to Juba in the southern Sudan where we embarked on the upper deck of the river steamer that was bound down the White Nile to Kosti five days away to the north.

The great river winds interminably through a primitive wilderness of savannah and swamp. Occasional villages of Dinka, Shilluk and Nuer tribesmen passed astern. The steamer pulled in at some of the bigger settlements where noisy mobs swarmed along the banks to join us in the journey north or to sell produce to the passengers: bananas, eggs, live gazelles or footstools. After an hour or so with a hoot from the bridge the armed guard of Arabs would begin driving the excited crowds back to the shore with shouts and shoves, some toppling backwards off the decks into the river, and the sternwheeler with its assortment of barges would resume its cumbersome progress downstream.

Eventually we reached the Sudd, the world's biggest swamp, larger than all England where the bulk of the White Nile's volume is lost to

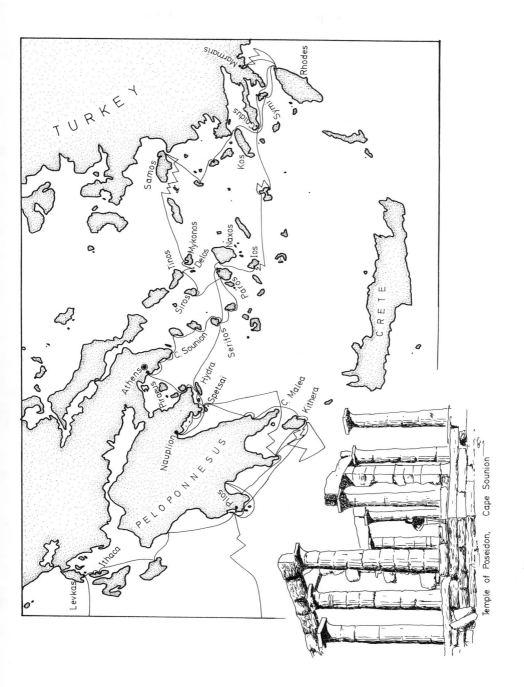

TURKEY

Marmaris

Rhodes

Symi

Nidus

Samos

Kos

Mykonos

Naxos

Tinos

Delos

Ios

Siros

Paros

CRETE

C. Sounion

Seritos

Athens

Hydra

Piraus

Spetsai

C. Malea

Nauplion

Kithera

P E L O P O N N E S U S

Pios

Ithaca

Levkas

Temple of Poseidon, Cape Sounion

evaporation. The river there disperses into a maze of changing channels lined with papyrus and choked with hyacinth. The steamer with its unwieldy retinue of housed-in barges had great difficulty getting through this tortuous mire. Each time a sharp bend came up the pilot simply put the wheel hard over and the barges, side-slipping through the water, crashed sideways against the banks of soft mud and papyrus.

The clumsy craft all came to a shuddering halt, backed off and then resumed progress in the new direction leaving the great scar of black mud and broken weed on the bank.

Emerging from this colossal swamp the steamer brought us out to the drier lands of Malakal. From there on Africa seemed behind us and we were again in the lands of the Arabs with a flat parched plain on all sides until to our vast relief we reached Kosti and debarked for the train ride to Khartoum.

Then came the excruciatingly long journey down the Nile to Alexandria, a journey unrelieved either by comfort or novelty. A mercifully quick passage on a Russian ship brought us back to Piraeus where the ferry to Spetsai lay waiting.

We had been gone two months and it felt wonderful to be "home" again in the creek aboard *Nanook* with *Thistle's* crew for neighbours, the myriad flowers bursting under the olive trees and the gentler winds of spring whispering to us of the islands over the sea.

III

Wine Dark Seas

During the early spring *Nanook* was made ready for sea. I tuned up the diesel as well as my mechanical ignorance permitted. Sails were bent on. I was robbed of 2,500 drachmas by one of the local boat yards for a two-day haulout, and in a short time we were ready.

After a few preliminary day sails taking friends out to anchorages around the island and trying to recompense them in this way for their many kindnesses during the winter, we set out up the Argolikos Gulf. The nights were still cool but the days were sunny and warm. Each morning before dawn a great comet with a luminous million mile tail appeared in the eastern sky.

We stopped overnight at little villages and uncertain anchorages till we reached the large town of Nauplion at the head of the gulf. We were grateful to get in there for as we approached a cold unpleasant wind reminding us of December struck at us out of the west and for several days it rampaged down off the heights. This Indian winter kept the townsfolk wrapped up in sweaters and jackets and prevented us from leaving the boat to venture inland as we'd planned to Epidavros and the ruins of Mycenae. We never even climbed the castellated ramparts of the Venetian citadel on the mountain behind the town but contented ourselves with scurrying ashore to the baker and the butcher and hurrying back aboard for cups of hot coffee.

Nanook lay quietly enough while the wind buffeted her. She was moored alongside the town's waterfront where according to legend Amymoni the beautiful daughter of King Danaos was out walking long ages ago on a sunnier day. A small deer ran out across her path. Amymoni shot at it with her bow but the arrow missed and instead hit a sleeping satyr who woke with a roar of pain, seized the girl and prepared to rape her. The god Poseidon heard her cries and came to her assistance driving off the now twice-injured satyr. This accomplished Poseidon proceeded to carry on where the satyr had left off. The result of this was the birth of a son Nauplios who later became one of the heroes venturing on the quest for the golden fleece. When he returned from that expedition he built the town of Nauplion.

For the present Poseidon seemed in a grumpy mood and treated us to chilly squalls and the gulf with roaring whitecaps. We thought on looking out one morning that the wind had eased and accordingly we cast off waving to the lone cadet on the quay whose raised eyebrows seemed to say "Are you sure you know what you're doing?" Just a short way out, but far enough to preclude a hard beat back, up came the wind again our dreaded Okto Beaufort and drove us down the gulf under bare poles to the safety of Spetsai.

Next morning spring had reasserted herself and with a soft northerly just filling the three big sails we stole across the water under the lee of Dhokos to Hydra, a long island with a 2,000 ft. central spur and a pleasant animated little harbour which is the centerpiece of the great three-sided amphitheatre of the town itself, its slopes aswarm with white houses. The Piraeus ferry delivered its cargo of tourists twice a day in the season, but as yet the town was as pleasantly quiet as in mid-winter.

We day-sailed from there to the town of Poros on the island of the same name, mooring alongside the busy waterfront like the *caiques* that lie there selling vegetables, for to go bow in would have left our stern warp in the ferry channel. The whitewashed houses and the twisty little staired streets of Poros seemed to us irresistibly appealing and as in so many other towns in Greece we found ourselves thinking, wouldn't it be nice to live in that house, or I wonder what this one would cost. But as Arthur Ransome said "Houses are but poorly built boats so firmly aground that you cannot think of moving them." No doubt we would quickly come to regret such secure moorings. In our little ketch on the quayside we already had the ideal house secured to the choicest site in a town full of nice houses and choice sites. And we had our freedom to boot.

Bound for Piraeus we left the land-locked Poros Channel at first light hoping for a breeze outside but scarcely any wind offered itself and the diesel pushed us over a slight oily swell past Methana and Aegina and the Doric temple of Aphaia. By mid afternoon the humid grey pall overhead was muscled aside by the drier air and blue sky from the east and in a short time another gale had come up which drove us towards the land and sent us surging with beating hearts past the breakwater and into the yacht harbour of Passalimani where we gladly moored in the fertile filth of the place amongst the glossy giants of the Greek charter industry.

We remained there eight days while various jobs were done to the boat. Sails had to be restitched, cockpit cushions and a new awning made, charts purchased and the compass refilled with fluid. Meanwhile to our great delight we took on board an unexpected guest. Harry Gerhart, our

Leaving the harbour of Syros, bound for Tinos, Harry Gerhart is at the helm.

recent companion who had shortened many a long mile with his wit and cheerful charm on the monotonous journey into Africa, appeared now at the end of the bowsprit still bearing his heavy rucksack and bearded grin. In Addis we had invited Harry to rendezvous with us in the Aegean but his arrival was premature for more troubles had broken out in the Sudan and he had to fly all the way from Nairobi. His time was limited but he hoped to see something of the Aegean before continuing home. This, as well as the sewage outfalls and the inordinate cost of mooring beside them, prompted us to conclude matters quickly in Piraeus and to set sail down the sunny Attic shore bound for the islands of the blest.

After a long afternoon of beating we turned at dusk into a pleasant little anchorage in the bay of Anavissos. By the time the anchor was let go daylight and the breeze had both gone and the full moon glowed over the peaceful place clearly outlining anchor, cable and *Nanook's* shadow on the sandy bottom. We waved a goodnight to our own shadows, they waved back and we all turned in.

We left again at dawn, breakfasted our way down the rest of Attica and stopped as voyagers in small boats must at Homer's "Holy Sounion the cape of Athens."

Here Katie surreptitiously lifted off a couple of small splinters of wood from the corner of a frame near her bunk and pocketed these as we rowed ashore. Cape Sounion is the headland on which the marble temple of Poseidon has stood for so many centuries, "a range of columns long by time defaced" and in the centre of the ruin Katie scraped away an inch or two of dust and buried the splinters, with no doubt a silent inward prayer for Poseidon's blessing, the essence of which in her case would have been simply "Dear god, let there be no more gales." This little pagan ritual was concluded by leaving a small pyramid of pebbles over *Nanook's* sacrificial flesh. Indeed there followed three weeks of idyllic weather when we drifted in sunshine from one island to another all the way across the Aegean to the Turkish coast and if the wind was not exactly what a gung-ho enthusiast like Harry expected, there was enough of it, and little enough of it, for Katie.

It carried us that same day over to Kea our first Cycladean island which looked from the sea dull arid and uninviting but actually had an abundance of oak forests, springs and productive little valleys where the islanders cultivate vineyards and market gardens. From our anchorage in Vourkari Bay we sailed on to Port Merika on Kithnos, an island which like Kea had little appeal to yachts and all we accomplished by going ashore was the purchase of some indifferent bread and a kilo of the rankest retsina in Greece.

We continued on to the more interesting island of Serifos which is entered on its southern coast where a wide inlet penetrates inland to the high hills. On the summit of one of these a great dollup of white icing seems to have been poured, spilling a short distance downhill in an uneven line. This is the *chora* or capital of the island, a town of little rectangular houses that crowd every terrace and cleft on the summit of the steep mountain.

Many islands have their *chora* perched in this way high up in the hills back from the sea. This was a defensive tactic against pirates, necessary up until the early nineteenth century when the British navy dispelled the marauders from the Aegean. Nowadays living on such an inconvenient ridge must at times be a thundering nuisance but happily the people have not succumbed to convenience and rebuilt around the more obvious harbour. No doubt the time will come.

Two days later *Nanook* entered Kamares Bay on Sifnos, the southern neighbour of Serifos. The three of us went ashore to the little town in search of meat but it was Good Friday, a big occasion throughout Greece. For some weeks the butchers had been out of business while the faithful confined themselves to fish. Now all the weekend lamb roasts were trussed up in yards and on cobbled corners bleating out their last hours before the slaughter. Katie finally located a freezer in a little shop and triumphantly extracted a hunk of frozen Argentine beef, a poor man's diet to the Greeks at Easter.

We didn't care much for the indifferent shelter of the barren hills around Kamares and we scuttled south for the night to the nearly-all-round shelter of Port Vathy, a sandy bay with a few scattered houses. Here on the beach we gathered sticks and driftwood for a bonfire and while Harry regaled us with his hilarious stories we celebrated the season with our own simple feast of barbecued meat, potatoes blackened in the hot coals, salad, fresh bread and retsina. Life has its compensations.

Sifnos has only a small population and makes no pretense of being anything more than a neglected backwater. Yet in ancient times it was the wealthiest place in Greece with a rich gold mine in its hills. The islanders at that time set aside each year a portion of their bounty for public works and the building of monuments, dividing the rest among themselves. The Syphnians once asked the oracle at Delphi how long their wealth would last. The oracle's reply was "Danger will come from a wooden host and a scarlet herald." Shortly after this a red ship from Samos arrived to request a loan of the rich islanders. The Syphnians refused so the men of Samos gathered a fleet and sacked the town and the prophecy was fulfilled.

While the Easter moon waned *Nanook* sailed on over the gentle Aegean and April numbered her last ten days by the anchorages we occupied, animated little white ports, sleepy quayside hamlets and remote coves, rocky and deserted. Days of sunshine and retsina and light winds. Poros where Katie gathered pen shells and fell for a little town of winding

A quiet corner on the island of Mykonos.

streets all asplash with whitewash. Syros where 20,000 people divide themselves between two hills, Catholic on one, Orthodox on the other and where *loukoumi* or Turkish delight is made, and sold like the nougat of Montelimar at prices inflated by fame. Tinos, the "Lourdes of Greece" where brightly painted caiques unload along the taverna-littered quayside and where generations of pilgrims have nourished an industry of garish religious trinkets and gew-gaws. Mykonos, an island we had rejected earlier as being unfit to visit on account of its poor harbour and appalling popularity with tourists but which we quickly loved on personal acquaintance.

And Delos. Once this narrow sliver of land, we are told, floated loosely on the sea, tossed about by waves, insecure and despised by men. Leto, a Titan's daughter, came to the island, pregnant from an affair with Zeus who had then rejected her out of fear of his ever-jealous wife Hera. The girl had been turned away from other countries and islands for the same reason; the people were afraid of offending Hera by giving refuge to her rival. But the little island welcomed her gladly and at that moment four enormous pillars rose from the bottom of the sea and secured the island forever. Leto gave birth to the twin gods Apollo and Artemis at a spot where later the temple of Apollo was built and so the most despised of islands became the holiest and most renowned in the Aegean, the centre of the Delian Confederation of island states. Once a stirring and populous capital it is now barren and uninhabited but it is still a place of extensive ruins that are invaded daily by the tourist hordes from Mykonos who come to stare at the theatre, the mosaics, the sacred lake and the terrace of skinny lions carved in Naxian marble, or scramble up the stone stairway to the top of Mount Cynthus to gaze down over the marble strewn land that has now reverted to cattle and goats.

> Such is the aspect of this shore
> Tis Greece, but living Greece no more.

A night passage took us north around harbourless Ikaria to Samos and the little port of Tigani hard against the shores of Turkey. The forested heights of Samos and the green productive farmlands between were in great contrast to the barren Cyclades which we had left behind. The shallow circular little port with its long outer mole may have inspired Tigani's name which means frying pan, but the Greek government was not amused by the resemblance and renamed the place Pythagorian in honour of the great mathematician who was born there.

Now, to our regret, Harry who was booked soon on a flight out of Athens prepared to leave us, but not before he had attracted around the boat a chattering swarm of young ladies down on a visit from the island of Chios. They liked Harry's beard and wondered aloud what it would be like to be kissed by it. They quickly decided that of the two males on board Harry was obviously the captain and addressed him as such. Had it been anyone else I'd have been glad to see him go.

On our own once again, Katie and I day-sailed south through the Dodecanese islands of Patmos and Seros, down to Kos and around the windy southwest corner of Turkey to Panormitis Bay in beautiful Symi, a poor rugged island close against the Turkish coast. Panormitis is a delightful place with all-round shelter in wild surroundings. A large monastery dominated one side of the bay but only two monks lived in the huge building. It was said that by tradition vessels entering Panormitis were always greeted with a peal of bells from the monastery. So as we passed through the narrow entrance we listened for Monk Gabriel to sound the welcome. But the bell tower remained ominously silent.

"I shouldn't have been sacrificing to Poseidon I suppose" said Katie as the anchor chain rattled out.

"I don't think it's that," I replied, "I imagine they'd just like you to get dressed," Katie was wearing the skimpiest of bikinis which by her own sea-going standards was cold-weather gear but in this part of the world a bikini didn't always cover enough and even her mini-skirt was indecent enough to have us driven from the gates of the enormous monastery that dominates the *chora* and the whole island of Patmos.

Still, we were forgiven. Katie put on her longest dress and we went ashore. A monument on the waterfront commemorated an uncooperative monk who was shot by the Germans during the war and as we gazed at this, Monk Gabriel came to introduce himself and invited us to tour his grand twelfth century domain and to join him in pieces of cake and a glass of peach and honey wine, all of his own making.

But you can't please everybody all the time and Poseidon, doubtless offended, kept us holed up in Panormitis for three days while hard winds buffetted us from the eastern hills, winds useless to us for we were bound east to Rhodes and the coast of southern Turkey.

By this time I was able to understand Greek well enough to follow the shipping forecasts on Athens radio and we tuned in to these regularly, even though they never seemed to be accurate. Versions of these were also broadcast in English, French and German but we found the translations as confusing as the forecasts were inaccurate. One entry in my log reads, "A system of pressures covers Greece with intense light winds over all seas. Present conditions are expected to continue changing."

While we were windbound we ran out of a number of supplies including bread. Katie was an accomplished bread baker from her years in the Arctic, but since we had no oven she decided to try her hand at soda scones done in a frying pan. The result of this first attempt was a heavy muddy yellow substance which however we undertook to eat. We subsequently suffered from upset stomachs and Katie belatedly acknowledged that the flour, last year's, was a bit mouldy and the baking powder was wet.

"I don't like soda scones," she complained. "They make me feel so disconsolate."

When subsequently I discarded the remainder of the batch into Mandraki Harbour in Rhodes Katie remonstrated with me for contributing to harbour pollution but I couldn't help pointing out that the holding ground on the bottom would be all the better for it. From then on her soda scones, little five minute miracles of puffiness, never looked back.

A morning sail brought us around the north end of Rhodes and off the reef-strewn entrance of Mandraki Harbour where we doused sail and motored cautiously past the ancient mole where it is said the great colossus once stood. Built to commemorate the wars of Demetrius the Besieger, the 105 feet of bronze stood there for only 50 years during the third century B.C. before being felled by an earthquake, and for 900 years thereafter it lay in the shallow water of Mandraki Harbour, to be sold ultimately for scrap to a Syrian Jew.

Throughout our stay in Greece we were surprised at the lack of other private cruising yachts. There were plenty of large vessels under charter but only twice did we see other private cruising yachts under sail. As usual at Mandraki we found the berthing area for foreign yachts almost deserted but a small cabin cruiser was moored there and as we lined ourselves up to secure beside it a man stepped from it onto the quay to take our lines and surprised us greatly by calling out, "Hello *Safari Too.*" It turned out that the young couple aboard the motor boat, Graham and Juta Townsend, had sailed from Australia via Capetown to Florida in a small cutter and had shared many ports of call along the way with the Frosts in *Safari Too.* Graham and Juta had made a voyage in their new boat across Europe and into the Black Sea by way of the Danube. They had arrived in Rhodes in December so they were able to help us with our shopping by recommending the best bargains in the white octagonal market across the road, the best restaurants and the shops within the walls of the old medieval city of the Knights of St. John.

In renaming our ketch we had, according to time-honoured tradition, invited bad luck on her and on ourselves. We had therefore rather shocked Kurt by changing the name he had chosen. Many other yachtsmen believe in these traditions and we now raised our friends' eyebrows by announcing one evening our intended departure from Rhodes the next morning.

"But you can't do that. Tomorrow's Friday," they pointed out in all apparent seriousness.

Friday or not, *Nanook* caught for once a good sailing breeze and romped across the straits to the Turkish mainland. A stiff land breeze came up in the approaches to Marmaris and after a hard beat through the narrows we found ourselves in a large fiord-like bay with here and there entrancing little coves and islands and the primitive but pretty town of Marmaris at the northern end. We were landlocked by green hills and they seemed so vivid and fresh after the treeless and well-peopled slopes of the Aegean.

The trouble about cruising Turkey we had been told was having always to deal with difficult officialdom in every port. So we anchored with some misgivings off the town with the Q flag flying beneath the red and white crescent and star of Turkey. It was not long before we received a crunch on the hull and a boatload of officials scrambled onto the deck and introduced themselves, harbourmaster, police, customs, immigration, health. We shook hands and invited them below where we exchanged pleasantries and cigarettes and after glances at passports and a little desultory form shuffling we were asked to go ashore and visit the offices of each of the five agencies in turn. They assigned a guide to us to lead us back and forth from one office to another for they were located on different streets. In some we were not to escape until a clerk had been sent out for refreshments and we had exchanged over cups of black coffee as much trivia about ourselves as our ignorance of each other's language would allow. One man told us in enthusiastic French that Scandinavians

Katie steps ashore off the bowsprit on the island of Symi.

The harbour of the main town on the island of Symi, looking seaward.

had now started to invade Marmaris in the tourist season and that local opinion had it that these visitors enjoyed an unrestricted sex life. What about England and Canada, he wanted to know, were such things possible in those countries? So to oblige the goo man we painted for him a vivid picture of unbridled license which seemed to gratify him greatly.

It was 2½ hours before we were through this entry process and I calculated that our arrival had consumed 11 man-hours of government time. But no doubt like all the world they need their jobs and if they had delayed us infuriatingly over their irksome scraps of paper, they could not have done so with more charm and goodwill.

The next day laden with fresh fruit and crackly new bread from the market we returned to find *Nanook* slowly dragging her anchor over heavy stones toward the shore so I swung the diesel into action and we left abruptly, bound for some of the hill-girt little anchorages along the west side of the inlet. There we were entirely alone except for an old man with an enormous handlebar moustache, and a boatload of boys who rowed some miles over the bay to sell us a bottle of beer and some onions.

Especially after this enticing glimpse of the unspoiled Turkish seaboard we had wanted to continue further east along the unsurpassed Anatolian coast, and we set out one morning bound east for Fetiye. The weather was clear and pleasant but the wind soon settled in the east, as soon, Katie claimed, as it realized which way we wanted to go. It seemed impossible to reach Fetiye before nightfall. We were already behind a self-imposed schedule for there was plenty of cruising awaiting us beyond Malta and we wanted to be in the Atlantic by September. Besides all this I was becoming impatient to have done with easting and to turn the bows symbolically to the west for that would be our general direction now for one and a half circumnavigations before we could return to our adopted home in the Arctic. With these thoughts in mind and a rising easterly to boot we eased the sheets and with mixed feelings steered off the wind to Rhodes.

Mandraki Harbour was an official port of entry and our only purpose in returning was to be reissued with the mandatory Cruising Log. But the Townsends insisted on a farewell dinner for us, a feast of *dolmades* (meat and rice wrapped in vine leaves) and local wine and after a final night with them in Rhodes we sailed next morning back to Symi, stopping this time at the main port and *chora* on the northeast coast, a harbour that seemed to me badly exposed to the northeast whence blows the fierce *meltemi* of the summer months, and a town that seemed the prettiest and most appealing of all the beautiful places we had so far seen in the Aegean, yet a town on hard times. For want of opportunity locally, the young and enterprising have emigrated to Rhodes and Athens and Australia. Half of the white or pastel tinted houses stood shuttered and empty. Anyone wanting a bargain retirement in lovely surroundings need search no further. A little boat building is done and sponge fishermen still leave the island for the summer diving season off Lybia, though in dwindling numbers. (As Katie said, "It may not be much but it's better than sponging off the government.") Tourism brings in a few pounds, dollars and marks, but not enough. It is the story of many Aegean islands.

We had intended to sail from Symi to Kalimnos, another island of sponge fishermen, but the winds were against that idea and we had discovered by then that when the winds of the Mediterranean had decided where they wanted us to go it was easier by far to take the hint. A motor-sailer perhaps could afford to argue. We drifted to a light air from ahead all day along the Turkish coast to Cape Krio with hopes of turning north there and reaching Kos for the night. But as so often happened as we changed course around the cape so did our head wind, coming at us now from the north and here it strengthened into the bargain. Cape Krio at the end of the Dorian Peninsula, the rocky Asiatic finger off which we lay had tucked in behind its lighthouse-capped bluffs a small pocket-handkerchief bay with two ancient moles protecting its southerly approach, one well preserved the other hidden beneath the surface having succumbed to two and a half thousand years of wave erosion.

I was a little dubious of our reception for we had left Marmaris without clearance and we knew that at least a few soldiers would be stationed ashore. But no other shelter offered itself before nightfall so down came the blue and white stripes of Greece and up again to the crosstrees went the red crescent and star as Katie steered between the moles. Inside the harbour the bottom was a thick grassy mat, and to be sure of the plough holding us up into the now-strong northwesterly I would have had to dive down and drive the point through the dense growth, but a small patch of bare white sand appeared ahead through the clear water and after three abortive passes at it I managed to drop the anchor squarely onto the six foot bull's eye. I then went overboard with the mask to make sure that it had begun to bury itself.

For me, frankly, the nicest moment of every passage is the end of it when the anchor chain stops its outward rattle, the sails are stowed, and the engine if used, can be shut off. Tensions evaporate and while we contemplate our novel surroundings a tranquility descends on *Nanook* and her crew that makes even the worst passage seem worthwhile. We now relaxed to gaze in wonder at the little harbour and its wildly beautiful surroundings. We had come to the ancient city of Cnidus.

Founded about 900 B.C. the Spartan colony of Cnidus grew into a walled city approached by a dual chariot-way, with two harbours, one commercial the other naval, two theatres, acropolis, necropolis and temples. But the city's fame rested even in those ancient times on the marble statue of Aphrodite the Goddess of Love by Praxiteles. That inquiring Roman, Pliny the Elder described the unrivalled nude marble goddess as absolutely perfect in form from every angle, a conclusion that suggests a fairly close scrutiny. Praxiteles' masterpiece at Cnidus was used as a model by so many sculptors of the time that 52 copies are still in existence.

Where now is the beautiful original? No one is sure but its discovery would be one of the greatest prizes of antiquity. One line of enquiry suggests that it was removed in the 4th century to Constantinople where it survived for a thousand years until its destruction in the fires that accompanied the invasion of that city by the Turks. But others dispute this and believe that the statue may yet be found in the ruins of Cnidus. The British archaeologist Sir Charles Newton made a careful survey of the site in the 19th century and carried away a number of relics that now lie in the British Museum. And the quest was taken up more recently this time appropriately by a woman named Love. On the day that Armstrong and Aldrin first stepped down on the surface of the moon, Iris Love stood among these ancient ruins and uncovered for the world the long-lost little circular temple of Aphrodite that housed the famous nude. But no statue.

We gazed over the silent ruins as the sun's shadows lifted up over the rubble-strewn slopes. No one now disturbed the place with trowel or camera. Only a couple of donkeys wandered around the terraced banks of the theatre looking for weeds and braying ridiculously in the growing dusk. We would have liked to come across a terracotta figure or a vivid piece of coloured glass as a souvenir. Erotic little statuettes and pieces of shell-decorated pottery come readily to light we were told and the ground is littered with shards for the ancients had monumental thirsts. But the soldiers had materialized and though they were courteous and friendly I felt constrained to leave the place to its ancient peace. We left in the morning, just as we had promised the officers, at 0530.

We were bound again for Kos and Kalimnos to the north but as the sun rose so did the northerly and soon the short steep little seas began smashing on the weather bow knocking our progress off and forcing us farther off the wind. We quickly took the hint and steered west for Astipalea, a high gaunt island whose inhabitants manage to export a few sheep and a little honey but otherwise are hard put to eke a bare subsistence from the unwilling soil.

Throughout our stay in Greece our bible had been H.M. Denham's excellent sea-guide *The Aegean* and on consulting this we made for the old pirates' lair of Maltezana, a pleasant deserted little bay with, as Denham said, "almost all-round shelter." Here we spent a sleepless night for the wind had discovered the one direction that made the place untenable and we had to reset the anchor twice in the darkness. To know nothing is bad but to learn nothing is worse and I had still not learned to pay out a generous enough scope. At dawn we battled out upwind to the east end of the island and as we then turned northwest along the coast so did the wind turn northwest facing us with an arduous beat along the rugged coastal bluffs to Porto Vathy where at 1500 we ran in through the narrow approach between the hills into a totally landlocked bay. The surroundings were barren and rugged but there were a few houses near the water, the modest homes of farmers and shepherds whose crops were being cultivated on hard-won stone wall terraces.

The wind increased to a gale and we were soon joined by a fishing *caique* seeking shelter and an American couple in their yacht *Xara* from New York. Frances Ann and Frazer were taking their yawl east to the Dodecanese and like ourselves they were finding sailing difficult. "Always too much wind or not enough." It was a familiar complaint. It was good to have their company for the gale lasted off and on for nearly four days. *Nanook* heeled over and snubbed at her chain under the gusts but the CQR was well buried and I made sure of a generous scope of chain so there was no danger of dragging.

We had run out of fresh supplies so I rowed over to the caique in hopes of landing a fish. A line of swarthy men leaned on the rail. I explained in very fractured Greek that we on both yachts would like to buy from them a little of whatever they'd been able to catch at sea.

"Oh of course," they replied, grinning down at me. "Pass up your bucket." They waved away my proffered drachmas and passed the bucket back. Inside were two little sponges.

The racket in the rigging eased on the third afternoon so I set the alarm that night for 0430, half an hour before daylight, and we set out at first light followed by *Xara*. It was still blowing a generous Force 5 from the northwest, not an easy wind for we were bound west for Ios but we were sick of our enforced idleness and we pressed on into the short seas, *Nanook* dancing westwards like a wild horse tightly reined, tossing a mane of white spray over her back. That may sound like an exhilarating joyride but to us it was nothing of the kind. All day long we sat in the cockpit wet and tense while *Nanook* reared and plunged, pounding endlessly into the steep vindictive seas. By evening as we came up to the south end of Ios the wind eased and I was able to smile at Katie for one half of her face and head, the windward half, was white with dried salt. It was long after dark by the time we came to anchor.

At sunrise we looked out the hatch to examine our new surroundings. We lay in a long attractive inlet with dry hills enclosing us almost all round. "Little Malta" the Turks had called Ios on account of this fine little harbour. The road leading uphill to the whitewashed *chora* was stepped with cobbles so that only donkeys and pedestrians passed us on our twenty minute ascent in search of bread and vegetables. This struck us as one-up on Spetsai where cars were banned but not motor scooters many of which set up a rasping racket that would deafen a chain saw. Returning from the cool crooked-laned *chora* we passed a train of mules as they hefted bags of cement up the hill from a *caique* on the quayside. Their master came panting behind them and I wondered if he might soon be trading his animals in for a truck. Ios seemed at the time on the verge of a tourist boom and progress does not tolerate inconveniences, however charming they might be. Typical tourists, we search diligently for the primitive and the simple, and the more we search the more certainly we destroy the very thing we seek.

After three days in Ios we sailed north against a light wind to Naxos the largest of the Cyclades. But we were in a hurry as we had a rendezvous with a friend Sue Pelham in a couple of days so as the log says "we 'did' Naxos in a cool fifty minutes" and sailed west to a deserted anchorage on the north coast of Paros, continuing next day to the *chora* of Paros and on to our old anchorage in Serifos.

Sue had worked for a time as nurse on an Indian reserve in northern Manitoba during the three years that Katie and I lived there. Since then she'd lived in England and we were glad that she had agreed to come cruising with us. We rowed ashore to the marine terminal and searched the faces as people streamed ashore from the Piraeus ferry and at last near the tail end came Sue, pallid from the English winter but pretty as ever and ready to go.

To a certain extent our intended route lay over already familiar ground, back to Spetsai and south around the Peloponnesus. We could have taken the more direct route to the Ionian by way of the Corinth Canal but I rebelled at the high cost of the canal dues and found little apart from Delphi to recommend the route through the rather shelterless Gulf of Corinth. Accordingly after Sue had sampled the delights of Serifos we made a dark and rainy night passage to Hydra and a day sail around Dhokos to Spetsai where we rambled again through the pine forests and filled the *galloni* for the last time with retsina from the cellars of Theodorakis. We then said goodbye to our winter home and motored south over the calm Aegean Sea.

The gaunt bull coast of the Peloponnesus between Spetsai and Malea is a vista of mountain flanks and remote valleys. There are few harbours along the way, but of the few Ieraka is by far the best. As we made our approach beating into a southerly towards a bare cliff face I hardly believed the chart which had assured us of a long inlet with a little village and good depths for anchoring. But the cliffs yielded at the last moment, stepping back on either side to let us pass into an attractive little fiord landlocked by a dog's leg in the approaches. Few cruising yachts come this way and the primitive little hamlet seemed to stare in surprise at our approach. As kerosene lamps came alight in the dusk we rowed ashore for a call at the taverna where fishermen called *"Kalispera"* (good evening) to us and where my "two wives" as the taverna owner put it began eagerly buying up locally made clay pottery.

An ancient town once dominated the approaches to Ieraka high above the cliffs. We went to inspect it in the morning sunshine. The ruins lay in a setting of olives and deserted pastures with a fine view to seaward. Homes and temples could still be traced and the usual litter of shards and marble chips lay all about ploughed into the thin soil. Little fields of parched scraggly grain had been shored up with terraces among the ruins and half buried in one of these terrace walls we came across a long marble frieze decorated in bas relief with running deer. Our fingers ran covetously over it, but we had no need of further ballast and much less of any lengthy prison term as a guest of the colonels in Athens so the thing stayed where it belonged.

An anticyclone had settled over Greece and the Mediterranean was living up to its postcard image of sunshine, calm blue seas and parched islands. Sue quickly turned a well-burned red, peeled a couple of times and then turned steadily darker until Katie and I looked pallid beside her. But the weather, so much to Sue's liking, was hard on the diesel and my temper. We motored for long hours on end and when a breeze did occasionally appear it was light, fitful, very local and always on the nose. Southwards we cruised to Paleo Monemvasia, and on beyond Cape Malea to Avlemona a dull barren hamlet on Kithera's east coast and from there to the island *chora* of Kapsali whose port we had tried so hard and so vainly to reach the previous autumn. Now not a ripple opposed our entry into the attractive little harbour. The *chora*, 600 feet above the port, a white town dominated by a massive brown stone Venetian fortress, is one of the most beautiful places in Greece but we stayed only one night and regretted again as we did so often that we did not have five years to devote to Greece alone.

We crossed the Gulf of Lakonia to Porto Kaio at the south end of the Mani, the promontory known as Taenarum in ancient times which offered a short cut to hell by way of a local cave, avoiding the River Styx. This enabled the thrifty natives to bury their dead without the customary coin in the mouth, knowing that Charon would not need to be paid for ferrying the soul to the underworld.

After poking about in the Gulf of Messenia we came round into the Ionian and back to our old landfall of Pylos. We felt sorry that Sue would soon be leaving us. She had enjoyed the cruising and had relished the few decent sails we'd had. She was browner and blonder than ever. Yet I felt without saying anything that there was something missing in all this and that she wasn't getting quite as much fun as she should. That missing "something" now showed up.

John Gubbels, late of the Mounted Police in Grise Fiord, had arrived in Spetsai in the course of his travels across Europe. There he had learned from friends what our itinerary had been, and with a little extrapolation decided that we would arrive in Pylos that very day, whereupon he hitch-hiked across the Peloponnesus and presented himself on the quayside just an hour after our own arrival.

Without this 6 foot 4 inch interruption Sue would undoubtedly have settled back into her prestigious professional career in London. As it was, her last few days on board upset the rhythms of the past, and though she did bid us and John a reluctant farewell at Ithaca to return to the daily grind, she promptly resigned two months later when John appeared in London, and the two were last seen bound across Africa to Timbuktu with a pup tent.

After cruising north through the islands of the Ionian to the home water of Odysseus we collected our clearance and reached across the windy channel between Ithaca and Levkas to the pleasant verdure of the little inlet of Sivota. Here, though we enjoyed all-round shelter, gusts struck at us from the hills and unfortunately the verdure extended to the sea bed itself where the green weed grew thick enough to keep the anchor out of the sand so that I had to dive and dig the point down through the roots.

Four fisherman's houses were set back under the trees. Three children played naked in the sunny rock pools nearby and a local fisherman rowed over to offer us a fine live lobster, but alas we had rid ourselves that morning of our last Greek drachma.

We left the next morning and with John still on board we set sail to the west. I gazed back regretfully at the receding hills of Greece and thought of the old fisherman who had spoken to us on Sivota. He spoke English easily for he had once lived in America.

"Where are you bound?" he had asked me and when I explained he gazed wistfully towards the sea and said, "How lucky you are. You have a nice boat. You are young and there's a whole world to the west."

IV

Returning to the Pillars of Hercules

Sicily was our intended landfall on this passage but for several days the wind held in the westerly quarter forcing us to the south so that we eventually abandoned Syracuse in favour of Malta. Although it was close-hauled slogging most of the way at least the diesel was kept silent and for the last 40 miles we picked up a spanking northeasterly that sent us surging happily across the glittering seas to the yellowed coasts of Malta and into Lazaretto Creek where we secured to the very bollard we had used on our way east, ten months before.

It was good to be back in a land of English beer, of well-stocked supermarkets at British prices, and of chandleries. John found himself a temporary job and moved ashore while Katie and I went energetically to work on the boat. A lot had to be done and most important of all was recaulking the decks for until that time whenever it rained we endured a soggy invasion of tar-stained drips on our bunks, books, clothes lockers, food tins, everything in fact below decks. I found some marine glue in the back of one of the chandleries and within a week the old filling was raked out, caulking hammered home, and with the new pitch poured in our decks looked a dreadful shambles of tarry dribbles which scraped away easily to clean straight lines after a few weeks of being tramped in.

Meanwhile Katie busied herself with long shopping lists. We planned to stow away enough tinned food for more than a year for we expected to be unable to find food as inexpensive or in such variety anywhere else between there and New Zealand. And with the exceptions of Gibraltar and the Canaries, so it proved.

The Malta Channel and Strait of Sicily tend to specialize in northwest winds and as we were bound beyond Cap Bon on the shoulder of Tunisia we expected a hard beat ahead, so we were delighted to find an east wind blowing on the morning of July 8th when we were ready to leave. Our food lockers were bulging, fuel and water tanks filled and at the last minute the customs officer had supervised the loading of two cases of bonded rum as well as one of gin which, though I seldom touched the stuff, I could hardly resist at 68¢ a bottle. At least it would make a cheap present.

At 1300 we cast off and motored out past the walls of Valletta. But by then the wind was back in the northwest right on the nose. With the appropriate charts aboard we were prepared to stop on either side of the narrowing straits ahead, either on the south coast of Sicily or the east coast of Tunisia. But the Sicilian ports can be unpleasant places swarming with noisy urchins by day and thieves at night, and the harbours themselves are generally filthy for, as elsewhere in Italy, these people can endure a degree of pollution that would kill a less resilient species. Having therefore sailed all night to the north well clear of the island of Gozo we went about on the starboard tack hoping for a landfall as far north up the Tunisian coast as possible.

For another two days we plunged westwards into big uncomfortable seas enduring much and seeing nothing, except for a time when we were surrounded by ships of the Sixth Fleet on exercise, and for an hour we enjoyed the sight of fighters catapulting into the skies from the deck of an aircraft carrier while swift grey hunters frothed across our wake in a confusion of ever-changing courses.

Having reached the Tunisian coast just south of Kelibia we beat up to the little port, dodging scores of local fishing boats that came streaming out past us for the night's work offshore. A polite young customs officer came aboard, gave us pratique without any fuss and kindly lent us 5000 dinars until we could change our own money next day. Kelibia was a typical dusty little Arab town and we were ready to press on after two days there, though some of the local people who had attached themselves to us were loathe to let us go. Two young men in particular, brothers, who had conducted us about the town now invited us to be the guests of their father who had a farm near Sfax, "for a week, or two weeks if you like" said the one, while the other who wished to suggest no limit to his father's hospitality countered "no no, for as long as they like." Not until we had actually cast off from the dock did they finally accept our repeated regrets.

During the night *Nanook* sailed slowly north with the land breeze and doubled Cap Bon at dawn. We altered course towards the island of Zembra and into the Gulf of Tunis bound for the new yacht club marina at Sidi Bou Said right under Cap Carthage on the outskirts of Tunis. We arrived just at dusk and were pleased to see friends hurrying along the jetty to wave us in and take our lines. Anne and Gunther Perlwitz from Dusseldorf had just arrived themselves in their sloop *Lord Jim* after sailing from Malta where we had first met them. We joined them for supper in unaccustomed elegance on the terrace of the club overlooking the bay and discussed our respective passages from Valletta and our future plans.

One of the disadvantages of being on a yacht was that we seldom saw much of any country beyond its coasts. But Gunther had hired a car in Tunis and now invited us along to see something of the country inland, so away we went next morning passing through Tunis at dawn just as the city was bestirring itself. We travelled far on to the south through market towns and farmlands and into the dry country at the edge of the Sahara where aqueducts and amphitheatres stand as a reminder that the lands of North Africa were once the breadbasket of Rome. The journey was a welcome break from the sea and we could not have spent it in more delightful company.

A strong southeast wind was blowing up when we returned to Sidi Bou Said, a wind we should not be neglecting. Katie's stomach was "all in a knot" with anxiety at the prospect of returning to sea. This hadn't escaped Gunther's sympathetic notice. Anne invariably felt the same way, he said, and the best thing to do was to put to sea as soon as possible. We were sad to say goodbye to such good friends.

We were bound for Sardinia. The quartering wind held nearly all the way so we should have enjoyed the passage but the sky had a hard menacing look about it and the air felt humid and to my active imagination full of ill omen so that Katie's earlier anxiety soon shared company with my own. Would this strong wind become a *temporale?* Would Sardinia become a dangerous lee shore? Would we understand the Italian forecast at 2200? Were our sails strong enough to haul us off in a gale? In the ultimate crisis, would our liferaft really inflate? We had already received by our reckoning a lot more buffeting at the hands of Mediterranean gales than we felt entitled to and this was beginning to produce in us a morbid preoccupation with weather forecasts and the statistical likelihood from pilot charts of more trouble ahead.

Nanook at least had the good sense to enjoy the unusual good fortune of being off the wind and she surged forward with her bow wave roaring happily through the breaking seas. "Why worry about what may never happen and which, when it does, will laugh at human speculation?"

The Admiralty Pilot quite rightly accuses the south coast of Sardinia of being addicted to fogs and heavy haze. The wind fell light as we approached the Golfo de Cagliari and when according to dead reckoning we were close in, there was still no land in sight through the thick pall of industrial smoke. But late in the afternoon the sun's reddened orb, still well up in the sky, was eclipsed by a jagged line, the invisible skyline of Sardinia, and till well past midnight we felt and smelt our way through the waters of the gulf from buoy to buoy and moored at last in the big commercial port of Cagliari.

It was 0400 before we finally turned in for a much needed sleep and by 0600 officials were rapping on our hull. We were occupying a place reserved for police vessels. Would we kindly move our yacht?

Having been thoroughly aroused, and the city itself becoming so, we abandoned sleep and set off to complete formalities with the officials and to explore the streets of the attractive but noisy place. It reminded me a little of Naples or Lisbon with its gaudy monuments and steep little streets like canyons with towering old tenements on each side tethered overhead to each other by a thousand flapping laundry lines, while priests and policemen and stolid black dressed women hurried about their business in the shadows below.

The morning sun shone brightly as we cruised a couple of days later down the west side of the gulf. The pleasant northwesterly breeze carried a big Italian sloop down towards us on a converging course and it straightened out on our own course as it came close. It was unusual to be in the company of other sails.

"Come on 'Nook," Katie said, "they're trying to race us."

The Italians scrambled to change to a bigger headsail, trimmed their sheets and studied us keenly through binoculars. Usually a sloop is a more efficient racing machine than a ketch so for the sake of one-upmanship we set the steering vane, left the tiller, and sprawled ostentatiously on the deck with magazines, as if to say to them "What a shame it is that you poeple have to steer like that all the time." One might as well put a cheerful face on failure. Why is it that we speak so disparagingly of the fox who sugared his disappointment with the cheerful conclusion that the unreachable grapes were probably sour anyway?

Not that it mattered. As the Italians began to creep ahead both yachts suddenly disappeared in a low bank of fog. Buried as we were in our magazines we had not noticed the approaching white bank. We held our course out of the gulf while the deck and sails and rigging dripped and dribbled and our hair turned white with dew. Two hours later we emerged again in sunshine and the sloop was nowhere to be seen.

Forty miles on, *Nanook's* anchor clattered to the bottom of the well-sheltered little harbour of Teulada. It was deserted but for a few summer campers. The wild surroundings reminded us of Greece. We had looked forward there to a night's sleep before setting off to the west but strong northerly winds gusted all night off the hills, keeping me awake and forcing me to lay out the second anchor in the middle of the night. By 0800 when we were ready to leave, the night wind had dropped right away and we left motoring into a faint southerly, an inconvenient and typically Mediterranean switch.

The passage to Menorca in the Balearics took 4½ days with a Force 8 *mistral* in the middle of it for we were then in an area under the influence of the much-feared tempests that are generated over the French Alps and the Rhone Valley and that strike south out of the Golfe du Lion to batter the coasts of Sardinia, Corsica and the Balearics. As usual we were hard on the wind and the steep short seas pounded the starboard bow endlessly. The wind broke reef points on the main and bronze hanks on the jib and carried the radar reflector into the sea in the middle of the night. Its halyard had chafed through but it was still well shackled to the downhaul and dragged along through the water at the stern. It was a struggle to recover it from the fierce grip it had on the water. Normally mounted on the mizzen the great clumsy aluminum reflector would make short work of anyone in the cockpit if it fell there and I was careful thereafter to remove it in strong winds and to keep an eye open for chafe.

We entered Port Mahon in Menorca July 28th motoring up the long arm of the landlocked inlet to the Club Maritimo, feeling pleased to be back in Spain. The great attraction of this rather low barren-looking island of limestone lies in its coasts that are carved and indented by the sea into a series of high cliffs, white beaches and deep peaceful inlets. Unfortunately all the attractive areas were being systematically carved up by urbanization schemes as in so many parts of Mediterranean Spain. The best that could be said was that we had arrived ahead of much of this "progress" excepting for the surveyor's pegs.

Mahon and its remarkable harbour deserved more than two days of our time but by that time we wanted only to get on to Gibraltar and have done with the Mediterranean. We left early one morning and sailed around to Fornells, a deep inlet on the north coast, deep that is into the land but very shallow otherwise so that with *Nanook's* draft of six feet it was hard to find a quiet anchorage away from the town and close to the shore. We settled finally for a place close in to a couple of little deserted islands, deserted except for a young French couple sunbathing naked on the grass. The clatter of our chain startled them into their towels but when they found that we were keeping our distance and in fact wore no more than they did, they relaxed and resumed their picnic. I spent the rest of the day with the mask scraping massive Maltese barnacles off the hull and rudder with the wooden porridge spoon while Katie cleaned away topsides.

Towards evening we decided to visit the little fishing village and track down a meal ashore. We motored across the inlet to the breakwater beside the whitewashed village and promptly went hard aground. This was my reward for accepting the assurance of a local fisherman that there was "plenty water" for our draft. Having stuck fast on a rocky bottom we were now treated to the opinion of all the other fishermen motoring in and out who declared to us loudly what was now sufficiently obvious, that there was not enough water for us; we would have to anchor off, and with that they left us to extricate ourselves as best we could which with the kedge astern and a warp from the breakwater around a sheet winch, was not too difficult.

The north coast of Menorca has a barren weather-beaten aspect, as well it might, exposed as it is to the Golfe du Lion. Even the shrubs bend permanently southwards. So having spent only one night at Fornells we sailed on in pleasant conditions round the western end of the island to Cuidadela, a beautiful town that is approached from seaward through a gap in the cliffs and then by a long narrow rock-walled corridor leading to a basin in the centre of the town. There we stocked up with supplies, stayed overnight and continued on next day to anchorages on the southern coast.

The bay of Galdana is a place of pine forest, white cliffs and pale beaches where we could see every pebble glistening in the sun thirty feet below the keel. It must have been idyllic until the previous year but within the period of one winter a multi-storied hotel had arisen. The beaches were covered with people. Passing swimmers gossiped with us in Midlands accents about their cheap two-week excursion rates. Plastic sailboats wove little wakes around us and even the cliff tops were peopled. Other anchorages were the same. It's happening all over Spain.

Being easily persuaded that Majorca offered much the same fare we sailed on down its southeastern coast and stopped for two nights at the rugged little island of Cabrera, uninhabited except for a small military garrison that kept an eye out for smugglers. A ruined castle looking like part of the mountain it stands on guards the harbour entrance. After scrambling up to its crumbly ramparts on the second day we returned aboard to catch a rising beam wind for Ibiza.

Once our shelter was far astern, the sky clouded over and the wind, typically, changed its tune so that I had to reduce canvas down to the double reefed main alone which still gave us over six knots, while Katie having been sunbathing on deck, lying ahull, so to speak, under bare poles, had to make canvas and trim her sheets.

After a tiresome night of too much wind and then none at all which left us leaping about in a confused slop, we motored along the enticing Ibiza coast to the main port where we moored with difficulty bow in on the outer mole amongst scores of other yachts, no one bothering to take our lines, fend off, smile or anything else. The Balearics are aswarm with yachts and indifference thrives in a multitude.

Ibiza of course swarmed also with all manner of spaced out flower children and other beautiful people of the western world. The streets bloomed with patched up jeans and sleeveless jackets, jangley beads and jeweled belly buttons; a wild assortment of beards, moustaches and frantic hairstyles extending at right angles to the scalp, or as the girls generally preferred, in long folksy tresses, straight and soulful, falling to the shoulders across ears, eyes or anything else that happened to be in the way.

A cruise ship was in so this provided an interesting contrast. Decent well-to-do folks in new holiday clothes fussed over cameras and traveller's cheques. Men ordered beer at shady outdoor bars. Middle-aged wives spoke loudly at shopkeepers, the better to make their English understood and some peered incredulous through their sunglasses and clicked their tongues at the fearful freaks strolling the streets, and doubtless wished they were young again.

Ibiza's harbour stank of raw sewage. To match this the weather was hot and humid. The high breakwater wall effectively cut off the sea breeze each day from the yachts parked inside. Our neighbors came and left in a cloud of diesel smoke but didn't improve on acquaintance in between times. So with nothing to detain us we sailed out past Formentera and set a course for Alicante, arriving there after an infuriating day, night and day again of no wind, light head winds, a brief gale and back to no wind again at the end.

We now left *Nanook* in the care of an English yachtsman in Alicante and went off for a fortnight in London, travelling overland by bus. We had a long list of chandlery supplies to buy there, as well as relatives to visit, a pleasant interlude if an expensive one.

On our return to Alicante we had *Nanook* hauled out on a local slipway. I had found that this would cost us only eight pounds and fondly imagined that by applying an especially strong antifouling this would be good enough for the fourteen month voyage to New Zealand without needing to haul out in the West Indies. While we were at it we put a new coat of enamel on the topsides and the bottom received its thick new coat of red poison of a well-known brand which claimed to be good for a year, and at the price should have been. Yet by the time we were in the West Indies the bottom to my disgust looked like a garden.

I had hoped at this point to sail south to the African coast and visit a number of ports in Algeria, but we were warned off by other yachtsmen. Officials, we were told, were hostile to yachtsmen. The red tape would be onerous and expensive, a military guard would be posted on board day and night and we would undergo a thorough search from stem to stern. If such a search revealed a tin of Israeli peaches or even a label from another country with a six pointed star on it the boat might be impounded. All this even allowing for a bit of exaggeration seemed reason enough to stay on the Spanish coast on our way west but I later regretted having been frightened off from what seemed like some fascinating cruising. As the Herero of southern Africa say, "The weak man goes only where he is smiled at."

We half drifted half motored in sunshine around to Spain's only natural harbour on this coast, Cartagena, or New Carthage, from where Hannibal of Carthage made his arduous march on Rome via the Alps. The place is taken over by oil refineries and in every direction the Spanish navy's oily wharves and repair yards. Oil lay on the water and smoke in the air.

Cartagena is the sort of place you hear and smell before you can see it.

Though cloud was forming over the high hills and the barometer had fallen we left after only one night preferring to take our chances with the elements and hoping to cover the 100 miles round to Almeria with an overnight run.

However an irritating calm seemed to have settled over the area and recalling the old sailor's notion that a breeze can be summoned with a whistle I let fly with a piercing New Zealand sheep dog call that quickly brought Katie out the hatch.

"What did you do that for?" she cried in dismay. In Katie's opinion whistling for a breeze, even though it might be only a bit of old superstition, still seemed too much like hurling a challenge at fate. What would be the result of that? A gale at the very least. It had happened twice last year, she reminded me, on our way east to Greece. Now it was likely to happen again. I tried to disabuse her gently of such fanciful ideas by assuring her that all the whistling in the world would not affect the synopsis one whit. But Katie was not persuaded, and to my disgust in a couple of hours a gale arose out of the west that lashed us for four days and nights without letup. There was little shelter on the coast and we preferred to do battle with the steep seas rather than run back to Cartagena. It would soon be over, I reasoned. On and on, day and night we slogged doggedly into the crashing seas, punching and smashing and cursing. The air above decks was filled with spray and below decks with unexpressed but implicit I-told-you-so's. I like to pride myself in scorning any and all superstition yet it must be admitted that it was a long time before I again whistled for a wind.

For all those four days we battled back and forth. We made long starboard tacks offshore at night and port tacks inshore during the day. A strong current from the Atlantic was setting east against us. It was strongest off Cabo de Gata and every time we came back in onto the coast we found that we had gained not one inch and the cape still lay upwind. In typical fashion the wind died suddenly in a few hours and we struggled west at last round the red rock cape under power. With the diesel full out at 4½ knots we only just gained on it.

It had taken us five days and nights to cover the short distance to Almeria. *Nanook* hopped from there along the southern coast stopping only briefly at other small ports. On September 17th in a lumpy sea with a southwesterly swell and a northeasterly wind and a hard current carrying weed and green water in from the Atlantic we raised the white and purple outlines of the Pillars of Hercules and at last in a grey levanter we turned to starboard under the gusty lee of the Rock, tearing the mainsail in a fierce willawaw and with a heartfelt sigh dropped anchor in the yacht basin of Gibraltar.

It felt good to be back. Always a crossroads for travellers between

Europe and Africa and for ships passing through the Straits, Gibraltar is also a major gathering place of cruising yachtsmen, a place where most ocean voyagers come sooner or later. There are many other such classic ports of rendezvous around the world, Horta in the Azores, Barbados, Falmouth, Auckland, Papeete and Cape Town are a few. Friendships are renewed in cockpits and club bars as ocean gossip is exchanged, storms compared, charts and lies swapped and boats mutually admired before each navigator sails away again and commits himself to the uncertainty and solitude of another long passage.

The new arrivals in Gibraltar included the usual batch in from England fresh from a dusting in the Bay of Biscay, one or two from the North Atlantic crossing and a few like ourselves coming out of the Mediterranean and looking forward to the steadier winds of the Atlantic. Quite a few intended world voyages that start in England get no further than Gibraltar and some don't even get that far. Financial troubles, friction between shipmates and the fright and disillusion of severe weather are the usual rocks on which dreams founder. A 30-foot trimaran lay near us, very neglected and going cheap. A movie version of a Viking longship had been in Gib the previous year, her young Canadian owners planning to sail her to the West Indies. Now she lay abandoned in a corner of the harbour stripped of her square sail and engine, her latter-day Norsemen long gone on some other quest. A Bristol Channel pilot cutter had just changed hands. The previous owner who had paid £500 for her had sold her, according to marina gossip, for £4,500. She was an enormous and colourful old ship but we wondered if the enthusiastic young American teenager who had put up all that cash had not bitten off more than he could chew.

My problem now was to get *Nanook* out through the Straits of Gibraltar. In the old days of sail many scores of square riggers accumulated in Algeciras Bay waiting sometimes for several weeks for an easterly to carry them out. The local winds tend always to be either from the east or west, a run or a thrash to windward, and the prevalent current is inflowing from the Atlantic, though a prolonged easterly wind, a levanter, can reverse the flow. That anyway is the pattern at the surface. The Mediterranean and Black Seas are so large and their huge drainage basins so modest in rainfall that surface evaporation from those seas is greater than the total amount of fresh water received from all the countless rivers that empty into them. The balance is made up by an inflow from the Atlantic. But evaporation increases the salinity and density of the sea and this heavy salt water lying beneath the fresher Atlantic water spills by gravity west over the sea bed of the Straits into the Atlantic. So normally there are two currents flowing one above the other in opposite directions. Curiously though there is much more water flowing in than out, there is an exact balance in the overall quantity of salt flowing each way.

Katie's shopping list was finally all crossed off and the lockers groaned with food enough to see us to New Zealand. That done I was delighted to see grey beards streaking off the tops of the Rock and *Nanook* swinging back to the east as a levanter set in. It was time to go.

Unfortunately the diesel thought otherwise. A dozen energetic swings of the starting handle resulted in a few polite coughs that subsided into silence. Until then the little auxiliary had been invariably faithful, but do what I may, prime the fuel line, heat up the cooling water, change the injector, there was no sign of life in the thing.

Practical landsman that I was I soon tracked down ashore the very thing I needed to get it running again: a mechanic. This fellow systematically spread the engine all over the cabin sole and produced a piston covered with salt, its rings gummed up and corroded. The valves were pitted. Bits of chromium lay in the sump. And there at the bottom of the manifold lay part of the Mediterranean Sea. The jacketed exhaust was leaking and salt water dribbled back into the engine every time it was stopped.

Unwilling to wait for a new exhaust to be made, I settled for the alternative of draining the manifold whenever I stopped the diesel and I kept up this tiresome procedure all the way to New Zealand.

Though nearly a week had passed in making repairs, the levanter still kindly obliged us and once clear of the gusty lee of the Rock *Nanook* surged along through the following seas under main and genoa, then reefed main and jib, then by progressive sail shortening till she ran out beyond Tangiers doing five knots under bare poles in a wild furious wind from the Mediterranean that seemed to shriek "Good riddance" to us, a sentiment that caused me in the middle of the night to turn back to the east and shout back upwind "And the same to you!"

We were in the open ocean, and the Mediterranean with its short seas and its vagrant and elusive winds was at last astern. "You get nine days of calm followed by a gale." So one sailor in Malta summed up the Mediterranean. One year there had been a tough introduction to sailing but it was over and we breathed a sigh of relief.

V

South from Barbary

We were bound now down the African coast and felt entitled to a pleasant quartering trade, but the wind fell light and progress was slow. Like California, South West Africa and other dry coasts on the east sides of oceans, Morocco has a high percentage of fogs caused by the removal of surface waters blown across the ocean to the west by the trades and the resultant upwelling of much colder water from the ocean depths. Each night before midnight the fog began to form and by dawn we were immersed in a soggy blanket of grey fog. Moisture dripped off the sails, trickled off the rigging and drifted across the decks, while ships near and far bellowed dismally like monsters in anguish.

Since I had cleverly foreseen the previous year that fog would never trouble us when once clear of the English Channel I had saved us the trouble and cost of getting a fog horn, but of course I now regretted this foresight. We felt acutely vulnerable out there waiting to be picked off by a passing ship. The traffic along the coast was busy and we had only the radar reflector to warn others off.

After five consecutive days of foggy mornings and sunny afternoons we came in to the large white city of Casablanca, mooring in the little yacht club basin. I was concerned here about the possibility of harbour thieves and before going ashore I even went so far as to stow sheets, lifebuoy and anchors below deck, a precaution I never took in any other place. But Katie had done some laundering and left some of it drying on the lifelines while we took a walk through the *ancienne medina* and on returning we found that it was all swiped.

Further down the coast we stopped in at the smaller port of Safi, mooring alongside a small French yawl which with a crew of five seemed more than sufficiently manned as French yachts are apt to be. Their intended course was to the West Indies and home the next year via the westerlies of higher latitudes but as we learned later the enterprise was abandoned when friction between the crew broke surface.

Fishing and phosphates had given Safi a modern port but within the walls of the old city the last several centuries seemed almost to be shut out. Dark visaged men swathed head to ankles in coarse homespun brushed past us in the market. In the narrow lanes off the crowded streets a water vendor with a heavy-looking skin of water on his shoulder beat his fist on the doors, and women with veiled faces followed us with their eyes.

We stocked up with bread, excellent honest crusty stuff as it always seems to be in countries that have known the French yoke. We should have left our shopping at that but while in the market we couldn't resist a cheap and tasty snack complete with raw salad, and sure enough down we both came with a bout of dysentery that seemed to thrive on the entero vioform tablets which at that stage we had still not learned to avoid. The debilitating disease later made our passage to the Canaries a misery.

The crew of the French yawl invited us to an overnight race to the fishing port of Mogador sixty miles south. This invitation was accepted, but as soon as the matelots put to sea and found themselves with a light head wind, they started the engine and powered straight into it, leaving Nanook to stand offshore close hauled all night.

Dolphins cavorted around the bows during the night helping to ease the monotony of our watches. Through the hull in the fo'c'stle we could hear their conversation of long high pitched squeaks something rather like the whine of a faulty fluorescent light tube. I wondered if they might be interested in what the transdcer of the echo sounder might have to say, for this emitted a high pitched sound downwards through the water. I turned the sounder on and the dolphins' squeaks showed up on the dial as a garbled burst of light scattered around the dial.

By dawn the wind had veered enough to let us lay our course. The sky was hazy but we had pleasant sailing and my dead reckoning was so accurate that, when still out of sight of land, I predicted a depth of 16 fathoms and Katie turned on the echo sounder, sure enough it was 16 fathoms.

Our dolphins returned to us at intervals and a variety of seabirds flew about, always in view. One bird seemed out of place. It was a rich yellow-brown in colour and was constantly trying to evade the attentions of a group of about eight gulls that took turns to swoop upon it. Eventually it saw Nanook and flew wearily towards us hoping perhaps to rest. It was a large handsome owl. We longed for it to take refuge on the rigging or deck, but it seemed uncertain of its welcome and the screaming gulls drove it off again. The distressed creature kept up its silent and hopeless evasions for over an hour to the almost equal distress of Katie who has a tender heart for anything small, shaggy and in need of mothering. We altered course to bring it closer but it finally fell towards the water a long way off, and we saw it no more.

Anchored in the bay at Mogador outside of the crowded fishing harbour, we were invited over to the French yawl for a supper of boiled skate and *"pommes de terre en robes de chambre"* or in other words unpeeled spuds. The French have a way of making the commonest thing sound elegant.

Returning aboard next morning after a shopping expedition we were hailed by our host the French captain. *"Mauvais Temps"*, he shouted, on local advice. We must move into the fishing harbour. A big swell certainly had built up quite suddenly. The glass had dropped and the sky had a well-blown look from a depression to the north. After three unsuccessful berths we finally established ourselves alongside a fishing boat for the night while spray thundered over the high harbour mole and slopped onto our decks. But the glass recovered and the sky cleared.

"Storm in a teacup," Katie snorted next morning as we returned to the open anchorage.

The pleasant whitewashed town decorated with high minarets, dark Portuguese forts and long beaches intrigued us and we delayed our departure two days to explore it further. Quite a few young people from various Western countries wandered the streets, for a sizeable colony of hippies had established itself just out of town. Morocco, with its liberal application of the law and tolerance of all the pleasures, has long been a haven for the playboy and the pothead. I was importuned at various points to provide myself with a supply of the "very best" grass and although this was something neither of us knew much about, I must admit I was tempted to take along a little stock to sample quietly on the long Atlantic run.

> Yield not to temptation
> For yielding is sin

So we used to sing as children in church. But in me the seeds of Calvin had long fallen on very stony ground and if we had never indulged in the weed before it was more from want of opportunity than from any objection in principle. There seems only one substantial case against the innocuous stuff and that is that it is very illegal. Too much pleasure (other people's that is) must be taxed, rationed or outlawed. One is reminded, like Macauley, of the Puritans who railed against bear baiting not because it gave pain to the bear, but because it gave pleasure to the spectators. Or of the duchess who upon asking her manservant whether the common people also had sex, and being assured in the affirmative, snapped "Then they shouldn't be allowed to. It's too good for them."

At any rate the delicate moral quandary was decided for me by the state

His tender nose protected with white ointment, Maurice scrapes away tarry dribbles after recaulking the deck seams.

of my pocket. I had bought an expensive camera in Gibraltar and had arranged for further funds to be sent on to Dakar in West Africa. Until then we had to husband our last few dollars like misers and sailed off innocent as ever to the Canaries. Katie, I think, was greatly relieved for she was obsessed with visions of *Nanook* being searched and seized in some god-forsaken land.

"Don't forget that old African saying," she said. "'Fear of jail is the beginning of wisdom.'"

Dysentery and an unfavourable wind decided for us against an intended landfall on the island of Lanzarote and we sailed on instead to Las Palmas anchoring in the oily sludge of the big harbour, off a grandiose yacht club that only just tolerated our presence. Nearby lay our old friend John Struchinsky of Winnipeg in his neat little Vertue sloop *Bonaventure de Lys* which we had seen last in Cornwall the year before. As we arrived, John rowed over to us with a supply of fresh bread, declining with the tact of a single hander to come aboard, "for," he said, "you must be tired and will want to tidy ship and have a good sleep before you're ready for visitors," which might have been true if it had been anyone but John.

Several other cruising yachts came and went in the next few days for Las Palmas was a favourite provisioning and jumping-off point for the trade wind passage to the West Indies and the season was starting up. We waved *bon voyage* to *Eric the Red* as her owner tacked her across our bows on his way out bound for Barbados. Only 19 feet long with unstayed masts and junk rig she was said to be built by her young English owner out of packing cases, floor boards, beer crates and church pews. A new arrival, *Pelagic,* had a very white-skinned skipper. "Must have come straight from England," said Katie. I rowed past later and asked where his last port of call was. "Plymouth," he replied.

Bill was taking his newly built sloop home to Seattle via Panama. He had bought *Pelagic* straight from the builder's yard in England. The boat had ambitions like so many stock designs of sleeping big numbers of people, an important selling point perhaps to the family man. But the bunks in *Pelagic* were all rather short and Bill himself rather long so that with five bunks to choose from he was forced instead to sleep on the cabin floor.

In a short time *Nanook* had acquired a thick film of black oil halfway up her newly-painted topsides for the commercial harbour was a notoriously polluted place and for visiting yachtsmen the final chore before departure from Las Palmas was removing the greasy filth with kerosene and a lot of hard rubbing. That completed, most trans-Atlantic voyagers would turn southwest and then west following the trades across the ocean. But in our case the fascination of Africa still held us and we were bound instead a thousand miles south to Dakar on Africa's westernmost tip.

At the beginning of our voyage the previous year I conscientiously recorded every navigational detail in the log believing this to be the proper and seamanlike thing to do. Looking back on it I read:

> 1445 hours. Eddystone bearing 162° mag. Rane Head 85° mag. 4½-5 knots under main, mizzen, jib. Course 210 mag.
> 1530 Barometer 1013. Wind veering. Changed course 235° mag. One reef in mainsail.

As the weeks progressed the log gradually changed in character from this mass of useless information to something more like a personal diary, while anything of relevance to the navigation department was recorded in pencil on the chart. My entries from Las Palmas to Dakar read:

> *18th Oct.* 1200 Bought eight loaves and a gallon of muscatel this morning, then after cleaning off the hull got the anchors up, waved goodbye to John and motored out. Glass has come up quite high so after three days of cloud, rain and southeast winds we're hoping for something better. Katie a bit queasy.
> *19th Oct.* 1500 Clear weather, nice going. Log 133 at noon. 1800 wind steady, getting a bit stronger. Took off main. Chili con carne for supper.
> *20th Oct.* Log at noon 260. Still good going but wind easing. 1700 Under full sail. A shade slow. A lot of ships are about; we're sailing right down the lane. Having to keep watches day and night. Constipated. (But that's a nice change after the passage from Morocco!)
> *21st Oct.* Spent the day sunbathing and reading. The sea here is full of plankton. Changed the engine oil. Still constipated.
> *22nd Oct.* 1730 Feeling very bored. Weather is pleasant but wind has eased a lot and we have a hard job making 3 knots. We motored for a couple of hours today, a sure way to get the wind back again. Spent an hour this morning photographing Katie's new found friend "Pinky," a nice fat little pilot fish who's taken up residence under the stern. He eats bully beef. We're close to Port Etienne, halfway to Dakar.
> 1900 Lactogen works!
> *23rd Oct.* Last night around midnight we slowed down and talked with a large fisheries research boat with a Norwegian crew who were curious to see a sailing yacht in these parts. At first as they approached I had thoughts of the Barbary pirates of old and was relieved to be hailed in English by friendly voices. Even so we were glad to be rid of them for they came perilously close. Bacon, pancakes and maple syrup for lunch.
> *24th Oct.* Winds are now stronger and we're making good progress, at times rather too good and because of the heavy roll life gets a bit

tiresome. During my midnight watch last night I collected four flying fish in succession off the decks. This morning before preparing for our first ever meal of flying fish I laid them all out on the dry deck to photograph them when we were suddenly swept by a freak wave that carried the lot of them out the scuppers and into the sea. Had a very silent lunch of baked beans and luncheon meat.

25th Oct. Having robbed us of our fish yesterday, the sea relented and delivered up two more during the night. Weather getting much hotter. Busy sewing torn sails.

26th Oct. 1300 We now have Cap Vert in sight on the port bow, having spent the morning trimming and changing sails to get every possible knot out of *Nanook* and taking sun sights to fix position. We have about 18 miles to go. Two more flying fish for lunch. Last night at the end of her watch Katie was struck on the head by one of these airborne missiles. It landed in the cockpit. *Mana* from heaven! 1700 We finally got into Dakar after a long beat on the wind around Isle Goree the old island fort where slaves were held in the old days for shipment to the New World. Moored just at dusk in the commercial harbour. Log 986 miles.

Dakar is said to be the Paris of Africa. It was certainly too French to be cheap and too modern to be typical of the Africa that lay inland. We anchored off the beach at the yacht club and stayed there only a week, of which nothing need be said except that Katie developed a consuming interest in collecting seashells and I contrived one day while manoeuvring in the main harbour to drive our bowsprit into the coachroof window of a nearby cabin cruiser while the Canadian ambassador to Senegal was visiting us aboard *Nanook* for a short cruise.

It dawned on us that a winter cruise beyond Cap Vert down Africa's west coast then up the Brazilian coast would be a fascinating venture if only we could have afforded another full year to do it in. As it was we could not afford even the time to go down the Gambia and we turned the bow west instead for the Cape Verde islands 400 miles out. The pilot charts seemed to promise us an easy starboard reach to the northern islands of the group but finding the winds well forward of the beam on that course I decided to settle instead for a call at the seldom visited southern islands.

With Suez closed, the traffic off Cap Vert was busy with tankers bringing Europe's lifeblood of fuel from the Persian Gulf. We were soon clear of the lanes and by evening we were quite alone on an empty sea with only the unwelcome northwesterly for company. With the shipping lane astern and the steering vane keeping us pounding up towards the west I decided not to worry about regular watches and we contented ourselves instead with glancing periodically out the hatch to survey the horizon.

I was dozing about 0200 when Katie happened to tumble out of her bunk to look out. She had scarcely finished shouting in anguish "Oh my god, Maurice!" before I was awake and fighting up past her on the companionway steps. A black wall of steel loomed on our starboard beam, silhouetted against the starry sky. The red port hand navigational light glowed clearly on one side and the green starboard light was just emerging. One of the masthead lights was eclipsed by the ship itself. A wall of white water advanced ahead of the silent colossus and in a few more seconds a monstrous tanker would have been upon us. I leaped to the tiller and heaved it down bellowing to Katie to turn on every light we had. *Nanook* swung round through the wind as I released jib sheets and steering vane, and went running off with the wind on the port quarter. With a deep roar the black silhouette swept high up behind us and thundered off southwards into the night.

It was a close call. I sat speechless and shocked in the cockpit watching the receding stern while my heart thudded hard in my chest. By that moment we might well have been dead. I could hardly believe it. I had assumed that we had left all the shipping behind us and I was reminded of the words of an old Devon sailor I'd once known. "Never assume anything at sea," he said. "Never take anything for granted."

Two days later just as a vast school of dolphins surrounded us, Katie sighted Ilha do Maio, the first island of the archipelago. Progress had been poor. We were close hauled nearly all the way and for eighteen hours we had sailed southwest on the starboard tack on a wind which according to the pilot chart didn't exist at that time of year. The sky remained milky, the air humid and the trade decidedly out of sorts.

By evening with all the wind gone we were close in to the harbourless southwest shore of Ilha do Maio and hoped to anchor for the night off Porto Ingles and to proceed next morning to the better harbour on Sao Tiago. But just as we approached the intended anchorage, the main gybed under a sudden southerly, an unwelcome onshore wind, so we abandoned the "English port" and sailed on instead across the strait to Sao Tiago.

The main port of the island and the administrative capital of the group, Porto da Praia lies at the southeastern corner of Sao Tiago. For strangers the entry by night is simplified by two red leading lights that guide mariners safely in clear of dangers. The port is protected from the normal trade wind but as we approached a heavy southerly swell rolled into the open bay and the gleaming flash of heavy breakers at the base of the dark cliffs a very short distance to starboard greatly upset Katie who was at the tiller, so that I had a difficult job persuading her not to edge away south of the line of approach. We dropped anchor in 3 fathoms not far from some small local craft. The lights of the little town twinkled down at us from the hills. We gazed at them as we sat in the cockpit with a final cup of coffee in our hands, happy to be at rest again and wondering what our reception would be in the morning.

Day dawned upon a barren landscape of cliffs and stoney yellow hills on which the town perched itself well above the harbour. A group of handsome government buildings stood prominently on the brink of the cliffs and we watched as the Portuguese flat was slowly raised to the martial sound of bugles, and unfurled in the breeze at the top of the pole. This little ceremony must have been going on at Praia for several centuries and no one could have known at the time how close the die-hard Portuguese Empire was to its death.

Beyond the imposing palaces of the Governor, the town straggled off along dusty roads with long lines of little stone houses all looking exactly like the simple square houses drawn by small children; peaked roof, one chimney, door at the centre with a path leading up to it, and a window each side of the door.

There was no sign ashore of any response to our yellow Q flag so about mid-morning we unlashed the dinghy, tossed it overboard and rowed to the landing jetty. A uniformed official waved us back shouting loudly to us. We must remain on board; it was not necessary to speak Portuguese to understand that much. So we rowed back over the swell and amused ourselves during the day by trying to talk to boys who swarmed curiously around us in rowboats. We tried unsuccessfully a second time some hours later to land, this time in a canoe full of boys and were again driven off with arm-waving imprecations as if we had been smitten with the Black Plague, as indeed we were in a sense for these naked black urchins had by then quite established themselves around *Nanook* and her strange white visitors.

However by mid-afternoon a posse of heavy-booted officials motored out towards us and the boys retreated discreetly away in their little canoes. We were politely welcomed in careful English, and after half an hour of form-filling and the inspection of our documents we were free to go ashore, which we did though not much was left of the day.

The following morning we found that a big freighter had anchored a cable seaward of us and general cargo was being offloaded into lighters which swept past us back and forth between ship and landing jetty. These lighters all worked under sail alone; rigged in the fashion of Arab dhows and each manned by several swarthy sailors who handled their engineless craft with great skill and waved cheerily to us each time they passed.

The sails used by these lighters were as many-coloured as Joseph's coat, much patched and full of holes but they did the job well for the boats had only to reach across the trade wind from ship to jetty. Flour bags were an important ingredient of these sails and the Northern Flour Mills of Minneapolis and a rival firm in Toronto would have been surprised to find their product so well advertised there.

The lively scene in the harbour was repeated in miniature in the shallows where the boys played endlessly with toy lighters made of galvanized sheet iron with clear plastic sails. Of girls there was no sign.

The islands may have their roots in Africa but there is enough Latin overlay for the girls to have a well-developed sense of "place." They were banished to the drudgery of the household, to caring for babies and to drawing water at the pump. But of boys there was no shortage. They paddled around us. They accompanied Katie along the coast in search of shells. They prowled the beaches and streets with no responsibilities and less education, playing endless games and dreaming I suppose of manhood and machismo.

Two more islands yet, Fogo and Brava, lay to the west of us before we faced the wide Atlantic. We hoped to call at one of these before leaving the archipelago but our minds were open on that score for neither island seemed to offer any easy shelter. With a sackful of bread, two stems of bananas, 3 litres of rank local rum and many other purchases stowed away we prepared *Nanook* for sea. We left in the afternoon in fine weather though the trade was blowing a shade too much for my taste and a great long trail of cumulus drifted downwind from the peaks of Sao Tiago to the far opposite horizon so that it took us two hours to emerge from under this sky-blanket into the sunshine.

All night we stood our watches as *Nanook* sailed toward and then south—around the symmetrical cone of Fogo. Normally shrouded in cloud, the great volcano, the highest peak in the whole group, loomed mysterious and dark but clearly etched in the full moonlight with just a thin collar of cloud half way up its sides. By Katie's dawn watch we were close in to the island capital but becalmed in the lee and *Nanook* leaped wildly in the confused swells that met each other from both sides of the island. Not caring for the anchorage there, I started the diesel and we steered into the channel towards Brava where we very soon found the trade funnelling fiercely between the islands at a full Force 7. Brava had a little pocket handkerchief harbour according to local account in Praia, but we had no chart of it and it lay on the windward corner of the island, so faced with these uncertainties as well as a powerful trade wind we were easily dissuaded from making the attempt and with mixed feelings we turned south off the wind to put the high, barren-looking island and the whole brown, cindery archipelago behind us. We had 2,100 miles to go to Barbados, our first ocean crossing. It would take us the rest of November and we hoped that the fates would be kind to us on the way for we had tempted them sorely at Praia by leaving port on Friday the 13th.

VI

Bound West for the Isthmus

Few yachts making the Atlantic run that year had fast easy passages, for the trades between the Canaries and West Indies were fickle at best. One catamaran took 42 days to reach Barbados, while the skipper of the charter yacht *Camelot* told me that the winds had been so poor he had actually motored all the way across. However we were a little further south than most and though the weather was changeable we still managed to average 100 miles a day and for the most part to enjoy the passage. Once clear of the Cape Verdes we set the yacht on course with the steering vane and never hand-steered another inch until our landfall on the other side. Despite our experience on the passage from Dakar I still persisted at that stage in the belief that the trade wind routes were empty, so we kept no watches and excepting for occasional glances at the compass and horizon, we slept through every night. The log entries tell the story:

> *15th Nov.* Now well clear of the islands. The weather is much better, typical N.E. trade. Have replaced jib and staysail with the genoa which is now working with the mizzen. Doing a good 6 knots. 115 m. noon to noon.
>
> *16th Nov.* Dull overcast day. Some rain at breakfast time and a bit too much wind. Changed down from genoa to staysail for a few hours in the night when *Nanook* began surging up to 8 and 9 knots in strong winds. Becoming boisterous but progress good, 132 m. noon to noon on the log. Cooking is a real chore. Everything goes flying the moment it's set down. Katie wants to make banana cake but can't face the struggle involved. We're having a problem disposing of food because it's all ripening at once, bananas especially but also apples, oranges and pineapples from Dakar, all ripe and ready to rot. A real fruit fest. Bread is also beginning to go off.

17th Nov. Another dull boisterous day. Much of the time we're sailing 5-6 knots under staysail alone. Have taken no sun sights since leaving Sao Tiago thanks to overcast skies and laziness. Life is taken up by lying on bunks reading, or gazing in distaste at the turbulent grey chaos outside. And eating bananas. I never get tired of bananas, only full of them. noon to noon 136 m.

18th Nov. Sky's cleared, wind eased a bit. Took sun sights. Noon position 33° 21' W, 15° 33' N. Got a huge load of water dumped onto my bunk at 7 a.m. to remind me it was time to get breakfast. Flying fish and chips for lunch. 1700. The wind seems at last to be mending its manners, and the sea is going down somewhat. We are tired of decks constantly running wet, severe thumps against the hull as maverick waves strike us and the stern being thrown bodily sideways by the fast following seas. Maybe that's because I've been carrying the mizzen with a small headsail. I'll have to experiment further. I now have the genoa up and pulling nicely at about 6½ knots.

19th Nov. Noon position 35° 26' W, 15° 29' N. Rotten bananas have been consigned to the deep. During the night I dreamed we were dragging out of control in an anchorage. I scrambled out of bed up the companionway and along the deck. I went right forward to the samson post and began fumbling with the anchor chain before I realized where we were.

20th Nov. Really beautiful weather though progress is a bit slower and it's our second day without flying fish. Both reading by the hour in the cockpit. Wish we didn't roll so much. The jam pot has upended in the food cupboard spilling its contents everywhere. The bleach bottle has spilt in the sink cupboard and likewise the bottle of cooking oil. While Katie prepared dumplings for lunch the bowl of batter went flying through the air and splattered onto the companionway steps. The poor teapot is collecting dents all over it. Noon position 37° 23' W, 15° 47' N. Ship's time put back one hour.

21st Nov. Perfect weather continues. The wind is steady on the starboard quarter and we're making 5½ knots under genoa all the time. No more bread, bananas or apples. We're getting down to tinned food and basics like potatoes, but thinking more of food, food all the time. Noon position 39° 15' W, 15° 27' N.

22nd Nov. Dull rainy day with one or two really ugly squalls close around us at various times. Spent the morning doing odd maintenance jobs and finished with a fresh water shower in the cockpit during the passing of a squall. Katie made delectable little scones for afternoon tea. We are now halfway across and feeling very pleased so Katie is making a special celebration supper.

23rd Nov. Latitude at noon 15° 20'. By dead reckoning we have come 100 miles since yesterday noon, but no way of checking this owing to miserable weather. Throughout last night we had endless downpours of rain and black, black skies which made me take down all sails except the little staysail (in anticipation of severe squalls). We have a few leaks around the companionway hatch and by devious means a steady trickle of drips have found their way onto both our bunks so spent the morning trying to dry out our bedding. Had a pizza for lunch and for supper a tasty tinned ham with raisin sauce and finished up with the last of the Dakar pineapples. Less than a thousand miles to go.

24th Nov. No sights, no sign of the sun, just hour after hour of grey gloom and passing showers. Both feeling imprisoned below behind shuttered companionway hatch. However progress not bad, noon to noon 123 m. by log. Clocks retarded one hour.

25th Nov. What started off as a pure blue sky at sunrise (albeit no wind) has now resolved itself into dramatic clouds, great towering cauliflowers of cumulus and black-bellied anvils rumbling angrily at our lonely little boat. We feel so vulnerable. At lunchtime we were engulfed in a hell of a downpour. But still no wind. Both feeling bored and longing for the trade to resume. We reckon we've used up two average years' worth of calms in the last week.

26th Nov. The sky is much sunnier with nice puffy little trade wind clouds. However instead of running free with the trade on the starboard quarter we are close-hauled on the port tack heading almost north. The wind is coming directly from Barbados to my infinite disgust. Katie is trying to appease me with pikelets and tea. Noon position 47° 10' W, 15° 20' N.

27th Nov. Position at noon 47° 58' W, 14° 40' N. The wind is now in the southwest of all places but at least we are now able to lay our course after a night of going south. We're enjoying gentle sunny weather with an atmosphere of crystal. At night the stars are clear right to the horizon so that I sometimes mistake a bright one low down for the lights of a ship. However we do have a dark cloud on the horizon, the diesel has packed up again. Ran it for two hours today to charge the battery but it won't start anymore and I can't remove the head.

28th Nov. Becalmed half the night. Another exquisite day but still not enough wind though it's at least going back now to the east. We could be sailing on a pond. Katie busy rearranging book shelves. I'm just being lazy. 49° 21' W, 14° 33' N at noon.

29th Nov. Pleasant weather, lightish trade. Every day seems hotter than the last, and we regularly cool off with buckets of salt water upended over our heads in the cockpit or on deck. Baked a sponge cake in the frying pan using asbestos mats top and bottom and switching them every half minute. It worked. Noon position, 51° 02′ W, 14° 25′ N.

30th Nov. Nice going. The trade has mended its manners. Katie has exhausted all her paperbacks and is now re-reading "Wind in the Willows." I'm busy restitching the luff of the jib and a few mizzen seams. Retarded the clock so this is our third 25 hour day. Noon position 52° 53′ W, 13° 55 N.

1st Dec. Both getting awfully bored with the crossing. I'm not getting enough exercise so I'm starting a training course, speed-walking clockwise right round the deck as many times as I can put up with. I did this 54 times today before giving it up as ridiculous. Noon position 54° 55′ W, 13° 54′ N. Only 280 miles to go. Katie is writing letters and sewing up the Barbados courtesy flag.

2nd Dec. Only 180 miles to go. We spend hours together eagerly discussing all the things we'll do once we get ashore. Movies, fresh water showers, T-bone steaks, beers, pastries are all high on the list. I struggled for an hour over the diesel this morning but it is dead. Drowned I suppose by more salt water.

3rd Dec. Nearly there! Sighted a ship this morning bound from the Antilles to Europe. Porpoises came to greet us after lunch, a sure sign of land. It appears we'll have to lay off for part of the night as we were only 55 miles off the coast of Barbados at noon according to my calculations.

4th Dec. Saw the glow of lights on the horizon ahead last night. We lay ahull for several hours and reset the genoa at dawn. Sure enough land lay ahead of us. The time lost was much regretted later on as in fact we were still quite a way offshore, and with the trade falling light after sunrise we were down to two knots and trying to get around to the lee of the island before evening without an engine. It's a rather low island but a lovely picture of smiling verdure after 21 days at sea. We sailed close in around Needham Point and after jilling around between other yachts, found a comfortable spot in five fathoms sand. I've poured myself a triple Cape Verdes rum to celebrate while we wait for customs. We are lying in a lovely little bay with friendly neighbours, a hospitable yacht club, sugary sand and clear silky water, and our first ocean is behind us. Log 2387.6 miles.

How good to set foot on land again! We dragged the dinghy up over the white sand clear of the surf and signed ourselves in at the little club where the secretary pressed a beer into our hands, and for several days while *Nanook* lay in Carlisle Bay we spent our time gadding about Bridgetown and savouring the firm feel of land beneath our feet.

With Independence the people had not lost their friendliness as it was rumoured they had on some of the other islands. We found their lilting jerky English a bit strange at first, almost like a foreign tongue until the ear caught the odd stresses of each word and phrase. The customs officers, the old ladies selling grapefruit on the streets, the busdrivers and the children riding donkeys on country lanes all seemed to have in their manner an almost Elizabethan grace. We caught buses around the island and spent long hours swimming at Accra Beach or helping the old women at Silver Sands to open up sea eggs. These were sold to be made into sea egg soup, a Bajan delicacy. "Orl de munts wit de R's," they told me when I asked about the sea egg season.

Mail was awaiting us in the old post office in Trafalgar Square. It was a chaotic place and we wondered if in fact we were really getting all the mail sent to us. As it happened, we didn't. Gunther our old friend of Mediterranean days had sent me a valuable chronometer watch as a gift. It vanished into the appalling parcel warehouse at Bridgetown and we sailed without it. Exactly a year later after several appealing letters to the Bridgetown post office it arrived at my address in New Zealand. "Inefficient but not criminal" Gunther remarked of the postal system.

One evening while sitting in the cockpit I noticed a large tender drifting downwind out to sea. The hotel authorities who owned the long jetty near the club had threatened just the day before to cast dinghies adrift if they continued to tie up there. No doubt they upset the guests. I rowed after the dinghy and had a long hard struggle upwind fighting for every foot to tow it back to *Nanook*. The owner was the skipper of *Camelot*, a large green wishbone ketch which had arrived in from the Atlantic crossing. Val was so pleased to recover the thing and to find that I wasn't claiming salvage that he presented us with a bottle each of Scotch and vodka and invited us aboard *Camelot* for dinner. He was an ex-test pilot whose party trick was water-skiing backwards amongst the yachts on one ski starting from a position completely immersed. The first thing to emerge was the backside.

Camelot was a superb yacht with everything a charterer could wish for: an entertaining host and a well-run galley, endless drinks and the sort of fabulous staterooms that charter parties appreciate, not only with double bunks but with full-length mirrors on both sides, the pillow end and overhead. The tender of course was called *Guinevere*.

Having repaired the diesel and refilled the rum jars with fine Bajan rum at $5 a gallon in bulk we wanted next to see something of the Lesser Antilles before going on to Panama. Time would not allow us to sail the full length of that island chain so we decided to be content with the French island of Martinique and all the British islands to the south, those referred to as the Windwards, rather strangely so for if anything they are further downwind than the so-called Leewards. The log of December 13th reads,

Marigot Bay on the island of St. Lucia.

"It was quite blustery in Carlisle Bay and we were sorely tempted to delay for another day as the passage to Martinique promised to be quite boisterous. Sailed up the coast to Speightstown and then to the northwest in alternate sunshine and showers, with more than enough wind. Now, 1900 hours, sailing well under full moon. A heavy shower has passed over and to the west is a beautiful complete moon rainbow."

But we had timed our passage badly and endured a night between Barbados and Martinique of rough seas and heavy rain squalls. The decks drained themselves constantly of wave crests and rain, and the motion was violent enough to dislodge an oar which was jammed, or so I thought, beneath the dinghy and it was lost overboard. Thereafter the oars were always stowed below.

With the dawn, grey silhouettes appeared ahead under the rain squalls, the first of the Windwards, St. Lucia to port and Martinique to starboard. Breakfast of Bajan grapefruit bread and tea was a perfunctory affair in the wildly unpleasant St. Lucia Channel while we hand steered in the cockpit in our yellow oilskins. A whale leaped several times clear of the water half a mile away and smashed solidly down again, probably to dislodge some parasites from its body.

The sun appeared for a time as we sailed towards a high green pinnacle in the sea looking like a great rocky tooth riddled with cavities. Diamond Rock has an interesting history. In 1803 the British in their never-ending feuds with the French set up a blockade of Martinique which the French managed to evade by slipping close along the coast, inshore of Diamond Rock. Commodore Hood then ordered a landing of men on the rock. His flagship *Centaur* anchored close in, and a detachment of sailors reached the top, itself no mean feat, rigged an enormous tackle from the top and hauled five cannon to the summit. For a year and a half 120 British sailors used these guns to harass enemy shipping until the French finally mustered sixteen armed vessels and attacked the small force with a loss to themselves of three gunboats and seventy casualties including thirty dead. The British, dislodged at last, lost only two dead and one wounded.

The British Admiralty, while recognizing French sovereignty, has ever since regarded the islet as a commissioned sloop of war, naming it *H.M.S. Diamond Rock,* and even now passing ships of the Royal Navy still fire seven guns in salute. Katie, never more ardently British than when in the proximity of Frenchmen, an ingrained habit I have tried in vain to break, now insisted as we sailed past in dipping our ensign, i.e. lowering it part way down its halyard, a sort of merchantman's salute to the fighting ships of the navy. But before the Canadian colours were returned to the top of the mizzen another squall hit us and Diamond Rock was lost astern in a torrential curtain of rain.

Like Guadeloupe, Martinique is an integral part of France, a department of the republic, a nice way of keeping your colonies without having colonies. Still the people, Creole with a slight Gallic overlay, seemed happy enough with the arrangement, more so it would seem than those of some of the semi-independent British islands.

Fort de France is an attractive green town spreading upwards into the wooded hills, but after three days the fast noisy traffic and the French prices sent us retreating across the bay to the comparative peace of the beaches not far from where Empress Josephine spent her childhood, and round the coast to Grand Anse d'Arlet, a protected bay with a fishing village at the head.

After two days at Grand Anse we raised sail and turned south for St. Lucia. Creole fishermen in little outrigger canoes were working for tuna off the Martinique coast. One close by gave us a cheery wave, not unexpectedly for his brightly painted pirogue was called *Plaisir de Vous Voir*. The others also had poetic names like *Mes Enfants* and *Souvenir de ma Jeunesse*.

The St. Lucia Channel was again in a grumpy bumpy mood. The fresh winter trade with all the fetch of the wide Atlantic slapped angry seas on *Nanook's* beam and we were drenched in a succession of squalls that called for rapid sail changes as rain began and the wind arose under the advancing curtain to a crest-ripping blast over the hissing seas. As each squall passed over, it left us wallowing for a while with hardly any wind at all. As one old West Indian sailor explained to me, "De rain she suck de win' out de air."

St. Lucia was lush and beautiful, spiked with sharp ridges and peaks. Castries the capital lay scattered around an inlet on the western or lee side. With the yellow flag flying we anchored off the harbour-master's office near the banana wharf. I was beckoned ashore by two customs officers, one of them already half corked in anticipation of Christmas and being myself infused with a spirit of seasonal goodwill I even contrived a wan smile as I parted with the arbitrary ten dollar entry fee imposed by the island government on all visiting yachts. I then rowed Katie ashore to explore the main streets of Castries and to discover whether the town might so easily rob us as the government had. To the contrary, Katie found the prices at the well-stocked supermarket to be so nearly reasonable as to warrant restocking our lockers with a few favourite lines of tinned food, while I for my part was happy to discover a den dispensing local rum to anyone equipped with a container and at a price to overcome any unreasonable objection that the stuff lacked mellowness or age. Throughout the islands since the days of Nelson the people have been assiduous in the cultivation of limes so that there is never a question what

Nanook approaches the Pitons, St. Lucia.

to mix with the rum. An old island rhyme has the recipe: "One of sour, two of sweet, three of strong, four of weak," or in other words, the juice of a lime, two spoons of sugar, three slugs of rum, top it up with water or ice. Stir. Delicious.

Christmas was now almost upon us and after a few practice celebrations with other yachtsmen lying in the tranquility of Vigie Cove not far from the town, we went on down the coast to Marigot Harbour for the real thing on the 25th in the merry company of *Aisling,* a small English sloop whose owner had lent it for a year to his son Mike and daughter Trish and their respective girl-and boy-friend for a North Atlantic circumnavigation.

Our old friend of Arctic days, Dick Vitt of the Mounties, now arrived in St. Lucia right on Christmas Day for a couple of weeks of cruising with us. He had flown straight out of the deep-frozen Yukon. On his way through Ottawa, Dick, a venerable bachelor, had picked up an old flame, a girl on whose garden gate he had swung as a boy, and Dick had plans I suppose to rekindle the fire. So the settee berths were rigged up and he and Mary signed on for the run down through the Grenadines. It was good to have them aboard.

In Castries, Dick (I think to the unspoken dismay of Mary) took care to stock the lockers with moderately massive quantities of his favourite brand of Scotch as an alternative to my meat and his poison, West Indian rum, of which I had laid in a sufficient quantity for all hands, and being thus provisioned we wassailed our way down the St. Lucia coast in company with *Aisling* past the high sharp peaks of the Pitons.

The main islands of this long chain were all independent of each other if not quite from their colonizing powers, so that the onerous formalities of entry and departure had to be observed at each new capital and up again went the Q flag as we anchored on the narrow shelf of the bay of Kingstown, St. Vincent, a quieter place than St. Lucia and not yet as adept at robbing the pockets of private yachtsmen. In a stiff wind and blazing sunshine we romped south from there over the straits to Bequia, the first of the Grenadines that extend sixty miles south to Grenada.

Bequia's Admiralty Bay is an old haunt of Yankee whalers and the people of the island are a nice blend of black and white with a long tradition of shipbuilding and seafaring. As she approached the anchorage powering up into the wind, *Nanook* was obliged, by the old rule that power gives way to sail, to weave a drunken course through a fleet of hundreds of little model yachts reaching across the trade wind to the opposite shore. The local boys' New Year race was on, most of their entries being just hollowed out coconut husks rigged with mast, sprit and sails and a little slice of galvanized iron for a ballast keel. They sailed well.

We were pleased to meet up with *Aisling* again in the anchorage. While in Kingstown the girls had bought three kilos of steak and cut it up for a good two- or three-day stew. Trish had bought a liberal quantity of

Katie bargains for a coconut husk boat from children of Bequia.

what she thought were mild salad peppers and cut them all into the stew. They turned out to be fiery chili peppers. The stew was ruined and had to be thrown overboard and poor Trish had to endure the passage to Bequia with her right hand immersed in a bucket of cold water to ease the burning on her skin, and to find medical help on arrival at Bequia.

But Trish was not alone. I had a heavy cold and Dick, pallid from wintering in the Yukon, had by that time thoroughly burned every decent square inch of himself and was unable to enjoy the New Year's Eve carousing in fancy dress on Princess Margaret Beach with the cheery quartet from *Aisling*. Dick's almost legendary good cheer and high spirits were well dampened and I felt guilty for having allowed him to sit so long exposed to the sun and sea. Meanwhile Mary, disenchanted perhaps with the islands, the heat, the confinement on board or perhaps just with our boozy bare-faced hedonism turned in at dusk and slept the New Year in. I wondered if the hinges on the garden gate might not be developing a rusty creak.

While in Bequia we met Lincoln Simmons, a sailormaker of the old school. My little jib had taken a deal of punishment in the contrary Med. and was becoming little more than a series of long patches so I arranged with Lincoln for a new jib to be sewn up at a very reasonable price and this done we set out again and for a week we drifted our idle way down through the sunny unambitious Grenadines.

At Union Island, Dick and Mary had to leave us. Their time was up and I think Mary at least had had enough of the Spartan confinement and the inescapable company that is intrinsic to small boats in remote places. From the nearby resort on Palm Island they flew home, Dick to the Yukon wilderness, Mary to her typewriter in Ottawa. The garden gate slammed shut and that was that. Still we were sorry to see them go.

Carriacou at the southern end of the Grenadines belongs to Grenada and there we made our entry to this last mini-nation of the Lesser Antilles, the officials taking our entry fees as if we were infernal nuisances and they were doing us a great favour. From the main port we sailed around to the snug anchorage of Tyrrel Bay for the night and there we again met up with *Bonaventure de Lys* and had John aboard for the evening. We also met there a Tasmanian couple, John and Julie Greenhill and their young daughter Lisa aboard *Moonbird*, a small sloop built by John in London. We were to see much more of them in the Pacific.

St. George's, the capital of Grenada, is a pretty town crowding the hills on three sides of the harbour or careenage. Restaurants and shops faced out along the waterfront where local trading boats tied up and small boys dived for small change. Close south of the careenage is a large lagoon that was once inaccessible to all except shallow draft dinghies because of a bar across the entrance. A channel was dredged across this bar and since then the lagoon has accommodated a huge number of yachts, many of them moored at the modern marina of Grenada Yacht Services. The lagoon was one of the main centres of the Caribbean yacht chartering industry where the well-heeled from North America set out to cruise the sunny isles while the winter blizzards blew back home. But an air of uncertainty seemed to hang over the industry. Various charter skippers that we met grumbled about Black Power and the punitive attitude of the local government towards charter yachts. The regime, they claimed, was riddled with corruption and malpractice of the highest level and all the charter fleet would soon be leaving for fear of more harrassment, more taxes or, worse, arbitrary arrest and crippling fines on some trumped-up charges. The things they had to say about the island's premier made the Haiti of Papa Doc seem like a haven of justice and democracy. They knew the island far better than we did but I still felt a pinch of salt might go well with some of the yarns. To us the island and its people seemed happy enough if still rather poor and apart from a certain amount of officious bumbledom on the part of the port authorities we met nothing but friendliness. The locals at least seemed to think a lot of their premier and he appeared to be well enough regarded abroad. Had he not just returned from London where he had been invited to take part as judge in the Miss

World Beauty Contest? The winner of the contest of course was Miss Grenada.

On January 22nd, equipped with official clearance and Venezuelan visas we at last left the lovely chain of islands behind, sailing downwind through a half mile fleet of floating wooden whisky crates. Scotch, bought very cheaply in Grenada in bond and sold at a fat profit on the Venezuelan blackmarket keeps many an industrious South American smuggler out of any other kind of trouble. Just why they invariably jettison the crates is a small mystery. It must make the offloading of individual bottles a fearful chore unless they are packed into some other innocuous container as a disguise.

Katie as usual after a longish spell in sheltered water began to feel queasy as soon as we drew out of Grenada's lee. So did the new hand; while buying kerosene in a small ramshackle grog store facing the careenage I had noticed a tiny grey and white kitten under the counter and since its mistress was anxious to be rid of it I carried the frightened little handful out to *Nanook*. Katie had been pining for a kitten for ages and fell in love with this one on sight. We named her Nutmeg in honour of Grenada's national emblem but this was generally corrupted to Meg or Nutty. Having been sick on the carpet this first day out, Nutmeg never again showed any signs of seasickness. She was the perfect sea-cat.

The trade was kind to us as we swept gently to the west. We were bound for Panama and the Pacific but were hoping to see something of Venezuela and Colombia along the way. Venezuela's island of Margarita lay conveniently close to our general westward course and since it had a port of entry I decided to call there. During my watch from 0130 to 0500 we passed over Cumberland Bank and with the echo sounder whirring away softly in the night I found it thoroughly unnerving to be sailing for hours on end over only thirty feet of water and no land anywhere, although in the blackness I thought I could make out Los Testigos, a small island group to the north of us.

On the afternoon of the second day we came to anchor at Pampatar on Margarita's west end, and the next morning, there being no response to our yellow flag we rowed ashore to hunt up the local officials. One or two policemen were lolling around on the steps of the *Palacio Municipal* in the sunshine, but when I asked where the *duanio* characters hung out they just shrugged their shoulders, told me it was *Domingo*, Sunday, and come back *mañana*. But after prowling the beaches and streets and having our fill of Pamatar's few delights we weighed anchor and sailed 24 miles west to a more remote but better sheltered anchorage. In doing so we were almost certainly breaking some law but I didn't expect anyone in the sleeply little place to do anything about it and having since heard various hair raising stories of the chicanery of the officials at Pampatar who have been known to slap "fees" of as much as $80 on visiting yachtsmen, I was glad we left when we did. A visit there would probably be more rewarding if one didn't have a boat to fret over, especially so if one were a Spanish-speaking bachelor; it is said of Margarita that only about ten percent of the people there ever bother with the formal nuisance of getting married and that for the rest, life from a remarkably tender age is a rip-roaring series of affairs.

Three Dutch islands lay not far off the Venezuelan coast further west and we decided to break the passage by calling there preferably at the first one, Bonaire, since the other two, Curacao and Aruba, are big smelly oil-refining centers. But shortly after dawn on the day of our expected landfall I noticed a pink line of flamingos flying due north which puzzled us because they could only have been heading for the salt marshes of Aruba and I believed Aruba to be well to the west. But an hour later when a sun sight was taken, I found that my bearing-by-birds on Aruba had been correct for a current had carried us well to the west during the night. By then Bonaire lay into the wind and we pressed on instead for Curacao.

Willemstad the capital is an 18th century-Dutch architectural delight. It lies astride the narrow entrance to a large and perfect natural harbour, the Schottegat and the two halves of the city were alternately joined and separated twenty or so times a day by a floating bridge known locally as Queen Emma, a rather charming nuisance designed in the 19th century by a resident American consul. Emma is supported by a long series of boat-like pontoons. Big diesels at one end power the bridge into action as it pivots on giant hinges at the Otrabanda, the Other Side. This is to allow tankers to pass to and from the great refineries in the Schottegat, but it badly disrupts busy street traffic. So with some perverse satisfaction we noted the long resigned queues piling up on each side while Emma inched her way around in a quarter-circle to let *Nanook* in.

Beyond Willemstad the channel opened into the great harbour of the Schottegat, a place encumbered in every direction with big ships as well as with all the stink and the mighty silver jungles of plumbing that go with the refining of oil. We were unable to find any anchorage in all this horrendous mess nor did we want to. We felt both puny and conspicuous like Gulliver in Brobdingnag and turned back towards the channel while black tongues of crude oil licked higher and higher on *Nanook's* white topsides.

Once back in the channel we moored alongside an empty quay to await Customs who eventually responded in the person of some junior function-ary. He wanted to know what firearms we had, (he was very particular about that) and whether we belonged to a yacht club. No firearms, no yacht club. I owned up to having a few bottles of rum. He left and we then thought we were entered. But shortly after, a more senior official showed up, uniform all nicely pressed, notebook in hand.

"Do you have any firearms?" he demanded. No, we didn't.

"But you have maybe a .22 rifle or a revolver?" he persisted. I repeated that we had no firearms.

"What ammunition do you carry?" he then wanted to know. I wondered what ammunition an unarmed vessel could be expected to carry.

"None."

"What yacht club do you belong to?"

"I don't belong to any yacht club." Ha, no yacht club. That was it then. In that case we would have to get clearance and leave immediately. We could not stay in Curacao beyond the hour. But first we would have to submit a complete manifest listing every item of equipment and supplies on board down to every last tin in the food lockers. But that would take a long time to compile, I pointed out.

The good servant of the people thought about that briefly. Well then, we would have to clear first thing in the morning after submitting the manifest. Otherwise we break the law. Fair enough; I didn't like the place much more than I liked its officials and meanwhile the black oil smear licked higher with the wash of passing ships.

We were then left undisturbed but next morning at 0630 just as we were having breakfast we were boarded by a heavy-booted official who announced that he would remain on board until we had cleared. Did they really think that if I had guns to sell I would wait for daylight before taking them ashore? Anyway armed with the typewritten manifest, a magnificent document, I hurried through town to the Customs building where yet more officials asked again whether we carried firearms and if we were members of a yacht club. I was escorted back aboard. The rum locker was sealed. (Curacao is a free port.) Clearance papers were stamped and handed over and in five minutes Queen Emma swung open again to let us escape back into the lovely open sea.

Many countries impose rather onerous and sometimes stupid procedures on visiting yachtsmen and all this must be borne with good cheer. Throughout all this I managed to remain polite yet nowhere else in our whole voyage were we treated with such inexplicable discourtesy. If they really thought we were running guns, why didn't they search us? At all events I did have the satisfaction of breaking their laws (illegal re-entry and pollution of coastal waters) for having cleared we then sailed five miles up the coast and moored Med-style to the jetty off the Hilton Hotel where I spent two hours in between beers rubbing the filthy topsides down with a rag and kerosene.

While we were in the Lagoon at Grenada we met a sailor, himself a Dutchman, who claimed to have perfected the technique of dealing with pompous overbearing bureaucrats and that was simply to be excessively apologetic and stupid. Ideally he explained, so that every possible snag might be glossed over, there should be no common language between skipper and officials, but this is difficult when one must obviously know English. It worked well for the Dutchman. He and his crew of three had crossed the Atlantic from Holland via the Channel. While in Portsmouth they had been asked by the harbour authorities to go ashore and pay harbour dues, a request which released a stream of affable Dutch, but the four never did manage to find their way to the appropriate office. They were eventually asked to move their vessel to a much more remote part of the harbour as they were obstructing traffic so close to the port. That would have meant a hard row into town.

"Ja, ja, very good!" they assured the man, nodding their heads and shaking his hand.

But ten days later when they were ready to leave they had still not shifted to the required location.

"Where are you bound for next?" the harassed official asked them. This they managed to understand and replied "Lymington."

"Very well," said the official looking closely at them and forming his words slowly and carefully. "Now listen. When you get into Lymington and you meet the harbour authorities there I want you to be sure and act just as stupid to them as you did here with me."

With its burning forest of refinery stacks, Aruba 70 miles distant, was visible all the way from Curacao during the overnight passage. The little island has the world's third largest refinery complex and one look at the place was enough to keep us sailing on our way west.

We had thought next to call at several ports in Colombia and after rounding the northernmost point of South America in pleasant weather we turned south east towards the city of Santa Marta. In conditions of great clarity such as sometimes precede bad weather we could make out far ahead the white skyline of the Sierra Nevadas when they were still 150 miles distant and the following day we could see the majestic range 18,947 feet high towering vividly over the hazy coastal plains, its snowfields glistening in the sunshine. From nowhere else on all the waters of the long Atlantic are such lofty mountains to be seen.

That night during Katie's watch when only an hour or so from the shelter of Santa Marta a sudden gale sprang up. After persisting on course for some time we smothered the sails and lay ahull hoping for the dreadful wind to go down, but our patience soon gave out and about midnight we began running west before the big breaking seas. I could have kept the reefed staysail up but the wind increased with every hour and I preferred to take all sails off while doing so was not too dangerous, and I let her run off under bare poles. "Any fool can carry sail on a ship."

We closed the hatches tight and left it to the steering vane to keep *Nanook* dead before the wind for we could at least be grateful that the gale was going our way. Gradually the roaring and the chaos outside increased and we felt thoroughly miserable as we lay awake by the hour listening to the baleful threnody in the rigging. Our blue Caribbean had suddenly gone crazy.

These wild conditions continued all the next day while we passed twenty miles from the coast through the muddy yellow waters of the Magdalena River. We had to forget about trying for Porto Colombia nearby and eventually lay ahull again in hopes of getting into Cartagena, but even that was wasted effort. We finally stowed our unused Colombian charts and with the tiny reefed staysail raised we resumed course for Panama, the wind still shrieking like a witch.

On the third day it eased a lot though it was still brutal sailing. My log reads, "Muggy and a lot more low cloud. Sailed part of the night with the jib. Progress good but poor *Nanook* took several quite stupifying strikes from seas breaking on her starboard side. Each time we wonder how the hull can withstand such violence. We're running by the starboard quarter. The scene outside is really awful.

"1400. The wind easing a lot, maybe Force 6, but I still think it's a bit strong for that lee shore at the San Blas 70 miles away. The decks are constantly running wet from the spray and the tops of waves sweeping aboard, and pitch is exuding out from between the swollen deck planks. Katie sick."

After a night of indecision I found by dawn star and planet sights that we were only twenty miles out from the entrance to the low-lying archipelago of the San Blas on Panama's north coast, and as the wind had moderated a great deal I altered course to close the islands which soon obediently appeared ahead exactly where they were expected.

There are said to be 365 islands in the San Blas group, all of them so small as to be ignored by most maps. Even our charts were vague enough. Yet many of these islands, some a mere acre or so in extent, are crowded to capacity with houses. These are the homes of the Cuna Indians, a proud people who have preserved much of their ancient culture and traditions in greater degree than most Indian tribes or other races that have been overwhelmed by the Western World. They live on the small insect-free islands and cultivate gardens on the mainland.

We stayed for only four days. While anchored near the villages we found ourselves quickly surrounded by canoes or stuck with a cockpit full of Indian women who may have been shy but who were determined anyway to lighten our purse. They all wore strange brightly coloured clothes and each had a black line down the centre of the nose and a gold ring through the septum. Their blouses were made up of successive layers of coloured cloth intricately cut into stylized pictures and patterns and sewn one over another, almost as a form of cloth sculpture. The women usually brought with them great numbers of these brilliant squares of cloth, or *molas,* and spread them all over the decks in the sunshine. Katie of course bought three times as much as we had previously agreed we could afford.

I was impressed by the well-developed commercial instincts of these women. Even the sight of a camera prompted some Pavlovian reaction that caused them to announce, "Picture fifty cents." They understood no English but I never heard anyone express themselves in American currency with greater assurance and clarity.

On our way around the jungled coast to the canal we stopped briefly at Nombre de Dios Bay and Portobello, the two ports that connected with the Pacific in the days of the *conquistadores*. What vast treasure, robbed from the Indians, passed through these places to the churches and the palaces of gold-gluttonous Spain! But the robbers were themselves robbed often enough. Katie, always mindful of English history, took the trouble to make up a small tinsel wreath and tossed it into the sea where Elizabethan sailors consigned the weighted corpse of Sir Francis Drake,

> Slung atween the round shot in Nombre Dios Bay
> And dreamin' arl the time a' Plymouth Hoe.

Once inside the mighty breakwaters of Cristobal we were boarded by a friendly American pilot who directed us to an out-of-the-way area called The Flats, a dismal place with poor holding, considerable fetch and a long hard row upwind to the port and yacht club. An admeasurer then came aboard and took all sorts of obscure internal measurements for the calculation of our tonnage. When we went to his office several days later to pay canal dues based on this tonnage we were pleased to find the bill amounting to only $8, and several months later a refund cheque for $2.35 from the Canal Company arrived at my address in New Zealand. There are few real bargains in this world and of those that exist not many can beat the dues on a small boat transitting the Panama.

After rowing and tramping some miles between The Flats, the customs offices and the yacht club carrying various signed statements back and forth we were given permission to moor *Nanook* at the breezily hospitable Panama Canal Yacht Club. To our great satisfaction a mountain of mail awaited us there as well as the facilities of the club, showers, excellent restaurant and bar, although this last being an all-male preserve we were given a reminder of the North American mores when Katie was politely kicked out of the place.

One of the transitting yachts moored alongside the club jetty was from New Zealand. She was the 36 foot ketch *Iorana*. We went aboard to meet the owners, Croix and Merle Grut. They had left New Zealand two years previously, sailed via the Indian Ocean and Cape Town to England and were then looking forward to the home stretch across the Pacific. Somehow they always looked to me more like Down Under farmers than world girdling sailors and in fact that's what they had been before leaving.

Croix had had *Iorana* built near the farm, gave up dairying and set off westwards with no other previous sailing experience than what he could get "in between milkings." They had a superb cruising yacht that was much admired wherever she went.

In addition to their own pilot, the canal authorities insisted on a crew of five for each yacht making the canal transit. Two line handlers were needed on the bows, and two on the stern as well as a helmsman. Not many yachts have that many crew aboard so a lot of teaming up was going on at the club and Croix immediately asked us to go through next morning with *Iorana* which we were glad to do, spending the full day on the transit to Balboa.

The next day we went through again, this time with *Chief Aptikisi*, a large ferro-cement ketch, a rather lovely traditional vessel when viewed from a distance but the closer one came to her the longer the face fell. The owners were also farmers, this time from Illinois. They'd never been to sea before and had built the boat themselves at home. Outlines of wire netting showed through the rough plastering on the deck and coachroof. The engine exhaust stuck up as an afterthought through a hole hacked in the deck and discharged its black fumes at eye level right behind the helmsman. The guard rails consisted of 4 x 4 wooden beams and common fencing wire. The world has thousands of better finished concrete cowsheds.

Tom, his father and another young man who at least *began* the voyage as a friend were bound for California where they confidently expected to sell "The Chief" for forty grand and begin a new life "homesteadin'" in British Columbia. But it didn't work out that way. After they sailed into some squally weather on the way to the Galapagos, the concrete rudder fell off. Apprehensive and unable to figure out an alternative steering system, they called up Panama for a tow back to port.

Necessity being invention's mother, it is worth pondering that had they not had a transmitter they might well have hit on a feasible jury arrangement and extricated themselves from their predicament. As it was, Tom could use his sextant only to obtain latitude so he advised Panama of his supposed position by dead reckoning. Unfortunately that part of the Pacific is subject to all sorts of strong and unpredictable currents and he was nowhere near where he thought. It took the salvage tug several days to find them and at $100 an hour by the time they were pulled back to Panama the salvage company in effect owned the boat so that the unlucky trio walked off with only their personal effects. End of voyage.

One sailor in the Caribbean had given me a hint about the transit. "Before you go through, they'll ask you what speed you can make under power. Say five knots, even if you can't manage that. Don't make it less otherwise technically they could refuse to let you go through." *Nanook's* little 4½ horsepower diesel seldom gave us much more than four knots and always very much less with any wind or wave resistance. "Five knots," I put on the form. No one asked whether we had a reverse gear. We did but it was so ridiculously underpowered as to be virtually useless. When entering the locks it can be pretty important to be able to stop quickly. The only alternative to a healthy reverse gear is to enter very slowly and to "slalom" or steer hard over in each direction with the rudder, port and starboard alternatively, rather a clumsy technique yet it is one used on some of the world's biggest tankers when an emergency stop must be made. Some "V.L.C.C's" (very large crude carriers) are so under-powered that it takes them two hours to reach their top speed of sixteen or so knots. For the same reason it takes up to ten miles to stop though by slaloming with engines full astern this can be reduced to two miles. Parachute sea anchors are being developed to slow these ships down more quickly. I had two buckets.

Merle, Croix and Tom spent a night on board *Nanook* after coming over from Balboa on the train, and at dawn the pilot came aboard. We had expected to go through "centre lock" like the others, that is secured to the centre of each lock by lines, two off the bows and two from the stern. But a couple of tugs lay alongside in the first lock ahead of us and the pilot decided to secure *Nanook* to one of these. The massive seven foot thick gates slowly closed out the Atlantic behind us and the inflowing fresh water turbulence from the next lock began. We gradually crept up the wall until the green water of the two lower locks settled at the same level. When the gates between them opened, the freighter ahead of us moved into its new position with the aid of electric mules. The tug to which we were secured then cast off and with a devastating burst of power rushed forward into the next lock dragging poor *Nanook* along as if furious at having this ridiculous sailboat lashed against her mighty fenders. Within seconds we were doing ten knots by the Sumlog. The nylon warps went bar taut and water burst out in plumes from the bows. I stared in horror, wondering what piece of equipment would give out first. But nothing did. At least at that speed our forward career was soon over and as the hair on the nape of my neck settled, lock hands secured the tug's lines to the wall of the second lock. Again the filling process began, lifting us this time to the level of the third. I asked the pilot to ask the tug captain to take it easy this time and we cruised into the third lock at a mere nine knots.

Few merchant sailors understand the limitations of a small hull and many a yacht has been severely damaged or towed right under by well-meaning big ships offering their assistance.

When the third lock had filled we were 85 feet above the sea at the level of Gatun Lake and with a sigh of relief we cast off from our enthusiastic neighbour and motored sedately past the open gates into the lake. The trade was fresh at this height so up went the sails and we bowled happily

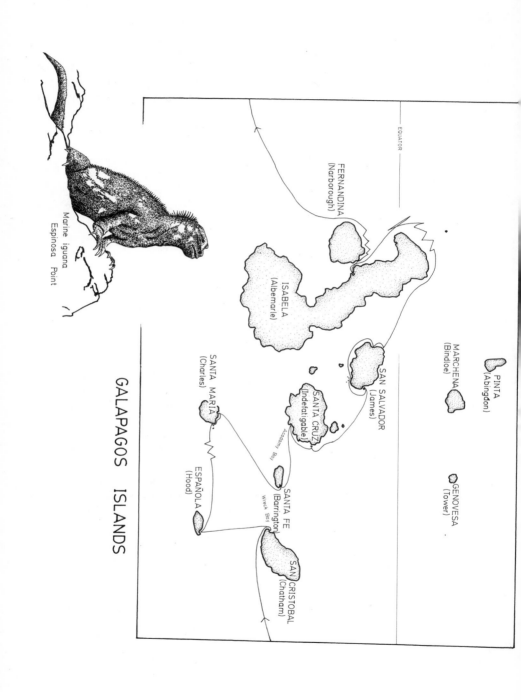

GALAPAGOS ISLANDS

EQUATOR

PINTA
(Abingdon)

MARCHENA
(Bindloe)

GENOVESA
(Tower)

FERNANDINA
(Narborough)

ISABELA
(Albemarle)

SAN SALVADOR
(James)

SANTA CRUZ
(Indefatigable)

SANTA MARIA
(Charles)

Academy Bay

SANTA FE
(Barrington)

ESPAÑOLA
(Hood)

Wreck Bay

SAN CRISTOBAL
(Chatham)

Marine iguana
Espinosa Point

along through the flooded forest, taking the unauthorized short cut through the "Banana Cut." Katie passed six plates out the hatch and we sat on the shady side of the deck eating our lunch of chips, salad and cold chicken as the islands and the grey trunks of drowned trees were left behind. *Nanook* rejoined the main channel and the lake gradually narrowed towards the mighty Gaillard Cut where the Americans had gashed open the continental divide early in the century. Once past the high terraced slopes of the cut we came to the Pedro Miguel locks ("Peter McGill" to the American pilots), the first of the three steps dropping us down to the Pacific. We then motored along Miraflores Lake and with all four and a half horses straining we passed a big ship against regulations and sneaked into the vacant first of the two Miraflores locks.

By late afternoon as *Nanook* lay against the walls, the final set of gates gradually opened up and the great Pacific at long last lay ahead of us.

VII

Passages to Paradise

Nanook had been slipped last in Spain and now stood in need of a new coat of antifouling. I had hoped to use the slipway of one of the yacht clubs at the canal but they were fully booked and the only alternative was to take advantage of the large tides on the Pacific side at Balboa and to put a new coat on while the boat was high and dry at low water. This was a procedure I'd never attempted before and it got us into some real trouble brought about as most troubles are at sea by bad luck and worse seamanship.

We tied up against an old steel barge, cleaned off the weed as the tide went down, put on a quick undercoat at low tide and finally a coat of American copper paint as the water came up. Unfortunately as the water rose, so did the wind. It came in from an unusual direction with a long fetch and blew hard on *Nanook's* exposed starboard side, holding the port side hard against the barge. This was of no great consequence until the water level was high enough to take some of the weight off the keel, and then no matter what I did I could not stop the boat rocking on her keel and slamming hard on her port side. The sharp frames of the rusty old barge chewed the fenders up like a crocodile having *hors d'oeuvres*. I was horrified. One after another, solid planks of wood inserted between boat and barge succumbed to a similar fate, grinding into pieces and floating off with the tide, and they were soon followed by the spinnaker pole. The cursed swell smashed heavily on poor *Nanook's* starboard side and to our great distress the rubbing strake and capping rail next began at one point to split and tear away against an exposed steel frame.

By this time it was quite dark. I struggled in a frenzied panic with the anchor chain trying to haul us forward into deeper water as each wave took the weight off the keel. Shudders ran through the boat with every lurch. Katie, in tears, paid out our mooring warps and kept the diesel thundering in forward gear and gradually we inched away. My heart pounded heavily from fright and heavy work. My legs quivered like jelly and my mouth was dry as an ossuary but after almost two hours of desperate struggling we won clear at last, and with two feet under the keel we re-anchored and made a nerve-soothing cup of tea.

At dawn back on our club mooring I surveyed the damage. The rubbing strake was fearfully chewed for over three feet of its length (but that after all is why it was put there), the capping rail ripped apart in one place and pushed out of line, and the main backstay rigging screw and fitting badly bent. Below water one plank had been gouged leaving a hole four inches long and half an inch deep. I spent two days repairing the damage as well as I could.

This incident while it lasted was the most harrowing experience we endured in all our long voyage. Compared to the bad times that others have encountered, it was nothing at all, but to us it was more than bad enough and we still tend to dismiss it quickly from our minds whenever the subject comes up.

Sailing out of the Gulf of Panama and across to the Galapagos can be quite a trick. Steer direct and as the sails fall idle the Humboldt Current will carry you northwestward away to the north of the archipelago and deeper into the doldrums. Steer instead towards the South American coast and another branch of the Humboldt will carry you backwards again into the Gulf. The whole region is one of baffling currents impinging on each other repeatedly and producing on the calmest day long excited lines from one horizon to the other of dark dancing wavelets chattering like a brook while all about the rest of the sea is an oily calm. From a distance these lines look like seas breaking white on a long reef. One crosses and recrosses them, some of them so sharply separating the two waters that as we crossed we were suddenly twisted around off course, the bow being caught by one stream while the stern was still held by the other. But if these great stirrings of the sea seem strange the tides of air in this region are no less baffling. Gone are the trade winds and one is left with sultry calms, light airs, dark thunder clouds and black squalls that may mushroom in from any direction.

We left the Canal Zone on the 25th February. A fair wind carried us out and though this soon fell light we at first maintained good daily runs with a 40 miles per day current going our way, so that I was surprised at dawn of the third day to find Malpelo Rock visible 15 miles ahead when judging from the previous day's astro sights it should still have been 60 miles distant. The sombre crags of Malpelo lie 200 miles off the Colombian coast. Malpelo has the inaccessible heights, the remoteness from land and the wild gaunt aspect that seabirds love so much. Gannets and boobies nested, fished and hovered in their raucous thousands. A few tufts of green grass sprouted on the guano and for the rest there was nothing but grim basalt precipices and the current foaming at their base.

A few miles on a 37-inch dorado, or dolphin, took our lure, a silver spoon and hook, and after a fifteen minutes tussle with the lovely irridescent creature we had him thrashing in the cockpit much to Nutmeg's satisfaction, and for three days we dined amply on fish. Food spoils quickly in the tropics but we found that by diligently boiling fresh meat or fish at least twice a day it would keep quite well.

For the next week the sailing was terrible with overcast skies, calms and light head winds. In one 24 hour period we made good only 11 miles, but I found this was because we were caught in the north-going coastal current so we stood out to the west on the port tack. The seacock on the galley sink drain then began for some reason to leak freely so that hard on the wind on the port tack we had a lot of sea water welling up past the closed seacock, overflowing the sink and getting all through the cupboards. The seacock could not be removed without first hauling the boat out. Meantime I hit on an easy solution. I let plenty of dirty dish water, cooking oil and food scraps lie in the drain pipe and put the plug firmly in. The resultant fermentation forced the water past the cock which jammed solid with putrid sludge. Nothing but gas remained in the pipe and this eventually blew the plug out.

We relieved the boredom of the long days by doing odd jobs about the boat while an amazing variety of sea creatures gave us something to stare at. Tuna leaped around us, though we could never catch any. Poisonous sea snakes slithered out of our way, and turtles abounded. One, his shell covered with red smears of antifouling paint from our hull, swam along behind us for several hours under the stern as we drifted along at one knot. We had no thought of disturbing these creatures let alone killing them and the time came when we could not even bear to troll for the beautiful dorado for those fish seemed to be so full of the joy of life, like the mammal dolphins whose name they share.

For four successive nights the wind dropped away to nothing and we motored till we tired of the heat and noise or slept on deck with the sails furled. But at midnight on the fifth of these idle nights I heard the halyards gently frapping on the masts and I quickly got up and raised main, genoa and mizzen to a light southeasterly. We had found the edge of the trade wind of the South Seas and *Nanook* seemed pleased to be on her way at last. We crossed the equator March 7th and three days later closed the surprisingly green south coast of the island of San Cristobal. The anchor went down in the sand of Wreck Bay where sprawls the capital, a dusty little shanty town with its face to the sea. The passage had taken 15 days.

Four other yachts which we'd met in the Canal Zone were in Wreck Bay including *Iorana* and it was good to exchange gossip and compare passages. Pelagic Bill arrived the day after us and as his yellow flag was unnoticed ashore I went to inform the port captain of his arrival. "I'm

At Post Office Bay in the Galapagos, Katie picks through the mail left in the old whalers' barrel to see what *Nanook* can deliver.

much too busy to see him now," he replied whereupon he locked his office, strolled along the beach and lay sunbathing in the sand. But if the formalities were tiresome and the visa expensive the graft at least was gone. Ecuadorian officials used to be famous for their chicanery and corruption.

After two days of worrying over the diesel which seemed to have lost a little compression, we left Nutmeg to stand guard over the boat and set off on foot to visit the community in the high country. All the Galapagos Islands are dry, with little but lava clinkers underfoot to wear away your boots and dry thorny scrub to tear at your shirt. But this becomes less true the higher you climb so that those islands that boast of one or two thousand feet of elevation attract plenty of rain on the heights. Here the vegetation is richer and on both Santa Cruz and San Cristobal farming communities till the fertile soil for market crops, coffee and the breeding of a few animals.

The character of the land changed rapidly after the first few miles. The grey lava rocks gave way to black soil. The dry scrub thickened into a green forest and suddenly we were amongst people again, the Ecuadorian dwellers of the green uplands. From the top of a hill we gazed far over the blue ocean. Other islands lay on the horizon. To the east of our hill not far away were two crater lakes of precious fresh water and behind us the poor little peasant settlement of Progresso, a place named, like the Pacific Ocean itself, in a fit of unwarranted optimism.

We each carried a rucksack full of green oranges the seven miles back down to Wreck Bay and while Katie began making marmalade I thought I'd try catching some of the little gray fish that hovered around the hull. In no time at all I had one of them on deck. Once out of the water it had a slimy look and began angrily grinding its teeth or grunting, I could not tell which. Though I didn't like the look of it, Nutmeg was all enthusiasm so I cut some pieces off for her and tossed the rest overboard. Katie was a little apprehensive for her kitten and started leafing through a book called "Dangerous Marine Animals." Suddenly she called out "Here it is!" and began reading the details. " 'Gulf puffer. Symptoms after ingestion of the fish . . . extreme weakness, nausea, vomiting, diarrhea, abdominal pain, twitching of the muscles, paralysis, difficulty in swallowing, loss of voice, convulsions and death by respiratory paralysis . . . It makes an excellent poisonous bait for stray cats.' " Quickly we looked on deck. Nutmeg sat licking her chops and contemplating the wet spot on the deck where she had just dined. Katie looked accusingly at me with mouth agape, perhaps stricken already with a sympathetic loss of voice.

"Well," I said, "perhaps the poison was only in the skin." I had thrown all the skin away, it being too tough for my blunt knife. Nutmeg retired below to Katie's bunk and apart from sleeping an unusually long time on her back with her paws in the air, a very dead-looking posture, she was

Playful young sea lions on Barrington Island, Galapagos Islands.

her usual self next morning racing up and down the main boom and, to my annoyance, scratching more great holes in the sail covers with her claws.

The greater part of a day of motor-sailing brought us south to Hood Island or Española as the Ecuadorians would have it. Each of the main islands of the group has an English name applied by the Elizabethan buccaneers who based themselves there to harry the Spaniards on their way to Panama, but in 1892 the Ecuadorians renamed the lot to mark the 400th anniversary of the first voyage of Columbus, even going so far as to officially rename the group itself the Archipelago of Columbus, or Colon, a name that might have been appropriately applied to the West Indies but hardly to a group of islands far into the Pacific.

To our delight a long line of black rocks on the brilliantly white beach of Gardiner Bay turned into sea lions as we came in to the anchorage. Heavy white surf crashed onto the steep beach, so choosing a suitable moment we surfed in on a comber and swept up onto the creaming beach amongst the sea lions. An irascible old bull raised himself up and stared balefully at us, shifting his weight from one flipper to another and barking grumpily. A few females humped across the sand out of our way and collapsed again as if the effort had overwhelmed them. Three juveniles playing together in the surf were fascinated by the extraordinary sight of us and followed us wide-eyed as we walked along the beach. The rest of the colony after giving us a brief inspection closed their big soft eyes and ignored us completely, their sun-dazed lethargy broken only by the occasional need to scratch themselves with their flippers.

But it was the Hood Island tortoise we had come to see. Giant tortoises once inhabited all the main islands and their Spanish name *galapagos* came to be applied to the whole group, certainly a more appropriate name than Colon but not as poetic as the original name of Encantadas or Enchanted Islands. The group was ideal as a laboratory of evolution, just close enough to the American continents to receive a few accidental arrivals in its two million year history and each island, with an environment peculiar to itself, just far enough from its neighbours to allow the development of its own distinctive species. An adaptable finch that arrived long ages ago has now evolved into 13 different species. When Darwin visited the group in *H.M.S. Beagle* in 1835 he noted and marvelled at this variety of finches each adapted to its own environment and pursuits and in due course Darwin startled the world with his theory of evolution and the origin of species.

But to return to the tortoise. The Hood species had developed a long neck and high carapace allowing it to reach higher for its food than was

A marine iguana basks in the sunshine of Barrington Island.

necessary on the wetter islands. I wanted to locate some of them and to photograph them in their dry habitat so off we set next morning hiking far across the rolling country, battering through scrub and scrambling over miles of sun-baked clinkers and brown furze. But no tortoises. In the late afternoon we returned to the beach by a different route and found that a party of Ecuadoreans had landed and were setting up their tents. They were sent out by the Charles Darwin Research Station on Santa Cruz to hunt goats.

"Oh you won't find tortoises here unless you're very lucky" they told me. "There's only one remaining on the island."

In the days of sail, whalers reprovisioned in the Galapagos as a matter of course. Tortoises were fresh meat and they co-operatively stayed alive for up to a year without food or water. So the numbers on many islands were quickly depleted. But man did far worse than that by introducing his own domestic mammals, cattle, donkeys and goats that stripped away the vegetation, rats, dogs and pigs that rooted up the eggs and ate the young. Many of the tortoise species are now close to extinction and the same is true of the land iguana excepting for those on a few small offshore islands where they can flourish in peace. The Research Station is grappling with the problem by breeding the reptiles in captivity while trying to exterminate the mammals on the various islands, but this is far easier said than done. All the wild creatures native to the Galapagos are ridiculously tame and trusting while the domestic animals that were introduced tame are now as wild as wolves.

We left next morning at dawn with hopes of reaching Santa Maria, or Charles Island before dusk, but the southeast wind soon died away to nothing and after motoring for several hours crabwise across a strong southerly current I stopped the diesel when it became obvious that we could not arrive anyway before dark. During the day a school of very large porpoises accompanied us, whistling under the bows where we watched them, and spraying us with their wet breath. After dark another group paid us a visit. The water was alive with tiny luminous organisms and as the porpoises hurtled past their bodies glowed with light and they left long trails behind like comets, intertwining with each other to form stranded ropes of glowing light.

A light breeze next morning carried us into Cormorant Bay on Santa Maria where we anchored beside another yacht containing a garrulous Frenchman who had entered illegally and was busy stocking up with turtle meat and 200 turtle eggs for his next passage. A salt lagoon nearby was home of a flamingo colony and after photographing this flock of pink orchids as they stood on one leg contemplating their reflections we returned aboard to motor round to Post Office Bay for the night. Before leaving, the Frenchman presented us with a bucketful of turtle eggs all of which Katie, incensed, promptly reburied in the sand at Post Office Bay.

It is thanks to people like that, that yachtsmen have since been barred from touching in at the archipelago, and I for one cannot blame the Ecuadoreans.

No longer do outward bound whalers leave letters in the old wooden barrel "post office" for collection and delivery by another ship returning home to Nantucket with a cargo of baleen and spermacetti. But that doesn't deter the tourists. Introduced to the archipelago ninety at a time by the Greek charter ship *Lina A* they descended in a horde at Post Office Bay to mail off postcard messages to all their friends. We found the barrel bulging. Heaven knows who cleared it or how postage was paid, but we picked up three for later delivery on our voyage, one to Australia, one to Brazil and one to Canada. The last two would have a long wait for delivery.

The barrel has now become a sort of cruising yachtsmen's shrine for it is festooned with wooden plaques bearing the names of sailing yachts that have called in the past. Many of them we recognized. The most recent addition was *Iorana* which had left only three days before us.

For a day we lazed about on the beach at Post Office Bay with only red crabs for company and big pensive pelicans, those "Sea Friars of Orders Grey," as Herman Melville called them. "Their elongated bills and heavy leather pouches suspended thereto give them the most lugubrious expression. . . . Their dull ashy plumage imparts an aspect as if they had been powdered over with cinders. A penitential bird indeed fitly haunting the shores of the clinkered Encantadas whereon tormented Job himself might have sat down and scraped himself with the potsherds."

After a supper of cod we sat in the cockpit in the calm evening listening to a request programme on the World Service of the BBC. The rest of the world seemed so remote except for that far away voice on shortwave from London. Suddenly to my astonishment the voice said, "And now we are calling the yacht *Nanook* somewhere in the Pacific. Birthday greetings are going out to the skipper from his wife Katie who has requested a record for you. I hope you can receive us clearly wherever your yacht is. How lovely it must be to sail around the world!"

It took all of a night and a day to cover 45 miles to the little harbour on the northeast corner of Barrington or Santa Fe where we stayed for four nights. It was an intimate little place protected seaward by a black lava peninsula that swarmed with sea lions and marine iguanas. We lay in clear water over white sand so that every link of the chain could be seen out to the anchor itself. Fish hovered around us, a pair of pelicans and a crane meditated on the nearby beach and turtles and black manta rays cruised outside the narrow entrance. Black lava gulls squawked over red crabs. But in all this profusion of wildlife, all within a stone's throw of our decks, nothing was quite as ubiquitous as the flies. They had reason to like the cove. A couple of dead sea lions lay on the peninsula and a huge bloated turtle carcass lay festering at high water mark on the rocks nearby. Katie looked several times at the glossy shell and hinted how well it would go with her burgeoning collection of sea shells so with some misgivings I waded into the stinking thing with a long butcher knife and lengths of rope. Clouds of red and black flies swarmed onto me as I disturbed the filthy quivering mass, but I persisted for fifteen minutes, rushing windward occasionally for breaths of clean air and returning to hack at the edges and hauling the putrid abdomen away from the shell with the ropes. But before I was half done I was so overcome with fits of retching and gagging that I retreated on board in disgust. "Turtles," I announced, "are *not* molluscs."

The crossing to the settlement of Academy Bay or Santa Cruz was courtesy of the diesel for the wind fell to nothing and the current was determined to sweep us southwest. We arrived in a dense tropical downpour, an unusual event, and many gallons of fresh water gushed out of all the scuppers as I dropped the anchor close in below the home of Karl Angermeier, one of the well-known family that left Hitler's Germany in the thirties to live in the Galapagos. Seven other yachts, all old familiars, were in the roadstead so we found it a little difficult to leave after only two nights as intended, but the mosquito swarms that came out at sundown helped stiffen our resolve. So having duly walked around to the Darwin Research Station to ponder the many great tortoises there and having taken on the last bread and water we could expect until reaching French Polynesia, we set out again around the southern coast for an anchorage on the east side of Santa Cruz in a slot between two narrow parallel islands called the Plazas.

Again we found ourselves entirely alone as to humans but surrounded by all kinds of interesting creatures. Sea lions snored and coughed on the rocks and played all around the yacht, some rubbing against the hull, others playing tug o'war with the dinghy painter. Like children they had to investigate everything. One clown thought he would try to squeeze through the narrow gap between the rudder and the trim tab shaft and when hardly halfway through he stuck fast so that I had to bend the shaft out a little and shove his shoulder back with my foot. The next morning the same scamp streaked with my precious red antifouling paint was asleep in the dinghy. After a time I came to take exception to this freedom with the newly painted bottom. The antifouling was supposed to last till we reached New Zealand so I took to driving them off with the deck broom, but I had to do this quietly while Katie was below for she would have none of such unkindness to creatures having such big, gentle, pleading eyes.

The Plazas were also well populated by land iguanas. They were about three feet long, slightly smaller than their slatey marine cousins and much more brightly coloured, orange, yellow and brown with a ridge of spines along the back, rather beautiful in an ugly way. Katie fed several with banana skins, a great delicacy that disappeared unchewed into their pink mouths in several slow deliberate gulps as if they all had sore throats.

A day's sailing, northwest through long rafts of floating pumice stone brought *Nanook* to Bartholomew Island and an anchorage dominated by an enormous column of lava rearing out of the water at one end of a golden beach like a great marlin spike pointing to the sky far over our masts. A colony of small penguins squatted quietly on a ledge at the base, cod and puffer fish hovered around our hull and a pair of turtles copulated in the water nearby.

In the evening we were joined by the red ketch *Aries* from Seattle and her crew asked us over to share their supper of boiled crab and fresh fish. The next morning we rowed ashore and leaving the dinghy amongst the many fresh turtle tracks on the shore we set off to explore the weird moonscape of Bartholomew Island. In every direction volcanic craters blistered the surface of the land, some several hundred feet high, some the size of a house and some just inches across. Well shod against the brittle cinders underfoot we scrambled to the highest point of the island and gazed in wonder over Vulcan's mighty kingdom. Far below us in one direction *Nanook* and *Aries* lay peacefully beside the mighty rock spire. Further inland inside a wide crater was an extensive field of fine cinders and there many yachtsmen over the years had recorded their visits by spelling out in big stones their vessels' names and the year of their visit. The old brigantine *Yankee* had recorded four separate years. The whole field was full of these giant names and as we sat far above reading them off we noticed two small figures walking among them and kicking the stones aside with their boots. *Aries'* crew, John and Verne, had decided that the environment had been disgracefully desecrated and spent a good hour trying to return some of the stones to their original resting places before giving up.

An even stranger place lay a half day's sailing to the south where in the company of Merle and Croix of *Iorana* we anchored between James Island and the island of Sombrero Chino, a volcanic cone that looked indeed just like a Chinese hat. Here we spent a couple of quiet days catching rock cod from the dinghy, skinny dipping over the side and scrambling with heavy boots over the tumultuous landscape of black lava. From this southern end, James Island looked as if a great cauldron of tar had spilled from the distant summits and slowly engulfed every visible mile. In all directions these immense deluges of black stone lay frozen in mid stream, so glossy and fresh as almost still to have the look of liquid. We hefted some twisted chunks of the stuff on board as souvenirs and left the rest to the blistering sun. No creatures, bird, reptile or insect, not even one solitary plant had yet dared to pioneer that forbidding waste, and looking at the chaotic tumbled stone underfoot it was hard to believe that it had not solidified just the night before.

After a couple of stops on the greener west side of James Island, *Nanook* was set on a night course to the northwest to pass around the northern end of the great island of Isabella, eighty miles long and ridged by a series of massive volcanic peaks. By dawn we had left Isabella's northern coast behind and watched the sun rising up over the cloven craters east of us. Having spent part of the night in the Northern Hemisphere we were again crossing the Line into southern latitudes. Of this exact spot Melville wrote "Did you ever lay eye on the real genuine Equator? Have you ever, in the largest sense, toed the Line? Well, that identical crater-shaped headland there, all yellow lava, is cut by the Equator exactly as a knife cuts straight through the centre of a pumpkin pie."

A breeze had carried us around the headland but it soon died and while I was taking a pre-breakfast nap, we drifted rapidly backwards to the north in an unexpected current coming up Isabella's west coast. We didn't reach the Equator at Cape Berkeley again until midday, motoring and muttering all the way. But with the northern peninsula astern we pulled clear of the current, caught a following wind and sailed all the way down to the sheltered anchorage of Tagus Cove. For three days *Nanook* lay resting under the high green escarpments of the cove with at first only the penguins for company, but joined later by *Iorana* and two big American yachts, *Tyrone* and *Santana*.

In the cove the grey volcanic bluffs were covered everywhere with white lettering inscribed in marine enamel from a hundred paint lockers for, like the barrel at Post Office Bay and the Bartholomew Island crater, Tagus Cove has long been a traditional visitor's book for sailors. Just as vacant landsmen like to scribble for posterity on vacant walls, so do sailors, the difference being that while landsmen always record their own names, sailors write only the names of their ships. There must be some deepseated psychology in this. The cruising folk we met everywhere tended to be known within their circle according to the name of their yacht. Thus the attractive family of girls frolicking on the sprit of the big green schooner nearby were known as the "Tyrones" whatever their real surname might have been. Likewise we were usually referred to as the "Nanooks." At all events, before leaving Tagus Cove, out came paint pot and brush from the bilges and *Nanook's* visit was recorded amongst a host of other ships' names famous and otherwise, including the still-wet names of our neighbours.

It was a month since our arrival in Wreck Bay and to our sorrow it was time to press on to the west. We had time for just one final anchorage at Espinosa Point, a black fork of lava on Fernandina Island where we photographed the incredible colonies of marine iguanas. Sea lions looked at us from rock pools and flightless cormorants stood quietly at the water's edge holding out their ragged useless little wings to dry in the sun while brine dripped slowly from their beaks to rid their systems of salt.

But at last on April 10th we brought the dinghy aboard and beat away to the west along the north coast of Fernandina, and in the evening turned south on a close reach down the west coast, hunting for the trade wind. Sure enough, after a good shower of rain in the middle of the night when I caught a bucket of precious fresh water to add to the tank, the edge of the southeast trade gently caught our sails and away we flew with Isabella looming dark over the port quarter and the Marquesas three thousand miles ahead.

We were now bound at last for the South Seas and the first outposts of Polynesia, the Marquesas. Our route across this vast and empty part of the Pacific would be a thousand miles greater than our Atlantic crossing and when on the first day out I marked off our first noon position on the small scale passage chart and compared that one tiny step out from Fernandina to the gigantic expanse of blank paper across the chart table to the tiny fly specks of the Marquesas, I felt overwhelmed by the colossal distance ahead. It seemed that reaching out over that chart in such insignificant steps would take many dreary weeks. Yet that part of the Pacific is blessed with a fine reliable wind, and I have never heard of a yacht that has found that passage an arduous or difficult one, excepting only for the one that went the wrong way, battling directly from Tahiti to Panama. On dropping anchor in Balboa, so the story goes, the skipper and his crew fought a pitched battle on deck during which the precious sextant was hurled overboard.

As we flew away to the west our latitude increased day by day away from the Equator and each day I added another little x on the chart showing the noon position obtained by a mid-morning sight of the sun and later a noon latitude sight as the sun reached its zenith. After a few days we came down into a west-going current and a stronger wind and then we increased our days' runs from 100 to 140 or 150 miles and then the little line of x's really began to march well out into the empty Pacific void.

At first there was plenty to see and do. As always on a long passage our thoughts dwelt a great deal on fresh food, but Nutmeg stayed alertly on watch all night and every night, so flying fish were off the menu for the rest of the crew. But bread, scones, pikelets and cakes came regularly out of the frying pan on *Nanook's* ovenless stove.

The first days out we had dorado and a few tuna and plenty of seabirds for company and occasionally a school of dolphins would come and play around us for a while before dashing off together on some other merry lark. But gradually the sea life thinned out until almost nothing appeared to enliven the long days so that coming up with an off-course turtle 500 miles out was a notable occasion, and even more so was the whale that we passed later the same day. It was only a boat's length from us. It seemed far bigger than *Nanook* herself. Its mouth was a great curved gash extending nearly halfway along its body. It appeared to be sleeping and we hoped it would stay that way. Whales can be a serious menace to ocean going yachts and no doubt the whale sleeping peacefully on the surface would like to say "Vice versa." We discovered a few weeks later that two young Germans on the same long passage to the Marquesas had their yacht holed and sunk by a whale at about the time that we were in the same area. After drifting in their liferaft for over a month they were rescued by a Russian ship and taken to Panama. The year before a single-hander was sunk on his way to the Galapagos and the next year another one again. Many other cases are on record elsewhere, like the New Zealand yacht sunk in the Tasman on her way to Australia. She went down so quickly that the only provisions grabbed up in the scramble overboard were a bag of onions and a container of kerosene. Luckily a ship happened by the day after. A great deal more sobering are the unknown cases that were not lucky enough to go on record.

There is no point in dwelling on an unpleasant subject except to note that as in all things prevention is better than cure and the only known prevention is not to put to sea. Some yachtsmen claim that pinkish bottom paints should be avoided; the colour chosen should make the boat look to a whale neither edible nor sexy, but so far as I know no one has yet consulted the whales as to what the colour should be. Some others suggest that a heavy layer of diesel oil on the surface will repel whales but you must then stay in the slick, just when you want to be miles away. One cruising man however who deserves the final word has developed his own Killer Whale Kit. This can be contrived by anyone, consisting simply of a fifth of overproof rum. Instructions: In the event of killer whale attack quickly uncork and take a good triple slug.

Katie who had always protested an ignorance of mathematics in which she once came in at the bottom of her class, now decided to apply herself to a study of celestial navigation.

"Never mind the 'why,'" she pleaded. "I don't want to know the theory behind it all, just teach me *how* to do it by steps." I had always pooh-poohed the notion that she could not master the subject properly and set about to teach her the whole process. Each day she learned a small but new step in the process of calculating and plotting sun sights. She began to speak in the secret, magic language of navigators, talking confidently of index error, declination, parallax and hour angles. Before long the entire sequence of steps was learned (if not the theory) and she could find our position each day on the chart without my help. Within a week she had disproven years of total conviction that for her celestial navigation was an impossibility. She found the most difficult part of all to be taking the sight itself on the rolling pitching deck, but even this tricky co-ordination she gradually acquired. I was happy with the result of this effort. A yacht on an extended cruise should have spares of nearly everything including even its navigator.

We had occasional spells of changeable weather with tiresome sail changes but we were able to catch the odd bucket of rain water in these unsettled conditions and this helped alleviate our concern at the water supply. By careful economy we found that we could keep our total consumption down to half a gallon of water a day and at that rate we had ample water on board for twice the distance but it is always well to carry a good surplus in case of emergency.

As the weeks dragged on we began to get bored. Our old radio companion of the Atlantic, the BBC World Service, was fading and we still could hear nothing of Radio Australia so we were stuck for our entertainment with the powerful but excruciating Voice of America, and even worse still the Voice of the Andes, a tiresome but tireless group of American evangelists trying to convert the world from their stronghold in Quito. So we saved nicely on radio batteries apart from time checks from WWVH, a radio clock broadcasting from Hawaii, and also the regular morning tune-in to *Iorana*'s frequency when we could hear Croix's cheerful voice two hundred miles behind us saying, "Good morning, *Nanook*," and giving us his position and news. We of course had no transmitter and were always sorry to be unable to reply to him.

There were always a few routine jobs to be done on board but we spent hours laying about the deck or cockpit discussing our first restaurant meal in Tahiti or the contents of the mail that awaited us there. Nutmeg's nightly vigils no longer rewarded her with a late supper of flying fish so she had to be content with tinned rations like the rest of us.

With so little to report the log entries became shorter and shorter, and so completely did one featureless day merge with another and another that we began to find it very difficult to recall clearly the mini-events of just the day before.

The highlights of every day were the meals. We drooled at the thought of food. We prepared it lovingly and we lingered over every bite, savouring every morsel and talking about it long after the dishes were put away on their wire racks. We drooled too over the things we didn't have. As the castaway Ben Gunn said, "Many's the long night I've dreamed of cheese. Toasted mostly."

However there was another matter that gave us something to think about: We were getting ever closer to our landfall. We had steered for the southernmost of the Marquesas, the small island of Fatu Hiva, thus putting ourselves in a favourable position to steer off the wind through the

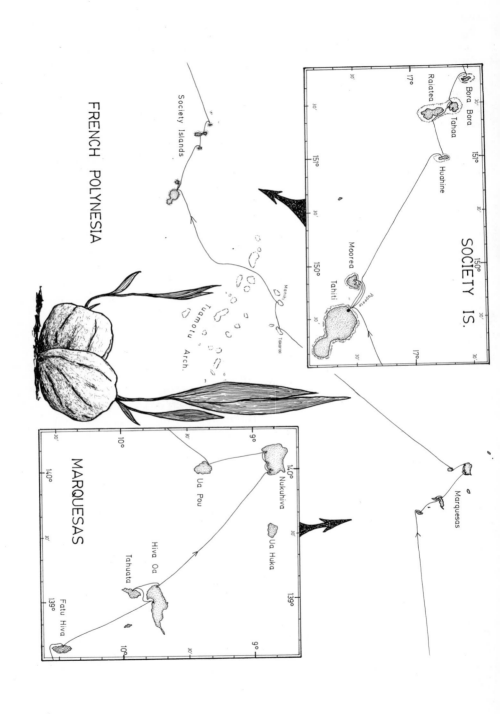

FRENCH POLYNESIA

Society Islands

Tuamotu Arch.

Manihi

Takaroa

Marquesas

SOCIETY IS.

Bora Bora
Raiatea
Tahaa
Huahine
Moorea
Tahiti
Papeete

17°
30'
15°
30'
150°
30'
170°

MARQUESAS

Ua Pou
Nukuhiva
Ua Huka
Hiva Oa
Tahuata
Fatu Hiva

10°
9°
140°
139°
30'

rest of the group, and as expected in the dawning of our 24th day at sea there appeared on the horizon ahead the grey jagged outline of Fatu Hiva.

For four hours our eyes never tired of sweeping over the growing spectacle of cliff and ridge and peak. We rounded Point Venus at the southern end and motored up in the lee of the mighty mountain walls to the Baie des Vierges. There at last we dropped anchor on a stony bottom where a verdant valley came down to the sea. Three thousand one hundred miles were on the log and the longest of all our passages was behind us.

VIII

Through the Heartlands of Polynesia

The islands of the South Seas can be divided roughly into three types. There is the high volcanic island rising directly from the sea without any barrier reef. The Marquesas are all of that type. There is the high island surrounded by a coral reef and containing inside the barrier a lagoon of sheltered water, a type well represented by Tahiti and the Societies, and the third type is the simple coral atoll, an ultimate development of the second type in which the volcanic land has completely eroded or subsided far beneath the lagoon, leaving just a ring of coral islands around the edge. The Tuamotus are of this third type.

Someone, I forget who, has likened these three groups of French Polynesia to three quite different but equally desirable women. The Tuamotus are like the plain, cheerful, unsophisticated girl next door, all sunshine, bare feet and freckles. The Societies are much more mature, alluring and overtly sexy, the *femme fatale* type. But the Marquesas are like a queen, even more beautiful than the others but remote, regal and full of dark melancholy. And so we found them.

Nanook lay in a narrow opening in the coast between high wooded ramparts which stood either side of a long deep valley. A small river emptied into the head of the anchorage and through the trees we could make out the first three or four roofs of a little village. We went ashore several times during the next three days, driving the dinghy backwards each time through a heavy surf, and wandered through the quiet village and up the peaceful forest trail far up through cool green glades past lemon trees and waterfalls to the high grass lands at cloud level above the

113

Nanook and *Iorana* share their first anchorage in Polynesia on the island of Fatu Hiva after the 3,100-mile passage from the Galapagos.

bush. The people seemed a little shy at first but when we returned down the valley they spoke to us in French and pressed small gifts upon us of oranges, bananas and lemons. After sunset of the first day a canoe load of youths paddled out to us, came below with their ukuleles and treated us in the cabin to an evening of Polynesian songs. Then as they departed they passed up to us a large sack of enormous green grapefruit each the size of a man's head. They were bursting with sweet juice and so large that we could only manage half of one between us at a time.

Iorana joined us a day after our arrival and we exchanged visits to compare impressions of the passage and to see how St. Vincent rum went with the Marquesan lemons.

The wind at this time rising over the knife edges of Fatu Hiva maintained the upper slopes in a shroud of dismal mist and periodically a tremendous gust of air exploded down the valley and across the anchorage, laying us far over. *Iorana*'s anchor dragged in one of these williwaws so Croix felt disinclined to go ashore and on the third day we decided to sail on together to Hiva Oa, 44 miles north where we could obtain official entry from the police.

Everyone has his own favourite island and the world is full of islands that are each, to someone, the most beautiful in the world. For myself, despite all its silent grey crags, deep forests and inaccessible solemnity I must cast my vote for Fatu Hiva even after a five year surfeit of beautiful islands.

Hiva Oa, a much larger island, has several anchorages on its coasts. We sailed into Baie Tahauku in the south beneath a range of cloud-hidden peaks, and anchored in an area totally protected from the trade wind. But nature had so arranged matters there that the heavy swell from the southeast was stopped short by a wall of rock and rebounded directly into our snug cove so that we rolled and crashed about as if we were lying ahull in a gale. Katie managed after some effort to get herself into the dinghy as it leaped up and down the topsides but try as she might she could not then get from the dinghy onto the small jetty nearby so I brought her back aboard and walked on my own into Atuona where formalities with the French police were mercifully brief. I then tracked down a Chinese baker who sold me some loaves of French bread from his primitive oven in the bush. With these under my arm and after a quick look at Gauguin's grave on the hill, I repaired aboard, and when Katie had had her fill of French crusts and English Marmite we lifted the dinghy out of the chop.

Next morning we left Merle and Croix and sailed on to Vaitahu on the island of Tahuata and after being boarded by a wench called Irene who swam out with a hibiscus flower behind her ear (on the single "available" side—I had to disappoint her), and then by the local policeman and then by sundry other brigands who all complained of a dryness of the throat, we paid the little community a visit.

Vaitahu was the place where the French navy first established a garrison in the Marquesas and took formal possession of the group for France. I was amused to find in the centre of the village a large bronze plaque reminding the populace of the deaths of numerous French matelots including their commander Captain Halley who died in a battle at that spot in defense of France. Not a word about the many more Polynesians who must have died in the same battle in defense of their little island, but perhaps an anonymous death was one penalty for being "savage." Apart from that plaque and the fierce williwaws that struck down at us from the mountains, we liked Tahuata, but the wicked gusts could not be endured while we had an alternative so after only one night there we turned north and came to an inlet called Hanamenu on the north coast of Hiva Oa where *Iorana* had arrived the day before. Here we stayed for six days.

All the islands of the Marquesas were heavily populated in pre-European times, and if early writers are to be believed the valleys rang with the laughter of a proud joyful race. But then Peruvian slavers came along and carried people away in ships to work out their lives in Andean mines. Whalers and traders arrived with their guns and devastating new diseases, the French with their colonial wars and the missionaries with their hot Mother Hubbard clothes for the body and wet blanket for the spirit, convinced as they were that of all this motley lot it was the naked primitive who stood in most need of conversion from sin as they defined it. And so the population fell away almost to nothing, in some areas in fact to complete extinction and elsewhere to a broken dispirited few, their culture and their whole past in ruins. Eden was at an end.

The valley leading down to Hanamenu was filled with reminders of this past. A long road bordered with fitted rocks led far up along the river and through the trees on either side were walls and high platforms of flat stone where houses once stood. Only one young family now lived at Hanamenu. Lucien Rohi, and his wife Marie Louise and their two children lived a quiet existence in their elegant little house of bamboo and fronds just back a little from the beach. They bombarded us with typical Polynesian hospitality during our days at Hanamenu and we found it hard to repay them adequately for their kindness. Shortly after we arrived they brought a present of fish out to us in Lucien's canoe and when we went ashore this was followed up by bananas and drinking coconuts. Marie Louise then invited Merle, Croix and ourselves to dinner in their little house in the evening. To our amazement a tremendous feast was laid out before us, steaming breadfruit, baked fish, rice, fresh water shrimps, lobsters, chicken, native spinach and coconut sauce. Not content with that, in the following days they brought out to us fresh eggs and an enormous eight pound chunk of fresh wild beef killed on the mountain.

The anchorage at Hanamenu was open only to the north so we felt entitled while there to expect good shelter from the southeast trade. Yet every morning about 0830 as the sun warmed the land to the south a breeze drifted in from seaward and by early afternoon it would be blowing fresh off the sea and up the valley. By that time *Iorana* and *Nanook* would be pitching wildly in the steep swell, heaving and snubbing horribly at their chains and sending things flying below so that life on board in the afternoons was intolerable. Then towards evening the wind eased and dropped altogether and we could forget our troubles again. I was always tempted to go ashore in the afternoon and pretend it wasn't all happening but I knew the anchor might drag and we had to stay on board on that account. Both Croix and I laid out second anchors on nylon lines to help take the strain and reduce the chance of the main anchor dragging, but when we finally prepared to leave Hanamenu for the passage to the island of Nukuhiva to the north, Croix found that his nylon kedge warp had parted leaving his kedge anchor lying somewhere on the bottom. The water was always cloudy, so poor Croix had to drag the bottom with a grapnel from his dinghy, raking up and down for hours across the sand in long straight lines.

"I wish you'd go and help Croix," Katie said to me. "He'd be helping us if it was our anchor down there." True enough. But there wasn't much I could do that he and Merle weren't already doing. They had a grapnel and

In a quiet corner of the Marquesas, Katie, with advice from Nutmeg, attacks the green weed that flourished on the waterline during the run from the Galapagos.

an outboard motor, while I had neither. Anyway, inspired by me rowing around making sympathetic noises they eventually snagged the line on the bottom and up she came. Again we prepared to leave Hanamenu. I went forward to recover our kedge and to my dismay found that our own thick nylon warp had also parted, having pulled out at what I thought was a good splice. So we started all over again (with Croix's help as Katie had forecast), and not till the following morning did Katie herself manage to find the thing, snagging the broken strands in the flukes of a small Danforth anchor.

Nukuhiva is the main island of the Marquesas and the one most usually visited first by incoming sailors. We had 80 miles to go from Hanamenu so this meant an overnight passage and by the next dawn we found the colossal dark precipices of Nukuhiva lying close ahead and *Iorana* outlined against the wave-lashed cliffs was beating us in. We came to anchor at Hooumi, the eastern arm of the Baie du Controleur a place offering complete shelter with no swell or downdraft from the hills. It was a most spectacular setting but so were all of our anchorages in the group.

Just around the corner from Hooumi and separated from it by a mountainous spur was Taipi Vai, the central arm of the wide bay where the great valley of Taipi drained to the sea. At least to me it was a great valley for it was the setting of Herman Melville's eloquent book "Typee," a tale based on his own experiences while held a captive by the inhabitants there early in the nineteenth century.

In one's adolescence certain things leave powerful impressions and I was hardly 15 when having read "Typee" I was permanently possessed by a romantic vision of an earthly paradise inhabited by Melville's companion, the beautiful Fayaway and a hundred other laughing nymphs "dressed in the summer garb of Eden." Heady stuff. I still cannot quite shake that vision. But alas, where is Fayaway now?

We rowed to the head of the bay to find out. Crossing a gravel bar we entered a slow-flowing river lined with trees, and rowed upstream paralleling a road and passing a few houses of hardboard and corrugated iron and a couple of heavy matrons doing their laundry. Several bends in the river brought us to fast water and a shallow bottom, so we left the dinghy and joined the road passing by a school and a playing field where a game of soccer was in progress between neighbouring villages. A few passers by smiled shyly at our *"Bonjour."* A boy on a Honda nearly knocked us over. A couple of French priests in white robes pointedly ignored us and a doctor coming out of his clinic nodded to us perfunctorily. The village shaded by coconut and breadfruit trees was strung out prettily along the side of the chattering river, but it was soon left behind and the road then became a trail leading far up the forested valley to where distant waterfalls tumbled over the mountain walls. There, far from the village, were the only inhabitants of Taipi that Melville would

Katie rows along the river that drains Taipi Valley on Nuku Hiva. She didn't know it at the time, but a stowaway rat was sharing the dinghy.

still recognize, a group of small squat pagan deities carved out of black lava, most of them unusually well-endowed males. There was only one female figure and she of course after so long a sojourn in such company was quite pregnant. Fayaway perhaps? But if so, she had gone very much to seed.

We stayed anchored only one night off Taipi Valley and in the middle of that night we were awoken by a tremendous racket in the cabin. A great scurrying, scratching and thumping had suddenly erupted near our bunks and we were both instantly awake. With my toe I turned on the fluorescent light switch at the end of my bunk and there on the carpet was Nutmeg gleaming with delight at the sight of a huge immobile rat.

Thank god for Nutmeg! Stowaways are never welcome on a yacht. Cockroaches, bedbugs and weevils are all equally intolerable but of all the things that ever decide to run away to sea nothing is more repulsive and disgusting to me than *rattus rattus*. I was afraid to get out of bed lest I disturb the tactical pause in hostilities on the carpet, because once mobile again the rat could easily locate various routes to the bilges and lockers here he might hole up for days or even weeks before being caught. But Nutmeg had the wretch cornered fairly close to my bunk so without getting out I slowly reached over, picked up the diesel starting handle and

Bread, sun-dried on the deck, would keep indefinitely at sea. We were fond of soaking one side of this dry bread in milk, and then pan-frying it with eggs or flying fish.

clobbered the thing with one smack. Nutmeg had more than earned her passage.

We were anchored an unusually long way from shore so the rat had had either a very long swim followed by a climb up the chain or dinghy painter, or, more likely, he had been cowering unnoticed in a corner of the dinghy when we returned aboard from the valley.

A short distance along the Nukuhiva coast lies the bay of Taiohae the administrative centre of the islands where we again announced ourselves to the police and remained at anchor three days enjoying the company of new faces, both in the friendly little town and in the anchorage for we had several other yachts around us. I spent part of a day diving down to clean the barnacles and weed off the hull until I was told that there were dangerous sharks in the area and that they were attracted to the bay by the zegular disposal of offal into the harbour every time a cow was butchered ashore.

Our Admiralty chart showed a land-locked anchorage called Tai Oa a few miles beyond Taiohae near the southwest corner of Nukuhiva. It looked on paper much too enticing to by-pass so we sailed along the coast searching ahead for the passage through high overlapping bluffs. It proved to be a scary approach running as we were before squally winds towards a dark wave-lashed precipice, a struggle between the instinctive fear of a high ugly lee shore and confidence in the veracity of a piece of paper printed in England, but the channel revealed itself and we were suddenly out of the heavy seas and round a corner into peaceful waters with hills ahead, great fluted mountain walls behind and thundering in our ears all night the sound of the heavy surf on the other side of the ridges.

In this peaceful deserted place we remained two days and nights relaxing and collecting shells on the fringing reef before proceeding south to Ua Pou, the last of our Marquesan islands and one noted, at least in clear weather for its fantastic fairytale skyline spiked with the eroded columns of vertical volcanic plugs. While we lay in the island's lee the trade wind smothered these improbable peaks in mist but occasionally one or other of them was unveiled, briefly revealing some dark basaltic phallus pointing to the heaven with an eternal erection. Or at least so they appeared in our imagination. As Oscar Wilde said, "A dirty mind is a perpetual feast." Our anchorage was a poor one so upon arming ourselves with long French loaves, coconuts and bananas from the pretty village ashore we weighed anchor and put *Nanook* on course to pass through the Tuamotus on the route to Tahiti.

The early navigators didn't call the Tuamotus the Dangerous Archipelago for nothing. They are the greatest collection of atolls in the world, a galaxy of coral and coconuts stretching a thousand miles across the mid-Pacific. They look on the chart like an endless series of necklaces and they read in the sailing directions like a recipe for a shipwreck. From seaward they cannot be seen from a distance greater than about ten miles and when sighted each atoll appears more or less identical to all its neighbours, simply a broken line of palm trees above a more continuous line of white breakers. The channels between the atolls are wide and clear but they are unlit and plagued with strong unpredictable currents. Unfortunately this dangerous fence of atolls is so wide that some night sailing must be done to pass completely through the channels to the open ocean beyond.

Four days out from Ua Pou I found by star sights at dawn that the atoll of Takaroa was only thirty miles ahead, and four hours later the tops of coconut palms appeared exactly where expected. A large rusty wreck on the windward side, the victim of a bygone cyclone, confirmed the atoll as Takaroa for the red hulk was marked on the chart as all prominent wrecks are. It was not till evening that we approached the pass of Takaroa leading to the village and lagoon. I'd intended to stop and secure to the wharf by the village but when I found that the current was strong in the pass and that in the low sunshine we could hardly see the shallow coral banks from a safe distance, I got cold feet and turned away. The result of this was that I spent the night muttering in disgust at my own timidity and steering a new course instead for Manihi for I was resolved to visit at least one atoll.

More by good luck than design we arrived at Manihi just at slack water the next morning. The people of the village saw our approach and raised the French tricolour on a flagpole above the palms to help indicate to us the postion of the pass and in a short time we lay alongside a long concrete wharf in the narrow pass with all the village out to gaze at us.

We loved Manihi from first sight. We sat under an immense shade tree near the wharf chatting to some of the adults. We visited the home of Linata and Tuarea and were plied with drinking coconuts and paw paws by their *grandmère* and we went hiking far along the motu under the palms, waded at the edge of the lagoon for shells, and returned to invite our hospitable friends on board for a visit.

Yet we stayed only six hours for the urge was strong to get quite clear of the dangerous chain. We still had seventy miles to the pass between Rangiroa and Arutua and only beyond there could I feel like relaxing. The weather at the time was perfect and there should have been no cause for concern, but fair weather only feeds my habitual pessimism for I then feel it can do only one thing and that is get worse. So in the evening we waved goodbye to the smiling folk on the wharf as *Nanook* shot seaward on the fast-ebbing stream in the pass. I set the vane to carry us through the night on a course between the atolls of Rangiroa and Arutua and by early afternoon of the next day we were clear of the group.

However just as we left the coconut trees of Arutua to port and came out into the open ocean again, the sky smeared over with a greasy grey film of cloud, and an awesome long swell rolled in towards us from the southwest. Later in the afternoon the wind began doing odd things, coming suddenly from north, backing through northwest to west, round again to the east. Eventually, one by one, I had to take the sails in as the wind hardened from the northeast. About 2200 the jib ripped almost in two. That was the last to come down.

The log for the next day reads, "2nd June 1000. We've never spent a darker night at sea than that 'un. The wind has been wild as hell and still is. Thank god it's at least daylight now if no better in any other respect. Still blowing a hard gale and raining like the devil. Visibility very bad, just one or two cables most of the time. Lying ahull beam on which isn't too bad (thanks perhaps to the Tuamotus being upwind) but a bit worried about our possible proximity to the island of Makatea. Katie's bunk is sodden and my clothes and leaky oilskins not much better. Occasional breakers bursting over the coachroof. The noise outside is fearful. A bottle of chutney has broken and distributed itself in the galley cupboard. Altogether we're feeling pretty awful."

Mixed up with the general misery was my increasing paranoia about Makatea. There was no way of finding our position under the leaden sky, and I kept imagining us carried off by a malignant current and drifting down onto a roaring reef in the middle of the night. But if we felt apprehensive we had less cause for it than Merle and Croix on *Iorana* who were sailing just a day behind us in the middle of the Tuamotus, fenced in on all sides by low atolls and unable to get sights. The gale drove *Iorana* down towards the line of atolls to the southwest so they steered for one of the gaps and having left one atoll to starboard and another to port they believed they were clear until suddenly in the murk ahead another line of palms appeared where there should have been nothing but open sea. The currents had carried them off course and they had passed through an adjacent gap. But at least they had done so in the daylight and were able to recognize their new position.

Meantime I had climbed into woolens and oilskins and started steering by hand towards the south-southwest as far south as possible with the wind a little on the port quarter, that being the direction offering us most searoom in all directions, especially away from Makatea and the Tuamotus. We made four knots without a stitch of sail up. By evening it seemed that the wind was easing very slightly but we still drifted on through the night barepoling downwind. The next morning I was able to raise the staysail and later as the wind moderated, the other sails too until by evening we were again bowling along towards Tahiti with a trade wind, a clearing sky and all our troubles and fears very conveniently forgotten.

The great mountain peaks of Tahiti shone in the early morning sun as we steered for the pass through a coral reef leading to Papeete harbour. A pilot came aboard to direct us to a berth and we were soon moored bow in, Med. style, amongst a line of seventeen other yachts along the gay noisy waterfront of Papeete.

Tahiti may not be quite the paradise of Cook and Bougainville, or the sexy lotus land of a hundred thousand jack tars since those first navigators but it is still a beautiful place and the people are still amiable, fun-loving and hospitable despite a nineteenth century invasion of black-robed preachers and a twentieth century invasion of jet-borne tourists.

For a week we lay idling in the pleasant Tahitian sunshine consuming great quantities of mail, ice creams, wine and fresh food and getting to know some of the other cruising folk most of whom were unknown to us, though we were soon joined by familiar faces on *Iorana* and *Moonbird*. Charlie and Marty Peet of *Santana* were already in after a cruise from the Galapagos to Pitcairn and the French island of Mangareva not far from the nuclear test site at Mururoa Atoll. Mangareva was very much out of bounds to yachtsmen but Charlie had wangled permission to stay there by the simple expedient of filling his bilges with sea water and saying to the local officials that *Santana* was sinking.

Our adjacent neighbour, the large ketch *Raipoia*, had just changed hands and was preparing to leave for her new home in New Caledonia,

With an anchor off the stern and the bow secured to a palm tree, *Nanook* lies in the tranquility of Robinson's Cove, Moorea.

and this fact occasioned a succession of riotous parties on board which as often as not we had to take part in, employing the ancient tactic of joining what cannot be licked.

The single-handed bachelor types were obviously enjoying their stay in Tahiti. Some had already spent a full season there sampling the delights of paradise, and one married American with an attractive wife commented wryly to me that "cruising in the South Seas with your wife is like bringing a sandwich to a banquet." But even if that were so he was at least having a far better time of it than one earnest young man from the American west coast who was bound west through the islands with his mother. The two were heading for New Zealand. John had built the boat himself and was emigrating to a simpler life down under, far away I suppose from the problems and pressures at home. John's mother was the no-nonsense type, not at all in love with sailing or with all the nonsense of the "romantic" South Seas, but determined to get on with it for the sake of the clean uncomplicated life ahead of them. She met us one morning in a supermarket where I was examining the display of French wines and when I pointed out a good brand to her she assured me that "we don't have that problem on our boat." Two or three of the other yachtsmen inveigled John ashore one evening in the hopes of plying him with a few strong drinks and a native girl or two, but as soon as he discovered what was afoot he excused himself abruptly and hurried off home. Unfortunately, John also had a cat and a huge German shepherd dog on board and when he later arrived in New Zealand and found that the animals were unwelcome there, he changed his mind and headed off home again the long way round.

Sundowners in the cockpit of *Nanook* or one of the other yachts each evening inevitably had us gazing wistfully westwards away from the town towards the high fairy tale peaks of Moorea silhouetted against the colourful sunsets. Perhaps it was just the rum, but Moorea always looked especially appealing and romantic in the evenings so that after a week in Papeete, tired of the noise of traffic, the crowds of pallid tourists and the French prices we decided to take a breather in the verdant peace of Moorea. I wandered over to the Customs building to explain ourselves to Gui Gui, the bluff personable official there who kept a fatherly eye on all the yachts, and with that courtesy completed we sailed across to Tahiti's kid sister Moorea, 12 miles to the west.

Like the other islands of the Societies, Moorea is surrounded by a sheltered lagoon and a barrier reef of coral. Two deep inlets penetrate the northern shore, and as if nature millions of years ago had in mind the convenience of ships and navigators, these two inlets are each matched by a wide clear pass through the reefs. We chose the western inlet, Opunohu Bay and brought up into a small cove facing inland fringed by palms and a sandy beach. Katie dropped a stern anchor into twelve fathoms while I rowed ahead with a warp and secured the bow to a coconut palm.

Here in Robinson's Cove we idled a week away never tiring of the dramatically beautiful setting. The needle-sharp peaks appeared and disappeared in the clouds and the freshening wind gusted occasionally off the nearby precipices sending catspaws fanning out to darken the water across the bay, but our little cove was so snug that these hardly lifted *Nanook*'s burgee. We were not alone. The cove is well known to yachtsmen and we were soon able to enjoy the company of *Iorana* as well as two American yachts, *Eolo* which was jointly owned and crewed by two married couples who incredibly were still quite compatible even after several years of confined living and co-ownership, and *Sayonara,* a new ketch built on traditional lines and owned by Dick and Iris Bellinger of Seattle. In the short time we spent with *Sayonara*'s crew, sharing anchorages through the Societies, we became fast friends.

Each morning one of us at the cove stopped the bread truck on the coast road a little way back through the palm trees and then rowed back around the yachts with an armful of long crusty loaves. Occasionally we hitched a ride round to Cook's Bay for an ice cream or a kilo of steak from the Chinese store. We went for long walks inland with Merle and Croix and

Nanook sails out from Moorea, bound for Tahiti.

snorkelled along the edge of the lagoon collecting shells or tackled a few minor jobs on board when the mood suited us, varnishing and going overboard with a mask to clean the hull. In the evenings we gathered aboard one yacht or another and spent long hours yarning about the sea and sailing for when they are together cruising yachtsmen will not be found to talk on any other subject for very long, and the taller the drinks the taller the stories.

Katie would have stayed in this little Shangri La forever but we still had great distances to cover if we were to be in New Zealand for the southern spring so at the end of a week in Robinson's Cove and a night in Cook's Bay we returned to Tahiti to complete our shopping and get clearance for the Isles Sous le Vent, the lovely islands of the Societies that lie further out to the west "under the wind."

In Papeete we moored bow-in again alongside *Raipoia* where the nightly parties were still in progress. Having spent a year in the Mediterranean we were well used to the intricacies of the "Med moor," choosing our position carefully and judging the direction if not the exact position of everyone else's anchor and we never once had any troubles there with fouled lines. So the next day we were a bit disconcerted to see *Eolo* come in from Moorea, and the crew, thinking that they could squeeze *Eolo* into the narrow gap between *Nanook* and *Raipoia,* dropped their anchor right over ours. It eventually dawned on them that they would have to try elsewhere and they began recovering their anchor again but in so doing they fouled our chain and up came *Nanook's* kedge anchor with their own thus taking all the strain off our stern. As luck would have it one of those infuriating little overpowered runabouts such as are found in sheltered water anywhere in the world on Sunday afternoons, now passed by, setting all the yachts pitching up and down at their moorings. *Nanook,* with the strain taken off her stern drifted in to the concrete quay just as the pitching started and down came her bowsprit with a resounding crash on the edge of the quay. The sprit bent upwards and at the waterline three half-inch bronze bolts securing the bobstay to the stem sheared off and the bobstay dangled uselessly into the water from the end of the sprit as those on board *Eolo* replaced our anchor into the mud. The air was blue.

This incident delayed us for several days in Papeete while I searched the town for bronze and for an engineering shop that could fashion it into three bolts and a new stem plate. It was a hideously expensive job which wrought havoc with Katie's carefully calculated monthly budget.

At last on June 25th with a strongly secured bobstay and a feeling of relief we cast off from Papeete's quay, cleared by Gui Gui for the outer islands. But at first we got only as far as our stern anchor for a single hander on *Miss Fancy V* had by that time arrived from the Marquesas and his anchor line was fouled around our own. I then made the mistake of passing our line the wrong way around his to correct the tangle, but finding that to be wrong I then passed it twice around in the opposite direction which seemed only to make matters worse. Finally Croix showed up with snatch blocks and line, Dick from *Sayonara* appeared with diving equipment (and one needed only to glance into the filthy sludge of the harbour to appreciate the gallantry of it) and while other friends took care of *Miss Fancy V* we lifted both anchors, separated them after a tedious struggle, said goodbye to everyone all over again and departed at last from Tahiti.

We were no sooner well clear of the island than the wind fell to a light air so that we couldn't even reach Moorea before dark. The Sumlog needle dropped to zero and for a while the booms had to be silenced with preventer guys. Progress was poor all next day but the sky was blue and the atmosphere so clear that we could see the islands one hundred miles apart lying on opposite horizons, Tahiti and Moorea behind us and Huahine and Raiatea ahead. To reach Huahine meant a second night at sea, part of it hove to waiting for daylight to reveal the edge of the island's extensive reef. At first light I resumed our course and steered round the southern end and up the west coast. A large dorado kept station with us just off our starboard beam. He shone in the sunshine with a handsome irridescent blue but whenever he darted off-course to go on the hunt his colours suddenly changed to black and yellow stripes.

I chose the first of the passes through the outer reef and felt glad of the good visibility for the land bearings recommended on the chart would have put us squarely on the reef just south below the pass. We brought up in a small inlet a short way from the main village anchoring in ten fathoms. The setting was idyllic and we were entirely alone.

Again our days were spent according to Katie's formula of a bit of work first on the boat then the rest of the day enjoying ourselves. We found the lagoon to be a rich area for shell collecting and the Chinese store to be well stocked with red wine and long brittle loaves. In the evenings we rowed across to the copra-scented wharves where the young people gathered, and sitting there on the grass we listened to them singing their songs of love under the palm fronds, thrumming endlessly on worn ukuleles and filling their throats with the rich sensual harmony that is heard all through Polynesia.

On the horizon to the west in Huahine lie the lovely twin islands of Tahaa and Raiatea enclosed together in the same lagoon and surrounded by a long barrier reef curving around the two tall islands like an hour glass or in the manner of a cell in the process of splitting itself in two. We kept glancing seaward towards these two and even beyond them to the distant pinnacles of Bora Bora. I am afflicted with a permanent impatience to be always somewhere else and Katie in that respect is no antidote. No sooner would our anchor dig in than we would be back at the chart table contemplating the next passage, figuring the mileages and deciding where next to anchor. There was plenty in Huahine to do and see, a variety of anchorages, archeological sites, long trails through the forest, extensive reefs and nice people. But there was always something new to the west and in any case time was pressing. The world is becoming small, it is said, but not when seen from a small sailboat and in five years of sailing around the world we never once left a country or even an island with the feeling that we had stayed long enough to do it justice.

So after the alarm on the chart table was thumped into silence we had a breakfast in the twilight of early dawn and motored out through the pass with the bow towards Raiatea. The expected southeast wind however was on holiday and we ended up motoring for six hours all the way to one of Raiatea's windward passes, Teavapiti where we anchored close by Taoru, one of the pretty little *motus* or low islands on the reef, a romantic deserted spot or so it seemed until we rowed ashore. There we were met by a sign warning that the island belonged to so-and-so and was *tapu*. But it was not this so much as the mosquitos and *nono* flies, or no-see-ums, that finally drove us back aboard.

The next day after making our way round Raiatea and through the channels in the lagoon to Tahaa, we found a quiet anchorage at the head of Hurepiti Bay, one of the long inlets that penetrate the island. After putting the anchor into black mud three fathoms down I found that we were just short of knee-deep water. A native man passing by in a pirogue spoke to us in Tahitian and a few scraps of French from which we finally understood that we were in a bad spot and we should go down to "Mekata" which I took to be a point halfway down the bay. But instead, Meketa came to us for he proved to be a man not a place. He came paddling up to us from his home near the point, apologizing in English for not noticing our arrival. We had come to a bad place he said (it was not all that bad) and if we liked he would pilot us down to the best anchorage by the point. As we made our way down to Meketa's point he explained that he had once sailed an American yacht as far as New Zealand and that he looked after any yachts that happened to come to Hurepiti Bay. He soon had us anchored in a quiet spot in ten fathoms with a long line ashore from the stern and there we stayed for several memorable days.

The people in the hamlets around the bay proved to be almost as helpful and hospitable as Meketa himself, and in a couple of days we were on the best of terms with several families each of which had invited us into their homes when we happened to pass by. They pressed on us small gifts of shell or fruit and offered us some refreshment, a plate of raw shellfish or a green coconut or a bowl of boiled home-grown coffee. We were at a loss at first to know how to repay all this spontaneous kindness but we soon found that the people were curious to see the yacht, so visits aboard *Nanook* became the in thing and our cockpit was seldom empty. They came out in their canoes always bringing some extra gift of food with them so that we began to accumulate embarrassing quantities of taro, large grapefruit and drinking coconuts. I took to storing these in odd places out of sight so that new arrivals bringing more of such things would not be embarrassed to find that they were bringing coals to Newcastle. We hated to accept such an unusable surplus from these kind people yet we felt that we couldn't refuse or devalue their gifts by revealing the abundance already on board.

Meketa came out to visit each evening and have a glass of rum and we enjoyed his company for he had a good store of local yarns most of them directed against the French. He always wore a hat on these occasions or took his glass below for the full moon was rising in the evenings and it always gave him a headache. The sun was okay, it was the moon, he told us. If left in the light of the moon fresh-caught fish will quickly spoil and babies exposed to moonlight have been known to die. He was a bit surprised that we didn't know this. As for Americans going to the moon, that was impossible and he didn't believe it. You can believe a lot of the things they tell you on the radio, but there is a limit.

The day before we left Hurepiti Bay, Meketa, after presenting Katie the collector with two buckets of assorted shells, took me far up through the bush behind the point. Here on the hillside overlooking the anchorage we arrived at some scattered plots in the bush. These weren't his family gardens, he said. These were planted by him each year for the use of visiting yachtsmen! I assured him that we were already well stocked and needed nothing more but he brushed that aside and started lopping banana trees down with his machete. My repeated protests were of no avail and we eventually re-emerged out of the bush with two large bunches of bananas, two more of *fe'i* or cooking bananas, a bundle of vanilla beans, a basket of taro, sweet-tasting seed pods that I couldn't identify taken from the branches of a high tree, and a small pile of drinking coconuts.

The next morning as I was recovering the lines, Meketa, who was sad that we were leaving, paddled out to us to say goodbye, bringing with him four more huge grapefruit. Finally as we sailed close by his house he called to us to wait so we lay off until he returned in his outrigger canoe. It was a sad day for him, he said, for we were leaving and he would never see us again. But he would always remember us. He then produced two long shell necklaces and draped these around our necks giving us at the same time kisses on each cheek.

What marvelous people are these Polynesians! Surely they are the most civilized people on earth. Kindly, fun-loving, sentimental and generous, they take nothing in life seriously except their friendships.

We sailed out the bay waving goodbye as we went and once through the pass through the coral reef we enjoyed an exhilarating sail over the sun-dappled sea to Bora Bora where we anchored all alone for the first night in a deep bay. Bora Bora is one of the loveliest isles of the Pacific, the classic Bali Hai of the South Seas, outlined with bold turrets of basalt and surrounded by a lagoon and a barrier reef studded in places with long deserted *motus*. I rowed ashore next morning for a view from the skyline. A shouting mob of happy young swimmers escorted me in over a fringing reef and after carrying my dinghy to the beach while I waded behind through the shallows they rushed for their clothes, not to cover their nakedness but to reach into their pockets for little gifts, pieces of buttered bread, chunks of coconut meat, shells and a lump of coral. Ten of these cheerful youngsters guided me up a track through the forest to the top of a hill where we could see both sides of the island and across the multi-coloured lagoon. From where we stood I could see several good anchorages in bays and behind *motus*. The best of all was at the south end of the island just out from a large tourist hotel built in the style of a thatched village. I was delighted with the sight of it because I recognized down there our old friend *Sayonara*. Dick and Iris had come over directly from Tahiti and they had anchored between the sapphires, cobalts and aquamarines in a patch of pale blue water indicating a bottom of white sand.

I returned aboard with my retinue who insisted on seeing all over "le yacht" and with them dispatched ashore again we made our way around the lagoon to the Bora Bora Hotel where *Sayonara* was lying. We anchored nearby in eighteen feet of crystal clear water, and while we admired our shadow and the indescribable colours around us, Dick who knew our priorities rowed over with a loaf of fresh bread from the bakery around the coast, and later while paying a return visit to *Sayonara* we were able to divide some of the masses of food from Tahaa that had converted *Nanook* into a floating greengrocery.

The hours on *Sayonara* went too quickly. Dick and Iris were re-freshingly honest about their cruising. They indulged in no heroics and made no pretense of liking the open sea or of relishing the passages ahead. Yet they put a cheery face on everything and we were sorry four days later to part company with them.

We were bound next for the Cook Islands and after only five days in Bora Bora having sated ourselves with snorkelling, hiking and cycling (on Dick's folding bike) we decided to leave the island to the growing tourist industry with its sprouting hotels and its Club Mediterranee. We went ashore to spend our last francs at the Chinese stores in Vaitape. Outside the lagoon a light wind was blowing and I set the steering vane to hold the bow to the southwest in the direction of Rarotonga.

On the fourth day we sighted the little island of Mauke, the first of the Cooks and a place devoid of shelter. Being now well to the south we found the trade wind to be less reliable and we spent another three frustrating days leaping about in confused seas on the way to Rarotonga. "Both writing letters, both bored, both full of bananas," says the log. At dawn of the seventh day we steered into the north coast of Rarotonga and the little pocket-handkerchief harbour of Avatiu at the western end of the straggling main town.

As always, how good it felt to be in. We had to squeeze into a tight berth along the eastern quayside where a crowd gathered to watch our approach and wonder at our antics with ropes. We were soon boarded by officials who took away what remained of our Tahaa fruit. They also asked if we had any drugs and they took away our passports. An attractive young journalist Bronwyn Webb then came aboard to interview Katie for the local paper and that done she invited us both to her parents' home for dinner ("tea" to the Kiwis), roast mutton and all the trimmings.

This was the beginning of a frantic social whirl that we still recall with amazement. Our intention had been to stay for only about a week but so involved did we become with several of the "expatriate" New Zealand families and their Maori friends that we had virtually no meals except breakfast on board for over two weeks when we were finally permitted to escape to sea. It so happened that various government-employed Kiwis on the island had known me or my family in New Zealand and between them they swamped us with invitations ashore to lunches, hikes, lectures, dances, dinners, picnics, drives and midnight parties until our heads reeled.

One of these people, Arthur Helm, was posted to Rarotonga to head an embryo tourist department for the Cook Island government, and he and his wife Jenny were insistent on taking us personally to see all the sights, pointing out all the old temples, the ancient road around the island that is as old as the Roman roads of Britain and pointing proudly to the pass in the reef where the Great Maori Fleet from Raiatea, augmented by the Rarotongan canoe *Takitimu*, departed for New Zealand over six hundred years ago.

These ancient traditions were passed by word of mouth with fair accuracy from one generation to another. One such story was repeated to us by an old man from Matavera village. A great Samoan warrior Karika while on a long sea voyage met a warrior from Tahiti, Tangiia, far out at sea. Karika invited Tangiia and his crew to a battle against the men of his own canoe. But Tangiia feeling that Karika might have the stronger side replied "Why fight out here in the middle of the sea where there is no one to witness the outcome and applaud the valour of the victors? Let us join our canoes and sail together till we find a land where we can fight properly."

Karika was pleased with the idea and they sailed off together. During the voyage the two groups became good friends and Tangiia meanwhile made sure of his position by marrying Karika's daughter. They eventually reached Rarotonga and after conquering the inhabitants they divided the island between the two leaders, the division being decided by a race. The two canoes sailed from one point on the coast in opposite directions till they met again on the other side. A line across the island from starting point to finish divided the land between the two chiefs.

Native tradition has it that the first Europeans to call at Rarotonga were the *Bounty* mutineers led by Fletcher Christian. The London Missionary Society established itself in Rarotonga early in the nineteenth century. In the absence of any other effective outside government the missionaries were only too willing to rule the people themselves which was easily accomplished once they had won control of the chiefs as they had done in Tahiti. There ensued a long period of theocratic dictatorship during which the people were forced into some sort of compliance with all the grim tenets of Calvinism, as well as into the payment of a tax, or enforced "collection" for the furtherance of mission work elsewhere. This was an era of the Blue Laws and even at the time of our visit remnants of these persisted in island council by-laws. The Cohabitation Law for example decreed that single people of opposite sex found together in suspicious circumstances could be arrested and punished. Incredibly this appalling law was not repealed in Rarotonga until as late as 1966 and was still in force on other islands even later.

Rarotonga looks like a scaled-down version of Tahiti. The islanders, despite the Blue Laws of the past, have the same cheerful zest for life, love and good times as their cousins to the east, and life in Avarua the village capital was apt to be the same spontaneous musical comedy that it was in Papeete twenty years earlier before the tourist boom. Alas, while we were there a jet strip was being torn across a corner of the island to bring an end to Rarotonga's isolation, so it was only a matter of time until the friendly intimate little world of "Raro" evolved into something a lot more commercial and a lot less charming. But that we are told is progress.

The harbour at Avatiu is an unsatisfactory little affair, crowded, shallow and wide open to the north. Late one evening the harbourmaster came down to warn us of a severe earthquake in the Solomons. We knew that seismic waves had wrecked yachts in Avatiu before, so after quickly calculating how long such a wave would travel over the intervening distance and finding that it would arrive if at all in the middle of the night, we quickly cast off and tied up for the night to a huge tanker mooring in deep water well out from the reef. Nothing happened and we returned sheepishly to our berth next morning. But we still felt concerned at the prospect of northerly winds blowing up. The island was just at the edge of the trades and the wind often backed from the southeast through north and right round the compass as depressions passed to the south. So though Katie would have stayed there forever we felt a sense of relief when we finally waved goodbye to the crowd of friends who had come to see us off on the quayside. We were given a typical sentimental Polynesian farewell and as we sailed away from Avatiu we both had long *eis* of pink frangipani blossoms around our necks and tears in our eyes.

The passage west to the distant island of Niue was a tough one. After one day of pleasant sailing we found the barometer dropping, the sky smearing over and the wind going round to the north. The only thing that pleased us was that we were not still sitting in Avatiu. On the second night the wind began to get really wild and the seas became increasingly high with a powerful vindictive sting. I clawed my way from bunk to cockpit to take in the mizzen and half an hour later I had to go out again to bring down the double-reefed main, and soon after that I had to smother the jib. This involved crouching on the bowsprit to drag the flogging cloth down the stay while the boat plunged into the seas, periodically burying me to the waist in frothing water. Except for my safety harness which was snapped onto the inner forestay I was naked and shivering from both cold and fear, dry mouthed and dripping wet. How passionately I loathed this awful life we were leading!

Dawn came without improving the scene any. As the wind was still rising I lowered the staysail and reefed it down to a tiny triangular patch. But during the day even that had to be taken down and we were then running under bare poles. *Nanook* rose beautifully up over the high seas and tossed the sweeping crests off her wet decks, but now and again she shuddered to the explosive impact of a breaker and cold salt water burst through chinks in the companionway weatherboards and spilled all over Katie's face and pillow. The wind vane kept us stern to the seas so there was nothing to do but huddle below on our bunks and listen to the horrible howling grey wet world outside. It was almost, as H.M. Tomlinson said, "enough to make a man feel that he ought to have a religion." Sleep by day or night was nearly impossible and though cooking was a tiring and difficult chore it seemed the only relief to the interminable hours.

We endured a second night and a second day of this treatment but there was no sign of any improvement and the radio station in Raro was still forecasting "gales and very rough seas. Outlook similar."

I now began to worry about two tiny reefs that lay ahead, Beveridge and Antiope, one north of our course and the other south of it, both nothing more than lines of coral at sea level hundreds of miles from anywhere else. In such a gale the reefs would be a mass of crashing white water, but even so they would not be visible in these conditions until within perhaps a quarter mile or less. This part of the ocean was subject to variable currents but in the absence of any sextant shots I had no way of judging them, if they existed at all. So once more I dragged from the foc's'le the enormous manilla warp kept there for the purpose and streamed this in a loop over the stern with one end secured on each of the two quarter bollards. I then added a long nylon warp with a small

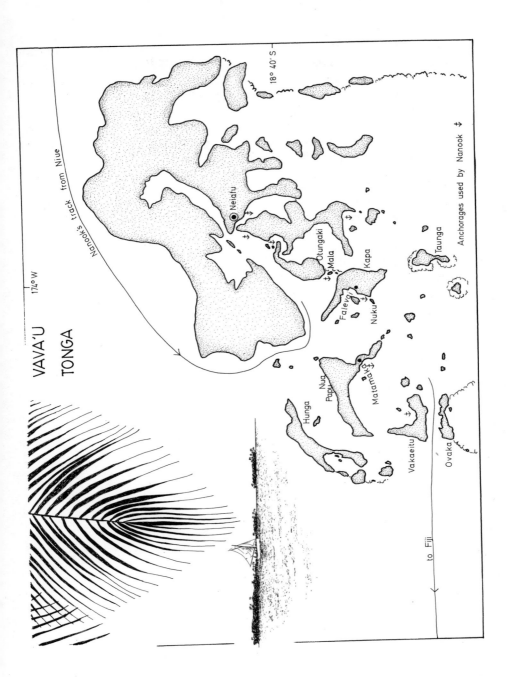

VAVA'U
TONGA

174° W

Nanook's track from Niue

18° 40' S

Neiafu

Otungaki
Mala
Kapa
Faleva
Nuku
Taunga

Anchorages used by Nanook ⚓

Hunga
Nua
Papu
Matamaka ⚓

Vakaeitu

Ovaka

to Fiji

Danforth anchor shackled to it and this also seemed to offer fair resistance so that between them the two lines held us down to two knots.

The following night I was able to get a sextant shot in the dark. The moon appeared through the clouds and formed a well marked trail of light on the sea up to the horizon. Mars happened to be nearby so I brought his little reddish speck down onto the surface of the moon trail and lo, we were exactly on course steering midway between the two reefs.

The wind on the third day was every bit as wild as ever, but I was at least able to snatch a couple of sextant shots of the sun, drenching the sextant in the process but confirming my position line from the night sight of Mars so I recovered the mass of rope from the sea and resumed running under bare poles.

Huddling below in our sordid dank closed-up cave we endured three more days of this miserable weather and heavy rain. It seemed utterly interminable. But on the sixth day out of Raro a cold front passed over us and a cool southerly blew away all our troubles. The hatches opened up and fresh air at last was allowed to dry out the interior. On the seventh day we sighted Niue's flat top, and secured *Nanook* at last to a mooring buoy in front of the village capital of Alofi.

IX

Islands Across the Dateline

Niue, an upraised atoll far from anywhere else, is a flat 300-foot-high slab of limestone, a bit of a Plain Jane as Pacific islands go, though the Kiwi hospitality there was equal to that of Rarotonga. Still, we stayed only one night as we were anxious to press on for Tonga while the nice weather lasted. "Look out for trouble in the Western Pacific," friends had warned us. "You can encounter heavy gales around Tonga and Fiji in all seasons."

The pilot charts didn't seem to be all that gloomy but then we had noticed on the part of *our* weather a nasty tendency to disregard pilot charts. We gazed astern as the horizon crept up the cliffs of Niue, and once we were so far on that turning back became pointless the trade wind failed us and the Sumlog needle settled back to zero.

After two days of sweaty exasperation, getting nearly nowhere on an oily swell we at last picked up our old friend the southeasterly. "We'll get a gale yet," Katie mumbled. "Tomorrow's the 13th." But if the Fates had especially reserved that date to give us an unwelcome treat, we cheated them. Pressed on by the gentle trade *Nanook* slipped over the International Dateline on the night of the 12th and the sun rose next morning on the 14th.

Tonga was not far ahead and we began tuning in to Nukualofa radio which switched periodically into English to give the national news. "The royal taro patch," one report went, "was harvested today on the island of Eua. Some of the taro will be displayed at the Agricultural Show next week; the rest will go to the palace to maintain the royal household. The royal taro will be replanted tomorrow. All the men and women of Eua are asked to appear tomorrow, the women to clear and the men to plant His Majesty's taro patch."

137

The island of Vava'u vindicated the navigator by appearing ahead more or less when and where expected. On its northern flanks, Vava'u presented a bold coast, high, steep-to, uninhabited and devoid of reasonable shelter. But to the south the shoreline dissolved into an intriguing network of bays, promontories, channels and islands. Once in the lee of the big island we found ourselves entering this attractive archipelago of deep sheltered water and tree-clad islands of all sizes. Katie, who had stitched the red and white Tongan flag together while we were becalmed at sea, now ran this up to the starboard spreader above the Q flag while I began beating in to the fresh trade that whistled down the long channel leading to Neiafu, the port and government centre of Vava'u.

Each tack brought us close in to a new sight. Villages appeared through the trees, channels opened up on each side, islands were passed close by, their limestone sides so steep and undercut by the sea that both access and anchorage were out of the question. Several miles from the open sea the main channel took a final bend to the south and opened into a large landlocked bay with Neiafu spread along one corner. Like many other South Pacific harbours this one was much too deep for anchoring except close in around the edge, but few other harbours can be in such an attractive setting or so totally tucked away from the sea.

Carefully picking out a pale patch clear of coral, I dropped the CQR close in to the town under the gaze of a large building calling itself the House of Nasaleti (Nazareth), a boarding establishment for school children, run of course by one of the churches which in Tonga goes without saying. "Hello *palangi*" (white man) the faces at the open windows called cheerfully. "Hello Tongans," I yelled back making a threatening gesture at them. The place exploded in shrieks of mirth.

A boat pulled alongside and a party of officials came aboard. They wore the *ta'ovala*, a woven mat strapped around the waist over their uniforms, rather an odd, cumbersome garment in such a hot climate for it is worn by both sexes on top of rather than instead of the usual Western garb. Encouraged by royalty and commonly worn around the streets of town, the *ta'ovala* is de rigueur for all formal occasions, and the more worn and tattered it is the more it is prized and respected.

After pratique was courteously granted us, we tossed the dinghy overboard and followed the officials ashore to the charming rag-taggle little town. That same sweet smell of copra drifted along the waterfront where a cheerful Polynesian gang bagged the dried coconut for export. Little sailing cutters disgorged cargoes of people after a hard beat up-channel from the outer islands. A few hopefuls gathered around us tugging our sleeves and pressing shells and basketware upon us but we had as yet no local currency and anyway first things first; at the end of any longish passage our first concern is usually to find a bakery and then, armed with fresh loaves and whatever else fresh may be offering, to retire aboard, put the coffee on and plot out a campaign. A couple of days in Neiafu would do, we decided, then we could go exploring amongst the islands. Deep water there was the rule but a perusal of the charted area seemed to indicate quite a few spots that would shelter us in reasonable depths.

Crunch! Our topsides took a nasty smack and we both peered scowling out the hatch. "Oh sorry," said a cheerful face. "You boat hit me canoe. Here some Tonga baskets. And shell. You want Tonga shell? I got lotta shell."

By this time a spry old man was established in the cockpit and spreading his wares out all over the deck. This was the first of many impromptu visits from people wanting to sell something or to trade, perhaps, a map cowrie for a pair of old pants or bananas for a tin of meat. It taxed our wits to know how to discourage them short of being obnoxious but after buying half a dozen map cowries, loads of textile cones, murexes and spider conches, enough drinking coconuts to quench a camel and bananas all through the rigging, one learned to say "No" with a little more firmness.

Business ashore was easily concluded for Neiafu is hardly the place where a yacht would reprovision unless with taro and watermelons. We took our passports as requested to the *polisi*, changed some dollars at the *bangiki*, got a 10-*seniti* stamp at the *positi ofisi* for a letter to *Nuu Sila* (New Zealand) and sailed down channel for a spot of exploring.

The Admiralty chart suggested good anchorage off the islands of Mala and Otungake, so, turning south of the main channel, I dropped the anchor in three fathoms onto white sand, in water so clear I could count the links.

"Seven miles," Katie called, glancing at the Sumlog. "That's my kind of daysail." We were in an attractive area with white beaches close around us and only a couple of houses ashore in the trees so that we stood a chance, we thought, of some seclusion, and went below for a quiet beer and sandwich before going ashore to prowl the empty beaches.

Crunch! A guy called Viliami (William) came aboard, helped himself to the end of the jib sheet to secure his outrigger canoe and announced cheerfully that he would sell us some shells and did we want any bananas or pineapples or did I happen to have a pair of old trousers I didn't want? I didn't. But Viliami was an amiable character and had a fine bag of shells which Katie immediately seized upon. We discussed terms for a few prize additions to her swelling collection and Viliami invited us to visit him at his house in the village ashore.

"That's a village?" I asked, pointing to the two houses by the beach.

"Oh yes," he said. "That's my village, name Telehau. Four hundred people live in Telehau." True enough, back in the trees were many more houses, rather poor affairs of palm fronds and corrugated iron mostly, but nicely laid out in well-kept gardens and shaded by breadfruit trees and coconut palms. It was recess time at school and Katie and I rapidly became a major attraction, fifty or so youngsters gathering around to stare, whisper *"Palangi"* or smile shyly.

In every village we were struck by the same phenomenon, children everywhere, hordes of them. What is to become of them all? Tonga's King George I last century enacted that every Tongan male reaching the age of 16 would be entitled to a country plot or *api,* measuring 8¼ acres. The system continues in theory but there are already far more applicants than *apis* and with a third of the population under 10 the situation gets worse every year. The government has started a much-belated birth control programme but the flood as yet shows no sign of subsiding. Never having been a colony, Tonga has had no easy outlet to a metropolitan country for her surplus population or much outside investment that might have diversified the economy away from the plot and the coconut trees.

In the afternoon when school was over, nine boys all in birthday bronze swam out 300 yards against the tide to *Nanook* towing behind them gifts of drinking coconuts. Katie put the boarding ladder out for them and after a conducted tour through the ship they sat politely in the cockpit for a sedate setting of cakes and orange juice.

As we were sailing around the northwestern end of Kapa Island next morning, we noticed two gaping black holes in the cliff, Swallow's Cave according to the chart. While Katie steered *Nanook* back and forth outside, I rowed the dinghy into the inky void. The black bottomless water sucked dismally at the dim limestone walls and the noise of the oars rattling in the rowlocks echoed eerily off the high roof somewhere far above. The walls glowed blue from the startling cobalt daylight shining up from the water at the entrance, giving the place a strange theatrical air. A water snake on a nearby ledge slithered suddenly into the water, and I was just as suddenly possessed of a powerful irrational urge to get the hell out of the place.

We spent two weeks in the Vava'u area visiting most of the possible anchorages. Generally a village was to be found ashore near these sheltered localities so that we were badly pestered at times by incessant streams of people wanting to sell garden produce and basketware or, worse, just wanting to come aboard out of a curiosity that always took several hours to satisfy.

"I'm never going to visit a zoo again," Katie, near to tears, said one day as we motored off to an uninhabited island for a day's respite.

Of all the lovely corners of the group, our favourite was off the southwestern tip of Kapa Island. A long white beach near the village of Falevai ended in a sandy point which continued underwater in a shallow bank to the small island of Nuku. One lone house stood on the point, a lovely traditional home of woven walls, palm frond roof and a floor of mats with tapa cloth lining the walls inside. Hala'apiapi and his wife Mele kept the house and surrounding grounds in a state of immaculate tidiness. Utensils and tools around the outdoor cooking area were kept in their proper places on racks. The outdoor stoves were cleaned after every meal, coconuts and taro stored in neat piles, paths were swept and the sand raked every morning. Everything had its place and stayed there, even the chickens.

Nanook remained anchored off this beach for several days. We were far enough from Falevai not to be unduly bothered by the usual canoe loads of curious visitors. Children swam out periodically to visit or dive off the bowsprit but we never minded their impish frolics and could easily send them packing if we did. When we wanted complete solitude we simply reanchored three cables away off the tiny island of Nuku, a lovely place replete with white beaches and shady glades. Nuku was a favourite picnic spot for the king whenever he made a tour of the Vava'u group.

Hala'apiapi and Mele often came out for a brief visit or asked us to their home to talk about their country and to teach us to speak Tongan. One morning during a visit aboard *Nanook* Mele presented Katie with a shell necklace. *"Meaofa,"* she said. "It's a present." Later the same day Katie went ashore and gave Mele a wooden bowl. *"Meaofa,"* she said. Next day in return for a shell bracelet and a fresh fish we gave them a tin of bully beef and some onions. Thus began a vicious circle of gift-giving that became more and more embarrassing until one day I carelessly expressed great admiration for the huge hand-painted tapa cloth that covered one wall of their house. To my dismay, it was immediately removed, rolled up and presented to us.

King Taufa-ahau at the time was visiting Neiafu during a tour of the northern parts of his realm. He was going to open the Agricultural Show at Neiafu and presumably to put on display there the products of his taro patch. We decided to return to town to see what was going on. The trade wind ripped down the channel as we approached, heeling us far over in the gusts, while up on the heights to the north of us the yellow royal standard fluttered proudly from a fine modern house overlooking the harbour. The king was in residence.

The eldest son of the late and much-loved Queen Salote, King Taufa-ahau Tupou IV had reigned since his coronation in 1964. Like all of the royal line he was huge. Queen Salote was 6 feet 2 inches in height, and the present king, just as tall as his mother, was a mighty 385-pounder. "Too much *kai*," Hala'apiapi had remarked, more with respect and approval than otherwise. In fact all Tongans are solid. The tall ones never develop as the string bean type to which I belong, but grow in proportion in a solid mass, out as well as up. It is said that the royal and noble families of Tonga are the largest people in the world, the men being an average six-feet-one-inch and weighing 320 pounds.

We were pleased to find a couple of cruising friends in the anchorage when we returned. The young Dutch singlehander Ivo van Laake had arrived from the Cooks in the little 19-foot plywood sloop *Vlaag* that he had sailed from San Francisco, and we met Klaus Alvermann again, another singlehander who had built his lovely little gaff sloop *Plumbelly of Bequia* himself, without power tools or plans, under a tree in the West Indies.

Time for us was running short. We were bound next for Fiji so we gave Klaus our surplus Tongan charts and went ashore to request clearance. But I had forgotten; it was a Saturday. All offices were shut and we would have to wait until Monday morning.

Sundays are a problem in Tonga. The people are devoutly religious and in order to hold the Sabbath sacred a Sunday Observance Act was passed long ago forbidding anything in the nature of work, play or even such idle relaxation as taking a swim. Stragglers were actually herded off the beaches on Sundays just in case they might have been tempted to take a dip. One item that came over the national news one day set us chuckling. "Two men who appeared in the Nukualofa court on a charge of stealing and eating a goat were yesterday dismissed and the charges against them dropped because of irregularity of procedure, the complaint having been laid and police investigations carried out on a Sunday."

All this could be a problem for Seventh Day Adventists, I thought. Many Tongans belong to that church and I asked one of them whether he felt victimized by having to endure, in effect, two such Sundays a week. "Oh," he said, "we don't go to church on Saturday. We go on Sunday like all the rest." I asked him how that could be. "Well, you see," he said, "the International Date Line was moved away east to give Tonga the same day as Fiji and New Zealand, ahead of Greenwich. But we believe that to be a man-made error. Tonga is actually in the Western Hemisphere and therefore behind Greenwich, so Sunday is really Saturday to us."

But however oppressive the Sabbath may appear to outsiders, the Tongans themselves seemed to thrive on it. The king of course led the way to the Sunday morning service in the Wesleyan church accompanied by enthusiastic throngs, while the opposition in the House of Nasaleti rang with joyful noises through the day and evening, serenading us at anchor with the virile vibrant harmony that seems to come so naturally to all Polynesians.

After getting our clearance we sailed around to Falevai again for a final visit with our friends Hala'apiapi and Mele. Towards evening as we lay at anchor offshore they paddled out in their little dugout calling loudly to us "Tonga *kai*." They passed up several mysterious packages wrapped in banana leaves which upon opening we found to contain various Tongan dishes, yams with coconut sauce, fish steamed in leaves, and a whole chicken dipped in coconut milk, wrapped in taro leaves and cooked in a ground oven. They were unbelievably good.

Ashore that evening in his home I asked Hala'apiapi if there was

Katie, in possession of a chambered nautilus shell, comes to an amicable agreement with the ladies of Niravuni, Fiji.

anything we could get for him when we arrived in *Nuu Sila.* "Well, yes," he said "it's my eyes. I can't see anything close. But I preach in church and I need glasses to help me read my prayer book. Maybe you could send me a pair of glasses." That was a tough one for of course I had no way of knowing what glasses would suit him. But later in New Zealand I gathered together from friends a total of 17 pairs of old used reading glasses of various strengths and mailed them away to Tonga.

We left there for the passage to Fiji the morning after our farewell feast. As the anchor came up the kindly old couple waved goodbye to us and the last we saw was the two of them walking together down the beach to a 7 a.m. midweek church service. Hala'apiapi was barefoot as always but he wore a white shirt and black tie and a formal black suit with satin lapels. A white frangipani was pinned to the left lapel and under his right arm he carried his prayer book. I hope since then he has been able to read it.

Gentle winds carried us westward past the green volcanic cone of Late Island, uninhabited except by wild dogs which according to the Tongans will attack human visitors. By nightfall we were again alone on an empty sea with only the stars and the equally countless sparks of luminous light in the water for company.

For two more days, Katie alternated between cockpit, galley and bunk consuming cheap paperbacks from Ivo's shelves and endless slices of Neiafu bread while I amused myself with the development of black and white films.

On the third day we sighted the island of Vatoa and the next day passed close by the southern islands of the Lau Group. We were in Fijian waters and bound for steamy Suva, the port of entry on the main island of Viti Levu. The Suva radio gave us plenty to worry about at this time as they sent out repeated small craft warnings of moderate gales. We needed no reminder that the trade was freshening rapidly to Force 6 nor that we were surrounded by coral and running towards the long reefs of the big islands downwind. It got up to Force 7-8 in the night and I held on anxiously in the cockpit through Katie's early morning watch, staring alternately at the sky and our one remaining sail, the little staysail on the foredeck, as water crashed loudly all around us and clouds swept quickly across the full moon. However the night was clear and with the wind easing towards dawn I found various lights appearing where they were supposed to appear and finally a long white line ahead under the grey shrouded mass of Fiji where the heavy Pacific swell rises up and hurls itself forever on the long barrier reef of Viti Levu.

With the main up, and the yellow quarantine flag, we made a quick gybe to the starboard tack and sailed through the passage into Suva harbour, enjoying again the never-forgotten feeling of satisfaction, subsiding tension and rising curiosity that comes after every long passage to a new land. It was a drizzly Sunday morning and though the Health officials boarded us without any fuss and gave us pratique, Customs would not clear us without overtime charges so we anchored near the yacht club expecting to spend the day cooling our heels.

However to our delight we found our old Aussie companions of West Indian days, John and Julie Greenhill of the little sloop *Moonbird*. They were full of questions and enthused about their voyage to date and about the prospect of returning to their home in Tasmania. They also enthused about the coldness and cheapness of the beer at the yacht club and about the mountain of mail awaiting us there so we eventually threw our dinghy overboard and rowed discreetly ashore to the clubhouse. The beer and mail were there alright, and so were friends from New Zealand. They were on vacation in Fiji and had been eagerly watching the harbour for our arrival for the last two weeks. They had to leave for home that night and were all agog to hear our news and see our boat. So having bent the law a little by going ashore without permission, we then had to bend it a bit further by ferrying them aboard for a visit and drink, and accompanying them ashore again and out of town in the evening to the home of an

Indian friend Ram Naidu for an exotic and sumptuous Indian meal cooked by Ram's wife, a New Zealander who was an expert at the art of Indian cuisine. Landfalls are marvelous.

For a week we idled around Suva, enjoying the town and its odd mixture of curry and copra, of Asia and the South Seas and the incredibly disparate races that manage to co-exist there, the big langorous musical kava-drinking Fijians who own all the land, and the small astute fecund family-centred Indians who own all the businesses, a very odd blend of people if you can call a mixture of oil and water a blend.

Other cruising yachts joined us in the anchorage and as always it was good to go aboard *Iorana* and compare passages and islands with Merle and Croix. They had gone north of *Nanook's* track after leaving Bora Bora, stopping at Suvarov, where they met the atoll's resident hermit Tom Neale, and American Samoa where they contrived to lose themselves in the jungle for two days and a night. "Just a simple navigational error," Croix explained, dismissing the subject breezily.

"Maybe a local magnetic anomaly," Katie suggested. "One with grass skirts and a big smile." But Merle averred that it wasn't so.

Santana showed up from Tonga. *Audacious*, *Tortuga* and *Vlaag* all arrived in and it was especially good to meet Ivo again, the golden haired

An anchorage in Fiji's Great Astrolabe Reef.

hippie of the engineless little *Vlaag*, who made love in the islands and poetry at sea, who refused to sanction any paperbacks of war or violence on his boat and who now offended some of the stalwarts of the yacht club by desporting naked in the anchorage around the little plywood sloop that he called home.

Cruising sailors don't generally set forth over far distant horizons in search of capital cities and commercial ports of entry and yet, take a look if you will, that is where most of them happen to be found, idling away the weeks. We wanted to be in New Zealand by October and we knew that we would have to leave Viti Levu and go island hopping if we were to see anything of traditional Fiji as it once was before airlines, hoteliers and travel agents co-opted the place. So early one sunny morning we anchored off the copra wharf to get a bit of paper called a Beetle Clearance. A certain insect particularly fond of coconuts infests some of the Fijian islands though not others, so the authorities naturally try to contain the pest by preventing it from hitch-hiking around the whole archipelago on boats. We accordingly collected our bit of paper issued in a perfunctory fashion by a gent who insisted on coming aboard but who showed no interest whatever in *Nanook's* beetle population. We then turned south out of the pass for the little islands away to the south inside the Great Astrolabe Reef.

The wind was moderate but well forward of the beam so that we pounded and pounded along all day at an unaccustomed angle, slamming repeatedly into the trade wind swell and sending the salt spray flying back over the boat and ourselves. Everything above decks was soon coated with salt, but this was washed off in the downpour of a wild afternoon squall as we sailed along in the lee of the isolated North Astrolabe Reef. Soon after, we picked up the long line ahead of us that marked the Great Astrolabe Reef, most of it at that point well submerged and visible only as a pale greenish line in the water. We passed inside this line through the dark gap of Usborne Pass and into an archipelago of peaceful islands clothed in forest and palms, garlanded with white coral beaches and inhabited if at all only by the people who truly belonged there, the soft-spoken Fijians.

We anchored in the lee of Ndravuni and lay there for three days. The village people came to talk to us under the palm trees and sold to Katie their chambered nautilus shells which they used as ladles when cooking. We revarnished our cockpit and guardrails in the early mornings before the heat of the day, and in the late afternoons we soaked the heat out of our systems as we lay like flotsam near the beach, knee deep in the little swell that came round the point, marvelling all the while at the crystal clarity of the water and the gentleness and gentility of the village people.

When the urge to explore was again upon us we sailed off for a day amongst the uninhabited islands nearby. But a sudden increase in the

Nanook lay for several days in the crystal waters off the island of Ndravuni.

wind sent us scurrying back to the better shelter of Ndravuni and there we lay for another five days while a near gale tore at the tops of the palms, tossing the fronds all over to one side as it would a woman's hair, and then whipped across the water and through our rigging so that it was difficult at times to get any sleep. But eventually the howling stopped, the palms straightened and the grey cloud and the whitecaps disappeared. The ocean recovered its tranquil sunny mood and it was soon hard to believe that it had ever had any other. The western Pacific is like that.

Eventually we coasted south around the points and inlets of the island of Ono, stopping wherever a thatched village or a deserted beach beckoned. At one place an old man called Tom came paddling out from the solitary little *bure* or traditional thatched house ashore and spoke with us in mission English to invite us to his home for "dinner." So we soon found ourselves under the dark cool thatch of his house sitting cross-legged on a clean woven mat and eating cooked bananas and coconut sauce with our fingers from a half coconut shell. To wash all this down Tom's wife produced some green drinking coconuts with the tops lopped off and when these were drained, Tom, who was eager for tales of high adventure in far away places, beamed hopefully at us and said "Now, tell me a story."

When we finally got away from Tom's pretty little cove, we took him and his wife with us and anchored at a village on Ono's south coast, a place where no yacht would normally choose to stop as it is quite exposed to the prevailing trade wind. But a low pressure trough to the south was giving us light northwesterlies and we took a chance in staying overnight. We had a wide-eyed reception from a large crowd that gathered on the beach as the four of us rowed in.

A handsome powerful-looking young man stepped forward out of the throng to introduce himself and to invite us to his house. Simione our host, who turned out to be old Tom's son, led us to his large *bure* ahead of the curious crowd and while we sat talking to the many people who gathered inside, Simione sent some young men into the bush for the roots of a certain tree and after these had been pounded into a pulp Simione produced a large ceremonial wooden bowl and began to prepare the traditional kava or *yanggona* in our honour. He washed and kneaded the root pulp in water for some time and when all was ready he dried his hands and ladled the earthy soporific tongue-numbing juice into coconut shells, passing them first to me as tradition demanded. I clapped once as also required by custom, drained the yellow-grey liquid at one long draught and clapped again. The cup was refilled and passed to Katie and the other adults. This kava-drinking went on for some two hours with long pauses between each round while we listened, fascinated, to their stories of olden Fiji, and they listened incredulously to our stories of the Canadian Arctic where people lived in houses of snow and the sea turned into solid white ice and the sun disappeared for months on end. During all this I began to see that Katie's somewhat tender digestive tract was in a state of crisis at the influx of all this muddy water so we excused ourselves graciously and retired aboard in the dark to sleep.

In fact I never slept a wink. The sky was heavily overcast and the night was black as pitch. Coral and solid land lay close about us but we were wide open to both east and west and I had a nasty suspicion that the northerly wind might back around through the west exposing us totally to the open seas north of Kandavu. But nothing happened. The welcome dawn returned over flat seas and although the leaden skies refused to lift we did go ashore again, wandering the long empty beaches under the palms in search of shells. Two beautiful dark girls, whom I recognized as having sat together through the kava ceremony in Simione's house, followed a cable behind us, almost, I thought for our benefit, singing the traditional "Isa Lei" and bursting the stillness of the solemn, calm, clammy day with a sensual uninhibited two-part harmony that the Sirens themselves could not have sung with more devastating effect. Here indeed was Fiji!

We felt worried about the gathering gloom in the afternoon and decided to retreat south to the all-round shelter of Kavala, a hole on the north coast of Kandavu, but our timing was bad and halfway across while motoring in the calm we were engulfed in a really tremendous thunderstorm that blotted out all the land around us in a dreadful cloudburst. Lightning repeatedly spat into the water fifty yards or so on either side followed instantly by the deafening and appalling noises of the rending atmosphere. We never experienced any thunderstorm as dramatic and severe as that one before or since and we were about as scared as we were wet. The dinghy sank lower and lower into the water as the rain cascaded into it. We could see nothing beyond the endless curtains of rain but by doggedly holding our course over the white sea surface we finally picked up the land at the entrance to Kavala and thankfully dropped the kedge on a warp in ten fathoms close by the black muddy shore of a mangrove swamp. Everything above and below was streaming wet and before escaping to a glass of rum below, I baled 22 buckets of fresh water out of the dinghy.

For three more days we drifted about in sunshine around the exquisite little islands within the reef. But time was running out. Spring was already in New Zealand and the cyclones would soon be coming to the islands. So we returned over the smooth seas to Suva (taking Simione with us for he wanted to visit the city), and after another week of abandoning ourselves to the pleasures of the anchorage we settled down to complete the formalities of clearing and to organise ourselves for the thousand mile voyage out of tropical waters and south to New Zealand.

We felt rather nervous at the prospect of this passage for the seas off the New Zealand coast can serve up some wicked weather and we felt that our sails and rigging were old and not up to too much any more. With this in mind as well as having to leave many friends behind both ashore and afloat in Suva, plus a persistent headache and a viral infection that I mistook at first for a hangover, I felt very depressed and reluctant to leave as we sailed out the pass in the reef and set our course for the last bit of tropic land, the western end of Kandavu Island.

Katie felt no better. She was violently sick in the choppy seas that smacked onto the beam and her little cat Nutmeg was gone. The authorities in New Zealand were very strict about not allowing any live animals or fresh foods into the country, so to avoid the obvious problem ahead of us, we reluctantly passed Nutmeg over to a friend, Richard Stephens on the New Zealand trimaran *Wild Lone*. He had planned to spend the cyclone season holed up in the New Hebrides and our plan was to rendezvous there with him the next year to collect the cat. As we learned later, however, he changed his mind, turned south himself for New Zealand and lost Nutmeg overboard, very much to Katie's distress.

My "hangover" didn't improve any. We passed Kandavu's Cape Washington in the moonlight with me being wretchedly sick into the bucket in the cockpit and Katie lying prostrate in her bunk below and calling weakly for her turn at the bucket. The seas were choppy and the trade wind was coming in very fresh and ahead of the beam. Sometimes, quite often in fact, ocean cruising in a small boat is absolute hell. It isn't merely, as some yachtsmen put it, "the most expensive way to travel third class." It really can be a hellish morale-draining torment. I wondered, sitting weakly in the cockpit, what in the world had taken possession of our sanity to drive us knowingly to this miserable existence. As Dr. Johnson said, "A ship is worse than a gaol. There is, in gaol, better air, better company, better conveniency of every kind; and a ship has the additional disadvantage of being in danger."

My unabated hangover-headache joined forces next day with, according to the log, "a toothache-earache-sore throat-sore chest." I had caught some infection or other and as my temperature went up I began worrying about a past susceptibility to pneumonia. We had Aureomycin tablets on board obtained in Canada. They were ridiculously outdated but better than nothing, or so I thought until I began taking them. From then on I really did become hideously sick. What should we do? Go back to Suva? We were slipping well west of the course. Suva now lay well on the wind and I didn't feel up to the hard slog back. Lautoka? I had no charts of the place. Turn downwind for Vila in the New Hebrides? From there the passage to New Zealand could be difficult or so I imagined. Noumea? A reef-strewn place and we had no chart of it. Brisbane? Might as well stay on course for New Zealand and be done with it. Which we did.

I decided though, after 48 hours on the old Aureomycin that I would rather switch than fight and I began a course of penicillin tablets. All this time I was unable to do any deck work for more than a shaky sweaty ten minutes and navigation consisted merely of occasional glances at compass, horizon and log before collapsing again on the bunk. Katie struggled to her feet to do the cooking when she could, but we were both too sick to eat anyway.

All this time though, the wind held steady and *Nanook* romped happily south. The penicillin (or at least the lack of the other drug) slowly took effect and I began to regain my strength and gradually to attend to the many little jobs that had been neglected, and by the time I was back to normal with my feet in my seaboots we had lost the trade and began working through a succession of cold fronts under the high overcast of the horse latitudes. Cold rainy southerly winds brought blankets out of lockers for the first time in years. We began driving close-hauled into the wind and I managed my usual trick in these conditions of neglecting to bring the genoa down until a heavy wave top had gone into the foot and torn an enormous rent in the rotten old thing.

For several days we made poor progress in changeable weather while a variety of things on board went wrong. The toilet started playing up so we were forced for a time to resort to the time-honoured procedure of "bucket-and-chuck-it." Seams in the mizzen lost their stitching. Jib sheet blocks tore loose out of the track. The seacock for the galley sink began leaking and allowing the sink to flood into the cupboards on the port tack, and on the starboard tack salt water invaded the full length of the cable to the Sumlog dial and ruined it so that I had to guess mileages for the rest of the passage between sights.

Gradually the water lost its tropic blueness. Billions of tiny jellyfish and Portuguese men o'war filled the sea for many miles on end. Each day albatrosses circled curiously around us or flopped lazily into the water astern and tried to keep up with us by paddling along behind. Dainty little petrels flitted endlessly nearby and black and white porpoises came to frolic at the bows.

Meanwhile, southwesterly gales were lashing most of New Zealand, Force 11 in the south, and *Nanook* rode silently over an awesome swell coming up out of the Tasman Sea, catching the light wind on the crests and losing it in the great yawning troughs.

On October 17th, fifteen days out from Suva we expected to close the New Zealand coast somewhere north of the Bay of Islands. But dawn found us enveloped in a dank fog which was the last thing I had expected to encounter. I reckoned that we were still well offshore and expected the fog to lift in the morning sunshine so being impatient to make harbour that day I put about intending to close the coast in an area free of offshore reefs. On the little direction-finding radio I picked up an aeronautical beacon from the town of Kaitaia and was using this for a bearing on the assumption that the beacon was located close to the town. In fact it wasn't and towards noon I noticed a patch of broken water appearing about 200 yards directly ahead of the bows. I leaped to the echo sounder. Eight fathoms. I yelled to Katie to take the tiller, swung the diesel into life and with chart in hand ran back to the bows to study the situation. The white water ahead was swirling over a nest of rocks that lay right on the surface. We turned back briefly on a reciprocal course while I studied the chart. Only in one place could I find such a reef, two of them in fact, isolated and well clear of the coast and that was in Doubtless Bay well north of our supposed position. The echo sounder tended to agree with all this. Not being sure which of the two sets of reefs we had come upon I altered course at right angles to the line joining them to close the coast, and before long we could make out white water, and hear it too, at the bottom of dark bluffs that loomed grey and gloomy out of the fog.

A local fisherman under power suddenly emerged to port. I still felt worried and uncertain so I swallowed my pride, I, Captain Cook, who had brought this little ship all the way out from England under my own command, and hailed him with the age-old cry of the incompetent navigator, "Where am I?"

But after all as one of my nautical texts pointed out "the prudent navigator will never miss an opportunity to determine or confirm his

Nanook under sail in New Zealand's Bay of Islands.

position," and to make me feel better the fisherman called back that, yes, we were in Doubtless Bay and that he himself had been lost for a time.

The little harbour of Port Mangonui lay at one corner of Doubtless Bay. We'd never intended to go there but luckily we'd received a chart of it from Ivo in Suva so I altered course to follow the coast around to the harbour entrance. Cold spring rain poured down through the dismal fog and inside our worn oilskins but we could not have felt happier. Within the hour *Nanook* had nosed into the pretty little port and the anchor was at rest in the sand. The fog slowly eased up the sides of the surrounding hills. Ferns and flax, sheep, green fields, red iron roofs, cold dark green water. No doubt about it. We were in New Zealand at last and my youthful dream of sailing out from England to the Antipodes was fulfilled.

Mangonui was no port of entry, and we rowed ashore in the afternoon to ask the local constable not to take our Q flag seriously as we were just waiting for the fog to clear before proceeding to the Bay of Islands. But instead we were met by George Thomas the secretary of the local cruising club who invited us to his home. The girl on the telephone exchange said the policeman had gone away for the day to play golf, and when she could not raise the postmaster she thought perhaps he had gone over to Kaitaia to visit his sister. That took care of all the officials in town so we settled down at George's to enjoy a few hours of convivial Kiwi company before returning aboard.

We beat out of Doubtless Bay next morning and proceeded by way of other anchorages to the town of Russell in the Bay of Islands where we made our peace with the New Zealand authorities. My mother who had waited many years for my return to New Zealand, and my sister Isobel, arrived in Russell for a joyous reunion with us and a week of sailing, a foretaste for Katie of the innumerable in-laws she had yet to meet.

We eventually sailed on to the hospitable little city of Whangarei. The first person we spoke to as we tied up in the town basin asked us home for baths and a party. The second one had seen us coming in and had come over to offer us the use of his car for a couple of days. "You might want to go down to Auckland or see something of the country," he suggested.

We remained in Whangarei a month while I attended to some of *Nanook's* accumulated ills. Katie found herself a job ashore working with a bunch of Maori girls in a hospital laundry, "but only," said the Administrator, "on the condition that you get yourself some footwear," for she was by then addicted to bare feet. Late in November I chained *Nanook* snugly between poles in the town basin and we left her to her own resources for the summer season.

X

Pandemonium

It was May of the following year before we were again on our way, homeward bound to the Atlantic. We had spent seven months in New Zealand, half of that time working the dreary routine of kitchen hands in a sheep slaughtering plant in the South Island (the only paid employment I undertook in five years) and the rest of our time either visiting unnumbered friends and relatives in the South Island or working on *Nanook* in the town basin of Whangarei.

She was given a new mainsail and mizzen, new sailcovers and fresh paint above and below the waterline. The diesel was overhauled and the leaky old copper exhaust replaced by a steel pipe. The old Sumlog too was replaced and so was the echo sounder. Chains and anchors were sent to Auckland for regalvanizing, all standing rigging checked or replaced, and new lifelines rigged. The cockpit got a new awning and new seat cushions. The liferaft was serviced at considerable expense by Air New Zealand, the dinghy was refastened, the lockers crammed with local tinned foods, the bilges bulged with tins of paint and varnish and liberal supplies of duty-free rum and the foc's'le was packed with items for trade in the islands, matches, clothes and candy; tobacco, torches, toys and tins of bully beef. We were bound for Melanesia, the black island groups of the western Pacific.

Most yachtsmen heading west from the South Pacific try to cover the distance to South Africa in one sailing season. We decided to take two, and to cruise through some of the more primitive island groups that are not so often seen. We had never budgeted on the extra year but we decided that it was well worth the belt tightening that was plainly necessary.

We were sad to be leaving so many kindly people behind. Long distance cruising, as one of our friends put it, is a constant succession of reluctant goodbyes. I felt especially melancholy at the prospect of saying goodbye again to my mother who had quietly hoped that we would settle in New Zealand. She was 72 but she was more active than most are at 40 and she sailed with us up the coast from Whangarei to the Bay of Islands, standing her trick at the tiller, never for a moment seasick and quite unperturbed when willawaws off Bream Head knocked us flat.

We were joined in Russell by my brother George, who first inspired me to sail but who had himself never been on a yacht, and by Isobel and her children. Together we explored many of the islands and inlets in the large beautiful bay. George, the hunter, kept us supplied with flounders, lobsters, oysters, clams and mussels, and Isobel with her endless good cheer and nonsense. But at last we had to go, and they did also, and after a tearful goodbye on a rainy day May 17th, we put to sea with a thousand miles to go to the first islands of the New Hebrides. I felt sad as I watched the Cape Brett light wink at us for the last time and sink into the sea astern.

The wind, an offshore southwesterly, was all we needed and then some, and I shortened sail progressively until we were flying along under headsail alone. The wind and sea increased through the night and life became a torment. The log entries for the next two days read "18th. Dirty, filthy stinking conditions. A terrible night of constant sail changes and dirty squally weather. During the day a prolonged squall of quite appalling force hit us like a steam engine and sent us flying with the Sumlog needle unable to get up past 10 and me out on the sprit fighting to get the jib down. The seas around me fairly smoked under the onslaught. I just cannot guess the strength of that incredible wind but it was much stronger than anything we have ever experienced before. The worst was soon over but the whole day was similar. Very strong winds, Force 8, 9 or 10 all day.

"19th. Unpleasant night running in big seas. However the wind has backed with the passing of yesterday's cold front and is getting progressively easier all the time. Took my first sight in a rough-and-tumble sea. Katie sick for the third day. Sea very lumpy. Katie's bunk has been inundated three times and is no longer habitable. The sky though is now clear."

By the fourth day Katie was able to sit outside in sunshine and hold food down for the first time since leaving Russell. Another front came along two days later but the weather remained fairly moderate. We caught the trade wind soon after and sighted Aneityum, the southernmost of the New Hebrides chain on the 28th May, eleven days out. The little island's volcanic outline and jungled textures were almost a physical relief to eyes that were sick of staring at a watery horizon. In the late afternoon we gybed around the southern fringes of Aneityum's coral reef and soon after dropped the anchor into seven fathoms close in to the thatched village on Coconut Ridge Point. Dark figures watched us from the stillness of the shadows under the palms. The smoke of evening cooking curled up through the trees and the only sound was the occasional flapping of a big tuna that had taken our line near the reef and now lay exhausted on the cockpit grating. We felt fabulous.

It begins near the equator, this great chain of Melanesia from little groups far beyond Manus down southeastwards through the Bismarck Sea to the huge lands of New Britain, New Ireland and Bougainville, islands inherited by Australia from Germany in 1918. Then come the Solomons, a double line of long mountain-ridged islands clothed in jungle and administered as a protectorate by the British. They are long narrow lands pointing like fingers into the trade wind, with grey-bottomed cumulus glued to their peaks and surrounded at their base by long reefs and intricate inviting waterways that demand investigation. The double chain converges at San Cristobal and breaks away to reappear again in the disparate scattered Santa Cruz group to the east. Southeast again, and only 80 miles from the last of the Santa Cruz islands, the first of the New Hebrides appear, little islands at first and then massive ones, aligned to the east of south like the Solomons and again the double chain converging this time at Epi. From there the impression of an archipelago is lost and each succeeding island rises isolated and out of sight of its neighbours. Little Aneityum is the last link (or the first) of this mighty chain and beyond that there is nothing but empty ocean.

Geologically the New Hebrides are relative newcomers to the Pacific surface. They have exploded up through the sea in volcanic upheavals that have still not stopped, and for the most part have still not had time to develop the surrounding coral reefs that protect so many other Pacific island groups so that, as in the Marquesas, harbours are simply accidental bends in the coastlines rather than waters that have become sheltered so efficiently by the coral polyp. An exception, however, is Aneityum. Apart from the wide entrance through the reef to the west, we enjoyed all-round shelter as well as the typically Pacific prospect of reef, *motu,* lagoon, beach and mountain.

Two hundred Melanesian people lived in the island's one village as well as one white man, an old Australian character who busied himself, and his "boys" with dragging kauri logs out of the bush and slicing them into lumber on a little sawmill. He was stoutish, a good cook and genial host, capable jack-of-all-trades and *raconteur,* and he went by the delightful name of Arty Kraft. When we first came in, Arty was off logging on one of the distant ridges, but he was no sooner back two days later than we were beckoned to his weathered old wooden house for a cold beer out of the kerosene fridge and the cook sent out poste haste with a hatchet to bring in one of Arty's goats and roast it in the company of sweet potatoes, manioc and pumpkin. It was a memorable feast.

Arty regaled us with tales of old times as a trader and of recent times

Tuna taken off the reefs of Aneityum, New Hebrides.

contending with the horror of cyclones. The islands had just endured a particularly bad cyclone season and though not as badly hit as some islands, Aneityum had not been spared the awful storms that unleash their fury in the summer months. Most mariners reckon the cyclone threat to be over by mid-April. We had arrived at the end of May and felt confident that there was no longer any reason to expect trouble from that quarter. So we were aghast next morning to tune in to Vila Radio and to learn that a cyclone code-named Ida was driving a path of destruction down through the Solomons and heading our way. Ida had already ripped straight down the full length of the long island of Santa Isabel, giving it a haircut that destroyed many millions of dollars in standing timber (to the chagrin of Japanese interests) and was lashing other islands along the way, destroying crops and bringing down many villages in its path. Local shipping was either holed up in total shelter, in distress or wrecked.

Panic! What should we do? I reckoned that we might have three days' grace with any luck. We could put to sea but the weather had already turned grey and dirty with a strong northeasterly wind. If Ida continued coming our way we could expect the wind to increase greatly in strength before changing much in direction. That gave us the worry of the long lee shores of New Caledonia (or its barrier reef which was worse) to the southwest. We could stay put in the anchorage but we were widely exposed to the west and the wind would come in from there once Ida went south of us. Eventually after much dithering I decided to wait and see, which in a way seemed to be just a decision not to make a decision.

The sky was filled with grey threatening nimbus and the humid sticky air that blew over us had the feel of the equator in it. Vila Radio began coming on at special normally unscheduled times to bring up-to-the-minute reports from further south. Warnings to shipping were put out regularly and Ida showed no sign of flagging or changing her direction. Next day she had moved south of San Cristobal, then the following day to a position north of New Caledonia. She seemed to have altered course a little more directly to the south away from east. By this time it was really blowing like stink at Aneityum from northeast and later from north, the wind switch indicating that the monster was coming abreast of us to the west.

I decided to move our few valuables ashore to Arty's house. The one local outboard-driven boat was used for the purpose as I could not row against the wind. I had to signal for it with a white hand-held flare and I burnt my right hand in the process. They are dangerous things and hard to hold in a high wind. The radio and sextant were packed off and our cameras and films, even the dinghy itself for that was just extra windage, and we stowed all sails below along with the wind vane and other movable things that could offer wind resistance. The liferaft was moved into the cockpit.

I laid out 35 fathoms of chain with the CQR bower anchor, 30 fathoms of nylon with the Danforth, the CQR kedge on 5 fathoms of chain, 10 fathoms of nylon and 20 fathoms of hemp and an 85 pound anchor borrowed from Arty on our new 30 fathom nylon line. Arty also offered me a couple of big old engine blocks to use as anchors but I had no way of getting them out to the middle of the lagoon where *Nanook* lay.

Slowly the wind backed around to the wrong side of the mountain peaks and came in from the northwest over the low land to the north of the pass. A huge swell began rolling in through the entrance ad the colossal seas that reared up and smashed over the reefs were adding their ominous roar to the screech of the wind.

Vila Radio followed Ida's progress like a reporter on a royal tour. She had just wrecked two local trading vessels on Tanna, the next island north. Then the good news, Ida had decided at last to alter course and go southwestwards as the textbooks said she would. The centre would pass well west of us, possibly a hundred miles away. As the long hours dragged on the wind slowly went west, blowing at last directly in from the open sea. *Nanook* reared up and yanked hard on her lines as each wave caught her bows and from the shore only her masts were visible as she dropped into the troughs. But between them somehow the anchors held and the

Mt. Yasur, on the Tanna in the New Hebrides, is probably the world's most accessible live volcano. Sailing by, *Nanook* was covered in dark ash.

wind which had at first come in from the west at fifty knots dropped perceptibly through the hours of night into a fresh wind at dawn and then to a breeze. By noon of the next day the heavy overcast was broken and apart from the continued roar of protest on the coral reef, all the world was quiet. Ida was off to Australia.

We for our part were off to Tanna, leaving our anchorage at 0330 well before dawn after a day of relaxing ashore. It took us until evening to get there motoring all of the 57 miles for the trade wind was still on holiday.

Tanna is a fertile island with a large population. A slot on the eastern coast formed by an old drowned crater was visited in 1774 by Cook who named it Port Resolution after his ship. It was there that we came to anchor. Our surroundings were wild, green and fertile. A geyser bubbled away making loud steamy belches amongst the rocks at the edge of the inlet and beyond that an active volcano, Mt. Yasur, filled the air with dark brown smoke and ash.

We set out early next morning to climb the cone. Mt. Yasur is probably the world's most accessible and safest continuously active volcano. It lay close by us to the north but we had to tramp a hot circuitous six miles along a jungle trail to reach Yasur's more approachable far side. Sooty brown clouds of ash burst from the crater every few minutes accompanied by hollow tinny-sounding explosions that grew louder and more threatening as we approached. We found that our eyes suddenly became gritty and sore at odd times though no visible ash was falling around us. At the bottom of the volcano's ashy slope lay the village of Whitesands and from there the climb to the top was a scramble a thousand feet or so upwards over loose purple-grey cinders. We stood exhausted at the top and ate our oranges and marmite sandwiches. The rim gave us a glimpse of the vast forces at work far below where cold crust and hot magma meet each other. Huge columns of ashy smoke and cinders burst with a roar into the sky every few minutes, blotting out the view. We didn't stay long for with all that airborne debris around we were afraid for our skulls. After the trudge back to Port Resolution we found that *Nanook* was covered with a heavy dusting of sandy black ash.

While we sat below with a cup of tea recovering from our unaccustomed exercise, our topsides took a heavy thud from an outrigger canoe and a man who had shared a coconut with us on the trail came aboard with a supply of taro for sale.

His eyes opened wide. "Number one ship," he exclaimed, gently patting the woodwork in appreciation. "All same house belong master."

We sat talking for some time. I tried to match the man's facility with Pidgin English but found it much harder to speak than to understand. Throughout the Melanesian islands with the particular exception of Fiji the native communities were so separated from each other for so long a time by mutual suspicion or hostility that a multiplicity of languages developed. Tanna with a population of 10,000 has seven languages. Pidgin was introduced by the traders of the 19th century and adopted and developed by the native people from New Guinea right through to Aneityum. The word Pidgin itself is actually a Cantonese corruption of "business" and refers to the special English used in trading in China. In the New Hebrides it is called *biche le mar*.

Our visitor pointed out "Captain Cook's rock" to us. I asked what Captain Cook had done with it but he didn't seem to know. He also showed us where Cook's ship had been tied up. I was skeptical of this for it was in shallow water but I learned later that an eruption of Mt. Yasur in 1878 had lifted that end of the island and made Port Resolution impractical as a shelter for large vessels.

The great navigator is still well remembered in Tannese folk history but with no particular affection. He took away a lot of stones, and stones have a special meaning to the people. The Tannese held extreme views of the sanctity of their land. Every rock, tree and blade of grass had a *mana* or power. It was all part of the soul-substance of the people, an extension of themselves. Early sandalwood traders visiting Tanna found that they could easily enough trade beads or red cloth with a chief in return for permission to cut down a certain sandalwood tree. But as soon as they began to haul the tree away, the sailors were swiftly attacked and killed. Stealing the tree was not part of the deal.

The stones carried away by Captain Cook had the power of wisdom. The only reason that Europeans live as they do in such ease and richness and are able to make such wonderful things, is that Cook stole the stones of wisdom from Tanna and gave them to other Europeans. Visitors, especially geologists, are now forbidden to take away or injure any part of Tanna lest by so doing they rob the people of their other great attributes.

So the sandalwood traders strongly distrusted the "treacherous" natives of Tanna, but the feeling was mutual and with some reason. Blankets used by smallpox victims were deliberately taken ashore as gifts at points on the coast, and one sandalwood master in 1860 boasted that "four young men have been landed at different ports [on Tanna], ill with measles, and these will soon thin their ranks."

Next on the scene were the "blackbirders" rounding up labour for the Queensland plantations in fetid old square riggers. These men used any method that seemed cheap and expedient for filling their holds with labour. During the blackbirding period close to 100,000 Melanesians from the Solomons and New Hebrides were captured, bought, taken by deceit or contracted willingly and carted off to Australia. Some in canoes were even caught by grapnels and there is the case of one swimmer who was taken like a fish with a grapnel hook through his cheek. The polite official term was "recruiting." Close to 50% of these recruits died from dysentery and other diseases on their way to Queensland and fewer than 20% were ever properly repatriated, and this not so much to disprove accusations of slavery as to preserve the status of a white Australia.

As if all this was not enough, the next group waiting in the wings were a breed of solemn no-nonsense evangelist missionaries of the old stamp determined to drive the devil out of these heathens with their message of sin, hellfire and damnation. Two grim Presbyterians arrived on the island of Tanna who set about to rule the populace with a rod of iron in the style of the severe and wrathful god they believed in. They were brave men, no doubt, but in their zeal they set up a despotic theocracy that sought to cut the people off totally from everything in their pagan past. If any traditional institution brought joy, pleasure or meaning to the lives of the people, that in itself appeared to be sufficient reason for its discouragement and ultimate suppression. Traditional art forms, dances, "custom" songs, accepted sexual values, old superstitions or religious beliefs, the drinking of kava, nudity and the old alternative to nudity, pubic covers, all were proscribed. Rigorous Calvinistic "laws" were proclaimed by these men of the cloth, a "police" force organised and "courts" established.

The original converts were largely a dispirited, passive, indolent lot but as their numbers grew there also developed a two-caste social system. The unclothed pagans were treated by the new order with unbounded contempt and deprived of the simple right to live undisturbed in their own land in their own traditional way.

By the early 20th century, Presbyterian power over the people of Tanna was absolute, and as for the present, the British writer Austin Coates observes, "throughout the New Hebrides a village which either is or once was Presbyterian can be identified by its silence by night and by the absence of anything of beauty or art by day." But in all fairness the same can be said of the other denominations. If one church was worse than another it was only a matter of slight degree.

With this sort of background it is no surprise to find that Christianity on Tanna is now in a state of decline. In its place a variety of cargo cult has evolved centred on a locally inspired deity called Jon Frum who was conceived as the protector of the Tannese people against the *mana* and magic of the white man. He was to bring immortality to the people and an end to earthly cares so that it was to be no longer necessary to till the soil or work for money. Once this idea took root all labour stopped, the churches were emptied and the people went on a bout of kava drinking and feasting, killing off their cattle, goats and pigs and neglecting their fields. Then during the Second World War the Americans arrived in the islands with their vast supplies and equipment that went far beyond all imagination, and this seeming magic encouraged the belief that Jon Frum would soon make good his promises, with however the help of the Americans who were seen as a superior kind of white man. These hopes have been repeatedly dashed of course but the cult of Jon Frum lives on, nourished by a century and a half of anti-white anti-church resentment.

The story goes on and on, and one could fill a book. I have indulged in this gloomy diversion to outline briefly some of the history of this one island because although the Tannese may not be typical of the people of the South Seas, their history is. Nearly every inhabited island group of the South Seas from the Marquesas to Torres Strait has its own similar tale to tell, equally as long or longer, and as often as not just as melancholy.

We sailed directly on to Vila the capital of the Condominium on the island of Efate and made our entry to the New Hebrides official. *Nanook* was moored in deep water with her bows to a buoy and her stern secured on a 30 fathom line to a palm tree on the small island of Iririki which stands in the harbour overlooking the attractive little town. Iririki seemed to be the stronghold of the islander Anglo-Saxons. The union flag of Britain flew from a staff on the hill behind us close by the British Residency, while the tricolour of the continentals waved in the trade wind at a suitably aloof distance on the mainland behind the town. The French had once been obliged to lop off a portion of their own pole when it was discovered that their flag was flying slightly higher than the union jack.

The two powers jointly govern the group with two parallel administrations sparring continually to maintain a delicate state of equilibrium. Let a Frenchman be appointed to head one government department, then a British appointment must follow to head another. If the British establish a school in a small remote village, *eh bien,* the French must put in a bigger and better French-speaking school. Both sides compete for position, influence and the affection of the natives, and at times, as people in Vila are fond of saying, the system seems not so much condominium as pandemonium.

The dusty little town has an amusing atmosphere of comic opera and for two weeks we idled about the place enjoying ourselves, shopping up and down the main street and driving off around the island with friends. We hadn't intended to stay that long but Katie's ever-tender digestive system fell victim to some local variety of gastric flu. I meanwhile had a stainless steel welding job to do on the windvane which had lost its counterbalance in the storm off New Zealand, so I occupied myself in daily pursuit of an Australian engineer who was suffering at the time from Katie's disorder and was therefore hard to pin down but who was the only person in town who could undertake the weld.

Several other cruising yachts were in port and we seemed forever to be sitting in someone else's cockpit drinking *vin ordinaire* and trading news of mutual friends. We loved the close-knit little world of these ocean-folk and we were glad as always to share in the camaraderie. "The best part of cruising," one of these friends remarked, "is when you are sitting in port going nowhere."

Two other yachts flew the Canadian maple leaf, the ketch *Honnalee*

Katie, and two of the girls, Carol and Susie Haigh, from the trimaran *Tryste*, peek out from a grove of slit gongs on the island of Ambrym.

from Vancouver and an old friend from Whangarei days, the trimaran *Tryste II* from Victoria with Ernest and Val Haigh and their four teen-age daughters. We were to see a great deal more of *Tryste* in the years ahead.

While in Vila we contrived one way or another to reintroduce cockroaches into the galley. We had rid the boat of the dratted pests in New Zealand and were dismayed to find a few sneaking about along the shelves down below. Some people adapt to cockroaches and learn somehow to live with them, but most don't and without a state of unrelenting war against them we would soon have been overrun. Cockroaches can thrive on a bewilderingly varied diet, paint, soap, toothpaste, newspapers, old shoes, wood, ink, bookcovers, even their own discarded skin or the soles of your feet while you sleep. It is not sufficient to sweep up the breadcrumbs in the galley food locker and assume that you are starving the little bastards. Katie especially could not abide the sight of them. I didn't mind them quite that much. Their most objectionable feature to me was the way their appearance evoked a sudden high explosive scream from Katie which in turn always caused me to leap in fright as if I were bitten by a snake.

One of these very screams rent the air on board about 3 a.m. one morning, but it was not brought on by the usual cockroach. We had both been sleeping peacefully until Katie was awakened with the awareness of a thing crawling slowly and carefully across her sheet towards her head. A rat! A fearful scream escaped her and she threw the creature off into the air. It landed somewhere and skittered away. I cracked my skull on the beams overhead as I sat bolt upright. I kicked the light switch on with my left foot and the fluourescent tube blotted out the stars. We searched right through the boat from the stem through all the lockers and the bilges to the lazarette. No sign of it. We wished Nutmeg was still with us. The thing could have been in a hundred inaccessible corners. I felt that it might have taken a hint from Katie's scream and gone back up the companionway steps. A brief prowl around the decks in the dark revealed nothing, but we slipped the weatherboards into place, closed the hatches and stuffed rags inside all the ventilators so that the wretch, if he had gone out, would not return. We knew that he must have found his way aboard along the big nylon warp that held our stern to Iririki Island. He was definitely a British rat and I hoped he would have the sense to go back to his island and stay there where he belonged. But after a long search in the morning through all the gear on deck I found him hiding under the cockpit grating. He was a big fellow and had already torn into several of our sweet potatoes that lay in the cockpit. I dispatched him with a wrench.

I noticed Katie at that point discreetly descending the rope rungs on the shrouds from half-way up to the port spreader.

"What the hell were you doing up there?" I asked, as she touched the deck.

"Just keeping out of reach of that brute," she replied defensively. "I didn't want it going for me on the deck."

"Don't be silly," I scoffed. "Why don't you relax? There's no harm in a rat. It wouldn't go near you if you were on deck."

"Why wouldn't it if it could go below and crawl all over me in the middle of the night?" she cried hotly. "There's no rat-free place on this whole blasted boat except up there in the rigging."

Katie's arguments were always largely unanswerable.

"Besides," she fired back, as with a sigh I tossed the corpse and the sweet potatoes overboard, "why else do you think they call them ratlines?"

Several days later, *Nanook* came into Havannah Harbour, a large inlet on the east side of Efate, and lay to her bower in Essema Bay, a well sheltered spot but "a bit mangrovy and dull" as the log records. Here we were joined by *Tryste* and *Honnalee* and for two more days had a pleasant time shelling and exploring together in the sunshine and sharing each other's rum, freshly killed goat meat and barracuda. The three ketches then sailed on together, rendezvousing at other overnight anchorages at the north end of Efate and on through smaller island groups to the little island of Emae. We were surprised and pleased to find that *Nanook* was quite capable of outpacing the two larger yachts, though this was probably attributable to *Honnalee's* unconventional navigation and *Tryste's* unfair load of six adults.

Emae was a disaster. It had a parched grey-green scrubby look from a distance and we could see as we came closer in that the forest had been savagely reduced to bare trunks and larger branches. Cyclone Carlotta had come visiting some months earlier and had passed directly over Emae lashing the island with unimaginable fury. Other islands nearby had suffered only slightly in comparison.

We went ashore and met some of the local people. They seemed rather quiet and apathetic. What remained of the houses, bits of torn corrugated iron and broken furniture lay scattered far and wide and the people were living communally in makeshift shacks and cooking in groups on the tree-littered beach. At least there was no shortage of firewood. The gardens were all destroyed and the coconut plantations stripped to bare trunks. There wasn't even a decent palm frond to start rebuilding the houses.

All this time our own weather was perfect. Each day was sunny and warm without being oppressive and the atmosphere sparkled with clarity. Many other islands were visible nearby and to the north the high cone of Lopevi Island threw its volcanic smoke constantly into the air from its crater nearly 5000 feet above the waves.

From Emae, *Honnalee* went off on her own and we never saw her again but *Nanook* and *Tryste* sailed on together to the island of Epi where the two yachts managed to ram each other in the middle of the night and then went on to repeat the feat at Craig Cove at the western end of the big island of Ambrym. Like Sicily, Ambrym is triangular and similarly dominated by a big dangerous volcano. Mt. Marum's eight mile wide crater has laid the island to waste several times this century, but it is still a fertile land and since the lava rivers follow predictable courses to the sea, people still cling to the jungled coastline.

We lightened *Tryste* to the tune of two girls and with this happy company in the cockpit we enjoyed an offshore reach up the northwest coast of the island. Landmarks along the coast were difficult to identify for a heavy pall of volcanic smoke from Mt. Marum lay in the air.

At Rannon Anchorage, farther up the coast, we decided to make a trip inland. Ambrym is one of four islands in the New Hebrides that have small inland villages still resisting the ubiquitous missionary and clinging instead to the pagan past. Fanla, some miles inland from Rannon Anchorage was one such village. Fanla's old chief Tain-mal had died a few months earlier and the new chief, Tofut, as I learned, was to celebrate that very day his inauguration as chief, as well as his attainment of a new *magé* or grade in the thirteen rung ladder of the old social order.

I had read of Tain-mal years before and was interested to learn that his son Tofut had proclaimed a feast and issued a general invitation over Vila Radio to one and all. That sounded slightly commercial coming over the radio like that, almost as if the travel agents were in on it, but Katie and I determined to go up and pay our respects anyway. The ash-laden winds ripping off the slopes of Ambrym struck down on our two vessels in heavy gusts. We were anchored in three fathoms over black, volcanic sand. I laid out 25 fathoms of chain and put the kedge overboard as well just for peace of mind but Ernest, ever drag-conscious, (as anyone must be who ties his anchors to a rope) decided to stay with the largely-chainless *Tryste* while Val and three of the girls made the long hike with us up through the bush.

For a couple of dollars a local man guided us several miles over steep jungle paths till we were a thousand feet above the sea. The rain forest crowded around us and blocked out the noonday sun. Gradually the trail levelled out onto a narrow plateau and we began to notice small banana and taro gardens opening up close by on either side. Then just when we thought we could hear the distant sounds of raised voices and barking dogs we came upon a small glade to the right dominated by several vertical figures nine feet high, carved out of tree trunks. These slit-gongs or *atintins* were hollow for most of their length, each with a long slotted opening running with the grain at the front and surmounted by a great concave face carved at the top. They seemed to stare at us with bug-eyed suspicion. So did a wizened little man in a corner of the glade. We wondered why he sat there on his own but realized why further along the trail when we heard him pounding the gongs. We were being announced.

Fanla consisted of a long string of thatched houses set back under tall trees with a well-pounded dirt road down the middle. We were as novel a sight as we were unexpected and we soon had a large noisy gathering around us. Our guide took us to a wide crowded compound at the far end of the village. At one side stood a small "custom" house or dwelling place for the pagan spirits. It was built specially for the celebration and was covered in flowers and brightly coloured leaves. We weren't encouraged to go near it but I noticed a carved face staring out from the dark interior. It seemed all very "tabu" and spooky.

Many of the people especially the women and the guests from the coastal villages were dressed in the dowdy cottons favoured by the moderns, but their faces were daubed with streaks of red paint that looked suspiciously regressive and decadent. Some were carrying away large hunks of bloody raw pork on green banana leaves, and pieces of pig carcass lay scattered on the ground.

The chief and some of his men stepped forward out of the crowd to shake our hands and welcome us. Like most of the Fanla men they were decked out in traditional garb. Pig tusks in full circles jangled at their wrists, colourful leaves were jammed into their frizzy hair and ear lobes and lines of greasy red dye covered faces and chests. Clothing consisted of nothing more than a broad bark belt strapped around the waist and suspended from this at the front a green leafy tube wrapped around the penis to hold it erect.

These penis wrappers were still being worn in the remote interiors of other islands in the group, Tanna, Malekula and Espiritu Santo but their use was dying out. They present a rather baffling mystery, since they seem to relate these people to some of the cultures of New Guinea where the penis wrapper reaches its highest point of refinement. In some areas of that island a gentleman's outfitting will consist solely of a 12 inch length of bamboo strategically planted and held up at an interesting angle by a string around the waist. In other districts a long tubular gourd is preferred, this rising sometimes nearly the full length of the body, narrowing to a point at the upper end and curling gracefully inwards towards the chest. How did the fashion spread to the New Hebrides? These hill people have no tradition of sailing and most cannot even swim. In the past they never even approached the sea, believing it to be poisonous.

Tofut's Pidgin was far too rapid for my still-unaccustomed ear so I used our guide to explain our presence to him. We had read before in a faraway country about the old chief Tain-mal, Tofut's father, and were sorry to learn that he had died. We had sailed to Ambrym and had come up from the anchorage to pay our respects to the new chief of Fanla and to wish him well. Tofut beamed at us and shook my hand a second time.

They all seemed a bit groggy. The feast was over, as Tofut explained apologetically (it had started at 4 A.M.), and everyone was now into the kava. But we were invited to join them around the bowl where a young man was wringing the yellow water out of a handful of pulped roots. Women are usually barred from kava drinking but the cup was passed to Katie, Val and the three girls in turn and they each downed the muddy stuff, not knowing whether they would give more offense by accepting or refusing.

I had half expected a strained silent reception at Fanla but Tofut was in a genial mood and seemed pleased not just at the importance of the occasion and himself but to have this confirmed by the arrival of white foreigners who had come all the way to Ambrym to join in. Somehow, as the guide mentioned after, Tofut had gained the impression that we six had come to Ambrym in one boat, not two, and that these five attractive women were all mine. Our guide knew nothing of how matters stood between the six of us so he had not disabused the chief. This regretfully false impression might have helped enhance my standing in the chief's eyes. Tofut himself, after all, had only two wives and the only other European to have come to Fanla for the celebration was a French Catholic priest, and he had no wives at all.

We stayed talking with some of the men while the crowds slowly dispersed down the trails to the other coastal and bush villages. We were taken into some of the simple little homes and at one spot under a large tree we were introduced to a large grumpy black boar that had survived the early-morning slaughter. Women and pigs are the symbols and substance of a man's wealth in Fanla (not necessarily in that order) and both are zealously guarded and cared for. Still I thought that crushing up the food and feeding the brute by hand a mouthful at a time was carrying animal husbandry a little far until our guide explained; the upper eye-teeth opposite the tusks had been knocked out when the pig was young so that the tusks of the lower jaw would not be worn down in the usual way but grow continuously. These ones curved outward from the upper lips and the points were already well embedded into the lower gums near their own roots forming an almost complete circle. It must have been painful for the pig as well as being a difficult business feeding the short-tempered creature, but full-circle tusks were very highly prized and no one seemed to mind all the troubles of producing them, not the least of which was having to refrain from eating the pig. It sometimes happened, though not often, that a man of prodigious patience pampered his boar long enough to allow the tusk to grow all the way round, out of the gums and into a complete second circle. Such double circle tusks had an enormous value to

Native fishermen of the Maskelyne Islands in the New Hebrides often came by *Nanook* to trade or visit.

the natives. Tofut, I noticed, had two that were a circle and a half and one very old man had a shiny white double circle tusk suspended from a neck string and outlined in solitary splendour against the black skin of his back.

Life is changing for the New Hebridean natives and the semi-sophisticates of Vila and other towns might now have to content themselves with store bought food, "four corner" for example as they call the bully beef that comes in the ubiquitous little oblong tins. But in more remote areas like Fanla life still revolves around pigs as it did long before Europeans came to the islands. In the villages, pigs are everywhere, rooting around at night, wandering and scavenging around the houses in the noonday heat when all else is prostrate. They come in all sizes and shapes and colours. There is even on Malekula and Espiritu Santo a remarkable breed of hermaphrodite pig. But whatever the breed a man's main preoccupation is with trading and accumulating the valuable creatures. They have a social as well as a meat value and the ceremonial slaughter of pigs and the clan feasting that follows are the means by which a man rises to a higher grade of society. Tofut's new status I discovered was the result of having slaughtered his 36 pigs and not the other way around.

The afternoon shadows were stretching well out before we finally left Fanla. Tofut and his cronies were well into their cups and perhaps for that reason the village had fallen restful and quiet. In the New Hebrides kava drinking is done usually at sundown and then children are kept quiet and conversation is carried on in whispers. It has a calming effect, inducing a state of introspection and euphoria. Any loud harsh noise or a sudden bright light, and the soporific calm is driven away. While drinking, one is said to be "listening to the kava."

We slithered down the long trail over the deep rich black loam of the rain forest, rowed ourselves out to the two yachts and slept like logs.

Tryste left early the next morning for Port Sandwich on the island of Malekula. We went ashore at Rannon for a while to talk to the local people who sold a yard-long incised bamboo flute to Katie. One man discovering Katie's interest in shells asked us to his home and furtively unwrapped a large golden cowrie, a rare shell in perfect condition, peach coloured with a white base and about four inches long. "Four thousand dollar" he announced hopefully. What he really meant was four hundred. We could not have afforded the thing even at one hundred, but Katie helped him write to various overseas shell dealers and he then presented her with another flute and me with a little spear.

The passage across the straits to Malekula was a slow reach over gentle seas. We arrived badly sunburned in the late afternoon ten minutes ahead of *Tryste*.

Port Sandwich is a long beautiful inlet on Malekula's eastern coast, one of the few natural harbours of the New Hebrides. The two yachts lay there for several days anchored in eight fathoms behind a sandy point that cut us off from the open sea. We were surrounded by beaches, coconut plantations and wild forested hills. The weather continued perfect with sunny skies and a light trade wind, and we busied ourselves with varnishing, sail sewing and cleaning the hull, or when not in the mood for work we swam or wandered along bush trails.

In the late afternoons, when by consensus the sun was over the yardarm, we gathered under the awning in one cockpit or the other and talked of distant anchorages and the ambitious dreams we all had for the future. Our ideals were similar. We loved the freedom of the open sea and we all wanted to continue cruising forever. But long distance voyages are an expensive undertaking and the shallowness of our pockets required that we all return to Canada before long. Katie and I had the Nova Scotian coast in mind. Ernest and Val had a piece of land and a barn on a small island of British Columbia so they were bound back to the Pacific coast, but they weren't sure how to go about getting there. Ernest was worried about apparent weaknesses in the trimaran wings and felt inclined to sail back to New Zealand, sell *Tryste* there and return to the barn in B.C. and build himself a "real boat" by which he meant a monohull. Perhaps *Nanook's* habit of snatching line honours from the overloaded multihull was beginning to exasperate Ernest, but if so he had his revenge when we turned out to tack upwind to the Maskelynes, a group of reef protected islands on Malekula's southeastern corner. *Tryste* could stand up to her canvas much better, as multihulls must, and she could sail more efficiently on the wind than *Nanook* so she was able to show us the way into the reef-ridden intricacies of the Maskelynes. We anchored for lunch near *Tryste* under the lee of Sakau Island, and after an hour of swimming and shelling there we all continued through the channels to a sunny attractive anchorage amongst mangrove-fringed islands.

Katie and the girls were not long in getting out onto the reefs. Their unfortunate mania for exotic shells was in full flower, and the situation in the cockpit was getting quite out of hand. The notorious "rot box" was filled to overflowing with marble and virgin cones, clams, tiger cowries, spider conches and other things. The insupportable stench in the cockpit was an offense to anyone unwise enough to row around our stern while we lay there to the wind, but it was worse for those on board so I took to lowering the putrid pile of shells overboard in a net bag to nourish the plankton and this helped to clean them and sweeten the wind.

With some reluctance we left the attractive Maskelynes and sailed west into sunshine along Malekula's southern coast with *Tryste's* red sails goose-winged behind us. By evening we were anchored in a circular bay with the pretty little village of Melipe spread along under the palms behind the beach. I was surprised to find that the people of Melipe still continued a few of the old customs. They were well missionized in many respects and all were regaled in dowdy mission cast-off cottons that made them look poorer somehow, less proud and more dependent than they really were. But inside some of the houses, primitive masks and figures stared balefully out at us. They were crude affairs of vegetable paste and black, brown and white "custom" paints. The faces were replete with chicken feathers, human hair and pig tusks sticking out of the mouths. New Hebridean art never reached the degree of sophistication found in other regions of Melanesia and I was surprised to find such a primitive art form surviving in a non-pagan coastal village. I liked the look of one mask and asked the owner if he could sell it. He would for eighteen Australian dollars which was more than I was prepared for, but he settled next morning for twelve dollars and a pair of trousers, a victory of sorts I suppose for the local mission, one less pagan mask, one more pair of pants.

The *Tryste* girls had set out that morning in the sailing dinghy to explore a nearby river, and Val and Ernest had followed in *Tryste's* other tender, a small plastic dinghy that looked like a baby's bathtub. So Katie and I set off ourselves in pursuit, rowing far up the peaceful stream which meandered endlessly through deep dark-green jungle. It felt strange to be suddenly surrounded by silent forest, black earth and fresh water, out of sound of the ocean. We sat on a log with towels and a lump of soap and enjoyed a fresh-water bath before returning downstream and back aboard to a glass of rum.

Both yachts left together again early next morning bound up the coast to South West Bay. The day was grey and humid and a big swell rolled around the corner of Malekula and piled up over the shallow channel inside Toman Island, so we followed Ernest's example and beat south into the wind to pass outside Toman and so avoid the more convenient inside passage. We caught a shark on the way and lost an expensive New Zealand lure to it, the fourth in ten days. I had still not learned that an ordinary hook with a white rag tied above it was just as effective as the shiny lures found in sporting stores.

We left South West Bay after two nights there. I had hoped to visit one of the Small Nambas communities far inland but the weather was drizzly, I had a cold and it was a twelve hour hike each way. The Small Nambas, or people of the small penis sheath, were pagan, like Chief Tofut's people and they still kept to the old stone age ways, their culture insulated from the 20th century by suspicion, distance and thick bush. Their old enemies the Big Nambas lived further north and closer to the sea and some of the Small Nambas too, and since my interest in the old cultures was undiminished I thought I might try for one of these villages, so we left early and made the long passage north in light following winds. The gentle clear weather had returned with only a lingering amount of cirrus in the anti-trade far above, and the inevitable dark dust drifting over our course from restless Ambrym. The main and genoa were goose winged and Katie as usual did the steering. I was forever reminding her that manual steering was quite unnecessary while we had a wind vane but so long as land was close by, abeam or ahead, she always remained determinedly at the tiller. Before sunset we were anchored over a white sand bottom in the pretty little cove of Espiegle Bay.

A few palm frond houses lay under the trees back from the beach and several of the resident natives came out in an outrigger canoe for a visit. One of these, a certain Simeonie, confirmed that there was a Small Nambas village three hours march back from the coast, and yes, he would take us there next morning if we wanted to go. Ernest was pleased to hear this when he arrived later in *Tryste*. He had missed the little expedition to Fanla and wanted to make up for that here.

W.A. Robinson, when he had sailed this way in 1930 during his circumnavigation in *Svaap,* had come to this very spot and after meeting up with some of the inland savages he was invited to dinner with them only to discover after the meal that the menu had consisted of "one fella Big Nambas." But times have changed and Simeonie assured us that "long pig" had been off the menu for sixteen years; no one had been eaten there since 1956.

For several hundred feet we scrambled up through scrub and low trees until we emerged into open country at the top of high limestone bluffs. I was interested to find old coral and sea shells embedded in the banks at this height, suggesting that Malekula had hefted itself up long ago out of the water but, no, Simeonie assured us earnestly, these things dated from Noah's great flood.

The trail we followed was well trodden and the grass on either side was trimmed neatly by long machetes. Closer to the village the verges had been thoughtfully cultivated with hibiscus and other flowering shrubs. All this suggested that our Small Nambas were a lot more civilized than we imagined. Sure enough when we arrived at the neat little village we were greeted politely by a well-dressed quiet-spoken group of adults who came out of their houses to shake our hands shyly and welcome us briefly in their language, Simeonie relaying into Pidgin. A chapel stood significantly among the houses, and from a large school building came the sounds of children obediently chanting their lessons. What they will do with their education is known only to God and the French but of course the school had to be built for if it had not, *les Anglais* would surely have stepped in to fill the breach.

The noonday sun was intense and we sat down on a bench under a large shade tree at the suggestion of a few adults who were not too shy to talk to us. School was soon out and although the teacher never appeared, the children, outfitted in cotton uniforms, marched out of the classroom, came directly over to us and by some general understanding formed a long

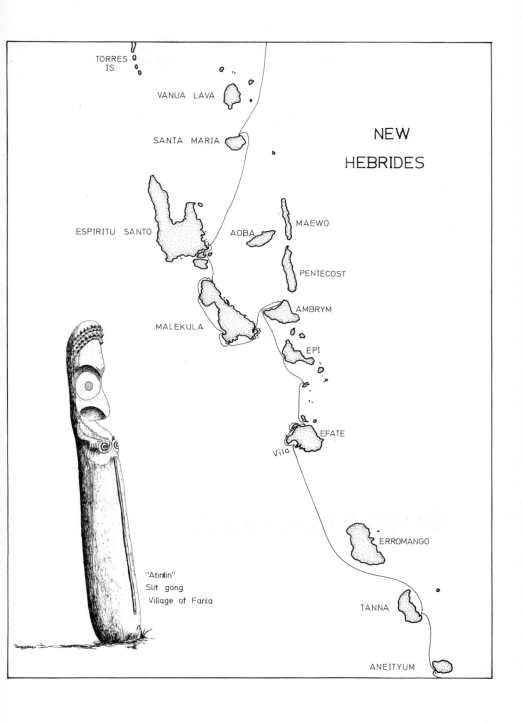

TORRES
IS.

VANUA LAVA

SANTA MARIA

NEW

HEBRIDES

ESPIRITU SANTO

AOBA

MAEWO

PENTECOST

AMBRYM

MALEKULA

EPI

EFATE

Vila

ERROMANGO

"Atintin"
Slit gong
Village of Fanla

TANNA

ANEITYUM

queue towards us. They all shook our hands, these children of cannibals, each one looking directly up at us and murmuring solemnly *"Bonjour Monsieur, Bonjour Madame, Bienvenu a Malekula."* Robinson would never have believed it.

Ernest, Val and the girls, disillusioned perhaps with the quality of my primitives, left early the next morning and we saw nothing more of *Tryste* and her happy company for more than a year. She returned to New Zealand while we sailed on alone northwards through the rest of the New Hebridean chain, touching in at other anchorages on the Malekula and Espiritu Santo coasts, and going on north to Santa Maria in the Banks Group before departing the odd little condominium at last for the British Solomon Islands.

XI

Black-Blonde Eden

Grey skies and squally humid weather carried us north and the rough seas gave us no peace. The trade was suddenly in a grumpy mood and the long moving crests lifted us high and frothed savagely around the stern, belching their white salty tops into the wind and all over decks, rigging and the few square feet of canvas that we cared to carry.

Luckily the passage was short enough not to require the use of the sextant for no sights were possible and after only a night of this treatment we came up on the first lands of the Santa Cruz group, passing to starboard of the high islands of Vanikoro and Utupua and putting them regretfully astern, not so much from a delicacy about proceeding first to an official port of entry but rather because the charted depths inside the lagoons were far too great for us. We continued instead on to the main island of Ndeni where in Graciosa Bay we came to terms with the British administration.

We had the impression here that cruising yachts were not an everyday occurrence. The dark-skinned people along the coast waved at us as we passed their villages and put out in canoes to pursue us. Even the District Commissioner, himself a Solomon Islander, was quite non-plussed at our arrival. He supposed he could give us official entry but he would have to consult Honiara first. At all events he sent out his chief of police, a kindly native man who gave the impression that he was embarrassed at having to snoop around on board as duty demanded. The medical officer Dr. Richard Lee was also despatched to make sure we were introducing no epidemic to the group. Richard brought his wife and another lady with him and for the rest of the day we enjoyed their company on board. The other lady proved to be Diane Hepworth who with her husband Tom had sailed out to the Pacific from England in the old Brixham trawler *Arthur Rogers* in 1949. Tom and Diane had spent many years since then trading under sail in the old tradition up and down the New Hebrides chain before settling as shore-bound traders in the Reef Islands north of Ndeni. We had read of their voyages many years previously and were delighted to meet Diane in person.

The only anchorage in the long deep bay was on a shallow ledge in the southeast corner where a small river emptied its crystal waters into the sea. We lay three miles from the government headquarters and the primitive little bush bakery where bread was sold, but we enjoyed the long walk under the palms and through the pretty little villages strung out along the shore. It was a relief to be doing the sightseeing ourselves for, so long as we remained on board, we were the object ourselves of a stream of curious visitors in dugout canoes. Some of these brought onto our decks great bundles of "custom" money for sale. This local currency was still used in property transactions and the purchase of wives. It consisted of long thick coils of fibre and bark gathered up like a sleeping anaconda. Over the surface of these coils many thousands of little red feathers were laboriously stitched. These came from small red birds that were snared in the forest and released after having their breast feathers plucked out. The work of making one of these long red snakes must take many months. We were intrigued to find such "money" still in common use but they were bulky items and not particularly attractive, nor was I in the market for extra wives so we had to disappoint the money changers.

Ndeni seemed remote, timeless and unchanging compared to the New Hebrides or even in retrospect to most of the Solomons and this struck us as very strange considering the history of the place for the little ledge of shallow ground off the river where we lay had held the anchors of the first ships to bring European colonists to the South Pacific more than two centuries before they came to Australia. In 1595 the Spaniard Mendaña, sailing from Peru with the grandiose purpose of subduing and colonizing the Isles of Solomon, chose Graciosa Bay as the site for his settlement. He could hardly have chosen a place less likely to fill his coffers with gold or a people more savage and less amenable to conversion, these being always the priorities of colonial Spain. But what with squabbling, bigotry, intrigue and a scheming wife, Mendaña accomplished nothing except to leave his bones on the island while the few that survived sailed on to their rescue in the Philippines.

Nanook for her part sailed on to the Reef Islands, a complex of atolls to the north. We wouldn't have considered going there at all for the charts are devoid of all detail, showing only miles of long jagged coral reefs and low islands. But Diane easily persuaded us to visit the anchorage behind Pigeon Island, the little three acre Hepworth retreat of many years. Diane herself was busy in Graciosa Bay setting up a new store, but she assured us of the Hepworth hospitality of Pigeon Island. Sure enough as we came into the lee of the little island Tom who was very surprised to see a sail approaching sent his three children paddling out in kayaks with written instructions addressed to "The captain of the approaching ketch" to tie up onto *Arthur Rogers'* old mooring and to come ashore for supper and also, if we wished, to bring our toothbrushes and stay the night in the guesthouse.

Pigeon Island lay adjacent to some of the main islands of the Reef group and depending on the tides the native people either waded or paddled over to trade at Tom's little store. The Hepworths were the only Europeans in the group. They started off with a deserted scrubby little island that was unwanted by the natives and said to be haunted. Over the years Tom and Diane cleared much of the bush, built a beautiful home and raised three children as well as an assortment of goats, ducks and chickens. They lived an apparently idyllic existence that reminded us a great deal of the Swiss Family Robinson. A little of civilization's technology was allowed to intrude this paradise. They did have D.C. power, a refrigerator and a transmitter radio. They also had a power boat that carried them over the thirty or so miles of open sea to Graciosa Bay for *Arthur Rogers*, the graceful old ketch that had brought the Hepworths from the other end of the earth was herself gone. Only her anchor and chain remained to hold *Nanook* in the lee of Pigeon Island. Tom had lost the old trawler in a cyclone some years before. This must have been inevitable eventually for she was kept anchored there through every season, sheltered only from the trade wind. When she was finally driven onto the coral-bound shore, the Hepworths got on the radio and called up the sea rescue service in Honiara using the two minutes of strict radio silence that is regularly imposed on normal radio traffic for just such emergencies. However the radio operator's job at Honiara had been "localized" by that time, in other words turned over to a poorly trained native and every time the Hepworths bellowed for help into the microphone, the operator answered insistently to "get off the air, Pigeon Island. This is a two minute silence period."

We remained at Pigeon Island for five days of delightful idleness. Katie waded the lagoons at low water to gather orange-spotted mitre shells, while I wandered further afield along the islands and through some of the distant villages. In the evenings we gathered outside Tom's home to sip rum and limes under the palm trees and to hear Tom tell of the South Pacific as it was in the unhurried fifties. He was soft spoken and gentlemanly and he insisted that we stay ashore in the guesthouse for as long as we wished. We were glad to do so because for all of those five days the wind blew in from the south and being denied the normal shelter of the Pigeon Island reefs, *Nanook* pitched horribly at her mooring, bucking into every wave as it came rolling in. I was unwilling in these conditions to place any faith in *Arthur Rogers'* old chain and I laid out our own two CQR anchors in addition so that we could sleep with easy minds. Tom was mystified at the weather. It was cool and cloudy, and day after day the wind blew directly out of the south. It simply never happens, he assured us. We smiled at that for it seemed we had heard such a remark often enough before. As another navigator once said, "local weather is never what it used to be."

From the Reef Islands our course lay south of west to San Cristobal at the lower end of the long Solomons chain. That meant having a wind forward of the beam while the southerly lasted but we grew tired of waiting for the normal trade wind and decided to press on anyway. We beat out past Pigeon Island waving goodbye to Tom and his little family and turned west, sailing in the late afternoon close by the island of Tinakula, a big active volcano that smoked and rumbled two thousand feet above the waves. As night fell, an eerie red glow shone from Tinakula's crater, and keeping this beacon astern all night we glided slowly over a gentle silent sea. By dawn the Santa Cruz group was below the horizon.

The sea is full of surprises. We had expected a wet passage, close-hauled. Instead the wind eased away to what the Victorians would have called a "ladies wind," and it backed just enough to come right on the beam. The seas were almost flat and the only sounds were the rush of water at the bow and the soft whirring of the Sumlog cable. I was amazed at the way *Nanook* could catch a faint air like this one on her beam, a light breeze barely perceptible to the skin, and rush along through the still water at five or six knots. Very seldom do such conditions exist in the open ocean but they are delightful while they last and not easily forgotten.

We came up on the San Cristobal coast after the second night at sea and steered for the little offshore island of Santa Ana where a large bay offered us shelter. We were surprised to find a small sloop putting out from the bay just as we approached. Cruising yachts were not very common in that part of the Pacific. It turned out to be a single-hander, David Field of Vancouver. We yelled to him to come back in to the island with us and to share stories over a drink and a meal. David was heading east and had the good fortune of an easy south wind, but he put about anyway and we enjoyed his company until he left again at midnight.

Santa Ana was one of those islands that season that had stood squarely in the path of a cyclone, and the place looked utterly devastated, worse even than Emae in the New Hebrides. Not a tree was left intact and every house had been levelled. But when we arrived the remaining tree trunks were beginning to green up a little. Vegetable gardens were again being tilled and the land was slowly losing its parched bombed-out appearance. Coconuts sent over from San Cristobal were sending their first green shoots up from the soil and the natives had reconstructed their village from the wood and palm fronds salvaged after the blast. The people seemed spirited and cheerful in their adversity, a refreshing change from the glum despondency of Emae. They laughed wryly at the appearance of

The centre posts are all that remain of the old pagan spirit house on Santa
Ana, after a cyclone devastated the island.

their temporary homes and the sudden changes in their diet. Some of them invited us to their homes and they swarmed persistently aboard in numbers that, as always, gave Katie a considerable pain, excepting of course for those with shells to trade. The cyclone had brought up a number of fairly rare cones onto the beaches and these were not long in finding their way into the swelling collection under the settee berths.

One of the greatest hardships for the people after the cyclone had been the nearly total lack of shade. People in the tropics place as high a premium on shade as cold climate populations place on sunshine. We hiked across the island one day to the south coast, a matter of some miles across a trail that is normally in shady forest but for us was entirely under the fierce sun. While visiting the villages on Santa Ana's weather side I was invited to examine the remains of the well known old spirit or "custom" house which had been preserved faithfully there since pagan times, one of the very few to have survived since the missionaries came to destroy such things. The carved centre posts were still standing like gaunt totems with naked male figures weathering grey in the unaccustomed sun and rain. Hollow carved sharks with mother-of-pearl inlay lay scattered about spilling their contents of human bones on the ground and piles of white human skulls grinned out from under the debris of the broken building. The people of the village had plans to rebuild the custom house but nothing had yet been done and it seemed to me that it would be more a museum than a place with any real meaning. However it still meant enough to the local people that Katie was kept strictly out of the way of it, for the old spirit houses were strictly taboo to women. She amused herself by trying to talk to the other women and bartering for old custom fish hooks.

The native canoes of the island intrigued us for they were completely different from any we had yet seen. The normal canoe of the South Pacific is a dugout with an outrigger. These Santa Ana craft had no outrigger nor were they dugouts. They were made of long thin planks bound together with sennit. The seams were caulked with a black glue taken from a local tree. The two ends curved very gracefully upwards into a carved fiddlehead and some were inlaid with mother-of-pearl. They looked light and elegant but the few that had survived the cyclone lay unused on the beach. They had opened up from too much sunlight and there was no more glue to be had from the trees that supplied it. Consequently whenever Katie and I returned aboard we had to share the dinghy with our visitors. Normally when we brought visitors alongside in the dinghy I remained seated on the centre thwart with a firm grip on the capping rail to prevent any accidents as they made the long step upwards over the guardrails and onto the deck. But here I noticed an odd reluctance especially of the ladies to go up ahead of me. I was stupid enough to be puzzled by this until eventually it dawned on me that of course they wore nothing under

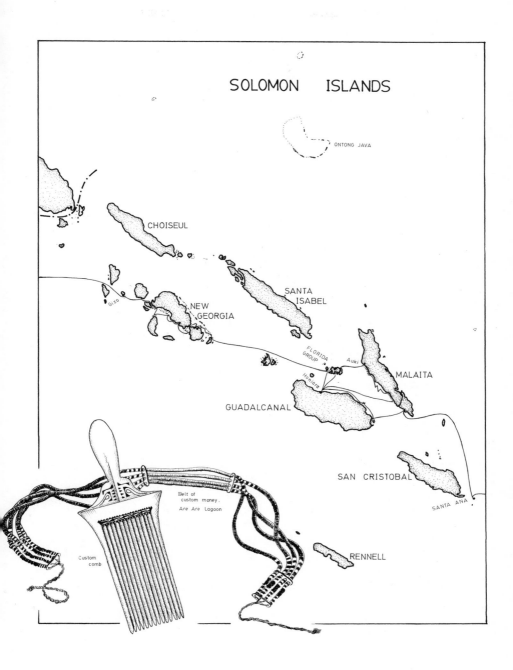

SOLOMON ISLANDS

ONTONG JAVA

CHOISEUL

SANTA
ISABEL

Gizo

NEW
GEORGIA

FLORIDA
GROUP

Auki

MALAITA

Honiara

GUADALCANAL

SAN CRISTOBAL

SANTA ANA

Belt of
custom money.
Are Are Lagoon

Custom
comb

RENNELL

their wrap-around calico. Thereafter I left them to find their own way aboard as best they could even though it resulted in two more breaks in the topside paint, a near capsize and one involuntary swim.

If we stayed more than a day or two in a place we usually found that one or other of the local people became a sort of unofficial host, usually out of a sociable nature and a facility with English. In Santa Ana it was an attractive young woman called Kala. She loved sitting on board regaling us with cyclone horror stories, or telling us of all the scandalous goings on in the little village and all about the yachts that had called there in years past.

We found the people surprisingly light in colour for Melanesians, presumably from a happy admixture of Polynesian blood in the distant past, and their easy generous personalities tended to confirm this. The women of Santa Ana are attractive and have always been very much in demand. Kala sitting in the cockpit with her friends recounted for us a ghost story from Kira Kira the district headquarters on San Cristobal concerning one such girl of Santa Ana who in 1809 at the age of thirteen was purchased by eight young bachelors from San Cristobal to be their common mistress. The girl was taken by the boys to their village on Kira Kira and for some time she managed to fulfill her heavy schedule to everyone's satisfaction. However a ninth bachelor appeared on the scene seeking her favours and when he was refused he threatened her with magic. But the girl's loyalty to her eight lovers was unshaken and the rejected suitor went off to a sorcerer and made good his threats. The girl then became covered all over with sores which set up so revolting a stench that no-one could stand being near her. She was expelled from the village and lived near the rubbish dump. She died at the age of twenty-three and her spirit entered the top of a tall tree which sixty years later was blown down in a cyclone. She then took residence in another tree which in 1930 against the wishes of the locals was cut down to make way for a government patrol house. She has haunted the house ever since, the enemy of all bachelors who go there.

Although we were bound for Honiara, the capital of the protectorate, on Guadalcanal we decided to go north first to the island of Ulawa before continuing west across the Slot. The natives of Ulawa used to have a strange practice. A group of them would creep up and surround a banyan tree in the dead of the night and at a given signal they would all scream horribly at the tree. After several successive nights of this treatment the banyan tree would die, presumably of fright. It's a hard one to believe but I wanted to go there and find whether the people still killed trees in this way. This meant a night passage, for Ulawa lay a long way off. Unfortunately we chose the wrong night. The sky clouded over and the easterly wind built up to Force 6 and then 7 during the pitch dark hours of early morning. *Nanook* rolled and crashed in the steep seas and well before dawn we began noticing a strong smell coming from the bilges. A quick perusal of the lazarette revealed that a gallon of dark tarry antifouling undercoat paint had tipped, lost its lid and spilled down the hull and into the already greasy bilge water under the engine. This made Katie even more sick than she was already but there was nothing to be done till we could get in to shelter. Ulawa lay not far to leeward in the grey dawn but we decided not to stop as the anchorage would be too exposed in such a wind. So after rounding the northern end we bore away off the wind to the shelter of a small jungle-shrouded cove on the island of Maramasike, Malaita's little neighbour, and here in this deserted spot we rested and cleaned up the awful mess in the bilges before continuing on to Guadalcanal.

Marau Sound at the windward end of Guadalcanal is a complex of reefs and islands and we had thought to do some shelling in the area but after a brief survey of the sound we gave up and continued on along the coast after one night at anchor. To our surprise we found a two knot east-setting current along the Guadalcanal coast, and as the wind was against the current and again up to Force 6 a wild steep sea was kicked up giving us a roller coaster ride downwind to the overnight shelter of the small low Rua Sura Islands and from there after a pre-dawn breakfast we sailed away in a soft pink dawn and drifted gently along the coast the forty miles to Honiara. In contrast to the previous day we had a gentle sail in perfect weather. To port the 7,000 foot peaks of Guadalcanal stood out clear to the tops. The sky was a hazy blue, the sea a vivid turquoise in the shallows of north Guadalcanal and the breeze just enough to fill the sails and keep the diesel quiet.

The anchorage at Honiara is wide open to the sea but for the modest shelter of a small spit of land called Point Cruz where Mendana raised the cross on his first voyage. On our arrival there we had a bit of fun mooring *Nanook* amongst a large collection of local trading boats but after anchoring three times we finally settled down with the stern secured by a line to an old sunken barge.

We loved Honiara. A friendly little yacht club spread its thatched awning to the edge of the beach by the anchorage and here we relaxed with cold beers and a mountain of mail. The weather remained clear every day, a bit too hot in the afternoons admittedly and then we had to endure a strong onshore wind from the northeast which set all the boats pitching unpleasantly into the swell until the sun stopped blistering the land. But we were compensated for this discomfort by the soothing coolness of a light breeze every night off the high land behind us.

We restocked the food lockers from the Chinese stores in the little town and at the invitation of new-found friends we went driving off along the roads to see something of the island and the development that has taken place there since the Americans seized the Japanese-built airstrip and halted the yellow invasion that was destined for Down Under. Guadalca-nal has the same ring to its name as Stalingrad and el Alamein in the ears of those old enough to remember. Now a more peaceful place could hardly be imagined. All that remains are a few rusting tanks, old barges half buried on the beaches and endless bits of perforated steel sheets that were used to surface the bombed-out airstrip at Henderson Field. These were being used as garden fences, driveways and ditch bridges. The police headquarters where we got our immigration clearance is just an ice-cream away from the yacht club. Yet it took the Marines from November 4th 1942 to January 21st 1943 to cover the same distance. Almost nothing remains of all this but the memories, and these too are rusting out like the sunken barges on the beach.

Next to the yacht club by the Mendana Hotel a beach notice warned that swimming was unsafe because of sharks, but a native fisherman swimming close by us with a net smiled at this and explained that although the sharks were really dangerous after the bonanza days of World War II they have now forgotten the taste of man.

Early one morning after a week of relaxing around Honiara and savouring again the easy pleasures of civilization, we let go the stern line from the ancient barge, lifted the anchor and caught the last of the cool night land breeze across to the old capital of Tulagi in the Florida Group which lies between the double lines of the big main islands. The pilots of wartime called this inland sea The Slot but the sailors who saw so many ships go to the bottom in the furious fighting called it Iron Bottom Sound.

Finding Tulagi to be a rather dull little town we continued on to anchor in the solitude of Tanambogo Island, a tiny scrap of land that was the scene of heavy fighting against the Japanese. Broken hulks and a great deal of other rusty steel junk lay around the beaches and we tried to imagine what the place must have been like thirty years before. Meanwhile to our amusement Japanese fishing boats criss-crossed busily nearby, sweeping Tulagi Harbour of its fish. A few token Solomon Islanders worked on these as deck hands.

"Look at that," said Katie. "There goes your Greater Asia Co-prosperity Sphere."

The Florida Group is an archipelago within an archipelago, and with its complex outlines and endless anchorages it seemed like the Solomon Islands in miniature. We meandered from one sheltered bay to another until we tacked into Utuha Harbour, a place deserted except for a Japanese freighter that was taking on water from a wartime pipeline. We anchored close by and went ashore to scramble far up through the bush and follow the old American pipe to its source in a limestone cave. Inside, a short way back from the entrance, the Americans had caught the stream in a little concrete dam that was dated 23 Oct., 1943. Here we threw our clothes aside and bathed luxuriously in the cool refreshing water that spilled over the dam and then sun-dried ourselves on the rocks while we gazed down through the tree tops at the little ketch and the big steel freighter lying far below us. Later we slithered back down the steep muddy mountain fighting our way over the tangle of fallen trees left behind by Cyclone Ida, and by the time we reached the bottom we were as hot and filthy as ever.

Of all the delightful surprises of the Solomons, few are as intriguing to the geographer or as inviting to the inquisitive mariner as the intricate channels that wind for no apparent reason through so many of the islands like salty vestigial rivers. One of these now opened up before us, Mboli Passage, which meandered north between the two main islands of the group. The tide carried us along many miles through steep forested hills and past mangrove shores and little settlements where the native people waved and yelled to us to stop and trade. We did anchor at one bend and rowed ashore to talk and pick over the inevitable bags of sea shells. The people were hard up as usual and had not recovered from the thrashing they and their gardens had received from Cyclone Ida, so that shells were all they had to offer. It seemed strange to be finding ocean shells so remote from the sea in this long valley, if valley it can be called when one land lies to port and quite another lies to starboard. We emerged at last into a pretty lagoon on the north coast of Nggela Island and after a night there we continued on for a rough and rainy passage to the big island of Malaita.

We found our way through the reefs to the harbour of Auki only by dead reckoning for the torrential rain blotted out everything in a grey curtain of falling water. Malaita lies more north and south than the other main islands and it takes the full brunt of the trade wind along its cloudy backbone. *Nanook* rested in a horseshoe of water that was fringed with native houses standing on spindly stilts right out over the water, and while we retreated below for tea and towels the heavens overhead applauded our arrival with claps of anger.

Malaita, or Mala as the natives call it, is not just the wettest of all the islands. It is the most heavily populated and historically the most difficult to administer. The Malaitans, as other islands are quick to point out, are a different bunch. They are the Irish of the Solomons, aggressive, loving, clannish and cantankerous. But being the best plantation workers in the group they were also ubiquitous exiles and generally disliked by people of the other islands where they were sent under contract.

There was no lack of opportunity to meet them for our track lay south from Auki down through the Langa Langa Lagoon, a long complex waterway between the hills of Malaita and a series of long low islands protecting the lagoon from the open sea. Villages dotted the whole area and wherever we went unless we carefully chose an anchorage hidden from the villages by islands, we were plagued with visitors in dugout

Like a figurehead decorating the bow, Katie pilots *Nanook* through the winding channels of Diamond Narrows in the western Solomons.

canoes. We stayed two weeks in the lagoon and after the first few days we became adept at spotting the quiet remote corners where we could expect a degree of peace and privacy. Yet the people themselves were fascinating and so were their villages, many of which were on small flat artificial islands built of coral blocks well out in the lagoon as a defense against their traditionally hostile mainland neighbours.

Very few yachts had ventured along this Malaitan coast and in the remote corners of the lagoon the people had never before seen a visiting yacht. Perhaps that was why we were so inundated. Boys wearing only a large land-snail pendant swam out to examine us. People stared from the shore or climbed trees for a better view while others piled into canoes and paddled out to knock on the hull and ask to come aboard. Sometimes a flotilla of fishermen in dugouts dropped by on their way home after several hours of pursuing tuna and on one such occasion we had twenty-three canoes tied up all around us or hanging on. To satisfy their curiosity we let them come aboard and we soon had dozens of these people sitting in the cockpit or standing on the stern jabbering excitedly and examining everything in great surprise and wonder, but as the invasion continued, *Nanook* began to point her bowsprit higher up towards the hills, and sea water began flooding up the cockpit drains and across the floor of the cockpit as the depressed stern went deeper.

The people were honest and well enough disposed but it was not long before we came to dread the nearly inevitable knock on the hull. Katie's tolerance on these occasions was a bit shorter than mine but she did at least enjoy the satisfaction of having several thousand shell gatherers scouring the long Malaitan reefs for her exclusive selection, or so it seemed.

The Malaitans had a strong commercial instinct and the one thing they consistently brought to us for sale was shells. Ida and the other cyclones of the past season had thrown a lot of unusual shells up from deeper down on the reefs and we were surprised at the variety that was emptied out from all those plastic bags onto our decks. Many we had never seen before. A pretty little shiny white cowrie with brown circles over its surface was offered to us for 10 cents each. They were worth $50 apiece as we found out later, yet we bought only a few from a woman who had a whole bottle full.

We were also besieged with strings of custom money which consisted here of thousands of little shell discs chipped laboriously out of oyster shell and strung together on long threads of natural fibre. Like the Santa Cruz coils they were still used for local trade and wife-buying. Katie ended up with a triple belt of the stuff around her waist which she was fond of wearing thereafter even at sea when she wore nothing else.

Nanook meandered south amongst big islands of mangrove and little man-made village-islands. Sometimes the lagoon opened away out into a wide expanse covered only by distant dugout canoes of tuna fishermen; sometimes it narrowed to channels hardly wider than *Nanook* herself.

The days were oppressive and I missed my daily swims over the side, but I had seen crocodiles nearby on two occasions in the remote corners where we lay anchored, so these plus the growing harvest of tropical ulcers on my legs kept me on board effectively enough. These great open infections which Jack London referred to as "Solomon Island sores" would begin to develop from the slightest cut or scratch. A mosquito bite casually scratched was enough to set one going. A red pinpoint the first day would expand to the size of a dime in a couple of days and within a week the thing would have consumed enough skin, flesh and tissue to swallow a quarter. Katie had only two of these, both brought on by coral cuts, but I had six, all on the legs. We found that the only way to heal them was to keep them scrupulously away from water or running sweat, to cover them with an antibiotic powder and to pursue flies with a furious vengeful heart. We often winced suddenly from a little pin prick of pain at the edge of one of these sores and found that some gross black village fly had been perched on the edge of the crater having a meal. This was another reason for steering clear of the villages except for brief visits. But even with these precautions our *"sitrong pela suwos"* (strong fella sores) as the natives called them took weeks to heal.

Still, despite the problems, it was hard to stay away from the villages because they were so interesting and attractive and their people hospitable and helpful. There was the little artificial village-island of Ta-alulolo, as beautiful as its name where the women and children came to greet us with broad smiles and ripe pawpaws. There was the village of Bulabu where Katie bargained with the ladies for an old wooden custom comb in trade for a fathom of calico while a gang of naked children played English cricket outside. There was the old man on Fanfala Island who retained all his pagan beliefs and told me stories of the old days when great wars were fought with the hill tribes and everyone was naked. His daughter, a pretty bare-breasted girl of fifteen, had studied *Nanook* from a distance and when I rowed to his house I found her small brothers playing in the water with a fine replica of *Nanook* that the girl had made, a model exact in many details even to the steering vane and trim tab.

The sun seldom appeared for us and every day towards afternoon the skies darkened and the grey clouds buried us in drenching rain so that even without swimming it was hard to keep our sores dry and we at last became so depressed with the monotony of wet humid weather and the never-ending streams of visiting canoes that we finally put to the open sea from the Catholic mission settlement of Buna and pressed on into the light head winds along the coast to the south.

It was a long unpleasant struggle down the coast with sails close hauled and angry black line squalls bearing down on us from time to time. One of these, a really frightful monster whipping the water white at its advancing base chased us back up the coast to the overnight shelter of Su'u. The second day brought us into the Are Are lagoon, a long complex waterway like Langa Langa but more landlocked and less populated.

Nanook must have looked pretty to the people of Rohinari, a Catholic mission settlement at the north end of the lagoon, for a crowd gathered on the shore as she carried all her sails in through the narrow entrance. We were interested to find that the canoes here were of the planked variety *a la* Santa Ana and similarly caulked with a black "custom putty" taken from the fruit of a tree. We anchored at some distance from the mission and towards evening the head man of the nearest village came paddling over and through an interpreter demanded three dollars for allowing us to remain overnight in the anchorage. This we politely declined.

"Silly old goat," Katie snorted.

Nanook again found herself next day wending her way amongst islands and motoring through tortuous channels, some of them so narrow that at one point she had branches reaching out to touch her rigging. We eventually emerged from this green maze into the wider waters of Wairokai Harbour and there we anchored off the village of Oio intending only to make a brief "coffee stop." But a sandy beach lay on one side of the channel opposite the village and Katie took time to row over and clean out the putrid shellfish from her rot box. Meanwhile a young man called Peter came visiting and I learned from him that many of the pagan Kwaio people lived close by on the other side of the harbour, so with Peter on board we motored over to visit their little village back amongst the trees where a small river came down from the mountain. I was delighted to find that these people were trying to preserve their culture in the face of the omnipresent pressure of government and mission. Four men were engaged in the construction of a custom house but they were not too busy to sit down and talk to us, Peter interpreting. None of them wore anything at all. The custom house being built was a place of spirits they explained and even at that early stage of construction it was very *tambu* (taboo) and the woman with me must not go near it. I assured them that she wouldn't. I asked if there was anything I could do for them. One looked at my camera and asked if I could make a picture of them to place in the spirit house to show who built it, so when I agreed they lined up stiffly and I eventually mailed the photo back to them through Peter.

The following morning we left *Nanook* on her anchor and rowed ashore again to hike far back into the hills to a more remote Kwaio village. Peter again accompanied us. We followed the river several miles back through the tall rain forest and open fields of cattle pasture. Our trail then began climbing up into a steep jungled valley. It was hot and sticky under the trees and I slipped at one spot on a root and scraped my arm which meant another two Solomons sores. The "village" consisted of only three houses far up on a hilltop. The people were very much like those at the harbour. They were rather astonished to see us but they greeted us kindly and showed us their homes and gardens and accepted our little gifts with grace and goodwill. We wondered as we left whether they minded their isolation and poverty up there on the hills and how long it would be before they abandoned their little plots for the easier life down by the sea. We slithered back down through the jungle, bathed in the cool river, sores and all, and returned aboard.

We continued on next day down the Are Are Lagoon but we found little more of interest. The grey wet weather was slowing down our progress as well as my earlier resolve to circumnavigate Malaita and we finally put out from one of the passes to the open sea and returned overnight across the Slot to Guadalcanal, following the island's strips of milky coastal water back to the civilized luxuries of Honiara.

We found it hard to leave the place. So many people had come out to visit us or to invite us to their homes. There was Wally Gibbons, the diver and shell collector who had discovered the location of a colony of the very rare *gloria maris* cone shells in the Solomons and was trying hard to keep it a secret. Wally had first noticed Katie cleaning her latest specimens at water's edge at the yacht club and he opened his home to us as well as a generous part of his enormous and valuable collection. Then there was Dr. Harry Cannon, a university professor from Vancouver who borrowed a dinghy to investigate the yacht with the Canadian flag. Harry and his wife May lived out on the hills near Henderson Field and they took us out there for meals, drives around the island and a couple of nights in a regular bed. We loved their company, the long conversations over long glasses of rye whisky, the skinny dipping in the pool and talking about the neighbours talking about us. Harry was on a year's contract with the U.N. to develop a science curriculum for Solomon schools, and he worked closely with the people in the nearby teachers' college. He confided his disillusion with the whole educational set-up there which he described as backward, traditionalist and conservative, and tailored to serve the interests of the powerful missions. At least 30% of time in all schools he said was being spent in reinforcing the teachings of the church. An interesting field for a humanist like Harry to try getting a little science going. And yet according to later reports his year there was very successful thanks no doubt to his proven ability to work within the established structure. He had for example once been appointed by a broad-minded minister as Canada's only atheist Sunday school superintendent.

Our crops of ulcers slowly withered in the dry air at the yacht club where we sat by the hour sipping beer, writing letters and talking to friends, but finally, armed with a magnificent fruit cake from May we cast off and put Honiara behind us.

To the northwest of us lay the island of Savo where the feckless megapode bird lays its eggs in sand and thereafter leaves its young to hatch, struggle to the surface and fend for itself. We had planned to stop at Savo but the shelter there was indifferent and finding strong winds offshore we changed course instead for Sandfly Passage in the Florida Group, stopping there for three nights while the bad weather lasted, and pressing on again to the western Solomons to explore the endless intricacies of the New Georgia group.

After sighting the volcanic peaks of the group close ahead in the light of dawn we followed the long cliffs of Gatukai and a succession of smaller parallel islands until we came to a gap where water from the Marovo Lagoon rushed out over a narrow bar. With some help from the diesel *Nanook* pushed in over the shallow ledges and into the lagoon. This shallow bar had once been a very deep pass countless ages ago when the surrounding cliff-girt islands had been long coral reefs under the surface. We found ourselves emerging into what is (though few yachtsmen or any others know it) about the most beautiful lagoon in the Pacific and in fact the largest island-enclosed coral lagoon in the world.

A short bend just within this entrance brought us into the lee of an island where we anchored in five fathoms, sand, with a yellow beach ashore, total shelter, green uninhabited islands everywhere around us and hot as blazes, a paradise in utter seclusion. Or so it was until our discovery in the afternoon by some of the natives of Bili across the lagoon who came to investigate and to urge us to visit their village to buy carvings, "any day except tomorrow," which was a Saturday. The people of the Marovo Lagoon are all very Seventh Day Adventist. They are also very good wood carvers but we were in no hurry to go trading. There were plenty of other villages ahead.

For several days we meandered along to the north, spending two or three hours each day on boat maintenance and the rest of the time in swimming, exploring, snorkelling over the reefs and relaxing under the yellow awning that shielded the cockpit from the fierce sun. We were completely alone with no other yachts and far from the villages on the mainland. At night we lit the kerosene Tilley lantern and went wading in the shallows in search of shells, beautiful vivid black-and-white marble cones, virgin and lettered cones, tiger cowries and a few other odds and ends. The ghastly rot box was in business again.

We eventually worked our way towards the mainland of Vangunu and were back into the old routine of receiving visitors. A knock on the hull. "Master. Good afternoon, master." (The "boys" in this part of the world still said "Master" and the "masters" still said "boy.") Some of these visits we enjoyed very much. "One fella old man Jack" for example who sold us an inlaid walking cane for $6 and brought his daughter Gloria to visit one evening under the awning and to tell us stories in Pidgin. One of these yarns explained the fate of the five Australian scientists who were lost from the yacht *Wanderer* on Guadalcanal in 1896.

"This fella ship he come shore long Wanderer Bay," Jack explained. "Alright this fella white man he like go up long mountain Tatuve. Olgeta [altogether] people long bush him he killim now. Him he dead finish. Olgeta people him he cookim body belong him for *kaikai* [eat] him. Olgeta cookim soup belong him. Him he good fella *kaikai* too much. Alright now olgeta tryem *kaikai* shoe belong him. Man long bush he savvy this fella shoe all same foot belong white man. Tasol [but] he no savvy *kaikai* him this fella shoe. Him he hard too much. One day behind [later] olgeta cookim more. Tasol tooth no savvy go long inside. Olgeta man loose him this fella shoe."

But many of our visitors were just plain tiresome like the native evangelist at the Batuna mission station. We had stopped there to buy bread when this fellow came along in his canoe to warn us that the Adventist church was God's only true church and that the cyclones of the past season were a sure sign of the second coming of Jesus. He gave us tracts which proved that God intended us to eat only animals which have both cuds and cloven hoofs, and only fish which have scales. All other creatures were unclean. Still in the end we came to appreciate this ridiculous dogma for it meant that we could buy the unclean lobster from the fishermen at all the S.D.A. villages for a mere ten cents each.

We left the Marovo Lagoon at Sege, a place that saw a lot of action during the war against the Japanese. We were laden with eggs, pineapples, bananas, grapefruit, bread and fish as well as some beautiful carvings in ebony and kerosene wood to send to friends in the lands we had left behind. *Nanook*'s course tacked south to anchorages on the west coast of Vangunu before turning west again to cross the Hele Bar, a shallow break in a long island-dotted-reef. As we crossed the two fathom bar we caught an unidentified ten pound fish that was the finest eating of anything we ever caught at sea in five years.

The winds on the New Georgia coast were unreliable and we found ourselves late one afternoon, although surrounded by islands, still a long way from any reasonable anchorage and much against my inclination we settled for a gap in the barrier islands of the Roviana Lagoon for the night. The lagoon itself was only a foot or so deep while the slopes around the barrier islands dropped away steeply to enormous depths. After motoring around the edges of the channels for some time studying the depths on the echo sounder we found one spot where the ground sloped away more gradually at about 45° and we dropped the kedge down on a short chain and rope from the bow. The bottom looked fearfully rough judging by the scattered light on the sounder dial and the anchor took an immediate and unyielding hold. We tied the stern to a tree and turned in hoping for a peaceful night. All sorts of jungle sounds were around us including a howling dog at a deserted camp nearby.

Katie at breakfast remarked that she had spent the night dreaming that the anchor wouldn't come up. Well, she was right. It was stuck down there as firmly as Gibraltar's Rock. For more than an hour we motored this way and that, reversed, charged forward, paid out line, charged again, reversed again. Nothing. We tightened up and tried again. I got into the dinghy hoping to unsnag the line from one direction or another. No luck. I dived down with the goggles till my ears hurt but could see nothing in the murky water. We motored again back and forth for another hour tugging this way and that, and finally collapsed on the deck to stare sadly at the empty anchor chocks on the deck and the rigid nylon line pointing straight down from the bowsprit roller. It may sound ridiculous but when an anchor has seen you faithfully through a lot of bad blows, you have a feeling of affection for it. But quite apart from all sentiment, we needed the thing. We had only one other hook apart from the ridiculous little Danforth and there was no prospect of replacing the plough in that part of the world. Still either it or its four fathoms of chain were securely snagged around something, and the whole lot was down to stay. I got the knife out. But before cutting ourselves free we decided to give it another final try and suddenly the line jerked free and up she came as sweet as anything. Were we happy!

This was the only time we ever knowingly anchored in very foul ground, and the only time we ever came close to cutting ourselves adrift.

While all this was going on the lonesome old dog over on the nearby island had swum across to us against the tide. He was dragged aboard and given some tins of pet food that still lingered in the lockers from Nutmeg's days. We were sorry for the beast. It was as hungry for company as for food but there on the island it had been abandoned and there was nothing we could do but take it back so I put it into the dinghy and rowed it over with some more tins of food. However he was soon swimming after me and I had to repeat the process. Once we were underway, the dratted mutt set up an unhappy howling and followed us for half a mile along the shore of the entrance channel crying at us all the way, and as we left the confined channel and put to sea so did the dog. It was a performance calculated correctly to melt Katie's heart. There was nothing for it but to turn back, drag the beast aboard again and take him with us to some inhabited place. He licked us all the way across the open sea to the lagoon on the island of Rendova where we immediately went ashore in search of prospective dog owners. The first people we met were a Polynesian couple from Ontong Java on contract to a local plantation. When I let it out that $3 would go with the dog, the man was immediately agreeable and he and his heavily tattooed bare-breasted wife took the beast under their wings together with six tins of cat food and some sticks of tobacco. It occurred to me later on reflection that the natives of Ontong Java are inordinately fond of eating dogs, but I was careful to say nothing of this to Katie.

We found that the nearby village was a Malaitan settlement, all the people being on contract to the local white "master" for a term of an incredible fifteen years. After the well-dressed ascetics of the Marovo Lagoon it was a bit of a relief to meet decadent Anglicans again, pig-eaters, tobacco smokers, chewers of betel nut and both sexes elegantly bare-breasted. The master himself, a gloomy Scot, lived in splendid isolation in a fine house at the edge of the lagoon. We heard him playing the bagpipes in the evenings but we saw nothing of him and learned anyway that he heartily detested European visitors.

As we left Rendova Harbour we noticed to port a really beautiful little *motu* on the reef, Kuru Kuru according to the chart, its white beaches sloping down into crystal waters, and finding that the winds outside were useless we turned back and anchored close in to the *motu* and tied the stern to a tree. Here we remained for two nights, relaxing, swimming naked along the reefs and writing in idyllic isolation. Only one canoe came by to see us, a family from down the Rendova coast on their way across the straits to Munda. John Kari, the father, introduced himself as "the man" (though he was not the only one) who rescued John F. Kennedy after PT109 was sunk by a Japanese destroyer. While we ate one of his juicy football-size pomolos in the cockpit, John told us the whole story including the sending by Kennedy of a letter written on a green coconut to his C.O. at Rendova. John got to deliver this coconut letter which was disbelieved at first by H.Q. until the coastwatcher Evans confirmed by radio that Kennedy's crew really were stuck out there on the little island of Gizo, and a patrol boat was then sent to collect them.

We crossed the straits ourselves shortly after John, to Munda, another area that filled the headlines of those days. Munda Bar, the crossing point of the sunken barrier reef, was identified for us by an outgoing Japanese fishing boat and after dodging shallows and coral heads we came to anchor in yet another beautiful island-studded lagoon not far from the wartime airstrip at Munda. There we stayed for three more days of luxurious idleness amongst attractive islands and friendly black-blonde people.

At this stage I had developed a very painful ear which I ascribed to my fondness for diving, over at Kuru Kuru. I could sleep only on one side and decided to pursue the doctor at the little hospital near the airstrip. His examination, out in the sunshine for want of other light, attracted a big circle of curious natives but neither he nor they could decide whether the ear was blocked, damaged or infected, for which I paid two dollars.

Katie fell in love with Munda and its lagoon. "It's the most beautiful place in all the Solomons," she said, and added only half jokingly, "Let's stay here forever." But we were already well into October by that time and with the approach of another cyclone season we had to press on to northern New Guinea to hole up there for the cyclone or northwest monsoon season. We had planned to spend that season in the Trobriand Islands to the east of Papua and to sail from there the following season around the north coast of New Guinea and through Indonesia to Bali. But somewhere along the way, I think it was while pouring over charts at the Point Cruz Yacht Club, I got to thinking that the Trobriands, which certainly didn't offer any kind of all-round shelter, might not be all that cyclone-free, and since we wanted to see that area thoroughly we decided to go meanwhile up to Madang on the north coast, a perfect harbour and too close to the equator to be bothered by cyclones anyway. We could then return east the following season and cruise eastern New Guinea before going on through Torres Strait to the Indian Ocean. We knew though that it would be almost impossible for us to get to Madang through the Vitiaz Straits once the northwest winds got going. Those straits separating New Britain and New Guinea so confine and funnel the winds and the very strong currents that it is extremely difficult to sail through them to the southeast during the trade wind season and just as difficult to get through the other way against the northwest monsoon which could have set in at any time.

So we put out from Munda early on the fourth morning there with pleasant sunny weather and mixed feelings. Our course took us into another of those long winding water mazes between big islands that make the Solomons so intriguing to the navigator. A fair tide carried us forward in the narrowing channel between the islands so we made good time towards the landlocked bottleneck of Diamond Narrows. The wind came and went and so did the villages which meant that clothes and diesel were on and off all day.

By evening we were at rest again in a little deserted grove on the island of Kolombangara. By the following evening we had crossed over the position of PT109's collision out in the straits, passed Kennedy's Plum Pudding Island and arrived at the little tin-roof town of Gizo, and two days later we sadly said goodbye to the most beautiful archipelago in the world. We were bound for the great land of New Guinea.

XII

A Diversion into the Doldrums

For several days *Nanook* alternately sailed and drifted westwards. It was near the end of the season and the trade had lost its punch. We managed to make good 100 smooth miles the first day out, but then the wind left us and for three more days we lay idle, or motored, or moved forward at a couple of knots with a faint breeze. But at last after the passage of a warm front that was laden with lightning and three hours of rain, a gentle easterly settled down to send us on our way again under blue skies, not briskly but we did have the help of an unexpected current. In fact I couldn't believe the sights taken during the next day until I'd taken so many that I had to be right. The Sumlog which had the human habit of slightly exaggerating, had measured off 86 miles from one noon to the next, but with the help of the current we had actually made good 139 miles.

Noon sights which gave us our latitude were taken every day and on one of these days I had the novel experience of finding that the sun's position where it strikes the earth at 90° was within a mile or so of our own position so that for a moment at noon I could swing the sextant right round in every direction and still have the sun resting its bottom edge on the horizon.

On the evening of the seventh day, a fix by Moon, Jupiter and the star Deneb put us just thirty miles east of Finschhafen in the approaches to Vitiaz Straits, and in the early hours of darkness I picked up the light on Fortification Point flashing twice every eight seconds. I then altered course to tackle the strait. We carried a fair wind with the odd heavy rain squall, a half moon and a good current. The only problem was losing the moon at midnight and having to make for the twenty mile gap by dead reckoning under a dark sky. But I needn't have worried, even when the wind headed us in the early hours of morning, for the current was flowing

199

through at up to four knots spilling us and our breakfast into the wide flat thundery Bismarck Sea.

It was good to see land again. And what land! Tall mountain ranges to port sloping steadily from the sea to 13,000 feet, and to starboard long volcanic islands offshore. In this setting we drifted for another day and night of long calms and brief breezes and on the ninth day, after eating the last of our loaves from Gizo, we caught an onshore northerly and went surging along in a rail-down reach through the entrance channel and into the wide intricate lagoon of the town of Madang, the place we had chosen as our home for the next five months.

After the usual flap-doodle of entry formalities, Ian Barton of Customs took us off for a tour of the town in his car and invited us out that night for supper where we met other people who also invited us out, and out of that evening came another invitation. This in turn led to my being roped in to address a local organization on the disparate subjects of living in the Arctic and sailing the world in a boat. And then having been introduced there to yet more of the mostly-Australian expatriates of the town, there began another round of invitations until we began to feel a little dizzy.

Few long distance voyagers touched on New Guinea's north coast and our arrival had aroused a lot of interest. Every other person it seemed, dreamed of getting a yacht and sailing around the world, though we noticed that most of these were too busy having families or buying homes in Australia or advancing their careers to actually cut themselves loose and do it.

Madang harbour is a complex affair and we anchored in eight different places before we found the right anchorage for the season, the only corner out of the traffic, undisturbed, close to the town and protected from the northwesterlies that would set in during the summer. But those were not the only attributes that recommended our little cove, for though we were not aware of it at the time, back in the trees ashore stood a large house where lived an Austrian artist, diver and dealer in artifacts and carvings, Rudi Caesar by name.

When we arrived in his little cove, Rudi was away off up country in the bush hunting up what he called "the good stuff," old traditional artifacts carved with stone tools long before the tourist boom in native carvings. He returned home after a couple of days and immediately called us ashore for showers and beer and threw his house open to us. We were glad of his friendship for apart from anything else we needed to cross his land to gain access to the streets of the town, but Rudi's hospitality seemed to have no normal bounds to it and we got into the habit of padding quietly past over his lawn without talking so that we might not be noticed. He was forever pressing us to come in for showers or meals or coffee or long conversations. He insisted that our laundry be done in his machine, that we take advantage of his refrigerator and make use of anything else we needed, so that by gradual degrees his home came to be ours. The house itself was a virtual museum, filled outside as well as in with all manner of masks, figures, spirit boards, bowls, lime pestles, food hooks, carved canoe prows and all the other amazingly varied art forms that characterized the native cultures of the north coast. Most of what Rudi had fell into the valuable "good stuff" category and was destined for galleries and private collectors in Europe and the U.S. But he was quite capable of seizing something off the wall and presenting it without ceremony to anyone he liked, and he was quite as insistent on acceptance as he would be utterly adamant in refusing similar gestures.

Katie and I knew that a season spent in New Guinea meant a fifth year to complete our voyage and since we had originally budgeted for only four years and had spent all our money earned in New Zealand on the boat, we immediately began looking around Madang at the few possibilities of employment there. Katie was lucky (or perhaps unlucky) enough to find a job within a few days working as a receptionist at the Hotel Madang, a place known locally in Pidgin as the *hausdiring*, or house-drink.

It happened that of all the varied itinerants who found refuge under Rudi's hospitable roof, there were two at the time, both young German doctors, who were passionately fond of the traditional art of the Sepik area. Rudi had already "sold" them quite a few excellent pieces at ridiculously deflated prices, but his accounts of a recent artifact-hunting expedition through the Schouten Islands had fired their fertile imaginations and nothing would satisfy them short of mounting their own expedition. Rudi suggested to them that they charter *Nanook* and he then approached me on their behalf.

We rather liked these two, the slightly bookish Michael and the cheerful debonair Hans Ludvig ("Halu"), and the upshot was that we agreed to take them from Madang on through the offshore islands of the Schouten group to the town of Wewak and to return then to Madang in a couple of weeks. We asked for a total of only $50 each per week, much to the horror of Rudi who had planned for us to make a big killing. But *Nanook* (as the Germans were to discover) was no high powered charter vessel with private staterooms and showers, and ice cubes to go with the sundowners. She was strong and capable, but she was also simple and basic with no frills and no privacy. The higher our price the more we would feel beholden to our guests and the more they would tend to expect. We had every intention of enjoying the trip ourselves, to be two of a group of four out for a good time, and we were quite happy to make a modest thing of it.

When Katie heard that we were going cruising again, she let out a wild whoop and immediately quit her hated one-week-old job at the house-drink. Then after a day of shopping and reorganizing the accommodation below, the four of us set off up the coast.

It was slow work. First we discovered a countercurrent with a northerly head wind, then a thunderstorm blew up which sent us scuttling for shelter into Alexishafen and when we finally got out again and clear of the straits inside the island of Karkar, the wind fell away and only the favouring current kept us company. Even that was no comfort for it seemed to promise a hard struggle home again to Madang. Yet surely, I thought, those northwesterlies must set in soon?

We drifted along the coast until the 6,000-foot-high offshore volcano of Manam appeared away ahead, and with the approach of night we steered to go seaward of it as reefs lay between it and the mainland. The whole coast was a poorly charted area and the few charts available which covered our waters were on so small a scale and so vague as to be nearly useless for close work inshore among reefs. We even found islands to the northeast of us, each several miles long, represented on the charts by vague oval dotted lines and beside them the letters "E.D." (existence doubtful). Yet these were up-to-date Admiralty charts purchased from the Australian navy the same year.

Manam, chain-smoking profusely, was behind us by dawn and we altered course for the first of the Schoutens, the little volcanic island of Bam. It was much smaller than Manam and less active but it was farther offshore, more remote and bristling with valuable old artifacts, or so Michael and Halu fondly imagined. We came round to the northwest side of the attractive conical little island out of the current. There was nowhere to anchor, for the ground dropped away steeply from the rocky shore, but we lay off a cable or so while carved dug-outs were launched from the rocks and we were soon surrounded. Michael who had perfected his Pidgin working in the *haus-sik* ("house-sick" or hospital) in Madang wasted no time with formal pleasantries.

"*Supos yu-pela gat planti samting workim long diwai* (wood) *me-pela laik lukim, aiting mepela bai-im long moni. Yupela kisim* (get) *planti moni bolong ologeta samting.*"

"*Tasol* (but) *me-pela no gat planti samting. Me-pela gat liklik* (little) *tasol* (only). *Behain* (before) *wan arapela man he bai-im,*" they replied.

"*He stop long we-a* (where)?" Michael demanded.

"*Me no savvy,*" they replied. "*Aiting long Madang.*"

"*Wusat* (who's that) *behain he kam?*"

"*Aiting naen* (name) *bolong im* Rudi."

Michael and Halu looked at each other meaningfully as if something was beginning to dawn on them. "Well let's go ashore anyway," Halu said, "and see what we can find."

A big swell from the northwest, coming from our elusive monsoon, smashed and sucked over the volcanic boulders ashore and I was not prepared to risk our plywood dinghy in landing our hefty guests, so they piled into the dugouts and went ashore for two hours in the little village that lay hidden under the palms at the top of the bluffs. Katie and I meanwhile lay offshore eating lunch while naked children swam around us or climbed our ladder to run around the decks and stare in amazed delight down the hatch to the "big-down-below" which was "all-same house".

Halu and Michael eventually returned aboard acknowledging that Rudi had done a good job, but even so they managed to bring back with them some carved bowls and paddles, bone hair pins, shell and tooth armbands and necklaces and canoe prows, and even with that they had been selective, accepting only those ancient looking items that they had judged to be "the good stuff." The fever must have been slightly infectious because the log records that I also indulged in a little haggling and from this I acquired an old nicely-carved paddle for a dollar, but I discovered later that it was so riddled with worm ("liklik snake" as it is rendered in Pidgin) as to be just a shell filled with yellow dust, and not wanting to keep such a thing on a wooden boat, I threw it overboard.

We pressed on in the afternoon to the island of Blup Blup but the wind failed us of course and the diesel got us there just after sundown. In the failing light I wasn't prepared to accept the proffered pilotage of various natives who were fishing offshore in outrigger canoes so I set course instead for the overnight passage to Wewak. But not before Michael had loudly impressed on the fishermen that we would be back in a few days and to be sure to tell everyone to have all their oldest carvings ready to sell. The sixty miles to Wewak took us not only all night but most of the next day as well even with the current bearing us along.

Michael and Halu had almost filled the lazarette with the carvings they'd bought from Rudi and the people of Bam. Their plan was to offer all this stuff for sale to European museums of primitive art so they busied themselves with ferrying it all ashore to be packed up in the town for shipment to Germany. Meanwhile Katie went off up the main street to restock the galley with fresh food while I busied myself with customs clearance and refilling the water tank, and while I was occupied at the landing with the heavy jerry cans a young Australian, Bob Lachal, drove up and introduced himself. Bob was a member of Wewak's modest little yacht club and a local *kiap* or patrol officer. He was tremendously interested in us and our boat as he was an aspiring cruising man himself and ours had been the first yacht to call at Wewak in two and a half years. I brought him aboard where he enthused at length over *Nanook*'s every detail. We liked Bob and easily forgave him when he reappeared with a gang of friends long after midnight to wake us up with a case of beer.

He was on the shore again at dawn ready to drive Katie off to the native market and help with our final shopping. This done, we hauled the anchor up to the bowsprit and sailed out of the bay, eager not to waste the wind that had suddenly sprung up, and for once we actually sailed to a fresh breeze with the sheets free, round the coast to the island of Mushu. The anchorage was snug and protected but the place was a washout from the point of view of artifacts, too long missionized and too close to Wewak so we continued on next morning powering to the west over the windless monotonous sea. Porpoises came to visit us but they soon left again when they saw how slow we were; natives came out to us from nearby islands but when we found that they had no old carvings we continued on. A big black thunderstorm built up during the day and we all scrambled up on deck, soap in hands and ready to strip, but it passed us by. Almost our entire voyage along this coast was marked by monotony and frustration and it would be tedious to dwell long on the passages.

Having motored all day we came in at last to the island of Tarawai and there a rather strange thing happened. It was almost sundown and difficult for that reason to judge the nature of the bottom as we approached the southern shore.

"Let me drop the anchor for a change," Katie asked. "You take the tiller."

This was a reversal of our usual roles but I had no objection and when we came in to what seemed on the echo sounder to be a flat patch at seven fathoms I called to let go. But by the time she did so the light was scattering again on the dial, indicating a rough bottom.

Michael and Halu swam ashore and immediately disappeared in search of villages untouched by time. Meanwhile I rowed around peering into the depths nearby. We were fairly close in and I wanted to ensure that there were no shallow ledges of coral that we might drift onto during the night if a breeze should come up off the mainland. Sure enough a shallow reef lay close ahead of us and we prepared to reanchor. I hauled fathom after fathom of chain back aboard into a pyramid on the deck until the chain outboard was vertical. Then with a heavy pull I tried to lift the 35-pounder and its seven fathoms of chain clear of the bottom, but as I feared it was stuck fast. "Damn," I muttered. "We're stuck in coral. We'll have to use the engine."

The diesel thumped into life again and Katie pushed it into forward gear. The chain tightened a little, shuddered, and then began moving forward freely through the water as we motored away from the reef.

"Out of gear," I yelled. "She's free." I heaved on the chain again but to my surprise it was still bar-taut. We both heaved mightily, sweated a couple of links over the roller and had to let go. Something down there, a coral head perhaps, was stuck on the anchor and I tried bumping it off by driving again several times towards the reef, but it was not so easily dislodged. We returned to deep water.

I put another turn around the samson post, donned mask and snorkel and dived overboard. There far below, dim now in the fading daylight, were the two long serrated edges of a giant clam at the end of the anchor chain. Katie had planted the CQR straight down into an open tridacna, the world's biggest shellfish, several hundred pounds of mantle, muscle

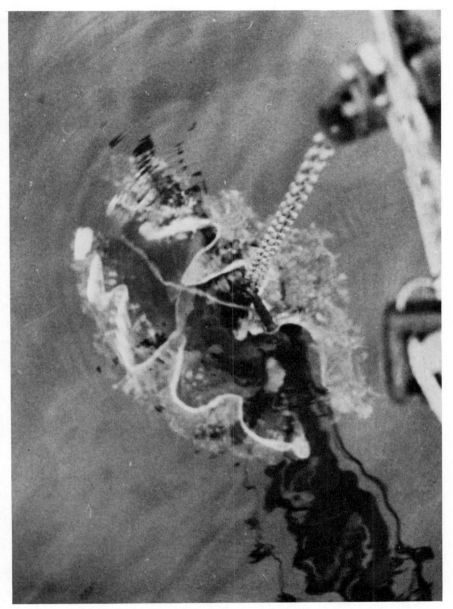

The giant clam that swallowed the anchor. Only a foot of the 35-lb. plow emerges from the enormous shellfish.

and calcium. Only a short bit of the shank emerged from inside the creature. It had literally swallowed the anchor and was torn in the process from its own mooring where it had been fastened to the bottom.

We had no windlass which would have given us the leverage needed to raise such a weight. I sat down pondering what to do next. Meanwhile, Katie who was delirious with visions of adding the monster to her already huge collection went whooping for joy up and down on the deck. This, I felt, was taking shell collecting just a little far.

Michael and Halu reappeared through the trees muttering together in German something about Rudi Caesar. While I rowed them back aboard Katie called "Guess what, guys. We've caught a giant clam."

"That's not exactly true," I countered. "A giant clam has caught us."

We then tried the chain again, all four of us but it was still too much for us and after easing the thing back down onto the bottom and setting the other CQR on its nylon line we turned in. But after sleeping on the problem and finding next morning that the great mollusc was none the worse for a night of severe indigestion, I rigged a block-and-tackle between the chain and a stern bollard. Then passing the free end around a sheet winch in the cockpit, I began gradually to lift the great weight off the bottom. After several full runs of the tackle from fully out to chock-a-block, we at last had the huge clam almost to the surface. It measured nearly five feet in length. I took a couple of photos of it. Katie was all for bringing it aboard and keeping the two shells but it was clear that together they would take up nearly as much room as the dinghy and weigh a great deal more, a difficult cargo in a small boat with all the world between us and home. Still we decided to try.

I should have put a rope around it there and then. Instead I heaved more on the tackle intending to lift the clam clear of the water and slip the dinghy underneath it. But fresh air (or its increased weight out of water) must have been the last straw for as soon as it broke surface the thing released its grip and crashed down again through the depths to its home. *Nanook*'s bow lifted an inch or so higher and I put her underway as Katie gazed in profound disappointment into the depths astern.

From Tarawai we turned east, bound for the island of Vokeo, 56 miles on and tacked all that day into a light head wind that died in the evening. We then split the night into four watches and began to motor, one steering while the rest slept on deck but it was not till the following afternoon that we reached Vokeo having sailed 50 extra miles to make up for the current.

The heat of the sun on deck was fierce but it was far worse down below with the noisy engine stiffling the torrid airless saloon with its awful heat. Katie, scornful as ever of convention, was topless under a huge sunhat while the rest of us settled only for hats and, abandoning even our beach towel "lap laps" we collapsed wherever the sails gave us shade.

Why people persist in wearing clothes at all under that equatorial sun has always been something of a mystery to me. The human form is sufficiently beautiful without them excepting in the eyes of the prudish. The white man of course has the excuse of necessity while he is under the tropical sun, being so subject to burning. My tender nose and a small but now-permanent brown patch of skin cancer on my left cheek were a perpetual warning to me to keep out of the sun's rays. But the dark people native to those latitudes have no such disadvantages, yet even they, naked though they were a generation or so back now demonstrate a coyness that would have done credit to a Victorian Methodist college for young ladies. It is an astonishing thing that the Europeans and especially their missionaries not only managed to bring their prejudices with them to the tropics entirely intact but have also completely succeeded in instilling a western middle-class sense of prudery in the minds of so many of the people of the western Pacific. The famous Sir Arthur Grimble of the Gilbert Islands, who abhorred the wearing of "filthy and unnecessary clothes," once wrote, "Clothes are now so closely associated in the popular mind with Christianity that an open crusade against them would be regarded by the natives as a deliberate assault on religion; they must now be regarded as an ineradicable evil, and the only hope to promote a habit of cleanliness and good sense in their use."

Vokeo managed to yield a few treasures to add interest to a dull afternoon in some dusty European museum. Long bone daggers were nicely etched with geometrical patterns. Michael bought a fine neck band made up of dogs' teeth and Halu bought a couple of old wooden mallets used by the women to pound sago. The handles were shaped in the form of a phallus while the two thick round knobs side by side at the end took care of the sago. They had a sense of humour in the old days. Still the haul was disappointing and in two other villages the next day there was the same story: Rudi (like Kilroy) was here.

So we left the rugged and unsheltered Vokeo and went on to Koil, the most important and attractive of the islands staying there overnight in the unexpected shelter of an offshore coral reef. From there we motored to the little island of Wiai, a place Rudi had actually neglected. But the people of the pretty little Adventist village there explained that the missionary had come over from the "big place" (mainland) and told them to destroy all their "images" "idols," and "devils," which they had done.

From Wiai it was only thirteen miles on to Blup Blup and one might be forgiven for hoping that the distance could be covered in six hours yet it took us from midnight to midday in the doldrum conditions and against the current. Upon her arrival, *Nanook* was immediately surrounded by canoes for of course she had been expected and the canoes furthermore were laden with artifacts and carvings. Michael and Halu had at last found the end of their rainbow, and once again the lazarette began to bulge.

We would have liked to stay awhile there but our two passengers were booked on a flight to Germany on the following Tuesday and we had to get them home to Madang. Neither current nor wind showed any sign of the monsoon and it looked like a long slow struggle. So off we set towards evening sailing on up in the direction of Bam. During Michael's watch that night he spotted the light at the mouth of the Sepik River but I found that its bearing disagreed with the position of the dark volcanic cone vaguely visible behind us which everyone assumed to be Bam. Not until my watch later did I discover that the island behind us was Kadovar and that Bam was still far ahead. For thirty miles progress on the log we had actually fallen back five miles. I then started the engine and turned onto the offshore starboard tack in hopes of escaping the current by crabbing away off to the north-east close-hauled to the light persistent trade wind.

By dawn Bam's cone was the only object visible and so it remained all day. During the afternoon the wind began blowing more onshore towards the mainland so that we could almost sail southeast on the port tack, and by evening Bam was at last ten miles astern of us, silhouetted against the setting sun. We were all sick of the sight of it.

Shots of Venus and Canopus at the next dawn made a mockery of the Sumlog, putting us after a full night of plugging doggedly to windward only ten miles upwind of our position of the evening before. What with making five knots tacking into the wind and against a two and a half knot current we were virtually standing still and only getting on to the southeast when the wind condescended to swing round a little.

A breakfast conference was held to decide our course of action. Getting to Madang by Tuesday was becoming out of the question. We reckoned there might be a Landrover at the end of the highway at Bogia on the mainland but that was upwind too and in a reef-strewn area within the straits of Manam where the current might be strongest. The only alternative was to turn back to Wewak and hope for a flight back from there.

This we did and in no time at all Bam was abeam of us, then Kadovar. We crossed the sharp line between ocean and Sepik River waters that swirled away to the west and in the late hours of darkness we anchored again wearily at Wewak. There were no planes that day and there was still another day and night of waiting for the next flight while *Nanook* pitched steadily into the steep swell of an onshore wind.

During this last day, the two doctors took the time to check over our medical supplies. They were horrified with what they found. Nearly everything we had, they said, was either inadequate, inappropriate or dangerous. Halu, serious for a change, told us to stop laughing and began to throw out a lot of what he unearthed. The two thereupon replaced our supplies with a variety of drugs which they'd carried with them during the voyage. We found later though that our new medical kit was even worse than before, for the instructions were all in German.

On the last morning we finally rowed Halu and Michael ashore to the airport bus and away they went. They were fun but as always two weeks were enough. Still I felt disappointed with the cruise. It should have been better but the weather and the currents gave us no breaks. We would still have to face that current ourselves but at least we didn't have the closely timetabled imperatives of modern landsmen.

Bob Lachal was there on the shore again to greet us. He carted us off in his official Landrover to see the sights, driving us out into the bomb-pocked countryside and into the hills behind the town where the Japanese had put up a last ditch stand till the American blockade starved them out.

Bob spent some time hunting around the town for carvings and finally took us down to the big carvings store at the R.C. Mission. He'd received an official request for examples of traditional Sepik art to be displayed at the Australian Embassy in Washington but they had delicately specified "no phallic carvings or naked ladies." That didn't leave him much room for manoeuvre and he was ignoring their proviso.

Interest in the rich art of the Sepik has grown enormously in recent years and with it there has developed a big trade in carvings. The missions have not been slow to join in. The R.C. carvings store occupied an enormous warehouse where the very things that were proscribed by the church many years ago are now eagerly bought by the same church and boxed up for shipment to the rich markets overseas.

"They came here to do good," Bob commented as we drove away, "and they've done bloody well."

Three days later we left Wewak again to resume the long struggle eastwards. For the first day we used a light northerly to sneak along the coast. There was no current and the familiar island cones offshore appeared at sunset. We then went offshore on the starboard tack and returned next day on the port tack expecting to leave Bam well to the west, but the current carried us relentlessly back directly onto Bam. Onto the starboard tack we went again for another night hoping to find the current easier further to the north and by morning all land was out of sight. But sextant shots showed that we had won almost no easting and we briefly resolved to return again to Wewak, and began doing so for a short time before changing our minds again and tacking on all day and all the next night.

On the fourth day a couple of very violent rain squalls presented me with two massive seam tears in the main which required some hours of stitching on the steep wet deck. I ran the diesel for an hour to charge the battery and to push us along between the squalls and after shutting it off I found that the whole engine was hot to the touch. The water pump had stuck and the thing had run for an hour without any cooling water. I opened up the water jacket cover and found that only a little water remained below the level of the cylinder. It had boiled almost dry and

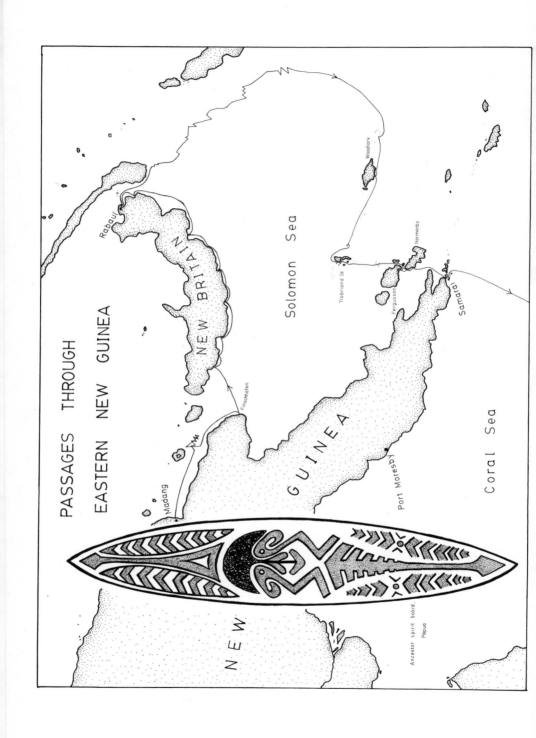

PASSAGES THROUGH
EASTERN NEW GUINEA

Madang

Finschhafen

NEW BRITAIN

Rabaul

Solomon Sea

Woodlark

Trobriand Is

Fergusson

Normanby

Samarai

N E W   G U I N E A

Port Moresby

Coral Sea

Antestor spirit board,
Papua

only the steam had been keeping the thing from cooking itself into oblivion.

A fair part of the next night was spent on the port tack heading for land, and morning found us a long way south but not much farther east. Manam lay immediately south of us and Bam was still visible to the west. Katie at first refused even to look at it, but the damned thing remained in sight all day mocking what little progress we managed to eke out of a light head wind. However by evening the wind had gone east and we were almost able for a while to lay our course. Bearings on the volcano at sunset even suggested that we were out of the current at last.

Then came another useless night getting nowhere and half a day wasted while we leaped about on a confused sea. But when the seas finally flattened we at last began stealing southeast on a light northerly zephyr so light as to be imperceptible to the skin yet for a few hours it gave us three knots until it again deteriorated into a strongish easterly. The following night we endured another series of fearful squalls from ahead which ripped the mainsail apart and I spent a wet two hours after midnight stitching a rough patch over the tear by the feeble light of the hurricane lamp.

Dawn to our disgust revealed that we had slipped back to our position of the previous noon.

But all things have their ending and two days later we finally caught a northeast wind and to our amazement no current at all, even in the Isumrud Straits where I'd expected it to be strongest, and we finally sailed in at last to Madang Harbour eight days after leaving Wewak having sailed 510 miles on the log to make good a distance of 220.

It felt good to be back. We dropped anchor again in the cove at the bottom of Rudi's garden, tied the stern to a mango tree and there we stayed throughout the monsoon season until March.

XIII

Through the Islands of New Guinea

It might be thought that sitting idly in port for several months would be boring, but it wasn't for we were never idle, and there was never time enough to do all the things we wanted. For one thing the maintenance list filled three pages of what we called the "Nanook book" and with our New Zealand antifouling paint more than six months old the first job on the list was to get *Nanook* hauled out and repainted which we managed in between the first great downpours of the beginning monsoon. Soon after that job was disposed of and *Nanook* returned to the mango tree, Katie contrived to get a typing job in one of the government offices. That was no small accomplishment at the time for independence was just around the corner and with the controversial "localization" of jobs in full swing Papua New Guinea was no place for the expatriate job-hunter. Even the "Old New Guinea Hands" who were the backbone of Madang's establishment were either packing up and going home to Australia or gloomily contemplating it. The good times, it seemed, were over.

It happened that Rudi at the time was also planning to go down to his other home in Melbourne but only for the summer holidays, and he asked us if we would like to move into his house and to take care of his two dogs in his absence. Would we? He had no need to repeat himself. In a short time we took up residence in the spacious house amongst the spirit figures and ancestor boards, and for seven weeks we luxuriated in the civilized comforts and the vast coolness of the place. Nothing could have been better. *Nanook* lay moored down at the end of the lawn where I could work on her. We had a modern kitchen, shower, refrigerator and double bed, all cool and airy and spaciously quartered behind mosquito screens under a leak-proof roof.

So Katie went off to work and I started on the maintenance list. All the interior varnish (and there was a great deal of it) had become soft and

213

gluey through age and tropical humidity, and the time had come to strip it off completely and replace it with five or six coats of an expensive but marvelously tough two-part synthetic varnish. That meant stripping the interior and filling Rudi's house with doors, rails, panels, table flaps and everything that could be unscrewed, and then working alternately between house and boat. Every surface had to be worked over and it was a long hot business especially on board. The monsoon season had set in with long nights of torrential rains. The days were usually sunny but there was no wind in the cove and the humidity and heat were so great that I streamed sweat from the moment I went below, and even though I kept a towel within reach I worked constantly in a pool of sweat at my feet. I eventually broke out in a fiery red heat rash around my waist and had to lay off the long hours of sweaty scraping and sanding until it cleared up. But at last everything lay covered under a glassy sheen of new varnish that accented the light and dark woods attractively, and after replacing everything we were delighted with the lustrous new appearance down below.

Then I turned my attention to the sails, reinforcing, patching and restitching by hand along many of the seams. Rudi's large living room made an ideal sail loft. We had bought a new mainsail in New Zealand but with my habitual frugality I had kept it stowed, and continued to use the old original main all through the islands. But the voyage back from Wewak had taught me a lesson and I retired the yellowed old main and bent on the smart new white one.

Ours was not the only cruising yacht seeking the shelter of Madang through the northwest season. Soon after our return from the Schoutens, two other yachts showed up, both of them American and both single-handed. One was the 25-foot Vertue sloop *Kittiwake* owned by Ed Boden who had spent many years slowly drifting his amiable way west from Britain. Ed was a great talker who loved to spice his tales with salacious limericks of which he knew several hundred. He had just come down from Manus and had had an even tougher time with the current than we'd had from Wewak, having spent ten consecutive days within sight of the island of Karkar. But Ed had no engine. He was a sailor in the purest sense, the only cruising man we ever knew who was a perfectionist for speed and efficiency under sail. After transitting the Panama Canal he was sick of his troublesome auxiliary so he lifted it out at Balboa and dumped it gleefully overboard. The strange thing though was that he was tremendously competent mechanically and could fix anything, a valuable talent that had assured him of the affection of islanders all the way across the Pacific. His vast array of tools was worth over two thousand dollars. Quite an inventory for an engineless little boat.

The other yacht was the little ketch *Mei Maru* owned by a young medical doctor Earl Hanson, who was a single-hander more in theory than in fact for he had the habit of signing on beautiful girls along the way and had arrived in Madang with an Australian girl Kathy who was not only beautiful but demure, intelligent and unaffected as well.

So the little cove became a kind of small floating community, a place where, with friends from the town, we gathered in someone's cockpit or on Rudi's porch for long rums and longer conversations. Earl and Kathy went off to the New Guinea Highlands together to work there for part of the season and left *Mei Maru* in our care.

At this time some of the larger towns of Papua New Guinea like Lei, Port Moresby and Mount Hagen were feeling the curse of growing crime and racial tension. We were glad to find that Madang was friendly and relaxed despite its size and comparatively long history. Native people greeted us pleasantly as we passed them on the streets or in the market and the commuters from Kerosene Island across the harbour smiled and waved at us as they passed each day on their way to work. These people all came from the Sepik River and being "one-talks" or people from the same area with a common language, they kept together in their own community on the island. They commuted to the town in dugouts and it seemed a strange thing to see well-dressed civil servants complete with white shirt, tie and briefcase slowly paddling their long river canoes across the harbour to civilization. As all the river people of New Guinea do, they stood upright, six or eight of them to a canoe and each with a paddle long enough to reach the water. They had no outrigger yet they never showed any signs of capsizing.

It was easy in such a relaxed place to improve our Pidgin, and I gradually came to use the language with some confidence. It differed considerably from the Pidgin of the New Hebrides. While in Vila I had bought a copy of the New Testament in the Pidgin of those islands. The book was titled *"Gud Nius Bilong Jisas Krais"* (Good News Belong Jesus Christ) and it was a useful introduction to the language and its orthography, but in Madang there was no need of texts. The ubiquitous language flavoured even the English of the expatriates. "Thank you too much," one would say in acknowledging a small favour, to which the other would reply "Oh it's something nothing." But for all its amusing twists of the English language it can also be poetic and imaginative. In what other language can you refer to berries and fruit as the children of trees *(pikinini bolong diwai)* or speak of fire shit *(sit bolong paiya)* when you mean ashes?

A man arrived on his "wheely-wheel" (bicycle) one day at Rudi's house to sell a *garamut* or carved snakeskin drum. I asked him if he could play music and he said oh yes he had learned once. He couldn't play the drum but while at the mission school he learned to play the *bokis-yu-paitim-tis-i-krai,* the box that cries when you fight (hit) its teeth. He meant a piano.

There was one job that should have been down on the maintenance list

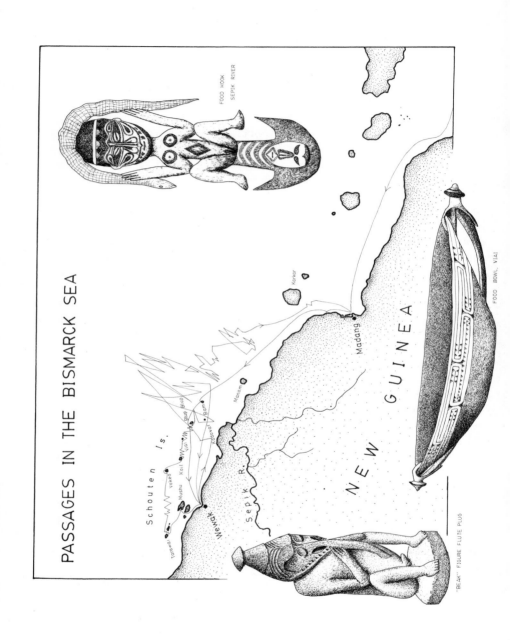

PASSAGES IN THE BISMARCK SEA

FOOD HOOK
SEPIK RIVER

FOOD BOWL, VIAI

"BEAK" FIGURE FLUTE PLUG

Schouten Is.

Tarawai
Yakeo
Mushu
Koil
Viai
Blup Blup
Kadovar
Bam

Wewak

Manam

Karkar

Madang

Sepik R.

N E W   G U I N E A

but wasn't. The two Douglas fir masts had always been sheathed in fibreglass but perhaps from being so long in the humid tropics the wood had swelled slightly and the sheathing was in the nasty habit of splitting vertically along the sides. Neglect could only result in rot entering the wood. I went aloft several times in the bosun's chair to seal up the cracks with resin and prevent the entry of moisture in the hopes that the problem would quietly go away. But of course it didn't and early in March just as we were preparing to leave Madang I finally decided that something had to be done.

So the masts came out. We were lucky to know a man who had Madang's one mobile crane and to have a friend in the fisheries department who gave us the run of his warehouse where the two masts were then stripped of all their hardware and sheathing. Katie by that time had quit her typing job in anticipation of departure and was on hand to help. I took the main and she the mizzen (that having been by tradition "her" mast since I never liked the idea of her working forward on the deck at sea) and together we sanded the bare wood, saturated it with an epoxy wood preservative and coated it with a tough two-part paint. When all was ready a week later we called on some local men to help carry the two heavy masts down to the waiting crane on the dock. Katie and three natives helped me first with the cumbersome main and after negotiating several streets and holding up the traffic on the corners we collapsed at the wharf to rest until the other gang showed up with the mizzen.

But the other gang never appeared. I walked back to the warehouse to find out what was holding them up but men and mast were all gone. I went out and looked up and down the road. There was no sign of them. I stopped motorists and asked neighbours if they had seen a bunch of natives walking down the street carrying a mast on their shoulders but all I got were stares and head shakes. Katie then appeared and we took alternate routes back to the wharf but without result. However our hired helpers were eventually located on the main road over half a mile away heading off at a half trot for the other side of town. Either my Pidgin wasn't as good as I believed it to be or someone in Madang was trying to build a boat on the cheap.

This incident didn't exactly amuse the impatient crane operator, nor was I in stitches myself, but my brother George in New Zealand managed when he heard of it to put the thing into this perspective:

> *Nanook's* mizzen mast went missin'
> When the main was on the beach
> And the skip' was fussin', cussin',
> And the mate began to screech
> "If the skip had not unshipped it

But had left it standing fast
Then it wouldn't 'a gone a-missin'
Would the missin' mizzen mast."

Yes the mizzen mast went missin'
And the mate was spittin' mad,
It was the worst by far, so far
Of all the trials they'd had.
"You abo rogues," the skipper yelled,
(Whose missus was a-fizzin')
"Bring right back here, you thieven' hounds,
The missus' missin' mizzen."

It was March and it was time to go. The seasons would soon change and we had to catch the last of the northwest winds out through the Vitiaz Straits. New Britain, the eastern end of New Guinea and the Great Barrier Reef of Australia all beckoned us on. So after a final frantic week of provisioning, of parties and of taking friends out for day sails and picnics up the lagoon we put out for the last time through the entrance channel of Madang's harbour and turned the bows east.

"We have lingered in Madang longer than anywhere else," the log records, "and we are sad to leave it. Particularly so since the weather is gloomy and we feel slightly hung-over from so much socializing in the past week. After shopping this morning for a few final things we went back to Rudi's and gave him a farewell gift of a book on primitive art. Unfortunately he then presented us on impluse with three assorted bottles of booze, worth more than the bloody book. We then lifted the anchor for the last time and sailed out. Now, sunset, feeling depressed as we watch the Coastwatcher's lighthouse flickering its goodbye astern of us."

We split the night into four watches and for that night and the next day and night we drifted slowly eastwards, watching out always for drift logs from the Sepik River that were by then so numerous along the coast. Early on the third day a light head wind from southeast came up over a glassy sea and this gradually increased. We tacked into this for most of the day but the seas became very rough and by nightfall conditions were dreadful, so down came the sails and we lay ahull all night in turbulent conditions.

The new 12-volt battery that I'd bought in Madang had been poorly secured and it tipped over during the night and spilled a lot of acid in the bilges, making a tremendous stink in the cabin. I had to turn out and add water to all the cells and flush the bilges with buckets of seawater. After that I was, as the Australians say, a bit off me tucker. One of the rigging screws came loose, the whisker pole fell from the lifelines onto the deck and began rolling all over the place, the chart drawer opened and spilled charts all over the soggy floor, and a wave struck and cascaded through

Fighting into a fresh trade wind, *Nanook* plunges into some wild water near Normanby Islands, eastern New Guinea.

the hatch and onto Katie's bunk just as I was slinking out to the cockpit to lash down a sail that had flogged itself loose.

In the early hours I found that Long Island was getting embarrassingly close under our lee so I raised the staysail to carry us south and the dawn found us exactly where we were 24 hours earlier. I was hoping for shelter somewhere along the steep mainland coast but the wind eased during the day and switched around to northwest when we were close in so we pressed on again for the Vitiaz Straits passing the Sio light at the entrance after sundown.

A heavy southeast swell persisted as did the unexpected northwest setting current coming at us, but the weather through the night was all from the west and as wild, wet and dark as it could possibly be, especially during Katie's watches as so often happened. We both got thoroughly soaked several times over not just from the rain but from the crashing wave tops that the conflicting conditions kicked up. Progress against the current was agonizingly slow. It took nearly all night to get out of range of the Sio light, and as the wind eased with the dawn I had visions of being carried back through the strait by the powerful current. By 1000 I had to start the diesel to augment the light wind and for two hours after that *Nanook* with her throttle wide open just barely managed to keep up with the land.

Great massive mountains lay to starboard, all terraced by ancient upthrusts, a long series of beaches all reaching back many hundreds of feet up the steep slope in giant steps. Strangely enough there was no forest, just a few trees in the gullies and along the coastline.

We edged inshore to cheat the current and found that we could creep forward there by infinitesimal degrees from one tree to another, then from one gully to another, fighting for every inch. Gradually we struggled up to Fortification Point and found there that we had at last pulled out of the cursed current. The remaining daylight hours then allowed us to cover the distance to the shelter of Finschhafen though only just for we arrived in fading twilight. We wouldn't have attempted an approach in full darkness. The little engine had pushed us at over 5 knots with no wind for the last few miles, saving us from another night standing watches in the falling drizzle at sea. I recorded in the log "Had a long rum to celebrate and a delicious curry supper. The satisfaction of winning that strait and of reaching shelter before another night makes it seem *almost* worthwhile to suffer so much."

We were anchored overnight in the outer harbour being afraid of the narrow entrance in the dark and the first surprise next morning as I took in the riding light was to find two other cruising yachts leaving port. Both Australian, they were heading together for Rabaul and we called to them that we would see them there in a couple of weeks. The second surprise was to find Finschhafen to be almost completely deserted. It had once been the German colonial capital and during the war with the Japanese it was for a brief time an enormous allied city. All that remained were gaunt old tumbledown warehouses and wharves slowly crumbling into ruin, and the rusty hulk of a Japanese munitions ship sticking out of the water in the middle of the harbour.

The anchorage was as peaceful as it was beautiful, totally landlocked and the sort of place any sailor would love in a cyclone. A few natives lived in the area and we ran into a couple of Aussie old-timers, Tom and Paddy, who filled us with beer and tales of the way it used to be. Paddy drove us in his Landrover one day into the nearest town nine miles away and there we stocked up with loaves of bread and ground beef. We hiked around, swam, collected shells and at sundown each day answered Paddy Watt's summons to help out with the cold beer in his "house-wind," a little building without walls that commanded a view of the harbour on one side and the ocean on the other. The house wind is a New Guinea planters' tradition. It is usually a simple affair roofed with thatch and open to the cool breezes, with a table and chairs and a view of the sea, a place to relax in for an hour and to regain a little sanity and perspective at the end of each day. We loved sitting there in the evenings staring across at the distant peaks of New Britain and talking to Paddy of the old days.

Tom lived on a pittance from a man who had made his million in Finschhafen selling wartime scrap. He was engaged at the time in removing calcium deposits from trochus shells before bagging the shells up for export to Japan. To do this he threw them into a cement mixer and the appalling racket of those heavy shells hour after hour crashing incessantly around inside the mixer finally sent us on our way through the narrow entrance and out into the quiet sea.

Our plan was to cruise along the seldom-visited south coast of New Britain till we reached Rabaul and from there make south for the many islands that lie to the east of New Guinea in the Milne Bay District. The weather as we left was exquisite. A ladies' wind filled the sails and the atmosphere was so clear that I could take bearings on peaks sixty miles distant.

The following morning we arrived in Arawe, a complex inlet near the coral-infested west end of New Britain. The one indifferent chart of the area gave no hint of where to anchor but some native men came out to direct us in to the spot used by coastal boats. A big crowd of natives gathered on shore to meet us and out of the crowd stepped a jovial English planter, Ron Wells, who asked us up to his fine home on the hillside for a huge evening meal.

We remained in Arawe for two days, absorbing the peace of the little place. Katie bought a number of shells and found some of her own after dark with the aid of the Tilley lamp. I spent half a day on the hot beach patching up the dinghy with fibreglass and paint. While the paint was drying, I swam out to *Nanook* for a cup of coffee and some of the natives, kids mostly and women who had overseen my labours with great interest, swam out behind me and climbed aboard for a visit.

A seven hour sail carried us across a small gulf to Mowe Harbour where we found the settlement of Kandrian, a small government sub-district headquarters. The log records "The plan of Mowe Harbour is the most inaccurate and misleading chart I have ever used." We anchored in three places before discovering next morning that despite what the chart indicated, we could easily moor in a cove close beside the delightful little settlement. It was one of the prettiest spots we ever saw. Katie joined some of the local women to wash the laundry in a sparkling stream at the head of the cove while I, male chauvinist, refreshed myself in a deep swimming hole further upstream. Some of the local *kiaps* joined us in the evening for drinks in the cockpit and carted us off to their home for a meal. This was a pattern of hospitality that repeated itself all along this quiet coast.

We put to sea again after two nights and sailed down Passismanua (passage man-o-war) between the mainland and a parallel line of high flat-topped islands, ancient coral reefs that had hefted themselves far up out of the sea aeons ago. By mid afternoon we were in Ablingi Harbour where we stayed two days. The next daysail took us to Linden Haven and the next brought us into the harbour of Fulleborn. At each of these places the same thing happened; the local plantation manager came to the beach to meet and talk with us on board, and invite us in turn to the hospitality of his home. They all seemed so surprised and pleased to see us entering and anchoring, a welcome interruption perhaps to the isolation and routine of their lives. We found as we proceeded east that people were actually expecting us before we arrived for we were being announced ahead of time over the little network of transmitters along the coast.

At one place in the long lagoon at Linden we anchored off a sizeable river and rowed upstream to do the laundry. After breasting the current for half a mile between walls of thick jungle we came to a dark limestone cavern. Here the river spilled silently out of the bowels of the mountains. We rowed far into the spooky cave disturbing clouds of black bats while the dinghy twisted around almost out of control in the upwelling water. At the cave entrance we climbed out onto the rocks and washed the clothes in the cold deep stream and then returned to drape *Nanook's* rigging with laundry.

After leaving Fulleborn we picked up an unexpected current that carried us east so that we made good passage times into the St. George's Channel, up to the little landlocked harbour of Put Put and on to the town of Rabaul where we anchored near the yacht club in a wide circular harbour surrounded by high volcanic slopes.

Rabaul was fun and we stayed there a week. The town was once the

German capital as well as the headquarters of the Japanese thrust during the Pacific campaign. The yacht club very kindly extended their privileges to us and there we met several other cruising yachts including the two encountered in Finschhafen and the red Belgian yacht *Tiare*. She was owned by Paul de Smet who had built the little steel sloop himself in Belgium and sailed her single-handed to Tahiti. Like many other single-handers before and since Paul found it hard to leave Tahiti, but after several years there he came west again with his Tahitian wife Vaiea and their son Petit Paul, or Liklik (little) Paul as he was known to the youngsters on the Rabaul waterfront. Like us, Paul and Vaiea were bound west for South Africa and the Atlantic. They were a lot of fun and we were glad that we could expect to see them again later in the Indian Ocean.

As always our budget took more punishment than it was designed for, but we had a lot of provisioning to do, charts, films, grog, rope, tinned meat, Primus parts and paint. I had to overhaul the capsized battery. Katie bought white and pink murexes at the huge Rabaul market and for our use in the remote islands that lay ahead we took on boxes of trade tobacco, long twisted strips of black tarry-looking leaf and a supply of betel nuts. These items were important because many of the little islands to which we were bound were populated by addicts of these things which they could not grow for themselves on their sandy atolls.

Finally, one more movie at the club, one more beer, and it was time to row out and stow the dinghy. Our last night in Rabaul was disturbed in the early hours by a very strange slop in the harbour which set *Nanook* dancing about her anchor like a ballerina. I was not usually bothered in my sleep by any amount of normal motion, but this had me wide awake at the instant. Next morning as we motored around saying goodbye to the people on the other yachts we learned that they too had been woken by the sudden agitation. It was caused by a sharp earthquake.

The weather while we were in port had remained clear, dry and settled but while at the club we warned our cruising friends to look to their anchors and their rain-catchment awnings, for, as I said, *Nanook* was ready for sea and that meant a change for the worse in the weather. Paul disputed that our departures could aggravate the Fates any more than his own did, but we were able to show him next morning for we were not even around the sheltering headlands before a furious rain-laden squall struck down at us and wiped out everything around us from view, all that is except the little volcano nearby at the southern entrance which was smouldering profusely in satisfaction at having interrupted our sleep.

An interesting complex of low islands, the Duke of York group, lay at the northern entrance to St. Georges Channel and we intended to take anchorage there until a favourable wind came up to take us southeast into the Solomon Sea. It was well into April and the trade from the southeast could be expected to set in at any time and according to the local Rabaul yachtsmen the channel became nearly impassable against the weather once the trade established itself.

On the chart the Duke of Yorks looked very appealing and the shelter they offered seemed even more so when a wide black wall of rain and wind descended upon us out of the north. By that time we were close in to the group and we had to decide whether to take shelter as we wanted to, or continue on as we knew we should. It looked like a very dirty night indeed but we had learned often enough not to neglect a fair wind, especially one at the end of a fair season, so we carried on south through the night, riding forward on a small storm just as we had through the Vitiaz Straits and by dawn we were off the southern tip of New Ireland. By that time our northerly had expired, the sky had cleared and we were confronted with an unexpected southwest-setting current coming down the east side of New Ireland. It was tramping along at three knots and cheating us of our precious easting so in the absence of a wind we had to use the diesel, steering due east and moving scarcely east of south.

The kindest thing to be said of the next four days is that progress was slow. We were bound south and I knew that the further south we went the harder the wind would be and the closer we would have to haul the sheets. So first I concentrated for two days on getting well over to the east against the coast of Bougainville so that the remaining miles would be across rather than into the wind. We found the sea flat at first until a chop from the southeast set in, heralding the trade. That made motoring pretty unprofitable. It is quite enough for a little engine rated at 4½ horsepower to push 11 tons of boat over a flat sea but it is quite pointless to fight a choppy sea, so we gave up on motoring and lay 45 miles off the Bougainville coast waiting, as the log says, "until Somebody does something."

That took another three days. We caught occasional breezes and we motored briefly till we grew sick of the noise, but we mostly lay becalmed while *Nanook* gradually turned in circles on the slight swell. Quite irrationally I would spend twenty minutes at a time holding the tiller hard over to one side or the other to keep the boat from pointing in the wrong direction, staring in frustration all the while at the compass. I am not gifted with the philosophy and patience of an Ed Boden and after three days of this I let fly with a whistle. Katie of course who always hated that old sailor's remedy for windlessness treated me to a sideways glance of horror and rebuke but within the hour we had the response of a nice breeze. *Nanook's* bow again resumed a healthy gurgling sound and away we flew.

The wind of course became far too strong during the night. Disgust and seasickness drove Katie below in retreat to her bunk while the sky smeared over and a near-gale kicked up big breaking seas. The next day was worse. With so much south in the wind we had to keep close hauled in order not to lose our easting and this meant a tiresome motion that was hard on the gear and worse on ourselves. There was no blue sky at all, and for getting positions I had to rely on dawn sights of the moon and one or two uncertain shots of the sun. The first of the many islands that extend out from the eastern end of New Guinea lay within a day's good sailing but with such uncertain navigation I began to consider the idea of lying ahull until the sky cleared. However the following night produced a few breaks in the overcast so we eased the sheets a little and pressed on nearly across the wind which had settled to a steady Force 6. Sights next morning were not much better thanks to cloud, violent motion and a tossing elusive horizon and each shot indicated a position only very slightly ahead of the previous one despite rapid sailing.

At one stage a big steep grey sea threw us far over on our beam. At the time I was waiting for a chance at the sun and in trying to protect the watch and the old brass sextant from spray, I lost my wedged-in position against the main boom crutch and went slithering violently across the coachroof. My right shoulder came up hard against the keel of the dinghy giving me a painful jolt and nearly jerking the sextant out of my hand, but at least it stopped me from continuing on into the lee scuppers or worse. I thereupon resumed wearing the safety harness which I had earlier discarded as a confounded nuisance. We both realized that if we ever had a "man overboard" in such conditions he would assuredly stay there. Katie might not miss me for an hour or more, and the chances of her returning on a reciprocal course and finding me were ludicrously remote. After that I was careful in such conditions to keep the harness on even if I wore nothing else.

My few rough sun sights and the steepness of the seas both suggested a current setting eastward into the wind and the result was that the landfall that I'd expected towards midday was finally made at dusk, a hard-won anchorage in the lee of remote palm-fringed islands. There we lay in blissful peace for several days while the sun shone out of a clear sky, a gentle trade hardly disturbed the tops of the palms and the great seas wore themselves out with crashing on the long coral reefs.

Our immediate objective was the Trobriand group to the west where we had planned the previous year to wait out the monsoon season. Time as always drove us on long before we were ready so that we gave the lagoons and islands of Woodlark only a cursory visit before pressing on again through the Marshall Bennett group to the little island of Kitava, close to the main islands of the Trobriands.

Kitava offered only one anchorage, a slot between the main island and a small islet offshore and we very happily took it for the weather was kicking up again by the time we got there. W.A. Robinson visited Kitava in *Svaap* and the place appeared to us to have hardly changed since those days except that the one white man of the island, a trader with a large harem of girls, had died shortly before, happily no doubt, and his house was in a state of ruin. The grass skirted girls it must be said looked quite as beautiful as they ever could have.

We had caught a fine colourful dorado while approaching along the coast. Part of this we gave away to the numerous kids who came out to visit us, each dressed in a green freshly picked loin leaf, and for a couple of days we dined on the rest, deep fried in batter, with boiled yams, while the tidal streams in the anchorage between Kitava and the small islet ticked off the miles on the Sumlog.

Katie had a bad throat and a slight fever all this time and she began taking antibiotics which gave the impression of helping her. But I felt concerned for her and decided after a couple of days to quit Kitava and press on to the main town of the Trobriands where medical advice could be expected. Katie came on deck rather weakly to help manoeuvre the dinghy onto its chocks and away we went again, timing our departure at 0315 to coincide with what I calculated would be a favouring tide around the northern end of Kiriwina the main island of the Trobriand group.

The following wind of course soon gave up, and the favouring stream of course was no such thing. To the contrary it swept us eastwards around the headlands as if it had urgent appointments elsewhere. But if we found this frustrating we were at least by then well inured to such things, and long perseverance eventually brought us around to the roadsteads on the east side of the island. Losuia the capital lay at the head of a wide shallow bay and we found that in the absence of any beacons to mark the one-fathom channel we could get no closer to the town itself than three miles out, and there with about six inches to spare under the keel we dropped the anchor. Half an hour of rowing along the shore next morning revealed a gap in the trees and in the hopes that this might reveal a road, we put in. Sure enough, not only was there a dirt track but by coincidence a Landrover as well, driven by an Australian *kiap* who was heading into town. Katie's charm halted him and while the Aussie filled us in on the local scene we bounced along between the trees past large villages on stilts and into the rambling administrative headquarters of Losuia.

No callow student of anthropology who has sweated his way through Malinowski's classic study *The Sexual Life of Savages* can possibly have failed to dream of a lengthy visit to the Trobriands. But any who do so now will be disappointed. The place has been discovered by the Australian mobs in Port Moresby and while tourism has flourished, so the traditional culture that brought the tourists in has fallen into decay. Always and everywhere it seems, it must apparently be so. Put in a big airstrip and a fancy hotel and say goodbye to the past. But at least for the time being all tourist traffic to Losuia (other than ourselves) had come to a halt. The hotel had burned to the ground.

Basically two things brought the tourists to the "Trobes." One was the culture and the attractiveness of the people, the women particularly who wear a short thick bouncy grass skirt slung low on the hips, sometimes with a provocative gap on each side. (In Losuia they wear dowdy cotton dresses.) The other attraction was the great variety of wood carvings made there, an art form that has changed to satisfy the demands of the tourist industry. These were far more formal than the Sepik styles, consisting largely of utilitarian objects, lime pestles, stools, utensils and the like, incised with abstract designs although there were many also that were simple illustrations of Trobriand tradition or even sardonic commentaries on modern life like the one we saw of a stern faced missionary attempting to haul apart a pair of copulating pigs.

We went to the post office to send mail off home, bought the usual loaves of bread and generally wandered around marvelling at the untidy boxy little houses, the dirty calicoes and the general havoc wrought on the culture by a few brief years of tourism. Katie obtained a little token tray for two dollars from the United Church which was doing a roaring trade in carvings and then we wandered back down the long road to the boat.

Losuia should have been put into perspective by a visit to one of the out islands, but these offered poor anchorages or none at all and since anyway we felt pressed for time we sailed away to the south to the shelter of the plantation island of Muwo.

As usual Katie trailed a fishing line astern but having no success at that she decided to go ashore to Muwo for hermit crabs to use as bait and to catch something for supper in the anchorage. However she caught supper of a different kind for on the beach she encountered the plantation manager and his wife, a kindly middle-aged couple who lived alone on the island except for a few transient workers from Kiriwina. They asked us to their house-wind for sundowners and later to their home for showers and dinner. We chatted on and on with them on a wide variety of subjects until quite late, enjoying their warm intelligent company and wishing that we could repay their kindness. Towards midnight we returned to the dinghy and as they said goodbye on the beach they gave us two dozen fresh eggs from the chicken shed, insisting that they had more than they could use.

South from Muwo our course lay for many miles over fairly shallow ground that was littered with scattered reefs and shoal patches, none of them marked. The passage was a navigational test that I had studied and fretted over for months beforehand. A few low islands lay scattered about but they would not be visible for the whole passage and would be useful as aids for the precise navigation needed only when close by them.

We left Muwo early in the morning with a nice trade wind that was not too far into the south. The sky was clear and I spent the whole day on deck with chart and hand-bearing compass, measuring off the miles, taking bearings and checking off all the shoal patches and ledges as we passed them. In the clear sunshine the passage proved simple enough for each reef appeared ahead as a patch of pale green or brown against the deeper blue and they ail showed up exactly when and where expected. Far to the south the little volcanic peaks of the archipelago of the Amphletts grew larger as we approached, helping to keep us on our course, and by late afternoon we had come up with them. The Amphletts were almost devoid of anchorages but with the help of an old American wartime chart we were able to drop the CQR in eleven fathoms close in against the sharp peaks of the little island of Wamea which looked like St. Lucia in miniature. This wasn't a comfortable berth by any means, but there we stayed the rest of the day while canoe loads of grass skirted natives came out to sell vegetables and hand-made pottery. Until early morning we endured the uncertainties of the place while wild rain-laden gusts struck down at us off the peaks and caused the long anchor chain to keep up a dismal sleep-disturbing rumble all night on the rocky sea bottom.

Before dawn we were away again with another long day of tricky sailing ahead. We had to weather the big island of Fergusson and that involved dodging a great variety of dangers, rocks, reefs and islands as well as an assortment of currents. Our course ran first through a scattering of rocky islets on the outskirts of the Amphletts. All of them were well smothered in white water for a big swell was running out of the southeast. Before we had drawn clear of this nest of trouble the whole lot were wiped out from sight by a drenching thunderstorm, thick, wild and prolonged. Compass bearings taken in haste in the early light before it engulfed us gave us a position and steering blindly by compass through the deluge we cleared the whole area before the ugly reefs and islands all reappeared again out of the grey curtains behind us. Seldom did we endure so much rain as fell on us that morning and never at such an inopportune time.

Gradually the wind then dropped as the grey pall lifted and we were left motoring slowly all the way round the east end of Fergusson Island. A line of reefs extended all the way from Welle Island across a narrow strait to Fergusson. We had to cross this barrier but we found the chart and the Admiralty Pilot equally unhelpful about finding a way through. To add to that problem we found on approaching the line that we had light grey skies, no wind and a glassy-grey sea surface which meant no visibility of shallows until we were right over them. Worse, a current was bearing us down onto the barrier. So we approached with very great caution. From the ratlines I caught brownish glimpses of banks close to starboard and indications of more further out to port. But a slight ripple ahead suggested a flowing stream through a gap and taking that as a cue we motored slowly into it, holding our breath while coral heads suddenly appeared under us, sweeping rapidly by under the keel. And then we were clear.

Shortly after getting through we were visited by some grass-skirted ladies who were fishing in a canoe. They wanted to trade for tobacco but all they had to offer apparently were some smoked fish. We accepted one for a stick of tobacco and had it for lunch. They'd no doubt intended it for their own lunch but they were pleased to settle instead for the tarry stick of nicotine. A customs officer with some years in the Territory later insisted that it was themselves who were the intended item of trade for the stick of tobacco, not the fish. Life is full of lost opportunities.

Another coral bar was then crossed but one that was well charted giving us four fathoms underneath as well as a large bonito on the fishing line, so we entered Dobu Passage not only with fish inside us but with 24 pounds more of it flapping in the cockpit. It was our experience that fish could easily be caught on or near reefs whereas the line might trail uselessly astern for many days in the open sea.

To port lay the island of Dobu. A big mission establishment lay among the palms on the island's sandy lee. It must have had quite a job to do in the beginning for the people of Dobu had a fair reputation in the early days for unfettered cannibal savagery. They had for example, after raids on neighbouring islands, the unpleasant habit of breaking the leg bones of their surplus victims and leaving them on the beach, not quite on the hoof perhaps but at least fresh and unlikely to escape. And there the meat supply was left until appetite restored itself. The early missionaries for all their narrowness and too-frequent abuse of power must have been very brave men.

At the end of a long day we entered a wide bay on Fergusson's south coast and anchored a short distance off Kedidia, a plantation run by Merv and Mary Preece. Merv came out to meet us long before we arrived telling us where to anchor and inviting us ashore to his ranch-style home for showers, beer and *kai* (supper). The same remarkable pattern of plantation hospitality repeated itself. We felt enormously indebted to so many of the kind Australians who lived out their isolated lives along the coasts of "P.N.G."

Merv was quite a character. He spent the evening passing what the Australians call stubbies, or small bottles of beer, and regaling us with fascinating stories of his years on Fergusson. His wife Mary produced for us a really magnificent stew. It tasted rather like beef but not exactly and we wondered what it could be. It turned out that Merv had been dugong hunting. Perhaps because of its flavour this great clumsy-looking mammal was once known as the sea-cow. The natives at any rate translated it that way. For some reason sea or salt water is rendered in Pidgin as soda-water and bull-o-m'cow means cattle. Hence in Pidgin a dugong is a "bull o m'cow belong soda-water." And that's what we had for supper.

From the sea we had noticed white columns of steam rising up out of the bush and we asked Merv about it. A short distance from the plantation, he explained, was a thermal area of hot springs, boiling mud and geysers that play at regular intervals, a sort of miniature Rotorua. We decided next day to look it over. After rowing a mile along the shore to a village we found several young folk eager to show us the way. Half an hour of steady hiking back into the bush brought us into a wilderness of noisy fumeroles, splashing geysers and smelly mud. Hot water flowing out of the pools built up crystalline terraces and flowed away in hot lifeless streams. It was an eerie place.

The next morning we sailed across the strait to Normanby Island and out into the open sea where we had hoped to get on south towards Goschen Straits. However a fierce wind was howling right at us up Normanby's western flanks. We tried fighting it but after plunging wildly into the steep seas for half an hour and finding it no easier away out from the coast we turned tail and scurried back to take shelter at the northern end of the island. But once in the lee of the mountains I managed to persuade myself that I was wrong, that the wind must be quite local and probably short-lived, so we sailed out again on the port tack. An hour later after an even worse thrashing over a sea covered with roaring whitecaps I felt sufficiently educated and we retreated to anchor in a small bay near Direction Island at the northern end of Normanby.

We were quite alone for there were no villages nearby. Katie started in on her old varnish routine while I put the pot of pitch on the stove and began attending to a number of insidious deck leaks, scraping the old pitch out and repouring into the seams. In the afternoon three girls came around the point to investigate us. One of them got a second-hand dress out of Katie. She was very thrilled by this and later after the girls had gone home her papa came paddling around the point to ask if we'd really given his girl the dress, or did she steal it? Having established that here were people who gave things away, he wondered aloud whether we might happen to have any tobacco, and being emboldened by a stick of the stuff he then asked for playing cards. Horrors! The Australian administration had long before placed a total embargo on the importation of playing cards into the country, for many of the natives proved inveterate gamblers. Yachts were sometimes asked to declare their playing cards upon entry, and these presumably were then sealed up pending departure. We did have a spare pack and we gave it to the man. He was ridiculously pleased at this and came back later to present us with a large bunch of bananas, four green coconuts and a big bundle of pumpkin leaves.

The wind eased up after two nights and we pressed on down the coast stopping in at little overnight anchorages until we had only one passage left ahead of us before clearing the country, the long sail down through Goschen Straits and across Milne Bay to Samarai.

Leaving our last Normanby anchorage just before dawn we hauled the sheets close to carry us towards the wind and across the straits. I'd neglected to lash the radio down properly before setting out and while we heeled sharply over it fell out of its shelf, crashed across the chart table,

Children of eastern New Guinea gaze in wonder at *Nanook*'s interior.

bounced off the steel supporting rail and thudded onto the floor. It then refused to work which didn't surprise us. We felt gloomy about it for Samarai was no place to hope for repairs and we needed the thing to confirm the chronometer for the very exacting business of navigating through the Great Barrier Reef.

Sailing through Jackdaw Channel at the extreme eastern tip of the mainland we watched for several minutes as *Nanook's* shadow raced with us over a shallow green bottom. We then eased the sheets and away we flew with a nice beam wind that sent us surging along at a steady seven knots. This was the only really decent sail we had since the passage from the Solomons the year before. It was our final passage in New Guinea waters and almost as if it was pleased to be getting rid of us a favouring tide carried *Nanook* easily down through the China Straits and into an area of many high islands, and there in the midst of them all we came close in to the little island, town and port of Samarai. Here not far from two big double-hulled sailing canoes from the mainland, we dropped the anchor.

The previous year when we then planned to enter the country at Samarai I had arranged for mail to be sent to us there and at my request this had been readdressed to us in Madang. While in Rabaul I'd written to the Samarai post office advising that we were on our way there and asking them to disregard past introductions and to hold all further mail. We went to the post office and sure enough my letter was ignored and all our mail was in Madang. We would have to wait.

This news was exasperating enough without the apparent indifference of the man behind the counter. Patience they say is a virtue easily fatigued by exercise.

"Never mind," Katie said. "He's quite right, we'll just have to wait." We cooled ourselves off with a stroll under the shade trees to the Customs building.

Samarai was our port of exit. When we first entered the country in Madang I'd been required as all tourists were to post a bond of $280 to guarantee our exit from the country, this despite the obvious enough fact that we already possessed the means to leave. From Rabaul I'd written to the Samarai authorities asking that they have my money on hand ready for the time of our departure. I now discovered that they had not taken the trouble, and instead the starchy young Australian on relief from Port Moresby insisted that we actually had to leave the country before we could expect the bond to be refunded. It could not be paid on departure. Since the intention of the bond was simply to guarantee our leaving, I thought this was a bit thick. It could be sent to us in Australia, he said, within two weeks of our departure. Knowing the state of tropical torpor that pervaded the civil service of the country I regarded that as rather optimistic. I pointed out that we were not Australians and had no address

Nanook received her regular six-monthly coat of anti-fouling paint on the Sariba slipway near Samarai, eastern New Guinea.

there. He suggested we get one. I then suggested that he didn't know his job and informed him that the Madang customs office arranged these repayments routinely to foreign-going yachts at the time of their departure, not afterwards, and in return for this information he then suggested that I was a liar. As it happened we were held up for a whole month in Australia waiting for the money, ample time to regret that I had not choked the wretch there and then.

> That which in mean men we entitle patience
> Is pale cold cowardice in noble breasts.

In disgust we sailed out of Samarai's lee to the overnight shelter of Kwato, a pretty anchorage formed where three islands converge. At least I accomplished something that day for before turning in I had the radio working again.

On the nearby island of Sariba was a boatyard with a slipway and engineering shop owned and run by an elderly Australian, "Bunny" Burrow who had lived most of his life in the area. It was half a year since our last antifouling in Madang and since we had to hang around Samarai for a while anyway we carried the tide upwind to Sariba to meet Bunny, and we arranged with him to have *Nanook* hauled and repainted below the waterline.

Bunny invited us to his home where Mum Burrow served us with delectable curried chicken. Bunny plied us with beer and his many recollections of the old days in Papua when life was tougher, simpler and more fun, and even Mum let drop a hint of nostalgia for the early days before the war when she lived in Port Moresby and knew Errol Flynn.

In a couple of days, *Nanook* had a new coat of copper on her bottom though not a very good coat as it later proved for I'd been deceived into judging the Rabaul factory product by its prestigious brand name rather than by its low price. The only difficulty was returning to the water, for the lower end of the slipway rails were well silted over and we had to awaken the "boys" in the middle of the night to help heave us off the cradle at high water.

While motoring into the dock next day to pick up the Burrows for a visit aboard we suddenly lost power as the diesel fell silent. This couldn't have happened at a better time for Bunny's shop was well equipped and some of the native men were competent mechanics. They hauled us alongside with a small island trading boat and soon had the engine head off and the problem traced to worn valve guides.

Repairs were made next day and the thing put back together again. The only problem arising from this incident was the fact that we were once again well and truly overrun with cockroaches. They were all over the decks next morning having boarded us from the trading boat alongside. They were under the cockpit grating, they hid in the furled up sails and

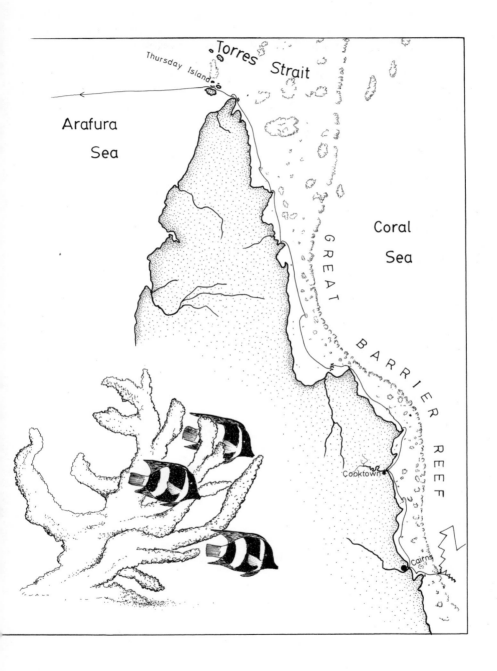

Arafura
Sea

Torres Strait

Thursday Island

Coral
Sea

GREAT

BARRIER REEF

Cooktown

Cairns

they skittered out from under the sail bags. Many had found their way below. We had completely rid ourselves of the pests while in Madang and now had to resume our old habitual state of unremitting war.

Our mail from Madang gradually dribbled into Samarai while we spent our last few days cruising amongst the many islands to the east. Katie gave away to the local people the remainder of our trade items, clothes and tobacco mostly, for it was now goodbye to the beautiful islands and islanders of the South Seas.

Reports of high winds and seas on the Queensland coast for the past week had helped soften our impatience with the post office but the weather picture improved just as the remainder of our mail arrived, so with clearance papers, minced beef and fresh bread on hand, we rowed aboard and stowed the dinghy for the passage to Australia. Just at sundown we sailed past the deserted and beautiful Dumoulin Islands which, as all remote uninhabited islands do, seemed to have about them an aura of mystery. In the dark we crossed over the long sunken barrier reef, several fathoms deep, that parallels the Papuan coast and set our course south into the Coral Sea.

XIV

The Coral Coast

Australia, me lads, is a mighty fine place
Heave away, heave away,
And to go there me lads is no disgrace
We're bound for Australia

So sang the British tars outward bound for New South Wales in the old days of convict settlements and square rig. We for our part were bound southwest for Cairns, the northernmost town of any consequence on the Queensland coast. I steered with the wind right on the beam well south of the rumb line so as to have some easting in hand should it be needed at the end when we had to thread the Great Barrier Reef. Yet I couldn't hold too much easting because long unmarked reefs lay awash upwind of the course. The Coral Sea is a dangerous place with an appropriate name.

The weather remained clear for three days and we were beginning to regard it all as a piece of cake until during my first watch of the fourth night a load of dark cloud came rolling up from the south, blotting out the stars, and a hefty wind soon got up from ahead, making it necessary to reduce sails and then soon after to reduce them again until for the last part of the night I took all sail off in disgust. After a rough and rainy night the wind suddenly dropped so I again hanked the genoa on the forestay in place of the jib, and raised the unreefed main. Soon after with the wind again increasing, I again replaced the jib for the genoa, reefed the main and started bashing into steep seas, hard on the port tack. Dense rain showers surrounded us. Katie was bunk-ridden and everything was thoroughly unpleasant. The following night, matters were not much better, and since dead reckoning put us fairly close in to the Great Barrier Reef I took all sails off and we lay ahull.

Dawn brought its own unwelcome surprise when sights of Venus and a star snatched through the fast-flying cloud above us indicated that we were 25 miles north of Grafton Passage, our gateway through the Great Barrier. This put us well downwind so I wasted no time in setting sails and

237

away we went close hauled on a hard wind and regretting every mile we had lost to the bad weather. The clouds allowed me to catch the sun twice later in the day and although these sights were not to be trusted they did suggest that we were doing battle with a coastal current. The conditions were really awful and I spent nearly the entire day crouched on the foredeck in my wet weather gear peering ahead through the rain and spray over the long high seas.

In that area the outer edge of the Great Barrier Reef lay 25 miles from the continental coast so in such thick weather we knew better than to expect to see the mainland from the open sea. The reef itself lay awash just at the surface. It had no islands on it, and it could be identified only by the white water that breaks perpetually around its edges, but only then when close in to it, perhaps a mile or so distant. Only one thing could help us find the passage, and towards the end of the afternoon I at last spotted it, a tall steel tower with a light on it, erected on Euston Reef, a little isolated scrap of coral at the entrance to Grafton Passage. There it was, a solitary little vertical pencil mark seemingly in the middle of the ocean, in a wilderness of grey skies and sea and spray. We were on the port tack when I saw it several miles away off to port into the wind. Our hearts lifted with great relief and I put about to tack up towards it, holding it in sight with the joy of gazing at something solid, though my happiness was dampened a little by a big whale that kept station with us for an hour and a half blowing his wet breath over the decks.

By evening we were close to the tower and I could see the first hints of white water on the reefs away to starboard. I had to decide whether to enter the passage in the dark or to stay out for the night. Katie was inclined to stay out. Normally a night entry would be no problem, for a powerful light on Fitzroy Island near the mainland guides ships between the reefs with its beam and when the Fitzroy light began to blink at us under the lifting murk, I decided to try the passage. But we were only four miles in when more rain blotted Fitzroy out again so before we lost sight of the light behind us on the Euston Reef tower, I turned back seaward. Some time later the same thing happened. Fitzroy light reappeared. I turned again to try the passage only to abandon the attempt three miles in as more rain blotted out the coast. I had no idea what currents might exist inside the reefs and I had no faith in groping our way by dead reckoning. By this time Katie was in tears. I sailed back out past the tower and punched eight miles out to sea on the starboard tack, far enough to overcome the estimated effect of the current during the night hours, and there we lay ahull the rest of a miserable night while torrential rain slashed over the decks and dribbled down onto the bunks in three new places.

Sleep was out of the question. I was worried that the Euston Reef was now lost from sight although it could hardly have been otherwise in such heavy rain. But I kept looking out for it anyway, as well as for ships. The masthead light was switched on for their benefit. Early in the morning I noticed that the bilges were making an ominous slopping noise and discovered they were filled with water almost to the floor boards. I baled them out with a bucket, dumping the water down the galley sink and then found the cause; the casing of the Sumlog cable had lost its clamp and slipped off the through-hull fitting.

An hour from dawn the rain stopped and the Euston light reappeared right where it was expected. I raised sail again, feeling life come back to the boat as she steadied her roll and gathered way across the waves. I steered for the light, passed its tower at sunrise, altered course in to Fitzroy and by midday we were running in sunshine through milky coastal water close to the hills of Queensland.

Before entering Cairns we sailed into the shallow waters of Mission Bay close to an Aboriginal settlement and anchored there to clean ourselves and the boat up. Everything above and below was wet and salty. The interior was a sordid mess littered with towels and ropes, dank charts, wet clothes, sailbags and unwashed dishes. I always found it hard to be methodical and fastidious in stormy weather. This awful mess was soon put to rights and in pleasant afternoon sunshine we sailed on up a long dredged channel to Cairns.

The harbourmaster waved us alongside his dredge and he managed to catch the Customs people for us before they closed for the weekend. We'd heard bad things of the Australian Customs but the formalities were brief and courteous and as our feet strolled the busy streets of the town our heads were in the clouds. No landfall to date had been tougher than that one and no arrival sweeter. We felt fabulous.

Cairns (pronounced as "Kens" in the Strine language) was a pleasant friendly town, retaining still the courtesy as well as the numerous verandahed two-storey pubs of earlier days. Shopkeepers took the time to chat to their customers and motorists (miracle of miracles!) pulled up to a halt at any intersection if we gave them so much as a slight hint on our faces that we wanted to cross. Not bad for a town that swarmed with tourists. It was June and Cairns received a deluge of sun-seekers from the cool drizzly southeast every winter season. The town was laid out on one side of a river that flowed down through the high hills from the tablelands inland. The other side of the river was a wilderness of mangroves and mosquitoes and it was on that side out of the traffic of the port that *Nanook* lay in line with a number of other yachts, her anchor in mud and mosquito screens over her hatches.

We had planned to spend only ten days or so in Cairns but several things conspired to hold us there for a month. Both of us stood in need of dental work as well as vaccinations for Indonesian visas. My chronometer watch took it into its head to stop and, new batteries being of no avail, the

On Fitzroy Island inside the Great Barrier Reef, Katie gets acquainted with the natives.

thing had to be mailed off to Melbourne for repairs. The same thing had happened in New Guinea and at first, thinking of the large repair bill and not wanting to throw good money after bad I went off in high dudgeon and bought a $5 alarm clock, resolved to use that to navigate across the Indian Ocean, together with another spring watch and the radio, but at the last minute I got cold feet and sent the thing off to the agents in Melbourne asking them to return it to me on Thursday Island.

A few memorable days were spent cruising out of Cairns to islands inside the reef. At one of these Katie made the acquaintance of a pair of wallabies and she soon formed such a strong attachment to these two, and vice versa, that I had some difficulty in getting her off the island and back on board, but in that I had the assistance of an old friend and colleague of Baffin Island days, Judy Wilson who had flown up from Sydney to join us for a few days.

We also had other friends right in Cairns itself. The town was popular as a place of retirement with many of the "old New Guinea hands" who wanted to remain in the tropics. Bill Lewis and his wife Pat were in that category. They had spent many years with the Lutheran Church in "the Territory" and retired from Madang while we were there. Now they devoted several days to driving us long distances back into the Queensland interior through sugar cane country, rugged hills, gentle green tablelands and parched empty lands of ant hills and scrubby eucalyptus.

There was a lot of shopping to be done for the months ahead on the Indian Ocean. (One of Katie's supermarket sales slips was seven feet long.) Some celebrating was called for too, our tenth wedding anniversary for one thing which fell in the middle of the month, and on *Nanook's* account there was the matter of her circumnavigation for she had crossed her own outward-bound tracks from Sydney when we came in through Grafton Passage.

As expected the landing bonds from Port Moresby delayed us longest. They had still not arrived when everything else was checked off the huge list of things to do. Every day we rowed crab-wise across the strong-running tides in the river to the wharves on the town side, and walked along to the Customs building where the money was to be sent, and every day the same man looked at us regretfully and said, no, there was still nothing for us from Moresby. Several telegrams sent off in that direction resulted in a grudging acknowledgement that payment had been "approved" (whose money did they think it was?). After nearly four weeks of this the man at Customs who had assumed from our persistence that we were more or less penniless, offered us a personal loan. I was as grateful for this as I was astonished at such concern for a stranger coming from such an unexpected quarter. Happily we were not all that hard-pressed for cash. However I had no intention of sailing on up inside the Reef thus putting ourselves downwind of the 280 dollars that lay gathering dust in the vaults of Port Moresby's lethargic bureaucracy, particularly when it belonged to no one but ourselves.

Still all things have an end. "Seek and ye shall find. Ask and it shall be given. Knock and it shall be opened unto you." Two more telegrams and a cheque finally arrived.

Once I had that all converted into traveller's cheques we stowed the dinghy and on June 30th we waved goodbye to new-found friends in the anchorage while *Nanook* caught the ebb tide downriver and filled away to begin the long passages up the coast.

With Cairns behind us we had little to expect but a long coast of strong winds and wilderness. The waters inside the reef are well charted. Generally the bottom is nearly flat with a slight outward slope from a fathom or so at the coast to around twenty fathoms along the inner edge of the Great Barrier Reef which lies from 20 to 50 or more miles out. The problem is that the inside waters are studded all the way along with isolated coral reefs, most of them unlit and most without even the virtue of dry land on them. Some people sail at night. Joshua Slocum sailed the entire length of the Reef with only two anchorages plus a small bite taken out of the edge of one reef. Even today that would be quite a feat for a single-hander. But quite apart from a question of seamanship, few yachtsmen who pass that way could be so short of either time or curiosity to want to barrel straight through in the fine style of Slocum, and we were no exception.

Nanook fled along, glad to be out of the river and into the wind. A sail lay far ahead of us and when we reached the shelter of the Low Islands forty miles on we found whose it was, a young couple on the sloop *Ticia*, a steel thing from further south.

"We are right on spring tides," so the log records, "so we liberated a few shellfish, cones mostly, at low tide from amongst the colourful coral heads, and rums later on board *Ticia*. The trade is a piping Force 6 and very cool."

We got away next morning ahead of *Ticia*, bound as she was for the Hope Islands. The weather was more changeable with rain squalls blotting everything out periodically. I had to make a number of sail changes initially to overcome a tendency on the part of *Ticia* to creep up on us. I have always felt a strong dislike of the ethic of competition, yet whenever I found a sail gaining from astern I could never resist taking all possible precautions to keep it there. We left *Ticia* well back and away off course and reached the Hope Islands in a drenching squall fifty minutes ahead of her.

Nanook and her crew at anchor in the lee of Green Island inside the Great Barrier Reef.

Despite a high wind we went ashore to retrieve a few more shells, deer cowries in particular from the sandy flats inside the reef edge, and oysters for supper as well as a few shrimps which, impaled on a hook, secured for us a couple of small fish that Katie flipped over the capping rail. These, with the oysters, soon joined a couple of Cairns potatoes and an onion in a chowder fit for Captain Cook himself.

The great navigator had passed this way two centuries earlier and had more than his usual share of problems when his ship *Endeavor* ran onto a reef. He was not even aware at the time of the existence of the vast Great Barrier to seaward. Divers had recently located the site and worked over it. While in Cairns we were interested to read an official Notice posted in the Customs building there.

Notice of Wreck

Jetsam in the form of an anchor with dimensions of approx. 13 feet in length and 5 feet in width between the flukes. Anchor reportedly jettisoned by Lt. James Cook R.N. at Endeavor Reef in 1770. Also one-and-one-half tons cast-iron billets in the form of ballast.

Endeavor Reef lay just six miles into the wind from our anchorage.

The crew of *Ticia* came aboard *Nanook* for long hours of interminable yarning while hard lashing winds and low visibility kept us pinned in the lee of the Hope Island. There we stayed for another day and night until in easier weather *Nanook* was able to sail into Cooktown, on the Endeavor River. This is where Cook careened the badly leaking *Endeavour* after his tussle with the coral reef. Cooktown became a gold rush centre in 1873 and was preparing to celebrate its centennial. More than a million ounces of gold were taken out of the area officially, and probably as much again smuggled out to China. Cooktown had been a city of over 20,000 and many more thousands of diggers lived along the neighbouring rivers. The gold field itself had 97 grog shanties and 163 brothels. The Centennial Committee, I thought, might be hard-pressed to match that. A few bedraggled passive-looking Aborigines hung around on street corners. If contemporary accounts are to be trusted the natives of Cooktown were cannibals a hundred years ago, not turning their noses up at the occasional white man although they preferred Chinamen for they didn't spoil themselves with rum and tobacco.

Cooktown seemed to us a funny sleepy little place with hardly a building that could have been less than forty years old. Somehow it seemed to me to lack the flavour of other gold rush towns like the Klondike, but as the man in the post office said, the romance of the past can best be rediscovered only after an hour or three in one of the two remaining pub bars.

My reason for going to the post office was to collect a telegram which some waterfront character happened to know was waiting there for us.

This confirmed that the chronometer was being sent on to Thursday Island and the cost was only $19. This was good news, especially as my new $5 alarm clock had taken it in its head to run for only three hours after each wind. Buoyed up by this news I wandered off up Cooktown's one street in search of the aura of history so recommended by the man in the post office.

However it was not out of any interest in the distant past that we came in to Cooktown unless old Bill Lewis himself could be said to personify ancient history. He and his wife Pat, our friends and hosts both in Madang and Cairns had been all eagerness to take us up on our offer of a cruise for two or three days, but as it was not convenient for them while we were in Cairns to come along with us as far as Cooktown they boldly asserted, to our amazement, that they would meet us in Cooktown and sail with us all the way north to Torres Strait. This took the wind out of our sails a little for we always felt that any long passage in the confines of a small boat imposes too great a strain on friends and friendship. We would not have dreamed of suggesting such a cruise ourselves, but these people at least we could not possibly refuse. Sure enough Bill and Pat showed up on time cheerful and eager and ready to go, Pat laden with medications for Old Bill, and Bill laden with fishing gear. And so we left, all four of us, bound for Thursday Island.

Our first anchorage out of Cooktown was in the lee of Cape Flattery, a wild area of rolling hills and snow-white sand dunes, a well chosen spot except that *Ticia* happened to be there already, having bypassed Cooktown, and as I expected, those interminable talkers were into their dinghy and rowing our way before we could get our own dinghy overboard and ourselves ashore. There are two kinds of talkers it is said, those who talk because they have something to say, and those who talk because they want to say something. *Ticia's* crew was the second kind. Still, Bill and Pat, themselves more advanced in years than in reticence, were almost a match for our visitors from *Ticia* so leaving the two men talking in the cockpit, the two women talking below and Katie sprawled on deck with a book, I rowed off in search of oysters and solitude. The cape itself lay at some distance and I returned two hours later after a successful reconnaissance of the area. Not that I found any oysters. *Ticia's* crew were still there, still talking, but they were finally driven away by the imminence of "tea", six fried trumpeters (for Bill had not been idle) and chips.

Each day we made another long step up the coast, anchoring usually behind one little coral key or another. We were surprised that the lands around us as well as the sea were so unlike the island groups of the open Pacific. They are exposed to the same southeast trade wind. But gone was the lush green tropical forest. Dunes, ant hills and open scrub took their place. Only once did we see a couple of coconut palms on the offshore islands and I suspected them of having been planted. Gone too were the crystal waters of smaller islands. Big lands mean big rivers, and big rivers mean silt. Despite it being the dry season the water was generally a milky pale green and some coral reefs right at the surface could be identified only by the breakers on them rather than by any changes in colour.

By the time we reached Cape Melville the steady dependable trade wind had miraculously stopped, almost like an electric fan in a sudden power failure. The seas fell flat and all the world was suddenly silent. The radio soon gave us the reason for this; an unseasonable low pressure trough had cancelled out the usual high to the south of us and was ripping the guts out of southern Queensland with cyclonic conditions that brought devastating floods to the land and havoc to shipping. But it's an ill wind that blows nobody good. We were now up to the Flinders Group, basking under a cloudless sky and decided to use the calm as an excuse to linger amongst the five high islands of the group, scrambling far up through the thorny bush to the topmost peaks and exploring the passages and anchorages among the islands and gorging ourselves on fish and oysters.

Bill was a keen sports fisherman, and the *aficionados* of Queensland liked to get out to the edges of the Great Barrier Reef where all the big ones were. But Bill was not long in discovering that *Nanook,* being in a bit of a hurry anyway, did a great deal more sailing than fishing and avoided even those reefs close to her course. We trailed his lines astern all the way north without much success but as soon as the anchor was down each day, he was off around the rocks searching for bait and casting around for one fish or another, and this he did so successfully that we never had to open a tin of meat all the way to Thursday Island.

Some yachtsmen who carry firearms are able to shoot the occasional goat on the offshore islands but we dislike guns with a passion and never carried one even for self-defence. The only "weapon" we carried for that purpose was Markusie's walrus penis bone which I kept hidden at the side of my bunk. A blow from that could have caved in the skull of a gorilla.

With the wind back in business, we were off again sailing northwards and lengthening our stride to sixty miles a day. Pat and Bill were adaptable to the life and good fun, and if they regretted our unremitting pace they gave no hint of it. For an active Lutheran mission worker Bill was gratifyingly liberal in his philosophy. He dissented openly from the stern strictures of the church and entertained us with raunchy tales of his own youth and with fascinating glimpses of the way life used to be in the New Guinea bush. All through the western Pacific I was constantly reminded that mission work was and still is largely the preserve of people whose minds if not exactly closed are at least greatly limited by background and doctrine. So very seldom is it the calling of such free-thinking people as Bill. He must have been an embarrassment at times.

Perhaps that's why he and Pat were stuck out there for so many years amongst the Kukukuku tribe, reputedly the wildest bunch of bush-whackers ever to prowl the hills of New Guinea.

The final passages were more of a problem than the earlier ones with stronger winds and a longer fetch from the far away Barrier Reef that lay 90 miles out into the wind. Also the distances from one sheltered anchorage to another became so long that we could no longer expect to cover the daily passages entirely in daylight hours. Still they gave us no trouble other than to provide me with my usual portion of wasted worry, and just eight days from Cooktown we gybed around the northernmost tip of the continent and came round into the lee of an island poised directly off the extremity of Cape York.

Here we ran aground. The cloudy tides sweeping through the narrow gap between island and cape had altered the sandy bottom since the old surveys and for a moment we were stuck fast. This was only our second accidental grounding, the first having been in the Balearics, and although we had a current and an offshore wind to help us into deeper water, as well as a rising tide and a forgiving bottom of sand, I was annoyed at my carelessness. Some people are able to take mishaps with equanimity. That may well be a good quality but it isn't one of mine. A few of our cruising

With the Pacific behind them Katie and Maurice stand near the top of York Island, a short distance from the northernmost tip of the Australian continent.

friends were famous for the number of reefs and shoals they had gone onto and they treated the resultant dents to their keels with as much indifference as they did those to their reputations.

We were not there long of course. *Nanook* lay slightly over at an unnatural angle while Katie held the tiller up and I hurried forward tripping over the sheets to unlash the dinghy and the kedge anchor. But meanwhile Bill had not been idle. As he explained it later, a quick silent prayer was offered up, "Please God, don't let it happen," and at that moment the keel slipped sideways off the edge of the bank and we were free!

Most of the next day was spent in the anchorage behind York Island waiting for a favouring tide to carry us on to Thursday Island. The tidal streams that sweep the reef-strewn channels of Torres Strait are complex in the extreme, seeming almost in some places to defy analysis or prediction. It pays to study the tables as carefully as the charts and we were pleased to find that a foul morning stream gave us time to explore the wild windy desolation of the Cape. It was a land of hot rocky hills, dry scrub and a forest of eight-foot anthills. From the summit of York Island we gazed down and across the narrow tide-ridden channel to Cape York, the end of the continent, and felt pleased that we had not sailed west from Madang but had come to Australia instead.

Twenty more miles in the afternoon and the Pacific at last was behind us. What a vast ocean it is, stretching back, in our vision, to the Miraflores locks on the other side of the world. What variety and interest it contains within its far-flung rims. Beauty and danger and the delight of discovery are still there in abundance and always will be. An amazing variety of island groups lie scattered over its surface. We touched on so few of them. What people live there on those islands, and how well they still understand how to live!

Change is the eternal condition. Tahiti and the Societies are being transformed by western investment into a new Hawaii. New Zealand seems determined to do the same thing to Rarotonga. Fiji is aswarm with hotels and jet-borne tourists. The old days are going out and age-old values with them and it's a great mistake to sail into the Pacific in search of the romantic lotus lands of Gauguin and Stevenson and Jack London. Even the G.I.'s of World War II would find their old Pacific gone.

Still, a few remote islands linger even yet, isolated as they are by distance and their own unimportance, where the 20th century seems hardly to have intruded. Only a yachtsman has much hope of reaching them and hopefully not even too many of them will disturb the rhythms of these quiet happy places. Some such places we visited and out of a love for them just as they were I feel reluctant to identify them. Yet before we turn our backs on the Pacific I must turn back briefly and mention two of these island paradises.

XV

A Backward Glance

We arrived at the little Melanesian atoll just at sundown. It had been a long hard passage to the place for it lay far upwind of its neighbours. We felt our way carefully in on the lee side not knowing quite what to expect for the chart showed only the dotted edge of the reef. The outer rim of the atoll was pounded by a tremendous roaring swell that exploded continually over the seething reefs. But the entrance was easy and the lagoon was crystal clear with a shallow sandy bottom. The usual necklace of *motus* or low sandy islands lay strung around three sides of the lagoon, seven of them covered with palms. Villages lay on two of them, and from their white beaches canoes put out to meet us and to gesture to us where we should anchor. Having no suitable chart, I was willing for once to accept a local opinion but there immediately arose a dispute between our self appointed pilots, each wanting us to anchor close to his own village. These were all equally sheltered so we settled the matter by choosing our own spot.

The dinghy was thrown overboard. I then put the engine into reverse to dig the anchor in and in so doing snagged the dinghy painter in the propeller. So overboard I went with the diving mask and began tugging at the tightly wound rope. Three native men joined me in the water and we worked away at it for half an hour in the failing light, communicating with grunts and bubbles. Finally, just as I went up the ladder for the bosun's knife to cut it away, my helpers wrenched it free. By then it was practically dark and as we were tired I made signs that we would sleep and with a smiling nod the men paddled back to their homes.

Next day, by some general understanding, was Visitor's Day. It started early and it finished late and at noon when it was at its peak a tremendous thundery deluge drove the whole kit and kaboodle below for shelter. Canoes were abandoned, decks were cleared and twenty-five people all agog at their new surroundings crammed below excitedly to sit out the

Melanesians, using their traditional pandanus leaf sail and carved outrigger canoe, sail by *Nanook* across the lagoon of their little atoll.

next two hours in the torrid confines of the cabin. The men and boys wore only the wraparound cloth or *lap lap* of the South Seas and the women and girls all wore grass skirts. Nobody on the whole atoll wore anything more or anything different.

The first day was something of an endurance test and when we finally got rid of the last canoe load Katie spent half an hour sweeping up bits of dry grass that lay scattered in and over *Nanook* from stem to stern. When she was finished she said wearily, "I wonder if we had everyone on board today. I hope so because I couldn't stand another day like that one." We hadn't, and for the next week the visitors kept calling, but they came in smaller numbers, less frequently and stayed briefly so that we enjoyed the times when they dropped by. The only problem was that no one on the entire island could speak English or Pidgin. One young man knew about 15 words of English and therefore considered himself fluent but for the most part we had to make do with sign language. It worked well enough. I began compiling a little dictionary of common words and this helped bridge the gulf.

From the start it was clear enough that what everyone wanted, and expected to get from us was one thing, tobacco. The whole population had an unbelievable craving for the stuff. Fortunately we had prepared ourselves for this beforehand by laying in a quantity of the twist tobacco that can be procured in any Chinese store in the western Pacific. I also had a bag of betel nuts mouldering in the lazarette and when I produced these on the first day and demonstrated that they were for all and sundry to take, there was an instant rugby scrum on deck, a mad scramble of grass and brown skin, and the nuts were gone in an instant. Areca palms don't grow on atolls. Some of the visitors emerged with large handfuls but most came out with few nuts and many scratches. There was no sharing with each other and as little thanks to me. They were perfectly honest, as islanders usually are; nothing was touched on board that shouldn't have been, much less taken, but they lacked the spontaneous joy and generosity of Polynesians. Everything was an item of trade. There was no store on the atoll and money didn't exist so while we remained there tobacco became the unit of currency. In just a day, the log records, we bought "three carved canoe prows, an ebony fork, a bunch of bananas, assorted shells, a lime pestle, a paw-paw, a yam, half a pumpkin and a young suckling pig," all for stick tobacco. The people were crazy for the stuff. It could buy anything that the atoll produced, fruit, fish, livestock or artifacts. It could buy not only a grass skirt, but also the beautiful dark wench inside the grass skirt.

Although these Melanesian atoll dwellers may have fallen short of the Polynesians in warmth, laughter and geniality they surpassed them in the beauty of their villages, in the great skill and care evident in the construction of their traditional houses and in the building of their ornate traditional sailing canoes. Round the edge of each village compound, the houses stood high up off the clean sandy ground on stilts. Each had two or three rooms. Floors were made of parallel slats, bound together with fibre rope and covered with woven matting. Windows were simple squares in the woven walls with rolled up mats ready to cover them in bad weather. Each house had a notched post for a ladder leading up at an angle to the doorway. There was no such thing as a nail, hinge or anything else not produced on the atoll, just as there was not on the sailing canoes. These lovely craft criss-crossed all day long as people went fishing or gardening in the far islands. The canoes were supported with outriggers and decorated with long strings of glossy white egg cowries and strips of a fibrous leaf. Intricate designs were carved into both ends of the canoes and the larger ones had a wide platform of slats between main hull and outrigger. The men themselves had given up the traditional pubic leaf for the cloth *lap lap* but there was still not one cotton stitch on any of the canoes. Each carried a pandanus leaf sail hoisted at an angle on a short mast and these performed well on the usual reach across the lagoon. They didn't look as if they could go to windward but when I went out with one of the men, I found that in fact they could.

Some of the large sailing canoes were still used on trading voyages to other islands far over the horizon to the west of the atoll. I wondered at first that most of our visitors were women until I discovered that many of the men were away at the time on such a voyage. After leaving the atoll, we met the crew of one of these canoes at another island. They had taken with them a supply of fish and grass skirts and were trading these for tobacco, manioc, fish hooks and cotton cloth. I asked them about the return voyage far upwind but they just smiled and said, with their hands, that they would wait for the wind to go more into the south and then they would be off. No problem.

The beautiful women of the atoll not only knew how to wear a grass skirt. They knew how to make one. They sent them off in the trading canoes to sell at other islands and it was not long before they began sizing Katie up for a new outfit. When in Rome, do as the Romans. I liked wearing the belted *lap lap* of printed cotton cloth from Fiji and I wore it whenever it seemed appropriate to local custom. But I thought Katie might draw the line at the topless, scratchy-looking fashions of the atoll. Yet in this I was wrong. A full flouncy looking mini was soon made to fit her and before long she was swishing her way around the atoll like all the rest, the trade wind rustling past her hips. No one of course paid the slightest attention when she first appeared topless. This Katie noted at first with great relief, and later with the faintest pique. Women are irrational. For the rest of our stay there she wore just the grass skirt but as we sailed away at last it was stowed by her bunk and never worn again. It felt, she admitted, exactly like wearing a bale of hay.

The other little island paradise further back in the Pacific was Polynesian, a small scrap of land two miles long and far from any other island, populated long ago by Tongans who were blown far away off course. As we approached this little land we noticed when still about ten miles out that we were being signalled by people on shore with mirrors. A sail on their horizon was evidently a rare thing and our arrival was something of a sensation to the little place. Before we were able to anchor in the lee of the high peaks, *Nanook* was surrounded by dugout canoes filled with throngs of people and more gathering on the beach. A few climbed aboard at my beckoning but the rest were held off by the first barrier of outriggers against the hull. We found hardly anyone who could speak English but later after sending the CQR and chain down into ten fathoms and rowing ashore in convoy, we met a man, Farava, who stepped out of the huge crowd on the beach to shake our hands and welcome us in English to the island. Farava, though not a chief himself, belonged to one of the ruling families and had picked up his English while fighting in the far-off campaign against the Japanese.

A big crowd gathered around us. Most were dressed simply in a "calico" or wrap around cloth (the *lap lap* of the Melanesians), some of them made of *tapa,* the only instance we ever saw of Polynesians still making and using the old fibrous material to dress themselves. Many of the children wore nothing. Both sexes were bare to the waist and many of the adults had long blue tattoo designs down the centre of their chests.

We explained who we were and where we had come from.

"Is the world really big?" one old man asked when he heard how far we had come.

I assured him of it. "We have sailed more than two years now and we are only halfway around it," I said. Gasps of surprise accompanied Farava's translation.

"Have many yachts come to this island before?" I asked.

"Oh yes," they said. "Many."

"How many?"

"Three," they replied. "The last one came six years ago."

"What does your own island look like?" another asked.

I tried describing Ellesmere Island. "It's a big land," I said, "where the sun stays below the horizon for 100 days every winter." (More gasps.) "It's too cold for trees to grow there. The people wear many clothes to keep warm and they catch animals to put fur around their faces so the wind cannot blow hard on their skin."

Utter silence while John translated. "On long journeys," I went on, "they sometimes make houses of snow, and the cold is so great that the sea freezes solid and you can walk on it." All this took some digesting.

"When the people want to drink do they eat snow?" one asked.

"No," I replied. "Big pieces of ice fall off the land and into the sea. Some are bigger than ten ships. Some are nearly as big as your island. Small bits are broken off by the people and melted on a fire for drinking."

This was discussed at some length and I began to wonder if I was being regarded as a more notable liar than traveller.

The old man finally said, "It is good you have come here. It would be better to be dead on this island than alive on that one."

Next morning Farava came out to bring us ashore to his house and to explain to us there that the island was owned and ruled by four hereditary chiefs. Custom required, he said, that we visit each of these in turn in his house and bring gifts to each one, for the island was theirs and it was by their indulgence that we visited it. He then impressed upon us the taboos to be observed concerning chiefs.

"When you are in the presence of a chief you must never turn your back on him." He repeated this several times. "When you go to the chief's house he will be sitting on the floor. You must not stand up when he is sitting. It is *tapu.* You must go in through the door on hands and knees

Katie surrounded by new friends on a remote little Polynesian island.
Behind Katie's left shoulder stand Farava and his wife Susana.

and then sit in front of him like this," and he made us do it cross-legged as
he did. "You must not stand. When the chief looks at you, say to him
'Laui te poni, te ariki. Koki alaui.'"

Farava made me practice this till I could repeat it to his satisfaction.

"Then give him your present. It can be just a small thing. Your ship is
small and you are only two."

We went through the routine thoroughly until he was quite sure we
would not shame him.

"Remember," he said as we were leaving, "when you go out from the
chief's house, do not stand up or turn your back on the chief. You must go
out on hands and knees and you must go out backwards. It is our custom.
It is very *tapu*."

So in the afternoon we went through the first village to the house of
"Chief Number Three." His house was undistinguished from all the rest,
long and low, built entirely of palm-frond thatch laid over a frame of poles
with three carved centre posts down the middle supporting the ridge pole.
The chief sat on a mat at one end, cool, hawk-faced and impassive as
befits a chief. He had shoulder-long hair and a woven mat strapped about
him. Some of his family sat at the back in the darkness looking at us

silently. In the face of so much dignity I felt slightly foolish trundling over the mats on all fours to shake the large brown hand.

"Laui te poni te ariki. Koki . . . er . . . alaui."

The chief's appearance of severity softened a little in appreciation and I removed myself at a respectful distance while Katie likewise mumbled a few Polynesian syllables.

Farava was right behind us overseeing our behaviour and pointing out where to sit. He began to explain to the chief all about us, while I produced our present, some tins of meat and two fathoms of calico. The chief accepted these ceremonial gifts with a gracious nod, set them aside without curiosity and began to ask all about us and why we had come to his island. (Were we lost?) After some time he spoke a few words to those behind him, something about *kai,* and two girls scurried out backwards through the entrance.

"We will eat now," Farava announced. We had just had lunch on board. But lack of appetite is no refuge in a Polynesian home and we were soon faced with a variety of strange pasty substances in half coconut shells as well as large lumps of cold cooked taro wrapped in banana leaves. To my regret we were given the lion's share and while our hosts nibbled we set manfully into it, determined to show how much we enjoyed it and to confirm for them the firmly held belief that their own island *kai* was far superior to anything we ourselves subsisted on.

"Eat up," Farava kept saying, "you must have some more," and before I had half finished scooping up with my fingers a half coconut shell full of a grey tapioca-like substance, the chief called for more to be brought to me. Apologies were made several times for the shortcomings of the meal. Various crops like bananas and coconuts had been destroyed by recent cyclones the chief explained, so these things were greatly lacking, and for this news, gorged as I was and confronted still with *kai* of various kinds, I made a valiant effort to sound sorry.

In all this, Katie suffered a deal more than I did. Not only did she have an appetite quickly satisfied but her tastes ran less to exotic foods, so I wasn't surprised when, walking home through the forest at the end of our long visit, she produced two large hunks of taro from the long sleeve of her dress and discreetly transferred them into the rucksack.

A similar ordeal took place next day, but this time we strictly avoided eating beforehand. Chief Number Two lived on the far side of the island. He received us with great solemnity and reserve and for three hours we sat cross-legged in his long dark house under the thatch talking and eating until we felt able to escape to the sunshine. I presented him with a flashlight and spare batteries as well as tins of fruit, and we carried away with us in the rucksack several coconut shells of unfinished food. Chief Number Four received us next day and Chief Number One the next, by which time Katie was too prostrate from over-indulgence to attend.

The chiefs were all of the same stamp, men of impressive dignity who were held in great respect by their people, and devotion by their families. They were marked by their intricate tattooing and long manes of hair brushed to the shoulders. Their families were just as mindful of the taboos we were taught as were the rest of the populace. They dressed much as everyone else did, both sexes having close-cropped hair and wearing a length of calico or *tapa* cloth wrapped as a skirt around the waist but nothing above it excepting only that they wore on a string around the neck, a *te manga* or little stylized fish hook fashioned out of turtle shell. This as Farava explained was a badge of nobility worn to distinguish them from "the rubbish people." They were interested to find that we came equipped with cameras and after each visit to the four chiefs, family portraits were requested and these I later returned by mail.

All of the people were fond of decorating themselves with flowers and fragrant leaves, and wherever we went they pressed on us crowns of frangipani or strings of scented leaves around our necks. They tucked woven fans or bunches of leaves down the back of their calicoes, and smaller bunches were pushed through ear lobes. Strings of blossom were worn around wrists or waist and changed daily.

We were never alone for long. Whenever we went ashore we were met by gathering crowds at the beach and dugouts followed us back to visit us on board and to marvel at the boat we lived on. They all brought presents of food, the same gluey dishes in coconut shells that were served to us ashore, but Katie was right off island food by then and I could only manage a small part of it so that to my very real regret, when the sun went down the little fish that hovered all day in *Nanook's* shade had a fine time of it.

From time to time "schools" of children set out from the edge of the reef and swam out to us, shouting and laughing in delight at the strange boat, and when I put the ladder out over the side they eagerly scrambled up to explore aboard and to sing their lusty island songs to us. At first, perhaps out of respect for the strange *palangi* they brought their calicoes with them, holding them high above their heads as they swam to keep them dry, but this delicacy was soon abandoned. At one time, as throughout the Pacific, the children wore nothing, but the missionaries managed when they came to the island to see to it that children adopted the wrap-around fashion of the adults. However the Anglican pastor was long gone, replaced by a local man, and while the children for the most part still retained the calico, it was more likely to be employed as a turban, a rolled-up necklace, a shoulder cape tied under the chin or a carrying strap for the baby, than as a skirt intended by the *palangi* to shield the eyes of the populace from indelicate reality.

We often rowed ashore to wander along the beaches or follow trails high up through the forest of the little island. It was almost impossible to

Stepping up the companionway, an atoll-dwelling Melanesian girl emerges after making an inspection of *Nanook*'s strange interior.

be alone. Some adult, if not Farava himself, would always join us and undertake to guide us around along with a retinue of excited children. We were often asked in to visit one home or another and to accept the gift of some morsel of food or to share in the chewing of betel nuts. This mild narcotic was taken by everyone and there were plenty of red lips and black teeth to show for it. The long slender areca palms were the strict and exclusive property of the chiefs whose right it was to oversee distribution to all and sundry. The nut is chewed in company with a green leaf and a quantity of powdered white lime, the result being a mouthful of bright red spit which may be either spat out or swallowed. I tried the stuff several times without discovering any narcotic properties and all I got for my pains was a well burnt tongue from hoisting in too much unmixed lime.

Farava never gave up calling us to his home when the opportunity came and he and his gentle wife Susana were gracious hosts, decking us in flowers, telling us stories of their island and teaching us to speak their dialect. Susana had a long intricate blue design tattooed down between her pendulous breasts from neck to navel. She always kept a fresh bunch of leaves in her ear lobes and a string of scented leaves around her neck. She was forever stirring up some concoction or other for us and one day after Farava warned us to be ready for a new dish we found her hard at work over a pit in the trees behind her house. The deep hole in the ground was lined with old leaves and filled with a sour-smelling yellowish mush.

"This is our cheese," Farava explained. "We are all strong on this island and it is because we eat this."

Breadfruit is taken from the trees in season, reduced to a pulp and then buried in a deep hole in the ground which is first lined with banana leaves. It is then covered with more leaves and finally with a deep layer of soil and left there to fester for half a year. The pit is then reopened, the breadfruit mush removed, the hole relined with fresh leaves and the sticky mess replaced for another extended burial. This happens three or four times until, after about two years have elapsed, the stuff is considered fit to eat. While we watched, Susana relined the pit and replaced about twenty buckets of the mush for its final bout of putrefaction, retaining a little of it however for our immediate use "to make us strong." It tasted both sour and sweet with a soft texture and a flavour nearly as concentrated as blue cheese. After the shock of the first mouthful it was not really unpleasant and I felt that a taste for it could be acquired with a little practice.

Every evening shortly after dusk, the drums began pounding in the village and sending their infectious rhythms out over the water and into the cabin. It was more than we could manage to remain on board. Crowds of people assembled on the white sand under the palms and began chanting out the old songs with hearty laughing voices and stepping out their odd posturing dance steps across the sand. Not just the dancing, but the music too had a strange alien faintly Eastern flavour, quite unlike anything we ever heard anywhere else in Polynesia. There were no guitars or ukuleles, only the hypnotic drum thumping its peculiar rhythms through half of every night. Nowhere else, even in the fun-loving South Seas, did we ever encounter such an endless fund of joyful exuberance. There was fun and laughter in everything the people did.

We didn't leave this little island of love as soon as we had planned for the simple reason that we were not *allowed* to. My first mentioning our departure to the people of the nearest village produced an explosion of objections and Farava in particular so vehemently opposed any such idea that we agreed to wait for three or four more days. However we finally won even Farava's grudging consent to leave and with that I climbed over the mountain to the windward side for a final visit with Chief Number One. While I sat talking with him in his house, his wife, a great laughing big-breasted woman with a pipe in her mouth, stirred up in a coconut shell a bright orange mixture of turmeric powder and oil, and began painting me all over, chest, back and arms with the brilliant greasy stuff. This, I was told, was a traditional mark of respect shown on special occasions. The newly initiated, the newly married, the departing and the dead departed all stand in danger of being smeared liberally head to foot with the stuff. It was intended as a mark of great honour, but I felt more than a bit conspicuous as I walked like a Day-Glo fluorescent beacon back through the villages to the lee side. White skin on that island was conspicuous enough.

I found Katie in Farava's house again and sure enough she was being painted by Susana with the same messy mixture. The house was crowded and Farava made a long speech which ended with him tying *te mangas* around our necks, elevating us from the ranks of the rubbish people to kinship with the nobility of the island and with himself.

We walked sadly down to the beach in the midst of a large crowd, a lump in our throats and unable to say much of anything to anyone. The dinghy had several little gifts of food in it to be added to the huge surplus already on board. Tearfully we shook hands and rowed away. "I will signal goodbye to all the people from the boat," I called to Farava.

Once the anchor was hauled up to the roller (and it was hard pulling from ten fathoms) I sent up three emergency parachute flares. They shot skywards with a whoosh and hung there burning bright red high up in the trade wind. A large crowd filled the beach and as each rocket went up so did a roar of surprise and pleasure from the crowd.

I got some sails up, smearing them (for all the trouble I took not to) with bright orange grease. *Nanook* heeled and slipped away downwind. We looked back and waved goodbye over and over until we were below their horizon and they were below ours.

It was an island of high spirits and great love. Someday we hope to sail back to visit those beautiful people. But sentimental journeys are usually a mistake and somehow I cannot hope to find that the raucous 20th century will have let them be.

XVI

Passages of the Indian Ocean

The exposed anchorage on the weather side of Thursday Island is not one to encourage voyagers in small boats to hang around longer than necessary, and given the attractions and facilities ashore not many would want to. Bill and Pat caught their plane south to Cairns and for a couple of days we relaxed on our own and made trips ashore to reprovision with fresh supplies. The post office was one of those few accustomed to holding piles of mail for yachtsmen for long periods. They handed over sacks of the stuff with an understanding smile and we were relieved to find not only the chronometer but engine parts from Japan, charts and wet weather jackets from England as well as many letters and other things.

Old wooden pearling luggers lay close around us in the anchorage. We lay pitching into the swell on 28 fathoms of chain while the decks ran wet with salt spray coming over the bow. Shopping ashore had to be timed to coincide with the favouring tides and for once I was defeated by tide and wind in my effort to row the two of us over to another yacht that had arrived in. The schooner *Kuan Yin* flew the Canadian maple leaf but her crew, Roger Clancy and his girlfriend Sheila were from Durban, bound home after a voyage out from Toronto. They were the first of a number of new acquaintances all bound like ourselves across the Indian Ocean. The rest were all behind us coming up the Queensland coast or down the channel from Port Moresby. They were all well known to Roger for they'd all crossed the Pacific from Panama in the same season, a year after *Nanook*.

Between ourselves and the distant land mass of Africa were seven thousand miles of near emptiness, an ocean of long distances and few islands and a place with a reputation for wildly unpleasant conditions. For a long time I had pondered the Indian Ocean crossing with some misgiving, regarding it more as a necessary evil than an end in itself like

Porpoises race joyously to overtake *Nanook* as she sweeps to the west over the Arafura Sea.

the other oceans. Then beyond that there were nine thousand miles of the long Atlantic and they were all to be covered in less than a year.

The strong winds of Torres Strait saw to it that we left as soon as we could manage. Rowing back aboard after a final shopping spree, we splashed our big loaves of fresh bread liberally with salt spray, stowed the dinghy and set off to wend our way through the last channels of the strait and out into the Arafura Sea. *Nanook* was bound for Bali.

But now after three days of harassment the winds that had driven us out of the strait decided to go on strike. By then we were well clear of the strait, and the islands were below the horizon, but we were still in the grip of tidal streams and as the wind dropped these began carrying us back the way we had come. The islands we had just left began again to peep over the horizon behind us. The stream was due to change towards midnight and since we were in only seven fathoms I put the anchor overboard to hold us in position till then. I was rather amazed at the way the anchor settled to the bottom in the still unrippled water and then seemingly shot out from under us and took a strong pull on the long nylon line while the water gurgled at the bow. It felt strange to be anchored in the middle of the sea. By midnight the anchor rode had slackened and a light breeze wafted across the moonlit water so we were away again.

Sailing can be an abomination at times, but on a few occasions it can also be pure bliss. That's how it was that night and for the next ten days and nine nights as we stepped west with our little noon-fixed x's across the chart of the shallow Arafura Sea.

While *Nanook* carried us quietly on to the west we did little and saw less. The Gulf of Carpentaria gave us a fright when we noticed what looked exactly like coral reefs all around us where none should have been, but these turned out to be large fields of some minute organism. We sailed close by the barren looking Wessel Islands of the Northern Territory and after catching our last Australian fish there, altered course slightly for the lands of Asia to the northwest.

Day by day *Nanook* ran goosewinged over the empty sea, the mainsail to starboard and the genoa held out to port by the whisker pole. The weather stayed clear with a moderate wind and the daily log entries became a bit repititious: "22nd July. Another fine day . . . 23rd. Clear weather . . . 24th. Another nice day . . . 25th. Superb weather still . . . 26th. Perfect weather . . . 27th. Perfect weather."

There were the usual hours of sail mending and varnishing to keep us mildly occupied. Even the bowsprit came in for three coats of varnish, a job normally reserved for quiet anchorages. The days were hot and sweaty and Katie was in the habit of plugging up the cockpit drains and half filling the cockpit with sea water for a cool bath. We had on board a slimy soft kind of American soap that lathered in the salt water as if it were an April shower.

On the ninth day out just as we sighted the great heights of Timor far to the north, a happy crowd of dolphins came rushing to meet us, squealing softly underwater and grinning up at us from the bows. The next day we sailed through several miles of strange little black crabs all swimming frantically at the surface, and the following night we were treated to a display of vivid phosphorescence that made each whitecap look like a flashing signal light. I spent my watches at the stern gazing straight down at the wake, a glowing galaxy in three dimensions with an occasional burst of light that spread several feet wide through the water and faded slowly far astern.

Watches were kept three hours on, three hours off, through every night for we'd expected to see shipping along the route but the seas seemed utterly deserted until on the tenth day out, just when I was beginning to believe we were being foolish in doggedly maintaining round the clock watches on such an empty ocean, a ship at last hove in sight. It was a mere speck on the southern horizon but its bearing was quite constant and before long it resolved itself into a freighter, from Freemantle I figured and bound for Japan.

It seems strange that two remote objects appearing over each other's horizon out of an otherwise empty ocean could be so fated as to be on an

Every change in wind direction called for a corresponding adjustment of the steering vane. *Nanook* here is on course from Mauritius to Durban.

exact collision course with each other, but that's what they were. Left to her wind vane, *Nanook* with all the emptiness around her to choose from would surely have smashed herself to pieces on the bows of the enormous ship. I held our course, fascinated by the improbability of it, just long enough to be sure of it. It was a clear gentle sunny day, and I felt that no one could fail to see us or to do us the courtesy if need be of throwing the wheel over to dodge us. A vast rolling wall of water heaved up ahead of the bows and the engines rumbled ominously at us, a sound without direction, coming not from the ship but up from out of the sea itself. Finally not wishing to confuse the Greeks on the bridge about my intentions I went forward, cast off the main boom preventer and gybed to port to let the onrushing monster pass ahead. A couple of fat officers strolled out along the bridge to stare idly down at us, a group of crewmen waved at us from the stern and the *KYPIAKH* from Piraeus went on her way.

This was a lesson to me in not overestimating the apparent emptiness of the ocean or the great improbability of a collision far from normal shipping lanes. In the early stages of our voyage we tended to assume that the empty trade wind passages were devoid of modern shipping, and at nights we slept accordingly with untroubled minds. But gnawing suspicions about that comfortable assumption gradually grew on us, and after this encounter we never again allowed ourselves the luxury of sleeping through the nights while on any passage. But quite apart from the question of keeping watches in the hours of darkness, the *KYPIAKH* reminded us that whatever the international regulations might have to say about giving way, there is really only one law that applies to a tiny sailboat even in the clearest daylight and that is simply that might is right. Ask any Greek captain.

Roti, Sawa, Sumba, Sumbawa. Outposts of Asia rose up in succession to starboard. A strong coastal current joined forces with the wind to speed us up along the Indonesian chain and I began to worry that with such gentle winds as they were we stood a fair chance of being swept away to the west of Bali. Lombok's enormous volcanic outline loomed next to starboard and after this, just at dusk of the 14th day, we set out across the Straits of Lombok for Bali.

The timing was right for an overnight passage to bring us into the port of Benoa by morning, and we had a full moon to keep us company all night. But the straits have a well-deserved reputation for powerful currents, and the full moon also meant spring tides, so we weren't too sure what to expect. Certainly we didn't expect what we got. All went well until my second watch after midnight. The weather was still fine with a light breeze and just a few light clouds covering the moon, but the sea began to get up as if from a sudden storm and before long I had to disengage the wind-vane and steer by hand. There was a lack of conviction in the wind and a lack of response in the vane gear that was getting worse with the jerky unpredictable motion.

By 2 A.M. matters were getting a bit out of hand. Wave crests were coming aboard and the motion was getting really violent. The waves seemed to have no clear direction to them. They seemed to leap up of their own accord out of nowhere and crashed into each other without pattern. The breeze in the sails no longer had any effect in holding *Nanook* on any sort of stable keel. By 3 A.M. Katie had been thrown twice out of her bunk and once out of mine, normally a near-impossibility, and I remained in the cockpit only by virtue of being firmly wedged between the coaming and the mizzen mast.

Poor *Nanook!* She leaped and bucked like a frightened horse, rising with half her keel clear at the crests and then dropping through the void into a deep and very temporary trough just as if she had been let go from a crane. We rolled and we pitched. Big wave tops swept across the decks. The preventer guy broke and the main began gybing violently back and forth, one side and then the other every half minute or so for the wind was behind us. I could do nothing about replacing the preventer without running the risk of being tossed off the deck like a cowboy off a Brahma bull so I changed course to bring the wind onto the starboard beam, steering towards the little island of Penida in the middle of the strait. The noise of crashing water was so great that when I opened the hatch to see if Katie was alright we had to yell at each other.

I couldn't hand over the last watch to her in those conditions. She couldn't have done any deck work. Even the tiller would have been too much for her. And I couldn't have got any sleep. I looked below at four o'clock and there she was wedged with cushions between the galley sink and the steep support bar hanging on to the overhead rope grip with one hand and watching the kettle come to a boil, gingerly returning it to the flame whenever it slithered across the stove. She stood in imminent danger of a scalding but she produced a cup of tea from it all, half a cup by the time it came out the hatch, and I needed it.

The vague dark outline of Penida by then had added itself to my worries. I began to imagine the island as being very close by. What the currents were doing to us I had no way of telling but I felt that we were being swept towards the island, for its form, a deeper black against the surrounding blackness, was becoming gradually higher and clearer, so I brought the bows around to the south, gybing over to the port tack and ran from the fearful shadow for an hour.

The moon sank to the west and disappeared in cloud leaving us to continue our stupefying ballet in deeper darkness. The wind remained steady but light. Yet not even in our wildest storms did we ever go through such disordered contortions as we did that night.

Speaking later to other yachtsmen who had crossed the same waters we

The Balinese seem to be incapable of creating anything that is not beautiful. Here, graceful double-outrigger fishing canoes lie on the beach of Benoa while, in the background, villagers return under sail from the mainland.

found no one who had found conditions anything like those we encountered. They all found a strong current and one was so unable to overcome it that he was carried beyond Bali forcing him to abandon his plans and to press on instead for Christmas Island.

The much-longed-for dawn arrived at last, just as the tossing waves were subsiding. No storm waves could possibly disappear as miraculously as those spring tide overfalls of Lombok Strait. We were not nearly as close to Penida as I'd feared and by the time the sun rose over the strait the waters were stilled to a near-mirror, although it was a mirror undulating eerily with a long deep swell that rolled into the strait from a distant storm far to the south. As we sank into each of these widely separated troughs Bali and Penida disappeared from view. Then we rose higher and higher over the long slope till we could see far over the other crests to the beautiful land ahead and the distant outrigger sailing canoes darting offshore in quest of fish, like a fleet of water-borne butterflies.

Far behind us was the line of white-water. The turbulent streams we had come through during the night had still not quite finished and I found that to reach Benoa I had to steer well north and crawl across the south-setting current that lay against the coast of Bali. But sunshine and peace had returned to our little world and sharing the sunshine were distant

Hindu temples and white beaches, large fishing villages and far-off sacred volcanoes. We passed through the swarm of double outrigger fishing boats that darted over the long swells under their high cotton sails. The break in the coral reef revealed itself and we followed the channel around the shoals and into the wide lagoon of Benoa.

The commercial harbour lay around an artificial island that was connected to the mainland and the main town by a causeway. There we could see the masts of a number of visiting yachts, so assuming the island to be the port of entry we regretfully left the handsome village of Benoa to port and came in to anchor amongst the small fleet of foreign yachts whose crews came on deck to watch our approach and wave a welcome.

"Hello *Nanook,*" came over the water at us and we recognized some of our old Seattle friends on a schooner that we'd seen last in the Marquesas two years before. Apart from our own, the only other maple leaf was flown by the ketch *Wapiti.* There was also the New Zealand yacht *Sunpeddler* met in Rarotonga, the 38-foot ketch *Mauna Kea* owned by a German couple, a New Zealand-owned Tahiti ketch *Karrie L.,* an enormous American trimaran *Asa Kaze* with a crew of 7, an American catamaran, two varnished Chinese junks lying like floating castles under their red awnings and the famous *Stormvogel* chartering out of Benoa. We had last seen her in Malta.

Most of these yachts were on short cruises with long protracted stays in port, and considering what Bali was like who could blame them for lying there month after month? The schooner wasn't quite in that category. The old boat had her problems. Her hull was tight enough but deep fissures were opening up in her six-way partnership of optimistic bachelors. The only happy yachts going long distances for long periods are those that are single-handed or sailed by a couple, and not all of those are happy. One of the schooner's co-owners had flown home after a nervous breakdown. A second was in jail after a police search on board for marijuana because a third had informed the authorities of a plan to smuggle Sumatran grass to Western Australia.

Mauna Kea and *Asa Kaze* were also bound westwards like us across the Indian Ocean but most of the yachts that comprised the annual migration to South Africa were still bringing up the rear.

Considering the storied touchiness of Indonesian officialdom we were careful not to leave the boat for some time or to go galavanting off in the dinghy to gossip with the other yachties. Instead we sat primly in the cockpit with the yellow flag flying underneath the red and white bars of the Indonesian national flag. But the only result was a visit from Roy Cummer of *Wapiti* and his girlfriend Doris, both of Alberta, who came over hungry for a chat with some real Canadians (though it was more a thirst in Roy's case) and being only slightly put off by our un-Canadian accents they asked us over for supper. Roy insisted that entry formalities were a breeze and that we could proceed ashore at our leisure. This we did and the procedures were straightforward though they took some hours and we were glad that we'd taken the prior trouble to arm ourselves with vaccinations, visas and cruising permits from the Indonesian navy.

Roy claimed to have been on his way home eastwards from Taiwan where he had picked up the yacht. But he was clearly having too good a time in the Far East to really mean it. He and Doris each had their respective offspring on board as well as a Celebes monkey that was fond of biting visitors when it was not fouling the decks. *Wapiti's* voyage south to Bali was a long series of misadventures. She had meandered slowly through the Philippines and many of the islands of Indonesia before reaching Bali. We learned later that after a half-hearted attempt to leave the Indies for the open Pacific via Dampier Straits and Madang they turned tail and returned to their beloved southern Philippines, a pirate-infested area thoroughly shunned by most yachtsmen, where they had earlier been boarded and robbed four times.

Den Pasar the capital of Bali lay just 11 km. along the road from the port and at intervals throughout each day a small vehicle called a *bemo* disgorged up to a dozen passengers and took on more for the ride back to town. All the yacht crews made use of these *bemos,* and an assortment of dinghies was always strung out at the landing place in company with sailing canoes from the fishing village. Roy lent us a map and a few hundred rupees and off we went to pay our respects to the Immigration Office, change some money and explore the exciting thronging town.

Bali is every Westerner's vision of the far eastern paradise. It is an incredibly colourful exciting place. The towns are a kaleidoscope of markets, temples, festivals, noise and colour. The Balinese are attractive, friendly and creative and their culture and religion are the fountainsprings of a perpetual outpouring of artistic expression. Music and dancing, carving, painting, cuisine and architecture. The richness of it all is breathtaking. One can't help wondering, why Bali in particular? It is only one of a long chain of islands. Yet none of the others will bear comparison. Why not Sumbawa or Flores or Lombok? The difference must lie in the fact that Bali is a Hindu land in a sea of Islam.

Having accustomed ourselves to the inflationary conditions of Australia and the Pacific we were amazed to find how many rupees our dollars could buy and how far the rupees could go. The ride to Den Pasar was only a few cents. A reasonable meal could be had for fifty cents in a restaurant and for a dollar we dined like royalty. Frogs' legs, skewered chunks of beef, pork and turtle in peanut sauce, bits of *betutu bebek,* (duckling in banana leaf), *bakmi goreng* (fried noodles) or *nasi goreng,* (rice fried with vegetables and spices). A glass of wine or a bottle of beer. The whole thing one dollar.

More yachts showed up in port as the days went by. *Kuan Yin* anchored nearby. *Skylark,* a big yawl from San Francisco, brought Bob and Christi Hanelt and their crew, and *Bebinka* from New York brought Scott and Kitty Kuhner. *Ard Sholas*, a concrete ketch from New Zealand, arrived and Klaus, the Dutchman in *Rik*, showed up after grounding on several well-charted reefs in Torres Strait.

The parties in the anchorage started coming thick and fast as crews became better acquainted. Groups began teaming up to tour around the island by car or motorbike. Katie and I joined forces with the Hanelts and a German couple on the yacht *Thalassa* to spend two days driving around Bali in a Landrover. Every mile produced its own sights, sounds, smells and exotic impressions. Temples and temple dances, water buffalo patiently sloshing across fields of terraced mud, little eight-year-old duckherders driving their flocks home from the wet paddies, volcanoes and crater lakes like those of Guatemala, fighting cocks set out in cages at the side of the road to let them watch the world go by, Hindu processions, *gamelan* orchestras, the elaborate preparations for a ritual cremation, decorated bamboo poles leaning over the road to announce a religious festival, temples carved out of a rocky gorge, naked bathers washing in a sacred spring, decorative flowers or little leaves holding a teaspoonful of cooked rice left on the ground at the crossroads as precautionary offerings to a carved Hindu deity against the chance of road accidents.

Each village had its own indigenous talents. Some were famous for their stone sculpture, some for their dancers. Katie and I travelled five times to Ubud, a village of prolific artists, in search of paintings of the kaleido-scope of Balinese life. That we went back so often was not because good paintings were hard to find but rather because there was such a bewilderingly rich profusion of fine work in the little place.

The vast market in Den Pasar was a constant delight. Every imaginable food could be bought there, including the vegetables of temperate climates, for the high hills of Bali offer a variety of climates. Some of the highest villages are downright chilly.

The yachties were not long in discovering that a certain local brand of gut-rot brandy was sold in Den Pasar for a mere 30¢ a bottle. Of necessity most long distance sailors have a nose for a bargain and upon this discovery being made sundowner parties were apt to carry through until not much short of sun-up. Meanwhile the little cafe at the dinghy landing did a roaring trade in ready-made meals. Bowls of *nasi goreng* for 25¢ any time of the night or day. Wash it down with a 30¢ quart of cold beer. And for the footloose and fancy free the waitress herself came at a reasonable price.

> Take me somewhere East of Suez
> Where the best is like the worst
> Where there ain't no Ten Commandments
> And a man can raise a thirst. . . .

The only flaw in this demi-paradise was the dysentery, or what Katie called "the Bali belly." I seemed to be blessed with a fairly resistant alimentary canal but Katie very quickly succumbed and so did nearly all the other crews. The attacks came and went. Cramps appeared and for a couple of days the victim gulped drugs and stayed close to the heads. Then the thing would seem to go away for a while only to reappear as soon as anything fresh or exotic was swallowed.

We stayed in Bali for three weeks. I could have stayed three months if time had allowed and Katie's physique could have endured the diet. But what with loose bowels and a tight schedule we had at last to leave and in the company of *Skylark, Kuan Yin* and *Bebinka* we put out to the open sea past the distant grey line of the mountains of Java, bound west for Christmas Island.

Many people have expressed great surprise that we should sail long distances without the precaution of having a radio transmitter. "What if you should get into trouble?" The truth is that I could not be bothered to afford the cost or space of such a thing and that if I had one I would rarely bother to use it. But my reply was usually to the effect that we were for much of the time out of range of other radios, that we had to take every precaution not to get into any trouble in the first place and that if we did get into it we had to be prepared to get ourselves out of it. All that is accepted with some reluctance. Nobody really expects you to be completely self reliant any more.

Nevertheless I have to admit that the passage to Christmas Island had me wishing briefly for a transmitter. Each of the other three yachts had one and at 0800 and 1400 each day they called each other up and gossiped about their day's runs, their sex lives, the cheap paperbacks they were reading and what they had, or expected to have for lunch. We tuned in each day to the little party line and enjoyed their banter and camaraderie and the occasional greetings made to *Nanook* in the hope that she too might be listening.

We copied down their positions and plotted their courses on the chart each day as well as our own. *Nanook* fell well behind the rest the first day out for there was little wind and a lot of motoring. But the second day we overhauled *Bebinka* and *Kuan Yin* although they didn't know it for we were far apart out of sight of each other from deck level. But since we knew their positions relative to our own I was able to climb the ratlines to the lower spreader on the main mast and could spot their white sails far away to the south of us. As for *Skylark* she was well over fifty feet overall with an enormous spread of canvas and none of the others ever came close to equalling her pace on any passage.

Dirty grey overcast weather overtook us on the third day, reminding Katie of our Atlantic crossing. Successive rain squalls blasted us and then for several hours we lost the wind and got nowhere. When it did resume it came in for a time from the west.

These massive rain squalls are a feature of trade wind passages and one just has to get used to them. Gazing astern at the dark onrushing blast I would make a quick estimate of its power and decide whether to hold onto our sails or drop them. Lightning would spit angrily into the sea and the electric air shout at us with the sound of tearing silk amplified a thousand times. As the falling curtain advanced a line of white would appear at water level and then the furious blast would strike, heeling us away over and sending *Nanook* suddenly rushing crazily through the smoking splashing water at eight knots, nine knots and while water streamed over my bare skin I would gaze upwards at the rigging in the fervent hope that she could stand the strain. The initial onslaught would usually last less than a minute and then settle down to a drenching torrent of rain. The wind would change direction and for a time we would go tearing off wildly 120° or so off course until I adjusted the vane. Gradually the wind would ease, the rain slowly pass ahead of us and we would be left finally to slat around, becalmed on the swell for hours sometimes before the grey anvil of cloud at the top of the thunderstorm cleared itself away and the trade wind crept back over the water to send us on our way again.

Bebinka and *Kuan Yin* passed us in this squally weather but once the sky cleared our progress shot up. *Nanook* rushed on with her sails pulling hard and a bone in her teeth and we took great satisfaction at the evidence on the radio that we were again creeping well ahead of the others. In one day's run, noon to noon, *Nanook* covered 190 miles. True she'd had a current to help her along. Her first owners claimed to have covered 200 miles in one day's run in the Indian Ocean but for us 190 was a record that we never again came close to repeating.

Ironically we more or less wasted that all-time record for our noon position then put us just 45 miles short of Christmas Island, just a little too far to cover the distance before nightfall and we were unwilling to attempt the restricted anchorage of Flying Fish Cove in the dark. Roger and Scotty on the other yachts discussed matters on the radio and to my chagrin both decided to make a night entry, with the people on *Skylark* who were already in staying up to help. I sheeted the mainsail amidships, lashed the tiller down and we lay hove-to the rest of the day and part of the night. I spotted *Bebinka's* sail late in the afternoon and felt disgusted as she passed by. She was a long way off and Scotty never noticed us lying there.

Golden tropic birds, the peach-coloured variety peculiar to Christmas Island, wheeled around us, each with a long thin tailfeather trailing behind. The common variety is white and known generally as the bosun bird, or as the French call it *paille-en-queue,* meaning straw in tail.

We came in at dawn. The others were there already as well as Peter and Beate Kammler, the Germans on *Mauna Kea,* and they all came on deck to wave as we rounded the point and came in to the narrow shelf by the beach. I laid the bower onto a patch of sand among the coral close to *Skylark* and rowed a stern anchor into shallow water. It was an uncomfortable spot but it was the best Christmas Island had to offer for the bottom sloped steeply away to incredible depths everywhere else. The Australian customs officers came out to give pratique to us as well as to *Bebinka* and *Kuan Yin* and to ask us all to make ourselves at home in the little yacht club ashore.

This we did. Peter Kammler had the key. Tables and chairs were set outside under the trees. There was a cold water shower and a barbecue grill. The fridge was full of Australian beer and a book lay beside it where we recorded what drinks we'd taken and paid for them later at Customs when going there for clearance.

Christmas Island at the time was still dependent on ships for everything from the outside world for it was still blessed with the curse of having no airstrip. The Australian authorities had bulldozers up on the plateau, busily correcting that situation but so far at least the little community was informal, friendly and happy. The Malay families smiled curiously at us as we wandered past their apartments near the beach on our way up to the island's one supermarket. We went up in the evenings to watch the free outdoor movies. The sergeant in charge at the police station asked us up to his house to do our laundry and have lunch. A geologist came down to the club in his Landrover and invited four of us to jump in and come for a sightseeing drive around the island.

It was a fascinating tour. The ramparts of the windward coast were an impossible wilderness of jagged limestone where the heavy swell constantly sucked and smashed itself into white foam or burst up through blowholes with a hollow roar. The whole island was mostly of limestone covered with bush but in some places it was a moonscape of yellow badlands. Phosphate deposits are the prize. These ancient metamorphosed bird droppings are stripped from the land, carted off over a railway, dried, processed and then loaded onto ships bound for Australia. Everything in Flying Fish Cove was covered with the yellow dust for it was there that the ships moored and loading was done from a gantry suspended over the water. Postage stamps are the only other export. We noticed that these all had printed on them "Christmas Island, Indian Ocean" to distinguish the place from its namesake in the Pacific. But it's the phosphate that brings people there, the contract employees from Malaysia and the managers and officials from Australia. If it were not for the phosphate the island would be abandoned to the golden tropic bird and the huge bright red land crabs that live in the bush. These crabs, our geologist friend Peter explained to us, pose something of a problem. Once every year when the urge is upon them they migrate *en masse* out of the bush in countless numbers. All doors are closed while gardens, paths and roads are covered with a seething red mass of crabs all scrabbling and scraping their way over each other in a blind atavistic impulse to reach water's edge.

"What's the idea of that?" we asked.

"It happens in the mating season," Peter explained. "They come out of the forest and down to water's edge where they copulate, then they return up into the bush where they live."

"Funny isn't it," said Katie. "It's the other way around with most islanders."

We didn't stay long at Christmas Island for our berths were uncomfortable and worrisome. At nights we were blasted with torrential downpours and an unseasonable swell rolled into the cove from the northwest so after only three nights we were prepared to leave. The supermarket up the hill was owned and subsidized by the Phosphate Commission so we were able to restock the galley at mainland prices or even less, while duty-free privileges were extended at the liquor counter.

Skylark, Bebinka, Kuan Yin and *Mauna Kea* all put out to sea bound for Cocos Keeling atoll, but we delayed because during our last night who should appear in the cove but our old friends of New Hebrides days, Ernest and Val Haigh and the girls on *Tryste*. It was grand to see them again. Ernest had decided after another summer in New Zealand that *Tryste* was after all quite up to the long voyage west around the world to British Columbia. Two of the four girls had jumped ship in New Zealand, so *Tryste* was carrying a lighter load. They had come direct from Torres Strait. We agreed to see them soon at Cocos and after recovering our anchors, waved goodbye and sailed away.

Cocos lay a little over 500 miles on. It was fast sailing but the sky was dirty and the sea looked exactly like my earlier visions of the Indian Ocean, high, dark, lashed by a strong wind and capped with crashing wave crests. We ran on under double-reefed main.

I managed to get some kind of odd unfamiliar infection a bit like a head cold for which I prescribed myself a course of antibiotics. Katie was sick and suffered from a sensitive front tooth. The hatch stayed closed most of the time shutting out the oncoming squalls, and the decks ran wet. "Oh what fun cruising isn't!" says the log.

On the fourth day at evening we were just 70 miles short of the atoll. *Bebinka* and *Kuan Yin* were similar distances and expecting like us to get in next day. *Skylark* was already there. The loom of the Cocos aero beacon confirmed our position for us about 0200 and shortly after dawn in fairly nice sunny conditions we saw ten miles ahead of us that familiar line of coconut fronds that mean, "atoll."

Even after just a few days at sea, landfalls are marvelous experiences. If we had made a thousand the last ten would have been as thrilling and satisfying as the first. We steered close in to Direction Island catching glimpses through the coconut trees of white masts and pale blue lagoon. The swell followed us around to the wide entrance. Again the scary thrill of a shadowy bottom flashing by underneath us at fifteen fathoms, ten, eight, and then the swell was gone and we were into the lagoon. Katie steered upwind over the smooth water while I conned from the bowsprit, directing her clear of the many dark patches of shallow coral and the suspiciously extra-pale blue places that indicated shallow water over sand. We anchored in exquisitely crystal water close in to Direction Island. Six other yachts lay around us, friends of other anchorages most of them, and in this happy company and this remote beautiful windswept place we remained for six days.

Direction Island itself was deserted. It was once the site of a cable relay station, but apart from the coconut trees and a flock of chickens all that remained there from those days was an old shack with a water catchment reservoir which was a boon to us all for we all had long distances to go and tanks to be filled. One of the yachts was bound for the Seychelles but most were aiming for Mauritius and South Africa.

Some of the other islands were inhabited. The Malay families who worked for the owner of the atoll, Clunes-Ross, lived on an island close to the south and the airport and administrative headquarters were over on West Island. But yachts are not welcome to the one and cannot find much shelter at the other so we remained where we were and the Australian officials came across the lagoon whenever they saw a sail coming in.

More yachts arrived including *Tryste* who anchored nearby. Every evening there was much rowing back and forth for cocktails in cockpits and one evening after an afternoon of spear fishing on the banks at the lagoon entrance we all gathered on the beach where a fire was lit under the leaning palms and Scotty put in charge of baking the five fish over the coals. The wives brought along a variety of dishes from their galleys, I unstrapped my guitar from its lashings over my bunk and brought it ashore, someone mixed up a rum punch and soon a rollicking party was underway, one of those happy occasions that are never forgotten.

I cleared my head next morning by going overboard with the mask and snorkel. The cheap Rabaul antifouling was already showing signs of losing its potency. Large goose barnacles waved happily about from their foothold around the rudder and green weed was growing along the waterline.

We must have hit a floating object somewhere along the way for one of the planks just below water level was scored near the bow and the wood exposed. This invitation to teredo worm had to be covered with a thick smear of antifouling paint, the kind I bought in London for such situations, intended as it is for underwater application. It was a tricky job applying it, working in slow motion and dodging the dark red globules of greasy paint that drifted off the brush, but it hardened nicely once it decided to stick. The trim tab attachments were checked too for signs of galvanic decay and one stainless steel bolt through the rudder replaced. It was riddled with tiny black holes as if worms had been eating it.

While I was huffing and puffing around the hull at these chores, Katie busied herself with baking up a variety of things to carry us through the first few days out for we expected them to be wildly unpleasant as indeed they were. A final meal with the Haigh family on *Tryste,* a final long night's restful sleep and on September 9th at midday we sailed out of the lagoon and away to the west.

Downwind the nearest land was the little island of Rodrigues, two thousand miles distant. Judging from the experiences of other sailors who had made the passage before, the conditions would be rather wild and rough beyond Cocos and the pilot charts didn't contradict them. The first day was moderate enough but on the evening of the second day I wrote in the log "This is awful. The weather is getting really filthy with one heavy rain squall succeeding another about half to one hour apart. Overcast most of the time. The————wind gets up ahead of the squalls and then falls light after them. I ought to be changing sails with every squall but————it. After one really prolonged and dreadfully violent squall two hours ago with the seas absolutely smoking from the onslaught, I've reduced sail to staysail alone. Might be a bit slow for the night but at least I might get some sleep, if the brown tar-stained drips over my bunk let me. 134 m. from Cocos at noon."

Katie of course was her queasy old self as she always was when a long passage had a rough beginning. She spent long hours lying in her bunk rather than risk feeling worse by getting up and moving about in the pitching rolling cabin. I liked to encourage her out of her bunk and into the cockpit at such times, for seasickness can be better held at arm's length outside with a fresh wind on the face and a view of the horizon. But this was no weather for sitting outside. Wave crests periodically smacked the hull and sent heavy dollops flying over the decks and into the sails. The hatches were kept closed and the motion was quick and unpredictable. Just sitting wedged in the cockpit was an effort. The best place was in either of the after corners with feet jammed hard against the opposite side but the heavy seas and the straining wind vane combined to keep the rudder always moving and occasionally in this position I collected a rib-cracking thump on the chest from the tiller as a big wave went under us.

For several days we endured these conditions. It was unpleasant and every last little task seemed to take on the proportions of a major undertaking, especially the cooking and the navigating. Drenching rain fell out of low leaden skies and I spent hours sometimes with the sextant against cushions on my bunk and the watch on my wrist waiting for a glimpse of the sun. Once while scrambling hopefully out of the companionway hatch in pursuit of the sun with the sextant held tight in my left hand I took a colossal wave crest full on the face and chest. I had only just opened the hatch and what didn't hit me cascaded straight down onto Katie's bunk. A howl of anguish and disgust rose up from the salty dripping mass of sodden sheets and pillows. I retreated below and reached for the towels. We mopped up the mess, half the Indian Ocean by Katie's reckoning, and replaced all the bedding with dry things from the linen cupboard. But that night a persistent leak developed where the deck meets the coachroof coaming over the bunk. It wasn't directly overhead, but with the yacht heeling to starboard in the wind each cold drip fell directly onto Katie's head so that she finally abandoned the quarter berth in towering disgust and took up residence in one of the two pullman berths over the saloon table, but not before slipping on the wet cabin sole and crashing down heavily between the galley and the horizontal support bar, scratching her right arm on the edge of the counter and bruising her left buttock on the diesel starting handle which had fallen out of its place and was at that moment slithering about on the wet cabin sole like Katie herself. These little things all helped her forget her queasiness and the pain in her back that she always developed after a few days of lying prostrate on the bunk.

I, meanwhile, tried to get a little mental relief from the infernal noise, motion, wetness and squalor by reading *The Hobbit* and by contemplating our return to Canada and our hopes of going back to a working life in the Arctic. Miraculous as it seems to me now as I write this on the deep-frozen coast of Cornwallis Island, far to the northwest of the northern end of Baffin Island, I actually revelled in the prospect.

The weather gradually improved. On the 6th day from Cocos I even confided to the log that it was a "nice day, still rather cloudy and blowing Force 6 but the cloud has cleared off a lot and gone higher. We covered 164 miles noon to noon and only 8 were courtesy of the current."

The next day September 16th I wrote "Much clearer weather and also cooler. The wind is still fresh but the sea has lost a lot of its sting. However decks are still wet as they've been ever since leaving Cocos. 149 miles noon to noon and still going well under double reefed main and jib. Busy restitching mizzen. Have actually been enjoying the sailing today especially with the nearly cloudless sky and brilliantly blue water flashing by us. This is our first day without flying fish for lunch. One or two birds are about, but there's nothing else to see excepting for Katie who's in the cockpit at last and working on her all-over tan."

The weather was more reasonable for the rest of the passage. There was always something to do and we never managed to find time enough to wish the hours away. I located on deck the source of Katie's bunk leak and stopped it with an epoxy filler. The toilet started playing up and had to be removed and repaired. We listened to our favourite programs from the B.B.C. now that we had lost the cheerful entertainment from Canberra on A.B.C. There was always baking to be done and fresh scones or cakes to be carefully divided into two exactly equal portions and ravenously consumed with afternoon tea in the cockpit. As Samuel Pepys said, "Sailors love their bellies above everything else."

There was the never-ending chore of restitching sail seams. The stitching on synthetic sails chafes readily and it doesn't bury into the material the way it does with cotton canvas. Prevention is better than cure. Where sails were concerned a stitch in time saves 999, especially in the Indian Ocean.

About this time it occurred to me that I'd recently been doing an inordinate amount of scratching. Apart from the reddened marks left by my own fingernails there was nothing much visible on my skin to account for this maddening itch. It was becoming more infuriating every day. There seemed to be nothing to explain it. The cockroaches were almost extinct and they didn't bite anyway. We didn't carry our own personal supply of sandflies and mosquitoes. It couldn't be coming from our clothes because for the most part we wore none. The odd thing was that Katie was completely free of the slightest hint of any itch, and that rang a bell! Back there in Ethiopia I'd endured several days of furious itching after a night with bedbugs while Katie was unscathed. Perhaps we were bed-bugged? There wasn't much to see on my bunk but we had noticed for some time and ignored a rash of little pin-point stains on the sheets of Katie's bunk. Close inspection revealed these to be spots of blood. But more startling discoveries awaited us close by. The deeply-stitched edges of the mattress, the tucked-away seams of the sheets and the unused blankets that were folded and stowed for extra padding at the side of the bunk were all colonized with tiny cities of little bedbugs, unpleasant slow-moving, tick-like little creatures that were small enough to escape the notice of the unwary. The egg-strewn colonies were more obvious but they were all cunningly hidden in crevices and undisturbed spots. A few scattered individuals who had not returned home after their night's feasting were still on the sheets. They might easily have been mistaken for bits of dust and casually brushed off. Some were bloated to double size and a slight squeeze resulted in a small splash of red blood or a darker shade if the meal was a few days old. The smaller the bug the darker the crush. My own bunk on further inspection did reveal a few of these tiny disgusting insects but they had established no colonies there. They had originated apparently on Katie's side and migrated across, pioneers apparently of a New World, but a very hostile New World as they were to discover.

We were aghast at these scalp-tingling discoveries and set to with a will to rid the boat of every last trace of them. We were lucky to have on board as one of our various cockroach treatments, a good supply of an insecticide powder. Cockroaches themselves seemed suddenly by comparison to be innocuous little household pets. We sprinkled the powder liberally all over both bunks. The bedding was removed onto the decks. Some of it we trailed astern in the water for an hour, rinsed with fresh water, dried in the sun and sprinkled with insecticide. Some of it we treated the other way around starting with the powder. But one way or another we successfully killed the lot. We suspected strongly that the insects had come aboard on the two grass skirts that still dangled by Katie's bunk. Katie couldn't part with these mementoes of happy days so they were removed, powdered and sealed up for several weeks in plastic bags.

This gave us something to talk about for a few days and my itching very quickly died away. Progress was good under clear skies, helped perhaps by quantities of blankets and sheets flapping about in the rigging.

On the 15th night at sea I reduced sail and we began taking much more interest in our watches for Rodrigues was only 55 miles distant at dusk. About 3 in the morning I was able to make out a dimness fine on the port bow and as this didn't blow away like the other clouds I knew it was land-ho.

By breakfast time we were close in off the north side of the island, feasting our ocean-weary eyes on the sight of it. Even from a distance it was quite unlike any island of the South Pacific. There was no green forest over its high hills. Instead little farms spread over the whole surface with modest little white houses and fawn-coloured fields enclosed by stone walls. It had the appearance of a stony man-made barrenness. But a few trees waved at us, the surf crashed over the reef in a smother of foam and we felt excited with the prospect of the new land before us.

Rodrigues is surrounded by an extensive coral reef enclosing a shallow lagoon that extends far out from shore. For the most part the island is unapproachable from the sea on account of this surrounding reef and lagoon. But at the main town of Port Mathurin on the leeward side the lagoon narrows to a quarter mile and at that point an artificial access channel six feet deep had been blasted out across the lagoon to allow small vessels to moor at the town dock. It was this place we steered for gazing through the binoculars at the little town and the narrow buoyed channel leading in to it. A diesel-powered lighter full of people pulled away from the dock and came out to us through the channel. Some officials were on board. It was low tide. Considering our draft they thought we should wait an hour before attempting the channel so they showed us where to anchor and said they would be back to tow us through.

While we lay there we gazed in dumbfounded surprise at what we saw through the binoculars, for there moored inside the little basin between two jetties was a trimaran that looked from a distance exactly like *Tryste*. Before we left Cocos Ernest had mentioned nothing about any imminent departure from the atoll. Yet here she seemed to be for we could see the Canadian flag on her stern and what appeared to be red sails stowed on the booms. The previous year in the New Hebrides our conceit was such that we almost came to take it for granted that *Nanook* would outpace *Tryste* on all but upwind passages. We had assuredly started first from Cocos 15 days before and apart perhaps from an initial reluctance to carry much canvas in the heavy weather, we had covered the distance I thought in reasonably good time. Nevertheless here before our eyes was *Tryste*. We could almost hear Ernest's deep throaty chuckles of self-satisfaction coming out at us on the wind.

The lighter appeared again and several people came on board, a police inspector, a helmsman, a doctor, a certain character called André. I recovered the anchor with difficulty for we were secured then to the launch and in their eagerness to help they carried us away forward and ahead of the anchor before it could be freed. We were then off at a dizzying pace. The helmsman impatiently brushed Katie away from the tiller, mere lubberly woman that she was, and away we flew along the 24-foot-wide channel. Some of the markers we were able to touch as we rushed by. The channel had a dog-leg bend in it and at that point I was sure that our pilot would move too late and put us onto the bank, but around we went at the last moment with inches to spare.

I realized later that we should have negotiated the channel under our own power but you never know these things till you've already been there, and it's always hard to stop people who are determined to be helpful. At all events we arrived without a scratch and for that alone I was grateful.

Hundreds of Creole people gathered on both the cement jetties to watch *Nanook* manoeuvre in and moor centre lock fashion between them. And there in the basin ahead of us truly enough lay *Tryste*. While the girls hauled the trimaran forward in the basin to make room for us, Ernest stood arms akimbo on the stern grinning widely out of his black beard and calling to us with exaggerated concern, "Hello *Nanook*. Whatever has been keeping you all this time. I hope you didn't have any trouble? We've been so worried about you."

We asked him to shut up and to come on board and join us below with the doctor, the police inspector, the pilot and André for a little celebration on us. The formalities were mercifully brief, the informalities pleasantly long and it felt good to be in.

The remarkable thing about Rodrigues is not the stony dryness of the place or the huge lagoon extending four miles out from the coast, or the poverty of the people. The thing above all that must impress every visiting sailor is the open-heartedness of the people. The very officials were like mothers to us.

Rodrigues belongs to Mauritius but while the Mauritians are largely of Indian descent the people of little Rodrigues are mostly Creole with a small number of Chinese and Indians thrown in. Both islands speak French despite 150 years of British rule since the Napoleonic wars. Not much love is lost between the two islands and for a year after the new flag of independent Mauritius was unfurled on Rodrigues it was regularly torn down or stoned. We never locked the boat for we were frequently reminded that there was no need. No thieves here, they said. Rodrigues is a very safe place—not like Mauritius.

Every day curious eyes watched everything we did. Some of the people we invited aboard for a look around, and our earliest acquaintance, André the dark visaged fisherman was a frequent caller, telling us a great deal about the island and his numerous family and glancing occasionally at the wine cupboard for he had a Brobdingnagian thirst, with which the police, so we gathered, had cause to be acquainted. I made the early mistake, perhaps, of giving him a bottle of Double Heart brandy from Bali which he wrapped in a paper bag and carted off under his arm swearing eternal friendship and promising us a fresh fish next day which indeed he produced.

All the islanders were hospitable but they were also very poor and we had to guard our indulgence in their free-flowing generosity. Sylvio, the police inspector, a genial gentleman if ever there was one, devoted a whole day to driving us off in a police vehicle across the hilly island to the limestone country on the south coast. There we visited a long cave, walking all the way through it with torches of kerosene-soaked rags burning on long sticks. We skirted stalagmite formations and waded through ponds of cold black water before emerging into the sunlight of a canyon at the far end. We then walked over empty unpromising grassland pastures for a meal at the Auberge de la Caverne before returning to Port Mathurin.

Sylvio asked us all to a dance up in one of the hill villages on Saturday night but Katie and I had already accepted the invitation of André to another dance at Baie aux Huitres, round the coast a little. This must have embarrassed Sylvio a little because he wanted us all to be together and André was one of his more regular customers. But somehow a compromise was worked out between the two and all eight of us went off in a Landrover on Saturday night to Baie aux Huitres where we enjoyed ourselves immensely until midnight. André was formally dressed and full of decorum and dignity, the perfect host. We then all went off together to the dance in the hills, an even more riotously successful affair than the first. The place was utterly packed and there was a carnival spirit of gay abandon about the place which infected us all, not excluding André who by then had abandoned all earlier pretense of decorum and formality.

The music was marvelous and the dancing never stopped so no one had much chance to overdrink except perhaps André who had switched to French and was holding forth at length to anyone who would listen. The whole crowd was well-disposed and convivial and our own little group gradually broke up and migrated elsewhere amongst the happy crowd. We all agreed later that we'd never enjoyed a dance so much in our lives. It was not till three in the morning that we found each other again. Ernest was located somewhere outside under the trees. Katie was still giggling to the two-step with her Chinese dance partner, the *Tryste* girls were run to earth and prised out from a knot of soft-spoken Creole boys. Sylvio after a long absence reappeared from nowhere to drive us away for a nightcap. Only André was missing, but he showed up later in the headlights of the Landrover. There was no need to stop. He was about to get a free ride back anyway. The road was lined with people and there was André lying on his back on the road bellowing like a bull in the middle of a scuffle with a couple of Sylvio's men. It seemed more polite just to keep going. We never saw him again.

After eight days we felt we had to leave though we were sad at the thought. *Tryste* too had to press on for the Haighs were hoping to find employment in Durban for the summer. Just as we were preparing ourselves for sea a sail appeared around the point and *Tiare* came sailing in so we delayed our departure for a while because we hadn't seen Paul, Vaiea and Lik-lik Paul since Rabaul and we were keen to hear their gossip. It was a tonic to meet them again.

Our three dear friends Sylvio, Ah Kee and Maurice came to say goodbye. They had showered us with great kindness and we felt sad indeed at the parting. It was such a strong feeling to have after only a week's stay. We cast off ahead of *Tryste,* went out the channel behind her and away we sailed from the little island of love, carrying the trade wind away in the afternoon sunshine, *Tryste* and *Nanook* on course together for Mauritius.

The sky was clear and the wind moderate and directly behind us so I set the full main to starboard and put the genoa out to port with the whisker pole and away we flew with *Tryste* nearby. The sun sank ahead of us to the west but our eyes and thoughts were all for the little island sinking astern to the east. Few other places had ever affected us quite so much as Rodrigues.

The wind was Force 3 and Mauritius was just 330 miles on. *Nanook* rolled gently to one side and then to the other in a lazy rhythmic swing while the water gushed cheerfully aside at the bows. Our days were sunny and uneventful and our three nights were quiet and starry. What could be more relaxing or pleasant than rolling along over such an easy sea with such memories and the company of friends within the visible horizon?

Nanook had overtaken and passed *Tryste* in the early stages and for the next two days at sunrise we were treated to the cheering sight of those red sails still four or five miles astern. On the third morning *Tryste* had disappeared completely but Mauritius on the other hand was appearing ahead. A current had set us north during the night so I had to bring the genoa over to starboard and start reaching across the wind to carry us between the tide-ridden channels between the offshore islets and the mainland of Mauritius.

I'd thought that *Tryste* might have sneaked past us during the night while we were off course, but as we motor-sailed up into the big commercial harbour of Port Louis for entry there was no sign of any trimaran. Moored freighters lined both sides of the channel and lighters scurried about carrying sugar out to them. The waterfront was a scene of mad bustle and the roar of traffic in the city added its own cacophony of madness. Some figures on the customs dock waved us over to a derelict fishing boat and called to us to moor alongside and wait there for clearance, and once the officials were gone we locked the hatches and rowed ashore.

Port Louis is an interesting if rather scruffy place with an ever-thronging Indian population. Anything more utterly different from Rodrigues would be hard to imagine. We had mail from the U.K. and New Zealand waiting for us in Port Louis so the post office was first on the list. How happy we felt to get mail again after months of silence. The news though was not very good. My mother in New Zealand was back in hospital and clearly ailing and I suddenly felt selfish for having sailed away from home after such a short visit there.

We stocked up with an excessive load of fresh food in Port Louis for the huge market sold mountains of every imaginable fruit, vegetable and meat and the fine sight of it all rather went to our heads. Upon returning to *Nanook* we found *Tryste* entering port and after they were cleared we took them ashore ostentatiously to "show them around." We were happy to be all together again. *Tryste* moored alongside *Nanook* and there we lay together for the night.

Port Louis is no place for a yacht so early the next morning we put out from the noisy port to sail up the coast ten miles to Grand Baie. Black ash from burning canefields scattered over us as we punched close-hauled up to the big circular indentation on the coast. Most of our friends of the earlier anchorages had bypassed Rodrigues so they were in already, anchored on the sandy bottom of the bay off the delightful and hospitable Grand Baie Yacht Club.

As we stepped ashore we were met by the genial club secretary, Gigi, who stood us a beer and an invitation to attend the banquet at the club the following day in honour of all the visiting yachts. The club was in a beautiful location. It wasn't large enough to be impersonal yet it had every possible facility and despite the increasing numbers of west-bound yachtsmen who must visit the island around October every year it was still extraordinarily hospitable. The members were mostly French, the descendants of the old land-owning class whose island history went back to the 17th century before the British take-over.

One of these members very kindly placed his car and chauffeur at our disposal for a day, so with Bob and Kristi Hannelt from *Skylark* we were able to make a tour of the whole island through barren limestone country, fertile market gardens and the extensive sugar cane lands where old stone cane-crushing windmills stand beside big modern refineries and where cane-laden bullock wagons still creak along the roads in competition with trucks. Sugar must mean a lot to Mauritius and labour must be cheap for cane is cultivated even on the drier lava-strewn lands. In some places rocks were piled up into long parallel walls leaving gaps of red soil between them hardly wider than the walls themselves and even in these unpromising strips the cane is planted and cut by hand. Our Indian chauffeur drove us on along the ruggedly beautiful windward coast and back finally across the centre of the island past the craters and the high volcanic pinnacles that give the island such a delightful skyline.

The eye infections that first began bothering Katie in New Guinea were recurring at this stage of our voyage and she had to find a specialist in Port Louis and have a minor operation before continuing on. There was the usual bottom scrubbing, maintenance and restocking to be done on board but most of our time was spent in the happy semi-idle luxury of Grand Baie.

Before leaving, the people on the cruising yachts bought a large Visitors' Book in Port Louis. Each yacht crew filled a page with photographs, drawings and a history of their voyage to date, and this was presented as a token gift to the hospitable club.

Nanook left at the end of her second week bound for Durban.

Some of the yachts were already gone ahead of us. The Haighs on *Tryste* had stayed only a week in Mauritius as they hoped to get jobs in Durban to help finance the final few months of their voyage to British Columbia. But none of the yachts could afford to delay much longer anyway as the cyclone season of the southern Indian Ocean was imminent. Cyclone Bernadette was already stirring up a lot of trouble in the Chagos Archipelago as we left and for several days we kept a close ear to the radio for signs that she might move our way.

The towering peaks of Réunion were passed close by after the first night at sea, but I felt we were already running a bit late and Bernadette put an end to any lingering temptation to stop. It would take several days or a week of waiting there for Bernadette to travel out of range and by that time we might have Charlotte or Carol or Cathy or some other hag screeching down our necks.

For six days we slipped along with light easy winds over an empty sea with just the occasional Cape pigeon circling us for company and once a great albatross that stayed with us for twenty minutes, a reminder that our south latitude was getting higher.

I hadn't looked forward at all to the passage to Durban. The waters south of Madagascar and off the African coast are subject to sudden fierce gales and when these are against the strong currents of those regions they can kick up some fearful seas. Doubtless some sailors have had pleasant passages on that route but I'd certainly never heard of a single one. Slocum wrote of those waters that the *Spray* "suffered as much as she did anywhere except off Cape Horn."

While in Fiji we met a French single-hander who had subsequently crossed the Indian Ocean one year ahead of us. In Mauritius he picked up a 21 year old French girl from another yacht as crew for the passage to Durban but south of Madagascar they were hit by one of these storms. The little yacht capsized in a heavy sea. The girl at the time was sleeping in the forepeak. After the yacht righted herself the owner called out to the girl but there was no response. He searched through the boat and found that the forehatch had torn off, and since there was no sign of the girl he assumed that she had fallen out the open hatch and gone overboard. He searched the stormy seas but found nothing. It was not until some hours later that he discovered the girl wedged down in a dark corner of the forepeak. Her neck was broken and she was dead.

I steered to leave the end of Madagascar a safe 70 miles away. Even so we found that the current suddenly increased and indeed so did the wind. A northeaster rose up for a day and a night until it reached 36 knots, but it was from behind and didn't worry us too much. The wind fell away after that until we were becalmed on a flat blue sea.

During the hard wind I'd leaned heavily against the Sumlog cable and broken it off at the dial end. This meant that we could no longer measure off the miles for dead reckoning, no very vital loss but for making an accurate landfall the log was very useful in between sextant sights. I rummaged around and unearthed an old cable fitting left behind by Kurt Frost. It was the wrong size but I attached it to the cable with epoxy glue and after giving it six hours to set I found to my surprise that it worked. It would have to be replaced in South Africa. "Our Durban list gets longer and longer," the logbook says.

We reached the southern limits of the trade wind belt and for several days we had poor progress with light fickle breezes, flat seas and sunshine. About twenty pilot fish took up station at the bow and a few on the quarter. I was startled one afternoon while stretched out on the deck with a book to hear what sounded like air escaping from the brakes of a big truck. A mist drifted over towards me as I leaped up and called Katie. A great pod of whales surfaced lazily. They were close all around us, each one puffing his breath out the top of his head. I could have prodded some with the whisker pole. I grabbed the tiller to steer clear if any should surface ahead of us for apart from ships and hard land if there was anything I never wanted to hit it was a whale. But in a moment they sounded and all were gone from sight.

By the end of October, eleven days from Mauritius, we found the weather worsening as the wind went round the compass through the west to south. The seas then rose quickly and conditions were bad enough to keep Katie in her bunk and me attached by my safety harness to a special securing line on deck rigged from bow to stern. This line allowed me to attach myself before leaving the companionway and to move the full length of the deck without having to refasten the harness to the lifelines and rigging at different points. That arrangement eliminated the dangerous moments when the snap shackle at the end of the harness line was being transferred from one point of attachment to another.

We steered westwards for the African coast under staysail and double-reefed main. At dawn after a wild dark night I clawed forward to find the source of a new noise amongst the louder noises of the wind and sea. The staysail, hidden from sight by the main, had shredded itself into unbelievable tatters. This was a sail which in Madang I had sewn up with self-defeating cleverness from the remnants of the old mainsail. The job had taken several days of hand stitching and I was quite pleased with myself when it was finished. But the folly of expecting too much of old cloth in bad weather was now evident.

Several heavy crests came over me as I groped around in the lazarette for the old original staysail that still lay rolled up there and after transferring all the bronze hanks onto it I set it on the inner forestay. *Nanook* responded and began again to throw the heavy swell off her

In a rising onshore gale from the northeast, *Nanook* roars along towards the narrow entrance to Durban harbour.

shoulders and forge ahead while the "new" staysail quietly sank astern. Another item for the Durban list.

Things settled down again for a few hours while the wind went round through the east, but the next day the barometer began falling while a hard northerly set in ahead of a cold front.

"Heavens," I wrote in the log, "how I wish we were in Durban."

The next day I wrote, "November 2. Solid overcast. Wind really going at it like a maniac out of the south. Gigantic crashing seas, the worst and the most fearsome I think that we have ever seen. We're working our way across towards the land with double-reefed main. Long way to go yet, 80 miles maybe to the coast, but position finding is impossible in this awful grey murk. Maintaining strict regular watches day and night and now picking up plenty of shipping. It's amazing how quickly these big oil tankers appear out of nowhere and how easily they smash their way forward through the big seas."

During my second watch the next night with a moderating wind I noticed a vague hint of light in the sky. Durban? It agreed approximately with a direction-finding radio beacon. Yet closer abeam was a light flashing intermittently from the coast north of the glow. It didn't agree with anything on the chart, nor with anything in the latest Admiralty List of Lights. This gave me cause to resume my habitual worrying. Where were we? Already past Durban? Drifting south too fast on the Agulhas Current? Should I continue? Lie ahull till morning? Close the coast? Sail up into the wind? Dark nights and high wild seas don't help logical thinking, but finally after much dithering I decided that the radio beacon wasn't a trick and that the vague hint of light to the southwest was Durban, and this was confirmed by morning. Dawn showed a long coast not far off, a leaden but lifting sky and a relenting wind. Far to the southwest was an odd line of white specks, the skyscrapers of Durban.

The sun greeted us at last as we sat in the cockpit having our ten o'clock coffee which Katie with her usual perverse Englishness always insisted on calling "elevenses." Because of the Agulhas Current that sweeps constantly to the southwest along that coast I had deliberately aimed north of Durban so that whatever the wind might be the current at least would be an advantage to us. For that reason we still had a fair way to go, thirty miles perhaps. The wind had fallen away with the dawn and I didn't see how we could expect to make port that day. But around noon a northeaster came along behind us freshening with every mile, and away we flew with happy hearts.

Thirty-one ships were all at anchor in the open roadstead outside the harbour waiting for permission to go in, and although the Admiralty Pilot reminded us that all vessels entering Durban Harbour had first to obtain permission from the port authority we sailed on through all of them shortening sail as we went for once again we had a sudden freshening gale under us. The seas became steeper with every mile.

Out of the east came another sail, someone, I thought smugly who had not aimed high for Durban for they were tacking upwind. They beat us in by twenty minutes. It turned out to be *Skylark*.

The seas got up steeply as we approached the narrow dredged neck of water leading into the harbour. We ran on roaring through the breakers that smashed themselves high on the breakwaters at the entrance and then we were suddenly in a wide smooth harbour surrounded by coastal hills and a big city. We joined *Skylark* for a while at the quarantine anchorage and at dusk were escorted by Customs men to the long jetty at the Point Yacht Club right in the heart of the city.

Many of our cruising friends were already in. *Skylark* and *Nanook* required some jiggling around of the other yachts which were all rafted together in three lines, and while all this shoving and fendering and casting off and yelling was going on I sat below with the Afrikaans customs man stowing all my Bali brandy in the boot locker where it was firmly sealed up until we left, and swearing that I had no Playboy magazines on my shelves and that we would not leave the vicinity of the city without prior permission.

Ernest was there on the jetty. "Ahoy, *Nanook*," he called. "You're invited out to supper. Be ready in fifteen minutes." We drove out with the gang from *Tryste* and a total stranger, enjoying the novel sensation of sweeping over solid land in a big relaxing car. Our host had a fine house in the suburbs and a large gathering of invited guests all sitting about elegantly with their cocktails and all wanting to know what sort of time we'd been having out there.

We felt scruffy and salt-grimed and our host after offering us a drink then added "But you are just in from the sea. You might like a bath first?"

"We'll have both," I assured him gratefully.

"Splendid," he said. "Which do you want first?"

"Both together," I replied.

"Good," he said. "Who wants the first turn at the bath?"

Katie replied "We'll have that together too."

As we lay there in the sudden steamy soapy luxury, glasses in our hands and feet by each other's head, our eyes met and we exclaimed in unison, "Isn't it lovely to be in!"

XVII

The Cape and the South Atlantic

This first introduction to Durban hospitality was typical of our whole six weeks there. The people of the city took great interest in the little fleet of overseas yachts that lay rafted together at the yacht club on the downtown waterfront, and great kindness was shown to us by many people.

Katie and I were especially lucky to have had friends living there. In 1962 I had sailed as one of a crew of seven on a schooner setting out from the Channel Islands on a cruise around the world. The owner was inexperienced and his boat was unseaworthy. She began sinking in the middle of the Bay of Biscay and only by dint of tough exhausting round-the-clock baling did we keep her barely afloat as far as northern Spain where the voyage like many another came to an untimely end. For me, two important things came out of this, one a determination to depend only on myself in future by having a yacht of my own, and the other the friendship of the young South African crewman Gerald Spence.

Gerald had since married and he and his wife Margaret lived with their two children in a beautiful home up in the hills of Durban. We had a lot of fun together and they showered us with hospitality. Once they drove us hundreds of miles up the coast to the edges of Zululand and the game parks of Hluhlue and Umfolozi to see the great variety of wildlife there, buck and buffalo, monkeys and stately giraffes and the primitive grumpy rare white rhinoceros which seemed to us nearly as massive as the elephant, and which stared balefully at us from their shady wallows like cantankerous tanks.

Life at the yacht club's congested jetty was quite unlike anything we had experienced before. *Nanook* lay tied between *Kuan Yin* and *Bebinka*. *Skylark* was behind us on the next line with *Mauna Kea* on *Skylark's* starboard side and another three outside her. Two others lay ahead of us

With the Indian Ocean behind them, the crew of *Nanook* relax in the saloon during *Nanook*'s six-week stay in Durban.

and two more on the exposed side of the jetty. We were a happy community, by no means similar in type but just as our boats were held together in a web of crossing lines, so in a way we felt bound by the common bond of our freedom.

Tryste being a beamy multihull was cast out of this company and consigned to the moorings some distance out, but we saw plenty of them and slept aboard her on a few occasions. Ernest, Val and the girls had hoped to get jobs in Durban for their funds were running low, but they were refused work permits and Ernest began muttering about having to get a bank loan from Canada.

As I said there was much interest in all the visiting yachts from overseas. Press reporters and photographers descended on the jetty in a stream and, primed with beer, some of the crews sat through a long radio interview for the national network. Crowds of city people came down during the weekends and the lunch hours and evenings to gaze down at the assembled fleet, to ask us all about our voyages and to learn for themselves what it was really like out there. Behind some of the questions there sometimes seemed to lie the deep-seated suspicion that something in their own lives was missing. But far from all were envious of us. Some were quite the opposite like the crusty old man who wanted to know how many times *Nanook* had capsized and whether we anchored every night at sea.

"Do you have far to go from here?" he asked.

"About 11,000 miles more," I replied.

"That far?" he said. "I suppose there will come many times yet when you will have to be rescued from the stormy seas."

"Oh no, I don't think so," I assured him. "We try not to depend on others. By and large we just have to look after ourselves and live by our own wits."

"Indeed," he exclaimed, looking at me speculatively. "In that case I am surprised that you have made it this far in safety."

There was much to occupy us in Durban and every day was filled with activity. The steering compass had become so murky as to be almost unreadable and I had to undertake the complicated job of cleaning and repairing it, and refilling it with clear fluid. I ordered a new staysail from a local sailmaker and had him restitch the jib. The mizzen backstays had to be replaced for the old ones were fraying, and the liferaft was tested, repaired and repacked. This last service was done entirely free for us as well as for three of the other yachts by a professional who understood how hard-pressed sailors often are for funds, and who was concerned that we might take a chance with our untested rafts for the problematical passage around the Cape. This was a gesture typical of the South Africans.

We both had dental work to be done. The problem was finding a dentist who had the time to take us on, but our friends Margaret and Gerald came to the rescue by petitioning theirs on our behalf, and their own doctor too for Katie's eye infection was back in business again.

There was a huge pile of mail waiting for us at the Spences on our arrival and a great deal to be sent off also for we found that the further on we sailed the longer grew the list of friends from places far behind us who simply had to be written to and informed of our progress. For this purpose Katie bought a big stack of postcards, each one showing the waterfront at the Point Yacht Club with several visiting yachts tied to the jetty. These were inscribed on the blank side with the caption, "Durban Yacht Mole, World Cruising Yachts in the Foreground." It was not till Katie returned aboard with these that she discovered that the most prominent of the yachts shown on the view was our own *Nanook,* or *Safari Too* as she was when she first visited Durban in 1967. She looked a bit different then, but she lay in exactly the same spot that she was occupying now on her second time round.

Six months had passed since *Nanook's* last antifouling and nearly two years since her last coat of topside enamel. I thought ruefully that if her bottom paint was showing its age as badly as the paint on the topsides, it was time for a haul out. The slipways of Durban were busy and expensive and we thought it would be more pleasant to get the work done in the

Cheap paint, hard wear, and polluted water combined to foul *Nanook*'s underwater surfaces and put her on the slipways in Durban prior to the passage around the Cape.

While hauled out in Durban, *Nanook* had her topsides stripped down to bare wood and a new coat of white polyurethane paint added.

quiet of the little fishing port of Mossel Bay away round on the south coast near Cape Agulhas. Margaret and Gerald knew the place well and their descriptions fired our enthusiasm. However my hull-scrubbing sessions in Mauritius had given me little reason to expect much more of our antifouling and after a month of lying in the murky polluted water of Durban harbour I was anxious to find whether we were fit to put to sea. So I put the mask on and went overboard between the yachts holding my face close to the hull to see through the murk. One cursory survey around the stern was enough. I climbed back aboard, astonishing the sightseers that I should want to go swimming there, and said to Katie "I'm afraid we have to haul out here. The bottom is an absolute jungle."

Wilson's yard arranged with luck to squeeze us into their well-booked schedule and the timing itself was lucky because their one rail slipway came up out of rather shallow water and *Nanook* required the few days either side of spring tides to get on and off.

We gasped at the amount of fouling that was all over the bottom, a heavy white crusty growth of calcium from a variety of worm coral that thrived on the nutrient sludge of the big city. But it wasn't the bottom that took up all our time. The topsides had several consecutive layers of different enamels. These layers were getting into the bad habit of peeling off each other, so a new coat involved first getting right down to bare wood. That was a long laborious business for the original epoxy coat ignored the blowtorch and we had to resort to a chemical paint remover as well as a lot of elbow grease, part of which was contributed by the two obligatory yard hands. These two cheerful black workers cost us only a few rand each per day, but they were so painfully slow that we began to wonder whether they were such cheap labour after all. Time and tide wait for no man, and *Nanook* had to be back in the water before the springs took off, so Katie and I with the grudging assent of the foreman did most of the work ourselves.

It was at this time while we lived on the rails at Wilson's Boatyard that Gerald came down one morning with the news that my family in New Zealand had telephoned the Spence household during the night and wanted to speak to me. The news from home had not been good and I knew before I took the call that my mother was dead. I spoke for some time over a bad line with my distant brothers and sisters and felt some slight comfort that they at least had been with her to the end. Poor Mum, she had always longed through sixteen years for my return home to New Zealand and always hoped that I would eventually "settle down." She'd had, as had Katie's parents, some considerable misgivings about our buying a boat and getting foolish notions in our heads about crossing oceans, but like them she kept her thoughts to herself and came eventually to accept the fact that if we were quite mad at least we were competent at it, and she became in the end, I think, quite proud of us. She was a great lady, and I grieved at her passing.

Nanook looked like a new pin by the time we were finished. After carefully lettering her name across the stern and paying our bill at the boatyard, I went off with three of the other skippers at the club to collect our clearance from Customs. It was the middle of December and it was time to go.

Strong currents and stronger winds, heavy traffic, high seas and a nearly shelterless coast, these things combined to make the 800 mile passage to Cape Town something of a challenge, a passage with a big question mark. It could be dangerous in the extreme as the South Africans were fond of reminding anyone who would listen. But it could also be, literally, a breeze as it was when *Nanook* made her first voyage around the southern end of Africa. As we motored out across the harbour we hoped for the same luck. Our friends from *Kuan Yin* and *Bebinka* drove out to the harbour entrance to wave goodbye to us for we would not be seeing them again, and just as we approached the open sea at the edge of the breakwater a fussy pilot launch raced up to inform us that we had permission from the harbour authority to leave port.

For several days we sailed quietly along the coast in the easy weather

Ready for 10,000 miles of the Atlantic, *Nanook* prepares to leave the Durban slipway.

we hoped for. One night we put in to East London harbour to take shelter from a forecasted southwesterly that never materialized, but otherwise we never stopped. We soon crossed the farthest east longitude reached 3½ years before in Turkey so that if we'd not yet sailed around the world at least we had crossed every meridian. Light southeasterly beam winds, calms, the occasional day of tacking, heavy haze and drizzle, sunshine; and always carrying us along was the welcome Agulhas Current, that enormous body of warm water flowing powerfully along the coast, driven southwest by the trade winds and deflected into the path of the westerlies south of Africa.

There was a never-ending stream of ships to watch out for. Some took only twenty minutes to reach us after first appearing on the horizon and all too often they came straight at us, great silent menacing things, pushing vast walls of water ahead of their bows. We kept strict watches round the clock, always ready for a ninety degree course change. The 12 volt signal lamp was kept plugged in ready for use and the diesel starting handle dangled at the ready.

Sweaters, jackets and blankets were dragged one by one out of remote corners as the weather cooled. The diesel at times was reluctant to start and a few times in calm weather when a supertanker's bows loomed towards us my first step was to set the kettle boiling on the stove and add the hot water to the cooling water jacket which made starting much easier. Cool southerlies filled the sails as we swept rapidly along the south coast and not wishing to neglect a fair wind we passed Mossel Bay by without stopping.

We steered south of all the traffic and enjoyed the relative emptiness of the waters well offshore where whales leaped completely out of the water and an occasional albatross, that "snow white ghost of the haunted capes of Hope and Horn," flew nearby over the long waves.

The life-rich southern seas glowed at nights with luminescence. One night coming on deck to relieve Katie I thought that we were being signalled by a ship, for the sails were lit with bursts of light, irregular long and short flashes. Yet no ships were in sight nor did the mysterious morse make any sense. The *Flying Dutchman* perhaps? I soon realized that the light came from the bows where white waves surged and spread and sank away again as we rushed on through the seas. These waves shone with a startling phosphorescent brilliance that I'd never seen before.

Around noon of the summer solstice, well out of sight of land, we reached the southernmost point of our voyage, 35°S, and later in gentle weather after passing Cape Agulhas at the end of Africa I altered the vane to bring us west and a little north into the Atlantic. We rolled along in the fresh breeze and bright sunshine and it was a good feeling to be entering the home stretch with only ten thousand miles of the long Atlantic remaining between us and the cool piney indentations of Nova Scotia.

Katie ponders the Cape of Good Hope as *Nanook* leaves the Indian Ocean behind and re-enters the Atlantic.

Penguins and seals leaped from one crest to another as we approached the Cape of Good Hope in the late afternoon but the high rocky peninsula blanketed our wind so it wasn't till midnight that we reached the approaches to Cape Town.

If we'd been smugly congratulating ourselves on an easy winning of the passage around from Durban, we now got our comeuppance. A pale white layer of cloud, "the tablecloth," lay over Table Mountain and a sudden southerly gale ripped down the slopes, across the city and out to sea. Our chart of the port was one of a few we'd inherited with the boat so it was several years old but I assumed it would still guide us in, even if a few of the details were out of date. In this though, I was quite wrong. I could make no sense whatever of the lights and general features of the port ahead of us. White lights and red lights occulted and flashed and beamed at us unblinking, but they bore no remote resemblance to those on the chart. The wind tore at us and I was blinded as much by the dust-laden gale as by the glaring city lights beyond the port but I was determined to get in and find a safe berth inside rather than having to endure the rest of the night hove to in the bay.

We tacked doggedly up to a narrow entrance between high dark massive moles, and just as we tried to angle our way through the entrance, a tremendous blast of wind laid us far over, burying one of the decks in the water. A huge stone wall loomed over us close by. Katie screamed.

"Bear away," I yelled from the foredeck. "For God's sake bear away." I scrambled back to help her and *Nanook* turned reluctantly off the wind and we ran off a little way to catch our breath and prepare for another try. Again the same thing happened and this time we came even closer to ramming the end of the mole. Katie was terrified and I cursed myself for not releasing the sheets as we bore away to allow the boat to turn more easily. I stayed with her in the cockpit for she'd almost tumbled out of it and into the water on the second knock down.

We tried again. I stood on and off waiting for another williwaw to strike and exhaust itself. Then we drove through at the difficult angle of approach dictated by the wind. *Nanook* left the high walls behind her at last and we found ourselves in a huge commercial basin which was devoid of ships excepting for a dredge working the bottom at the far end. Clearly, a lot of changes had been made since our chart was published, and the big port was undergoing massive expansion. We tacked back and forth wondering where to anchor for there was no place to tie along the high unfendered concrete walls. But I found a mooring buoy at the far end of the basin and after securing to it with a heavy nylon line we collapsed with all our clothes still on into our bunks. We couldn't remember ever being so scared before, and the experience at the end of an unrelaxing passage had worn us right out.

"When in doubt, stay at sea." That had been our maxim from the beginning, and it seemed to me as I lay thinking in my bunk that I was beginning to forget it. We slept for two or three hours but it was a nervous sleep with a hair trigger release, and when a police launch approached to investigate us at dawn I was on deck like a shot. They might have thrown a number of books at us but instead they simply asked if we were alright, and did we need any help? I explained that we'd entered in the gale during the night without up-to-date charts and we didn't know where the yacht club was. So they kindly threw us a line and towed us through the commercial basins and deposited us at the club jetty. It was December 24th and we could have wished for no better Christmas present than to be safely into the hospitable shelter of the Royal Cape Yacht Club.

Skylark was in as well as three or four other acquaintances of earlier ports. *Tryste* appeared on Christmas Day after sailing around from Mossel Bay where she'd grown tired of waiting for *Nanook* to join her. A few days in Cape Town were enough to make us regret having spent so much time in Durban, despite the good times there. As it was we could afford only a week.

Local yachtsmen took us on long drives to show us the beautiful wine country and the rugged mountains of the Cape Peninsula, and to lecture us for not having the time to do greater justice to their country. The *Tryste*

Under the able command of her owners, the Haighs of British Columbia, the trimaran *Tryste* leaves Cape Town in company with *Nanook* for the passage to St. Helena.

girls climbed up the face of Table Mountain while Val and Ernest accompanied us to the summit on the cableway. Katie gathered clumps of wild heather at the top and brought them back to secure them in the cabin to bring luck, she said, to our last six months of sailing.

Twice more we observed the well known phenomenon of "laying the cloth" that had greeted our night arrival. A white cloud would form over the flat surface of Table Mountain as a southerly buster blew up and before long we would all be heeling and bobbing around in the little club basin as the sudden wind lashed about us. White tongues of mist ripped away off the edges of the "cloth" and tore rapidly down the precipitous ravines at the back of the city. A percussion band of frapping halyards added itself to the din at the club while clouds of coal dust and grit from the railway tracks coated our rigging, masts, decks and every other possible surface. I regretted not going aloft with a rag before leaving Cape Town, and Durban too, for both cities contributed a great deal of grey grime to our previously white sails.

On the last day of December, Ernest and I went to the customs shed and collected an impressively official-looking document sealed with red wax, clearing our vessels for sea. We left there, *Nanook* and *Tryste,* in the late afternoon sunshine of New Year's Eve. Many friends, yachtsmen and townsmen both, were there to call *"Bon voyage"*, to help us with our lines and to cast streamers over us as we left. We felt sorry to be leaving so soon. Blue streamers fluttered from our rigging as I raised sail outside the entrance.

While we sailed out to the northwest in *Tryste's* company I gazed back at the city and the great backdrop of Table Mountain, and wondered what might become of South Africa in the years to come. It seemed impossible that anyone could go there and not love the place, and yet there it is with all its racial distinctions, Black; White; Indian; Coloured; racial divisions even within the legal racial divisions and a remarkable set of laws designed to separate one human from another so that they will not have to urinate down the same drains, ride the same buses, rub shoulders at the post office or (heaven forbid) sleep together. Yet everybody mixes together on the streets and in the stores and our impression on the surface was that there existed no more real ill-will there than in most places of mixed race. In their day-to-day dealings, most individual white South Africans are no more stupid or less considerate of their fellows than are most other Europeans, rather it seemed to us to the contrary, and it is difficult to understand why self-interest alone does not suggest to them the urgent dismantling of laws and institutions that stand as a towering insult to the rest of Africa.

The sun sank westwards for the last time that year while *Tryste* disappeared in the gloom and the hills of Africa faded to the east. We were all alone again with only the wind and the sky and the sun around us. We were bound across the South Atlantic by way of St. Helena to the seductive delights of Rio.

"It's nice to be ploughing the Atlantic," says the log on the first day out. "Katie celebrated the arrival of the New Year by being sick in the red bucket. I was asleep. A fresh wind came up this afternoon and we're now sweeping rapidly through the seas, even up to nine knots or more on the crests."

Southerly winds drove us on day after day and the cold Benguela current kept us covered up night and day until we were well inside the Tropic of Capricorn. Then gradually one blanket after another came off the bunks as we returned to tropical conditions. Strangely we never seemed to get the trade wind sky, filled with puffy rags of cumulus against a blue sky that typified the trades in other oceans. High grey overcast blotted the stars each night and persisted until the afternoons when it would break apart and partially disperse only to close over again in the evenings.

We did little apart from refibreglassing the dinghy and preparing sumptuous meals from the supplies taken on at Cape Town, concentrating at first on the things easily spoiled, the chops and cauliflowers, peaches and fresh milk, and the daily gift of flying fish, and later turning our ravenous attention to the dried smoked beef, the salami, carrots and potatoes and ripening stalks of bananas. We enthused at ridiculous lengths over every meal and as soon as one was over we began planning the next, discussing it in every detail for hours beforehand. Nowhere have we ever appreciated food so greatly as on such passages at sea (nor at certain other times could we have appreciated it less).

On the ninth day I took my noon sight looking south instead of north for *Nanook* had by then crossed the line of the sun's declination, and the next day we crossed the meridian of Greenwich into the Western Hemisphere. We carried as much sail as possible at all times. The mainsail and the genoa were wing and wing most of the time, even when the wind came in fresh, for *Tryste* was surely somewhere about us and this would be our last passage in her company. This was hard on the venerable old genoa. It was ten years old and pulling hard on its second circumnavigation, but by the tenth day it was feeling the strain, torn, worn and rotten as it was, so it finally had to come off for some major surgery before it could ever again be considered a sail.

We hove to for six hours on the night of January 12th for the little island of St. Helena lay somewhere ahead in the darkness, and at dawn, there it was, a high rugged barren-looking pile of ancient cinders with a few hints of grass on its heights. Here and there stone watch towers and gun

The seas build up behind her as *Nanook* settles into her stride towards St. Helena.

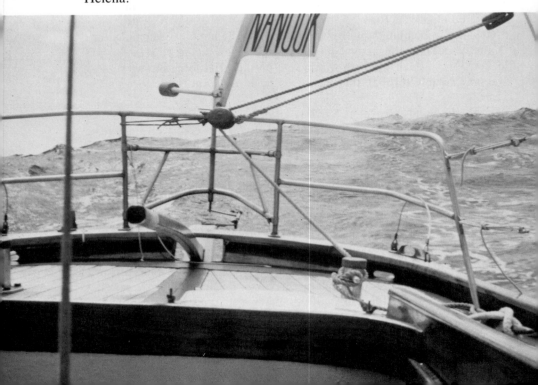

emplacements warned us of troubles with the French. A big swell rolled in to the little anchorage at Jamestown. Fishing boats bobbed about and white waves exploded against the landing stage. But it was Jamestown or nothing so we came carefully in with the guidance of a man and boy who suddenly appeared in a rowboat. We put the anchor down where we were told in seven fathoms. We had taken 12½ days to cover 1,720 miles. There was no sign of *Tryste* and we were the first yacht in of the season.

The customs officer was not long in coming out to give us clearance and to stay aboard for a long pleasant visit. What better things are there to do in such a little place on a quiet sunny morning? The boatman who had first directed us in carried us all ashore. He was almost a permanent fixture of the anchorage being hired by one of the trading firms as a watchman over the boats in the anchorage. He was always within hail and although we put the dinghy overboard for the sake of ventilation we never used it for going ashore. The landing stage was constantly awash from the heavy swell. It had steps at three levels and a couple of long ropes dangling from a frame overhead as well as lifebuoys nearby. While the boatman rowed slowly in stern-to with a canny eye for the waves behind him, his passengers stood on the stern supporting themselves by an upright post set permanently into the stern thwart and if their timing and confidence were up to it they were able to step neatly ashore at the top of a wave just before the boat sank behind them into a deep trough.

The whole island supports five thousand people and the British taxpayer supports the whole island; for with the dying of the flax industry there is no exportable product at all except postage stamps, and almost no tourism. Jamestown the capital was strung along the narrow bottom of a dry steep-sided ravine that reached far back up into the hills. I had the feeling that if anyone should sneeze he should do so quietly or the whole crumbly mountainside might come crashing down on top of Jamestown. Such a thing happened years ago as the local people are fond of recollecting and many people died in the avalanche.

A fortified wall lay across the narrow valley at the seaward end. This was built in Napoleon's time to discourage any French expeditions that might be bent on rescuing the emperor, for of course it was here on St. Helena's uplands that Napoleon was held after Waterloo. Just inside the gateway was the Castle where in a dusty little government office we changed a traveller's cheque and paid our "port dues," a peculiarly British invention imposed as it is in England on any overnighting yachtsman who happens to drop his anchor on the sea bed, but at least in friendly destitute little St. Helena we could not possibly have begrudged the few dollars they asked.

The attractive little town had a timeless unsophisticated charm about it. We wandered through it till we reached a branch road that doubled back up the south side of the valley to the heights above and from there descended the 699 steps of Jacob's Ladder back to The Castle. I then picked up a couple of loaves of bread at the bakery while Katie laundered a few things at the water tap by the landing and we returned aboard on the watchman's ferry just in time to see *Tryste* appearing round the end of the island. Quickly we rigged a line between the shrouds and set the laundry dangling in the breeze to give the impression of long-established residence.

"Hello *Tryste*. How good to see you!" Katie called as the trimaran came within hailing distance. "But wherever have you been? We've been ever so worried about you."

Several taxi drivers pursued us next day with their services so that we could visit Longwood where Napoleon spent his last years in easy if not luxurious captivity. *Tryste's* crew were keen for us to join them in a taxi charter but I was reluctant to cash the necessary extra traveller's cheque at The Castle and felt anyway that we needed the exercise and would enjoy the walk much more. Jacob's Ladder had shown us how out of condition the easy voyage from Cape Town had made us. So we walked.

St. Helena is a dry cindery desert at sea level but the rains fell nicely enough in "the country" as the folk in Jamestown call the green uplands. The climate and the air gradually changed as we tramped up out of the hot valley. Grass, flowers and bushes took the place of stones and we came up eventually into pastures and cultivated gardens and long hillsides of New Zealand flax. It was a long way to Longwood but every climbing crooked mile was worth it. The French consul in charge of Longwood was absent at the time but the garrulous local caretaker showed us through the fine old house himself, sparing us no detail of what he knew of the Corsican and his last years in the rustic and remote spot. We staggered back to Jamestown in the evening and by the time we returned on board we were ready for bed.

In one of our forays through Jamestown, Katie and I encountered a short jovial woman called Dot who ran a cafe, a primitive little back street affair frequented by the down-at-heel and also, according to the graffiti on the walls, by every cruising yachtsman for many years. Dot was a thorn in the flesh of the more respectable element in Jamestown. "Free love and good times," she reminded us, "are the recipe for life." Her other recipes were just as good, especially her spicy, deep fried, thyme-tested fish cakes. Before leaving we stocked up with a good supply of these. We stayed only four days and nights and then *Tryste* and *Nanook* together recovered their anchors and sailed away.

A Russian spy ship bristling with electronic gadgetry had come into the anchorage on our last day and as we sailed out past her she dipped her red flag to us, a salute which we returned. This was the only time any large ship ever so honoured us.

Tryste accompanied us for a mile or two down the coast and then after a final farewell we went our separate ways on different courses slowly diverging until we were lost to each other. This was the last we saw of the Haighs on *Tryste*. They were bound for the West Indies and home via Panama; we were "rolling down to Rio." It had been fun cruising in their company and for a few hours after, we both longed to forget Brazil and alter course instead for Barbados. *Tryste* returned eventually to the Canadian west coast. Strangely enough although she had spent five years in her travels around the world, only seven months of that time had been outside of the Pacific.

Nanook was now bound south of west. From a glance at the map it might appear strange to be going all the way north from Cape Town to funny little St. Helena when the main object is to get to Rio. But the fastest sailing time between two points is not necessarily over a straight line, and to follow such a direct or great cirle course from Cape Town would take very much longer than detouring far north and following the trades. Out of the southeast the winds bowled us along at 135 miles a day and exactly as we expected them to do, they slowly backed around day by day from the quarter directly onto the stern. Then we really were rolling down to Rio. Still, imperceptibly the wind edged more into the north until at last a week and a thousand miles out of Jamestown I hauled the mainsail in and gybed over to the starboard tack.

The weather stayed fair and life took on a featureless monotony so that it was sometimes nearly impossible for us to remember what it was that we did with ourselves the day before. Perhaps one of us would remember something and say, "Oh of course you made pikelets" or "Don't you remember? You stopped the leak in the heads."

We continued to indulge in prodigious meals and since it was Katie's ambition to do the navigating for our last ocean crossing she undertook all the daily calculations. The only incident of note during this time happened one night when having neglected the retaining lee cloth on my bunk, I landed hard against the support bar several feet away and then hard down again on the cabin sole, but even this bone-breaking flight did nothing more than provide me with two or three unimportant bruises.

The winds fell lighter as we moved in tiny daily steps across the wide Atlantic chart and the air became hotter and more humid. On the tenth day in late afternoon sunshine we came up on the Martin Vaz Islands, a small formation of steep rugged improbable-looking pinnacles that stick high up out of the ocean. They were entirely inaccessible, a remote republic of seabirds. I had no chart of them but I was hopeful of a fresh fish around their edges so I steered close in under the brown cliffs, but on discovering that we were in horrifyingly shallow water I quickly altered course. The visible rocky bottom passed on underneath the keel for a long way across an extensive shelf of a mile or so before we were again over the bottomless blue. I found at such times that I was stricken with the same

Arrival in Rio after the South Atlantic crossing. Here *Nanook* passes beneath the Sugar Loaf on her way in to the Rio Yacht Club.

feelings that I would have standing on the edge of a high mountain precipice, feeling both strongly attracted and strongly repelled by the idea of looking down. I caught no fish but instead lost two good lures to some large sharks, a loss that bugged me out of all proportion as for some reason it always did. On the horizon far ahead of the Martin Vaz Islands lay the long high island of Trindade, an inhabited bit of Brazil, but the place offered no prospect of an easy anchorage. It was dark anyway when we came up with it so we kept going.

Seventeen days out of St. Helena in the pre-dawn darkness we passed the light of Cabo Frio and filled our eyes with the sight of the long white beaches and tall green ranges of Brazil. Flanked by bare rock mountains, the dense agglomeration of high rise apartments and hotels at Copacabana rose up out of the sea like a striated white cliff. Behind the cliff stood the peak of Corcovado and to the right, guarding the entrance to the large harbour was the Sugar Loaf.

In the late afternoon we passed the tide-swept harbour entrance, turned sharply to port under the towering bare bulk of the Sugar Loaf and anchored in 2½ fathoms well out from the Iate Clube do Rio in Botafogo Bay. Suddenly, from being "alone, alone, all all alone" out there on the empty Atlantic we found ourselves in one of the world's most stunning anchorages, surrounded by a roaring, excitingly beautiful metropolis, fringed with green jungle and white beaches, divided into many parts by sparkling bays and tall, bare, convex mountains that reared up with collars of green over the white magic city.

Here we stayed for a month. The Iate Clube do Rio extended their privileges to us. This elegant club occupied half a mile of prime water frontage in the heart of the city close under the Sugar Loaf. It had a great complex of buildings catering to the boating and social needs of Brazil's elite. The place offered no encouragement to the common herd. Quite apart from the heavy monthly dues it cost $10,000 just to join so that took care of the riff raff. We were anchored on the outside of a sizeable fleet of elegant yachts, all of them maintained by full-time professional crews. Ashore there were restaurants and repair shops, bars, swimming pools, slipways and car parks. There were armed guards at the gates, a resident doctor, several hundred yard and catering hands and for every suave grey-haired Latin tycoon there was a bevy of beautiful golden-skinned girls.

But the Rio Yacht Club didn't have them all to itself. The whole city seemed to be filled with beautiful brown girls. They covered the beaches, these magnificent nymphs, in the siesta hours and late in the sunny afternoons. The closer you got to a sandy beach the more you saw of them and the more of them you saw. The Brazilians have perfected the bikini down to a narrow black membrane trimmed to the barest few square inches that nature here and there insists upon. All the rest is deeply tanned, lithe sensuous skin. The bikini was accepted on the streets so long as something else was worn over it. So for that purpose the towel, intended more for wearing than for drying, was slung low on the hips like a Polynesian *pareu* and pinned in front. Katie, not to be outdone by all this beauty, scoured Copacabana until she came up with her own outfit which instead of the more common fore-and-aft strings sported little plastic picture windows at the sides.

Rio was an exciting place filled with vitality. Every day we rowed ashore to absorb more of it. We joined the downtown throngs and wandered the back streets and marvelled at the architecture and lost ourselves on the buses. We rode cheap taxis all over the place and we walked for miles through the mountain tunnels and highways to Copacabana or round Botafogo Bay past the drinking fountain statue of the little boy urinating fresh water for the thirsty, round into the enormous outdoor food market where we greedily filled our sail bags with vegetables. We gazed down at the spectacular city from the summit of Corcovado where the 40 metre high statue of Christ raised its arms high above our beautiful anchorage.

But if Rio was exciting it was also noisy, polluted and perilous. The long curving auto route from the club to the city centre was a race track for tens of thousands of Volkswagens and colour-coded buses. You crossed a street at the peril of your life. It wasn't much better at the anchorage for the Brazilians operated their power boats the way they drove their cars. They roared straight out from shore at top speed through the fleet and woe betide the dinghy that didn't get out of the way. The weekends were the worst. The professional crews then left off their polishing and painting and changed into whites. The owners came aboard by launch with guests and food hampers and servants, and while they relaxed in deck chairs, the crewmen attended to the menial chores of steering and handling sails and setting canvas. Wealthy Brazilians live very well indeed.

After some time in this rarified society it was a pleasure to meet the English single-hander Brian Craigie-Lucas who anchored his modest little engineless sloop *Mouette* nearby. Brian had sailed down from the English Channel for a few months in Brazil and planned to return to England when his money ran out. He'd been in Rio for several weeks and suggested to us that when we tired of our spectacular setting we would find better company at the small Iate Clube Icarai in one of the bays of the quieter eastern shore across the water from Rio.

In this, Brian wasn't wrong. Although his anchorage was still within sight of Rio across the water it was a peaceful almost rural spot compared

Seventeen days out of St. Helena, *Nanook* approaches the high hills of Brazil while Katie gazes in excitement at the Sugar Loaf and the white ramparts of Copacabana.

to the metropolis. *Mouette* and *Nanook* lay in a large bay surrounded by high hills and fishing villages. The commodore of the Iate Clube Icarai came aboard to present us with his burgee and the hospitality of the club where a family atmosphere prevailed and where we soon came to know many of the members. One of these was a white-haired old man who called us "his children" and who became known to us in turn as Vovo, meaning grandfather. Vovo took us on long drives in his car far along the coast and back into the hot hinterland, and we in turn took him cruising about in the harbour.

Brazilians tended to regard a yacht more as an occasional pleasure and symbol of wealth and status than as a serious means of conveyance over long distances. We were therefore something of an oddity to our friends at the I.C.I. For a mere two people to actually cross an ocean in such a small thing was incomprehensible to them. Why endure such hardships? There are such things as ships and planes if you must travel so far. This reminded us of the point of view of Mediterranean people. Why travel so far, and why anyway choose the least comfortable and most perilous of all methods? Perhaps the attitude was understandable in the Brazilians. They had their paradise already (or so it seemed to us). Why leave it?

We attracted a certain amount of newspaper publicity and this resulted in our meeting two very delightful people, Thais and Roberto da Silva, both reporters for the big daily, *O Globo*. They came aboard first for an interview and later for a sail and they took us many times to their apartment in Rio which was just a short stroll from the yacht club in Botafogo Bay. For that reason as well as the imminence of Carnival we established *Nanook* again on the Rio side and were pleased to find that by then *Tiare* had arrived in from the South Atlantic crossing. It was grand to meet Paul and Vaiea again, and Liklik Paul, especially since *Tiare* had had the bad habit of arriving in nearly every place west of Thursday Island just as *Nanook* was leaving. This had happened at Cocos, Rodrigues, Mauritius and Durban, and when it again happened at the entrance to Cape Town's harbour on New Year's Eve we very nearly turned back in with them.

There were a number of other foreigners in by then, all having, like us, timed their arrival for Carnival. There was an American trimaran with a crew of eight and a British concrete ketch with a crew of six, both rather unhappy boats as tensions ran deep between members of their crews. Then there was the Durban boat *Brer Terrapin* which was on her maiden voyage after five years a-building. But though she was not over-crewed like the others, *Terrapin* had an incompatible wife, or the wife perhaps had an incompatible house, so Rio was the end of the voyage. One boat for sale.

Apart from this assortment, there were also several very large yachts taking part in the Whitbread Round-the-World Race. We went aboard some of these and got to know their crews. The yachts were absolute

Katie steers amongst the islands of the Baia de Ilha Grande.

racing machines and no expenses had been spared on them. The two big sheet winches on *Great Britain II* had cost as much money as I had paid for *Nanook* herself. We went sailing one day on *G.B. II* and we were fascinated to find such a different attitude to sailing and to life generally in this company of racers. They seemed for example not to be profoundly affected that a crewman had been lost overboard on passage. It was very unfortunate of course, but it was something that had to be expected when you are holding on to all your sails, genoa and all in a Force 10 gale down in the roaring forties. They had been to sea a long time and they looked forward to the finishing line in England and the celebrations to follow. In every sense their world was a different thing from ours, and for me they were welcome to it.

For several days, samba schools practised along the streets gathering crowds of happy supporters about them and their infectious rhythms drifted out over the water of Botafogo Bay. And then suddenly Carnival was on, four days and four nights of continuous noise and colour and gaiety, of endless processions and non-stop partying. A spectacular ball was held in the yacht club where it seemed that all the rich of Rio had congregated for an all-night affair of incredible spectacle. The men dressed simply enough but the women were decked out in a bewildering variety of unbelievable costumes from long flowing silk robes and feathers and towering headdresses and sequined trains many yards long down to narrow strips of dark cloth trimmed to an inconceivable brevity. There was no pause in all this merrymaking and people slept where they fell, on the streets, in the parks or propped up in doorways. After 48 hours we gave up, rowed wearily back to *Nanook* and collapsed.

In a few days we were off again, bound west past the fashionable beaches of Copacabana and Ipanema, past bare-rock islands and green mountains to the bay of Ilha Grande, an intricate unspoiled cruising area of islands and protected waters sixty miles from Rio.

The currents and light winds of this coast saw to it that we arrived inside the large bay after dark, 24 hours out from Rio. I anchored just within the entrance to the bay but on finding that we were in a strong tidal stream that gurgled menacingly over a nest of rocks directly downstream of us I decided that I'd sleep better anywhere else and we reanchored a mile to the north well out from the land that surrounded us. Even there the tide added seven miles to the log before morning when we hauled in the anchor and set off over the smooth blue waters of the bay, waters familiar to *Nanook* for she had taken the Frosts to Ilha Grande six years earlier.

She now took us into a cosy green cove carved out of the high green flanks of Ilha Grande, and there we anchored. A house was set back in the trees behind the sandy beach at the head of the cove and as I stood head and shoulders out of the companionway hatch furtively studying the place with the binoculars I found a figure under the trees studying us in turn through his own binoculars. He came hurrying down to the beach, launched his runabout and was soon alongside.

"*Safari Too*," he cried. "*Nanook*, I mean. I'd know her anywhere. Welcome back to Ilha Grande. You must be Katie and Maurice."

This then was Peter Thuridl the German American who had thrown in his career as an airline pilot for a few acres of Brazil. Pat and Kurt Frost had spoken much to us of the delights of Ilha Grande and of Peter and the good times on his banana plantation, and it was this image as much as the appeal of Carnival in Rio that had enticed us downwind off the beaten track to these shores.

"She looks as beautiful as ever," Peter said, rubbing his hand over the varnished capping rail. "Make yourselves at home ashore. There's coffee in the kitchen, showers out back and books in the living room. Be ashore sometime after six for cocktails and we'll eat at eight." And with that he sped off to spend the day fishing.

Peter's plantation has become a haunt of the off-shore cruising set who divert to southern Brazil, a place like the home of Arty Kraft of Aneityum, the Preeces of Fergusson Island or the Angermeiers of the

Galapagos, a place with open doors, spoken of with affection in cockpits on the other side of the world.

We put in a full day of work for a change. I poured fresh pitch into some of the deck seams, and dived overboard to clean barnacles off the hull while Katie tackled a mammoth laundry ashore with plenty of *borrachudas* to hurry things along. These infuriating little insects are the curse of the bay, the one flaw of paradise. *Borrachudas* ignore ordinary repellants. They bite silently and painlessly especially around ankles and feet. The bites swell, become itchy and septic and in no time you have a fine harvest of sores for a souvenir. Katie also attracted the attentions of Claudia, Peter's big woolly monkey from the Amazon. Claudia was particularly fond of laundry days and kept walking off with wet underwear or stealing the soap. But at sundown she made up for it. We came ashore and lounged on the verandah where a dugout canoe with one side cut away hung suspended from the roof by chains. Claudia picked hopefully through Katie's hair for livestock and then curled up on her lap while we sipped our *cuba libras* and talked with Peter long into the night about far away places. We had to leave the next day for the town of Angra dos Reis so we said goodbye to Peter and promised to return in a week's time. When we walked back down to the cove we found the dinghy on the beach to be half full of bananas.

Next morning we sailed slowly round the coast to the Isle of Monkeys where we enjoyed a couple of hours scrambling over the windy hilltops ashore. It would be hard to find a more attractive area than this and one so unspoiled despite its proximity to a metropolis of many millions. Yet seclusion, tropical verdure and grand vistas are not money in the bank. Several peasant families lived ashore and we were startled at their poverty. These folk lived in little huts of their own making and coaxed a subsistence out of the tired soil on the steep hillsides. They seemed to be silent and introverted, unwilling to make any contact, hopeful that we might pass by without noticing them. Brazil still endured the two extremes of great wealth and widespread poverty and perhaps these people regarded us with our fine sailing yacht as belonging on the other side of that unbridgeable gulf.

Would that we were! It was well over four-and-a-half years since we left Canada to go cruising and our funds were running rapidly out. Plainly we would have to return soon to our old haunts in the Arctic and begin the unwelcome uphill struggle to find a job, settle down ashore and start our savings again from scratch. I had spent over $150 in Rio on a long phone call via satellite to the Canadian Arctic to discuss job possibilities with the school authorities there. But that exercise seemed to have made no impressions at all, excepting on the man behind the counter at the telephone company office in downtown Rio. "*Senhor*," he said as he gathered up my wads of paper money, "you are always welcome here."

But the evil hour of settling down after all those years of freedom was not quite yet upon us, and to help stave it off a while longer we hurried on our way to Angra dos Reis because there at midnight we had arranged to meet our *carioca* friends, Thais and Roberto. These two had dreamed up a scheme to write an article describing our voyages and to have it published in *O Realidad*, one of the nation's leading magazines. We could share in the proceeds. I had suggested that they come cruising with us in the bay of Ilha Grande where in a couple of days we could firm the article up, pick out a few slides to illustrate it and at the same time have a lot of fun exploring the area together.

They showed up in Angra as expected and they brought with them one of Brazil's top professional photographers, Armando Rosario, who declined our invitation to a bunk and settled instead into a hotel. "It is on the expense account," he assured us.

Armando and his Nikon were waiting on the beach at dawn before the rest of us were half awake. It was another fine clear day but one without wind, a good day for photographing anything except a boat under sail. So we powered up and down the mainland coast anchoring here and there for a swim or a drink until noon. By that time Armando had exposed three 36-exposure colour films and his thirst was in full flower, so we anchored in a pretty bay and went ashore for lunch at the elegant yacht club, an outpost of the Rio Yacht Club, all five of us on Armando's expense account.

Such a "lunch" should have laid us all low for the rest of the day but an onshore breeze came up and Armando's instincts with it, so away we went under full sail, tacking up and down amongst the green wooded islands in sparkling sunshine and laughing as the salt spray flew over us. The afternoon wind freshened and when *Nanook* heeled sharply to the gusts, Thais gripped the cockpit coaming tightly and cried "Please Maurice. Will *Nanook* tip upside down? Tell me truth!"

By evening another four films were finished and *Nanook*'s anchor was back into the mud at the bottom of the harbour of Angra. We should not have been unduly hungry but Armando complained that the exercise in his index finger had given him an appetite and insisted that we all go with him to dine ashore. This we did, the five of us meandering through the cobbled streets to Angra's best sea food restaurant where Armando ordered only the most expensive dishes and threw in a selection of the best wines from the German districts of southern Brazil. I never had the luck to discover a cheap restaurant in Brazil, and this one was more expensive than most. Yet the bill which seemed colossal by our standards was breezily consigned to Armando's long-suffering expense account and after a couple of convivial hours with us he wished us all goodnight and went off in pursuit of his chauffeur for the road back to Rio.

Thais and Roberto stayed aboard for another two nights. The gypsy life

Motoring out from Angra dos Reis in the Baia da Ilha Grande, Katie searches for a breeze.

of the sailor was a new world to the fun-loving *cariocas*, a dangerous and alien life it seemed to them, but one full of excitement and discovery. We took them farther afield exploring the inlets and beaches amongst the many little islands of the bay while Thais scribbled volumes of notes for the article and Roberto struggled manfully with the daunting task of teaching me to speak Portuguese.

Eventually they left for their reporters' desks in Rio and we were left alone again to relax into our old routines, to wake-up when we wanted and go where we wished with no thought for the schedules of landsmen, to cook only what we felt like cooking and to eat as much or as little as we required, to work or to play as the fancy took us, to wear anything at all or nothing at all, and to talk without restraint about anything or to relapse into companionable silence.

Slowly *Nanook* meandered back to the coast of Ilha Grande and we explored a variety of anchorages. In some places access to the shore was denied us by the insects that came out in eager droves to plague us as we approached so that we had to retreat below in the humid thundery heat behind a series of screens. But in other places the mosquitos and *borrachudas* permitted me to wander ashore and even to meet some of the local people and to inflict on them my kindergarten Portuguese. One old man asked me to his house to try a cup of his home-grown coffee so he could introduce his family to the *commandante do barco*. He lived in a small house with walls of mud and saplings and a roof of palm thatch. Banana trees and corn grew nearby. Water flowed down from a spring high on the hill through a long series of bamboo tubes feeding into each other and draining onto the stones near the doorway. It was pleasing and attractive from the outside, but the real story was inside where the silent woman of the house seemed to struggle despondently with her dull and difficult existence, trying to make do on a dearth of everything except flies, dirt and children. I gave a pocketknife to the man as a parting present and left, wondering how people can be so different from one place to another. Here they had as much as most Polynesians and more than many. How happy they could be if only they had the energy and laughter of the South Sea folk. Perhaps the spirit is missing. "What poverty," I wrote in the log, "but what coffee!"

There were three yachts in Peter's cove when we came to anchor there, the two South Africans *Brer Terrapin* and *Windsong*, and the large German yacht *Magdalena*, and in honour of these visitors Peter had hoisted the South African and German flags to the top of the flag halyard on his most prominent coconut tree above the beach. The honour in *Magdalena*'s case was an uncertain one, for the flag displayed was that of the old German Empire, whether as a joke, a snub or an act of defiance I was unable to detect. At all events the maple leaf was hoisted in this company only moments after we came into view and again we were welcomed to Peter's hospitable threshold where we collapsed with coffee, showered at the side of the house where the walls of a little alcove dripped with bougainvillea, and in the evening gathered on the lawn with Peter and all his company of cruising folk to share in a feast of mussels from the south coast of the plantation and to talk about distant places, times and friends. It is worth sailing a thousand miles of empty ocean for such moments.

We finally left Peter's place early one morning with a lump in our throats and an embarrassment of bananas in the dinghy, bound the sixty miles back to Rio. It took us 33 hours to get there.

By this time it was mid-March. We had to be in Canada early in the summer and plainly we had to get moving. Even so it took us a week to get away from Rio. Armando surfaced from his den in Copacabana to take us prowling the back streets in search of diversion and lounging at sidewalk tables to sip cognac and watch the girls along the Avenida Atlantica. We in turn took him sailing out of the harbour and across to the beaches of the eastern coast. We took Thais and Roberto harbour sailing too, and also Vovo who had driven us far and wide outside of the city and had taken in hand for us the problem of a blocked exhaust pipe that had to be cut open, cleared of carbon and rewelded.

Before putting to sea we went over to anchor away from distraction off the little fishing village of Jura Juba, and while there I went aloft in the bosun's chair to make my usual pre-passage survey of masts and rigging. I then discovered that the starboard spreader on the mizzen had rotted badly away at the end where it butted against the mast tangs. One bolt still remained in firm wood though and as I was in a frenzy to get away I decided to delay repairs until we reached Salvador.

For six weeks the weather had held clear and sunny but now as we put out towards the harbour entrance the air had a sticky humid feel to it and the lowering grey skies smothered the mountains and cast a blanket of gathering gloom over the city which matched our own spirits exactly. *Nanook* was carried rapidly forward by a strong ebbing spring stream, past the fort at the entrance where an ominous swell crashed heavily over the smooth rocks in the gloomy premature darkness. There was hardly any wind and the rain began to splash around us.

"Let's go back," said Katie, nearly in tears. "I don't like it. Just for one more night in Rio."

I looked all around. To starboard a break in the clouds revealed that statue of Christ up there on Corcovado holding its arms out as if signalling to us. And then it was lost again. What did that mean? "Come back, you fools, come back"? Perhaps I should after all fix that spreader. A fierce squall struck at us out of the southeast. I put the helm over and we plunged against the stream back to Jura Juba where we lay all night listening to the thunder and the pelting of the incessant rain.

Vovo found us there next morning after driving round the bay from the club to investigate, and called to us from the shore as I was glueing a new splice onto the spreader. He came aboard to gaze at my handiwork and he clucked his disapproval that we should think of putting to sea in such weather and in such a state of disrepair. Katie laughed and said there was no need to worry; the statue on Corcovado had appeared to us just at the right moment and had sent us hurrying back.

"Ah yes," Vovo replied, "it is always up there standing on watch and I'm afraid it sees a great deal more wicked folly than yours."

Having put ourselves downwind of what Katie called "the Brazilian Bump" for the sake of the fleshpots and allure of Rio, we now had to face the long struggle to the northeast against wind and current. We were short of time and my impatience to get moving wasn't soothed any when it took us an agonizing three days and two nights of light head winds and scorching heat to reach Cabo Frio, a mere sixty miles from Rio, and even there we could do no better than sail close hauled off to the southeast while the coastal current bound for Argentina carried us rapidly sideways the wrong way.

There was no point in staying on the coast. It offered hardly any shelter whereas well offshore we could hope to find less current and less north in the trade wind so we stood offshore and by next morning according to the log we were "out of sight of land, powering slowly along on the port tack, close hauled to a faint northeasterly and falling ever further south of Cabo Frio."

But then the log becomes more cheerful:

26th March. Miracles! At dawn I found that we were sailing slightly north of east. The wind had backed a little and in a few hours it was blowing out of the north and we were then on the theoretically desirable course of 070° magnetic. The wind has gradually continued round into the northwest. Such winds according to the pilot charts hardly ever happen. It's still backing slowly and *Nanook* is roaring up into the northeast at six knots. The watchkeeper on Corcovado must still be taking care of us.

27th. What a lucky break this wind is. We're still bowling along on course exactly where I expected to have a hard slog upwind. 135 m. noon to noon with a nice quartering wind, grey skies.

28th. Our helpful wind eased last night and went into the south, finally dying away in a burst of rain today at noon. Now a gentle easterly is coming in and the sky is clearing. Meanwhile the B.B.C. news on shortwave has given us a clue to the unusual winds. Brazil has had widespread flooding both in the northeast and south of Rio. Eight hundred bodies recovered from one town alone. Katie has painted the dinghy. I replaced a Primus burner and did a bit of sealing along the coachroof coaming. Both dreaming of the West Indies. 96 miles noon to noon.

30th. Less said about the past two days the better. Lots of rain (did the laundry this morning in the cockpit with rainwater as it fell), grey skies and very little wind except under the squally clouds. Result: only 90 miles made good in 48 hours. There must have been some wild offshore weather recently. We've had a plague of moths on board today as well as a number of dragon flies and two species of land birds. Yet we're 140 miles from land.

Four days later, days of frustration that had best be left unrecorded, at dawn of the 13th day out from Rio, we edged forward against a foul tide past the lighted headland of the Bahia de Todos os Santos and came to anchor off the Bahia Yacht Club on the outskirts of the beautiful black city of Salvador.

We should have stayed in Salvador a year, but we stayed only four days. Money was running out and time with it. I began to get the uneasy feeling of being caught at last at the outer edges of the inescapable vortex of work. Wistfully we strolled the streets of the splendid city, or, bending over the chart table, poured our eyes over the chart of the great bay with its islands and estuaries that would have to go unexplored. At any rate until Next Time Round. If only we'd seen more of Salvador we might have begun to satisfy a craving we had to stay on and on; if only we'd seen nothing at all we could have continued north in the happy ignorance of what we were missing.

We had looked forward to meeting *Tiare* again or *Mouette* who'd both left Rio before us. But *Tiare* had spent 21 days struggling north so she stayed only 36 hours in Bahia and had left the day before us. Brian on *Mouette* was still somewhere to the south. We learned later that it took him 28 days to cover the distance from Rio sailing hard against the coast. Our few tribulations seemed like nothing by comparison.

Still, we were not without the best of company. As we lay at the uneasy anchorage of the yacht club a small catamaran came in from a day sail inside the bay, lowered her tan sails and lay to a little hook nearby. A voice called to me as I lay sprawled on deck writing letters.

"Hello Maurice. Hello *Nanook*."

I waved and rowed over to investigate. Ivo van Laake himself! Ivo, the young Dutchman with the golden curls whom we had last seen in Fiji, who had crossed the Pacific from San Francisco to Auckland in his funny little plywood sloop and who was remembered by many a brown skinned girl in the islands that lie between the one city and the other. We'd expected never to see him again. Yet here he was living on the coast of Brazil.

Ivo and his young American friend Reid Stowe had worked together to build their little craft *Tantra* in South Carolina. They had then crossed the

Nanook catches the afternoon onshore breeze on her way back to Rio from Ilha Grande.

Atlantic to Portugal, followed the northeasterlies down the coast of West Africa and crossed from there to Brazil. *Tantra* seemed to us hardly more than a pair of canoes lashed together. For living quarters the two companions had a hull each and they needed it for there was hardly room in either to do more than contain a few basics and to allow the occupant to stretch out and sleep.

A wooden grating formed a low deck between *Tantra*'s two hulls. Here at sea the boys kept watch as the ocean swept visibly by beneath them through the grating. Here also in harbour under an awning they sat cross-legged by the hour painting in acrylics and carving in wood, cooking their vegetarian meals or meditating in the fashion of the eastern religion that appeared to have seized them, a religion that seemed as kindly and gentle as they were themselves, for while it abhorred cruelty and excess it still allowed them to enjoy a sundowner with us, to swim naked about the harbour, to take their mulatto girls out sailing or to lie at anchor with them through the soft black nights of Bahia.

How good to be young and free! In all our voyaging we never met one yachtsman who could confirm for us that the bigger the boat and the larger the income, the happier was the life on board. Ivo and Reid seemed very hard up even by our modest standards and certainly I wouldn't have wanted their catamaran for even the briefest coastal passage. Yet we never met any cruising sailors who got more simple joy out of life than those two.

> When all the world is young, lad, and all the trees are green,
> And every goose a swan, lad, and every lass a queen,
> Then hey to boots and horse, lad, and round the world away,
> Young blood must have its course, lad, and every dog his day.

After only one night at the yacht club we were driven from that exposed spot by an ugly black onshore squall and with *Tantra* we went scurrying off further into the bay to the shelter of the main port. We anchored close by an old island fortress where slaves were once received off the ships from Africa to be held there until market day, and our minds cast back to Dakar where we had seen just such a stone fort where the black captives were held before shipment to the New World. We tied our dinghy to the stone steps and wandered all over the gaunt, decaying, empty old fort. From the slit windows of the big empty cells we gazed out over the harbour to *Nanook* and *Tantra* and the high-masted sailing luggers trading at the waterfront, and up to the big vibrant voodoo city that we had to leave so soon.

Katie bought a few charms from the handicraft market, I bought bananas from the trading boats in the harbour and coarse manioc flour to throw over the stew the way they did in the sidewalk restaurants. Sixteen

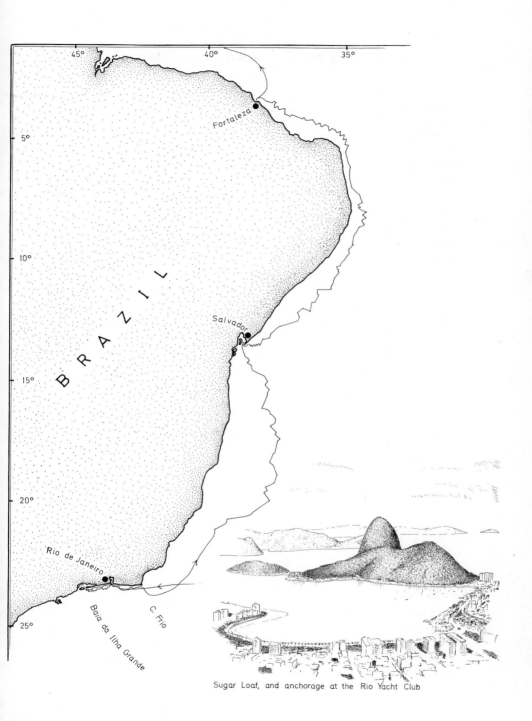

45°   40°   35°

5°

Fortaleza

B R A Z I L

10°

Salvador

15°

20°

Rio de Janeiro

25°

C. Frio

Baia da Ilha Grande

Sugar Loaf, and anchorage at the Rio Yacht Club

loaves of bread, four more bottles of rum and we were off, carrying the ebb stream past the yacht club, past the lighthouse and out to sea.

If the passage from Rio was difficult the passage from Salvador was more so. The glow in the sky from the lights of Salvador were still visible the second night out. But the next day, 8th April, I was able to record "Progress better and the wind a little steadier from the east. Katie busy sewing flags. I've put a big patch on the genoa and developed black and white films, two last night, two tonight. I have to wrap the bottles of chemicals in wet towels and set them outside in the wind in order to lower the temperature for processing. Chicken from the Salvador *supermercado* still on the menu."

There was no entry for the next day but on the 10th I wrote "Bloody awful conditions the past two days. No trade and conditions like the doldrums only worse. Last night we were treated to an appalling downpour that went bucketing on and on for many hours—nearly all night, millions of tons of the stuff thundering into the sea like an endless cascade. How can the heavens hold so much water? All this of course is accompanied by a heavy slop from ahead and lightning zapping into the water around us while the skies split open with awful bursts of thunder. I rushed around attaching copper wires to the shrouds with bulldog clips to ground the rigging directly to the sea but whether of any earthly use I don't know. Being close to the coast we cannot just pull the hatch closed and forget about it. There's shipping to watch out for. Today has improved slightly but we're now being treated to a series of squalls, plenty of wind, then no wind, with all the appropriate sail changes. Am having to nurse the mizzen as the repaired weather spreader isn't to be trusted."

Next day I recorded "Terrible night last night with fearful squalls and countless sail changes." But things then gradually improved while we came slowly up to the easternmost tip of the continent. We remained out of sight of land but each night I was able to identify various towns along the coast by the glow above them in the sky. Near Recife I found that the South Equatorial Current that flows across the Atlantic and bends southwest down the continental coast was at this point split into two, sending a branch to the north and carrying *Nanook* along with it.

We had intended to stop in Natal to rest and reprovision but our arrival would have been in the early hours of darkness and I didn't like the idea of putting any trust in the charted approaches with their silting depths and undependable lights. The Easter holiday was about to begin anyway and provisioning might have been difficult so we kept going bound for Fortaleza on the north coast. Katie gave the remaining loaves of Salvador bread another quick scorching over the stove to keep the mould at bay.

Nanook was no sooner back on course than an unexpected west wind came at us off the land. "Now what?" asks the log.

A local trading scow heads out under sail past the old island slave fort in Salvador harbour.

14th April. Lousy day, lousy weather. Sailed north with the westerly abeam all night in a hideous rainy black hell of a night—and since then have been enduring sullen leaden skies all day, hard on a northwest wind right in the . . . teeth. How can this be? The pilot chart doesn't even acknowledge the possibility of such a wind. I left the galley sea cock open today and flooded the shelves behind the sink with sea water including three precious loaves.

15th April. Dear God, will we ever reach the lovely northeast trade and the distant West Indies? Not at this rate. At present I don't even know if we can make Fortaleza. It's an exposed anchorage in these conditions for one thing. Still very overcast. Sat on the coachroof today for 1½ hours waiting to catch the sun through the cloud cover. The northwest wind continued all night and early morning. At 0900 a tremendous black front came along giving us a beam wind from southwest for a while and then dense overcast, steady rain, light airs and universal gloom. We ought to be going into Fortaleza but how can we when we're in the grip of an unknown current, can't get the slightest glimpse of the sun and the D.R. radio is packed up?

Had a fright this morning just before that front arrived. I was a bit puzzled that there should be whitecaps on the horizon to the

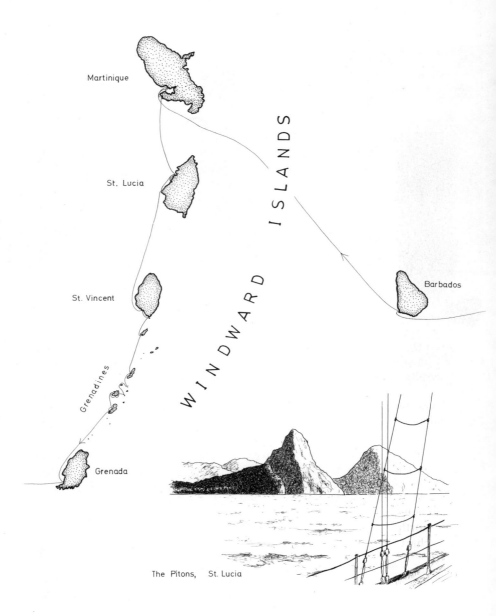

Martinique

St. Lucia

St. Vincent

Grenadines

Grenada

WINDWARD ISLANDS

Barbados

The Pitons, St. Lucia

northwest and more close by. Soon after I noticed a large patch of brownish water near the edge of normal wind-blown water to the north, and suspiciously smooth oily water on our side of it. Visibility was poor and I immediately assumed we had been carried onto the coast inside one of the offshore reefs. I rushed below for the lead, but finding no bottom at 21 fathoms I knew by the nature of the coast that we must be quite clear of any dangers. The "reefs" turned out to be a line of convergence between two strong currents.

17th April. No entry for yesterday and now I cannot recall even the slightest incident that might have occurred. It's almost as if yesterday never happened. At any rate the squally northwest wind persisted right on the nose and still does. We are always close hauled and always under cloud, low and dark or high and white. Navigation is a real trick. Can't do any boat work to speak of but Katie keeps herself amused sewing flags.

But two nights later *Nanook* reached Fortaleza after all and found anchorage in the dark amongst the fishing fleet. After half a night of real sleep we surfaced to gaze around at a nondescript city to the west, sandy hills to the southeast, a commercial port nearby and a picturesque if run-down looking lot of fishing boats festooned with bamboo traps.

Our last slice of Salvador bread was shared for breakfast and then to our delight a red-hulled sloop appeared from north of the docks and *Tiare* came and anchored beside us, Paul, Vaiea and Liklik Paul waving furiously. They rowed over to sit in our cockpit and to share with us the recollection of the tiresome passages from Rio, and then we went off laughing happily together, catching a bus into the city to do our shopping, to send off some mail and spend our last cruzeiros at the *panaderia* and the *supermercado*. Bread, cake, bananas, biscuits, sugar, a pineapple and a roasted chicken.

Fortaleza had nothing about it to delay us further and we left in the afternoon, some hours ahead of *Tiare*, for the passage to Barbados. The afternoon sea breeze died as the sun sank in a rosy glow over the Amazon.

XVIII

Higher Latitudes

"Red sky at night, sailor's delight." Perhaps, we thought, the elusive northeast trade was not far away. For a night and a day we motored slowly north through green coastal water under a clear sky looking in vain for a hint of wind while a strong counter current on the continental shelf carried us southeast. Yet a regular tradewind swell rolled gently onto the starboard bow and late on the second day the first few fingers of a light northerly came along to darken the mirror of the sea. The mainsail which till then had been serving merely to dampen *Nanook*'s roll, filled and went to sleep as I set a course to the northwest. The other sails were hauled up, the diesel was silenced and the only sound in our suddenly quiet gentle world was the chuckling of the water at the bows as *Nanook* settled into her stride.

The northerly remained with us and I soon knew it to be the outermost edge of the trade wind. By the next morning we were in blue water and the wind had turned slightly east of north. By imperceptible degrees it edged further and further into the east. The windvane was adjusted several times a day and the sheets were eased out inch by inch until we were at last rollicking along with a fresh wind just forward of the beam. How *Nanook* loved it!

On the fourth day I wrote in the log "We crossed the equator just half an hour after the noon sight much to our satisfaction."

"During the afternoon we found many thousands of tuna desporting all around and keeping pace with us. Scores of them were surfing inside each big wave. I put the line overboard with a stout hook and white rag and immediately got a bite. However that got away with the hook as did two more before I dragged a huge one into the cockpit. Have removed big fillets each side and thrown head, skin and skeleton overboard. Tastes really beautiful, just like chicken.

"We've had a big tanker exactly abeam of us all day since 0200 this morning. Black smoke pours periodically from her stack. I guess she has engine problems as she's only doing 5½ knots. Our day's run 130 miles."

Each day the wind went a little further east and the noon positions on the chart stretched out until we were covering 170 miles a day. Watches were kept around the clock and though we saw little shipping we had reason enough to stay awake. The nights were clear and starry and a "thousand thousand slimy things" glowed and sparkled in our wake. One night we came very close to being clobbered by a tug that was towing a barge far behind it. We were on a collision course. The various lights shown by the two vessels exactly in line were thoroughly confusing. The tug at last recognized our lights and my urgent flashes on the mainsail, and took avoiding action to starboard. But at first I thought from the appearance of lights on the tow that she had turned to port so for a moment I turned that way too until I realized what I was doing and put about again with a beating heart. The signal lamp was working overtime. The barge took a long time to respond to the new course and with a rush of white water she loomed up and swept very close by us behind her lethal invisible towing wire. It was another close call. We could so easily have been smashed into oblivion and it took us some hours to recover from our fright. The recollection of things like that help keep you awake on even the dreariest of watches.

At last the trade wind eased and went behind us and with the dry weather and easy motion I spent long hours raking out the old tar from the deck seams, hammering the cotton caulking home and pouring in new pitch. It was a messy job but a satisfying one too for *Nanook* had a series of Canadian winters ahead of her and we wanted her to be tight. Katie meanwhile dragged out all the musty-smelling clothes that littered our lockers and washed and scrubbed and rinsed until our ship looked like a floating Chinese laundry.

On the 2nd May I wrote in the log, "A day of deck raking with Barbados on the horizon. The wind died away to nothing by noon. Katie in her enthusiasm for clean laundry and in anticipation of a landfall has sucked out our water tank completely dry, so for want of both wind and fresh water we are motoring in towards the land."

And a later entry: "After coasting the familiar Bajan shores we rounded the buoy off the Hilton Hotel just at sunset and anchored finally in Carlisle Bay amongst various other unknown yachts. How blissful after the long struggle from Rio to be motionless at last with the chain hanging into the limpid water and *Nanook* for a change going absolutely nowhere. Log from Fortaleza 1552 miles."

"We have now crossed our outward bound track and accomplished what so many sailors have dreamed of doing; we have sailed around the world."

Katie steers as a dawn squall sends *Nanook* hurrying through the Dominica Passage.

We were, as I said, out of water and rather than wait on board till morning for official clearance I rowed ashore to the yacht club to fill up a couple of plastic jerry cans. But in the dark I misjudged the swell that rolled in onto the beach and a big dark wave lifted the dinghy up on end and tipped me and my jerry cans into the surf. This had never happened to me before, so remembering that a winning skipper is traditionally dunked by his crew I took it as a kindly-meant compliment from the sea that I had at last circled the globe, crossed my tracks and returned finally to familiar ground.

A few people were sitting drinking beer on the upstairs balcony of the club and as I thrashed around retrieving oars and jerry cans from the water I heard them laugh gleefully at my upset. I emptied the dinghy on the sand and as I groped around in the dark beneath the balcony looking for the fresh water tap, I overheard someone above me saying, "A lot of them are like that in the Caribbean. They fly down here for a couple of weeks of charter cruising, but they don't understand a thing about seamanship. They can't even row a bloody dinghy, some of 'em."

For several days we remained in Barbados and enjoyed the funny little place as much as ever. The prices were a shock, but everything else seemed just as it was, the same untidy market, the same polite ladies selling bananas and limes on the streets, the careenage crowded with trading boats, the lilting accents, the red Canadian apples and the pallid Canadian tourists.

Tiare caught up with us two days after our arrival. Paul and Vaiea were bound for Paul's home in Belgium but his heart was not greatly in it and we knew that the winter would bring them back to the Pacific where they belonged. We were sorry to bid them goodbye but we were bound ahead of them through the Leeward Islands and we saw *Tiare* no more.

For thirty hours *Nanook* roared along with wet decks and a beam wind, and then gybing over to the port tack she swept through the wind-whipped channel between the flat pancake island of Marie Gallante and the wild green mountains of Dominica where we came in to anchor off a palm fringed beach in Prince Rupert Bay.

We might have lingered in that beautiful spot for a week but that we'd received confirmation in our mail in Barbados that Bob and Audry Christie, old friends of our days on Ellesmere Island in the High Arctic had accepted our invitation for a cruise and had arranged to fly south to Antigua to meet us the next day. So off we set again crossing the Dominica Passage at midnight and into the long tiresome lee of Guadeloupe and out of it again without stopping into the choppy blue seas

The crew enjoys the final trade wind passages through the Leeward Islands before heading north for Canada.

for the long hot sunny salty ride over the ocean swell to English Harbour in Antigua.

We'd read of English Harbour enough not to be surprised at its total shelter and its beautiful protective bends that open up so suddenly out of the bluffs along the island's south coast. What we hadn't expected was to find fully 167 other yachts in there ahead of us. Antigua's Race Week was in full swing, and yachts of every description littered every corner of the little harbour. Gone indeed were the lonely remote corners of other oceans. We felt suddenly projected onto the doorsteps of North America, a part of the holiday crowds, the owners and the girlfriends and the crews who jet in from Boston, Toronto and Miami, who drink beer and talk with loud voices and wear funny hats and Bermuda shorts and ostentatiously nautical shirts.

Nanook squeezed into a spot opposite Lord Nelson's old docks where she could lie to the wind without touching her neighbours. We washed the salt off ourselves, rowed ashore to find Customs and ran smack into the Christies. It was five years since we'd seen them last but they were as refreshing as ever and we felt happy to have them at last on board.

For four days we stayed in Antigua. The old dockyard of Lord Nelson's days were full of interest, setting aflame Katie's passion for British imperial history. She led us eagerly through the stone museum and the sparsheds, and old magazines and gun ports overlooking the harbour approaches, and she went off scouring the hills for broken shards and bits of rubbish that had become treasure to her for having lain there for a century and a half.

Bob, the geologist, was more fascinated by the shells and coral growths and the variety of marine life in the water, tropical forms that he had found often enough in ancient sedimentary deposits in the Arctic.

"What are those round dark things?" he asked, pointing down towards a colony of spine-covered sea urchins.

I explained. "But for goodness sake don't touch them," I warned. "Those spines are sharp."

Later that afternoon, we were swimming ashore to a beach when Bob who had reached shallow water let out a fearful yell. He had set his foot down squarely onto a sea urchin. In pain he half hopped, half floundered onto the beach and turned his foot up for us to see a huge crop of fine brittle black spines embedded all over the sole. We tumbled him into the dinghy and rowed him back aboard. He was in some pain. The tweezers brought two or three of the spines out but most just snapped off and stayed put. A quick row around the anchorage yielded a few folk remedies, vinegar, hot melted wax, lime juice or urine applied topically to the affected area. But the only one that seemed worth taking seriously was a good slug of rum, prescribed orally. Bob limped about thereafter over on the side of one heel and I felt worried that his geological field work

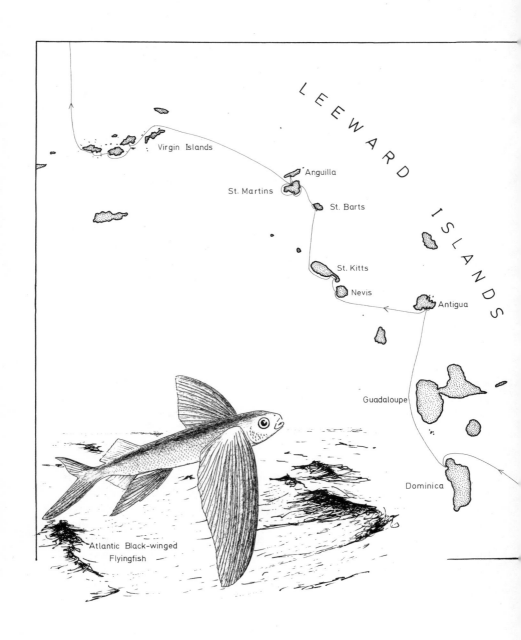

L E E W A R D   I S L A N D S

Virgin Islands

Anguilla

St. Martins

St. Barts

St. Kitts

Nevis

Antigua

Guadaloupe

Dominica

Atlantic Black-winged
Flyingfish

along the northern extremity of Greenland in the coming summer might be affected. But the pain slowly went and the limp slowly disappeared and he was nearly back to normal by the time he and Audrey flew off back to Canada.

We were not long in tiring of the Race Week crowds, so one day before leaving Antigua we sailed *Nanook* out and set her plunging upwind into the swell till we had tacked up to the entrance to Indian River, an inlet similar to English Harbour but with a rather more difficult entrance, less room inside and, of all miracles, not a solitary other yacht there, nor even a house ashore. Scrambling over the hills behind the inlet amongst cactus and thornbush we marvelled that such a dry island could be so close to the rain forests of Guadeloupe, Dominica and the other islands to the south. But in this chain every island makes its own climate according to its elevation and in the case of Antigua what might once have been moderately fertile land (witness the crumbling remains of old sugar cane windmills on the heights behind Indian River) had been further reduced to a dusty wasteland by goats.

We sailed on past Montserrat to Nevis and St. Kitts. Entry at Nevis was effected at the post office at Charlestown where we handed in our Crew List. The guy said "Have a nice visit," and that was it. Leaving St. Kitts before dawn we splashed our way north to the happy little French island of St. Barts where in the once-Swedish port of Gustavia we had to moor fore and aft to keep out of the way of other yachts.

Barbados rum sold in St. Barts for five dollars a gallon, cheaper than in Barbados itself, so I took the trouble to load five one-gallon jars of Mount Gay into the dinghy and stowed it securely in the bilges, padding the jars carefully with sheet rubber.

At the leeward end of St. Barts is a bay protected by wild craggy hills where one of the Rockefellers has himself a mansion. *Nanook* lay overnight in this remote spot before sailing on to St. Martin, an island half Dutch half French with an invisible and meaningless frontier across its middle. In Barbados I'd received a cheque from an American magazine for the sale of an article so while in Philipsburg on the Dutch side I bought a Nikon camera with the proceeds. Philipsburg is one of those honkey-tonk duty-free places well-suited to its purpose of catering to shiploads of tourists, but it had nothing to detain us and we sailed on across the clear channels to the flat island of Anguilla and back to Baie Heureuse on the French side of St. Martin, a deserted spot where we all went skinny dipping, and finally to Marigot the French capital where we said goodbye to Bob and Audrey. They had been aboard for two weeks, much longer than the usual limits imposed on tolerance by the confines of a small boat. But instead of breathing the usual sighs of relief to be on our own again we felt rather empty after their departure and had to put it all behind us by making an overnight passage to the Virgins.

Dawn of May 23rd revealed Virgin Gorda and various other bits of land appearing on the horizon to the west, and before long *Nanook* was rolling along down Sir Francis Drake Channel leaving a lane of islands on either side until we reached Roadtown the British capital where we entered and cleared all at once, bought a loaf of bread and a chicken and sailed away again to a more peaceful spot on Peter Island.

The Virgin Islands are littered with coves and beaches and attractive anchorages. The wind is just right for sailing. The islands are interesting and beautiful wtih a history of buccaneering and the distances are modest. No archipelago in the world could be found that so well suits the needs of vacationing charterers as the Virgin Islands. The only problem therefore is that everyone else is there too. Bare boat chartering is big business and rented sailboats criss-cross in every direction. We found on arriving at Peter Island that we had to moor fore and aft because ten other yachts were spending the night in the same confined anchorage.

Nanook made her entry into U.S. territory in Cruz Bay and several days later we arrived at Charlotte Amalie on St. Thomas, our last tropical anchorage. We had planned to go on to Puerto Rico, Haiti and the Bahamas, but a phone call to Canada revealed that if I wanted a job back in the Arctic again I had to be in Halifax in mid-June for interviewing. That gave us just barely enough time to get there, sailing direct from St. Thomas. So we sadly stowed away all our unused charts of the big islands to the west and went ashore for the last time to collect our clearance papers which certified that the "Master of the Canadian ketch *Nanook*, mounted with no guns, navigated with two men, foreign wood built, bound for Halifax and having on board ballast, hath here entered and cleared his said vessel according to law." The dinghy was stowed and lashed, the sail covers removed, the fresh food stowed away and the balance bar set up in the saloon. There remained nothing to do but recover the anchor and set off on the long passage home. It all seemed so final that we hated to get on with it.

Katie hauled up the main while I washed the mud off the CQR and lashed it to the bowsprit, and away we sailed through the islands to the west and round the western end of St. Thomas where a sharp turn to starboard brought the trade wind onto the beam. I engaged the vane on its new setting and off *Nanook* flew across the trade wind bound home to Canada.

For several days the wind held fair out of the east while I occupied myself with pouring more pitch in the decks and tracking down leaks. Katie was intent on sewing up the end-of-voyage "paying off" pennant, a long ten foot triangle with a white polar bear on a blue field.

The third day out we covered 152 miles. The next day 143 miles, then 98, then 77 and then 29. The trade wind was behind us and we were entering the horse latitudes and the perpetually circulating waters of the

Sargasso Sea. Yellow sargassum weed lay in clumps everywhere on the sea surface. Great splotchy lanes of the stuff ran across the blue in the direction of the wind. We passed occasionally through whole fields of it. And as we exhausted the trade wind and our pace fell off, the little yellow crabs that inhabited the weed patches would strike out towards us to investigate us, completely miscalculating our speed of two knots or so, and two equally yellow fish took up station on the stern.

Watches were maintained strictly through every night. Steering was simple enough; the course was due north so the pole star lined up with the main mast led us straight for Halifax. We made no westing, so noon sights of the sun were taken at the same time by the clock every day.

To our surprise we saw no ships and I began wondering if this really was the North Atlantic. "Perhaps," Katie suggested, "the Bermuda Triangle has taken care of them all." The seas were flat and the only things of interest were bits of congealed tar, a floating 45-gallon Shell drum, the occasional seabird and the omnipresent weed. Soul music and ridiculous weather forecasting from Bermuda irritated me and we began tuning in to the Canadian shortwave services. Even the French and the Eskimo programmes sounded good.

On the 8th day out I recorded, "Better progress, 72 miles by noon. Typical horse latitudes conditions, dry with a high broken cloud ceiling and a slightly cool edge to the air which has us sitting around naked and complaining of how cold it is, or putting on long pants and shirts and enjoying the novelty.

"We have now drawn abreast of Bermuda. Just as well we hadn't set our hearts on stopping there as the wind is from that direction, northeasterly earlier, now east and going a bit south."

The tedious work of filling all the deck seams was finally finished in the next three days and some drizzly showers showed the seams to be tight. Katie's bunk however still took its usual portion of every shower. I'd sealed every possible chink I could see or imagine and still the maddening drip, drip, drip continued.

"Infinite fiddling," Ed Boden used to say "will fix every problem." I went back at it while the bedding hung to dry in the rigging and finally spotted two tiny pinholes in the black rubber sealant of the cockpit coaming. Once they were filled the leak stopped.

The days became longer, starting at 0430 and ending at 2000. We put blankets on our beds, and our bucket baths became exercises of self-will. Yet even at 38° north, twelve days out, the weather was still surprisingly tropical.

Four Mother Carey's chickens stayed around us for three days and a pair of pilot fish kept station at the bows. The sargassum weed had a lifeless appearance to it by then but it still persisted. But like Lord Nelson holding the telescope to his blind eye, we saw no ships. The smokey atmosphere was the only thing reminding us that the U.S. was not far upwind.

At the end of the second week with only 200 miles remaining I recorded, "We noticed this afternoon a definite change on the sea surface ahead, the meeting of two currents, the Gulf Stream from the Caribbean and the Labrador Current from the Arctic. Having crossed over the line of convergence we found the cold inshore current to be much smoother, moving along as it was with today's northeasterly wind, and naturally much colder, 49°F at the surface compared with 67° in the Gulf Stream. The wind today has been blowing more or less parallel to the line of convergence and I was interested to notice that in the vicinity of the convergence the wind locally trends northerly or even northwesterly, exactly like a land and sea breeze effect, bending around to blow locally from the colder onto the warmer surface. This plus the fact that we want to enjoy the benefit of the Gulf Stream for a while longer has caused us to tack back out across the line and into the warm water."

My next entry, June 15th, reads: "Terrible progress but otherwise a pleasant and unusual day. The wind has fallen to the very faintest air out of the northeast. Not enough to ripple the surface of the glassy sea, yet it does keep the sails filled and we can still manage two knots or more surprisingly. The seas are flat, the sky clear and sunny and the whole world seems utterly still. Birds are everywhere and the water is filled with plankton. A big pod of pilot whales has kept us company for much of the day. It is so quiet that we can hear their exhalations from a mile or more away like distant gunfire.

"Last night was *very* cold indeed, and today was only tolerable once the sun got busy warming up the boat. We have the stove burning away steadily. Even so everything is ice-cold to the touch. The inside of the hull is covered in beads of condensation and the cameras got steamed up when I brought them out to photograph the whales and the sunset."

The next day was one of unrelieved greyness under a smothering dank blanket of heavy overcast and fog. My little direction finding radio no longer worked and no sights were possible all day, but I found early in the afternoon that we were in soundings of 35 or 40 fathoms. I took this to be the Roseway Bank. We still had the same light northeasterly wind but the forecast was calling for strong southeasterlies so in anticipation of night and onshore winds I put *Nanook* about onto the offshore tack. But as I did so I noticed that the fog was lifting slightly above the sea surface and that a thin grey line appeared to the north and northwest. So we went about again and sure enough this slowly materialized into land. Not any land that we'd ever seen before, but Canada anyway, our land of milk and honey, and I began singing and jumping up and down on the deck in excitement as the thin line resolved into a landscape of spruce-covered promontories and islands, inlets and shoals and wave-lashed rocks. By

Beyond the northern edge of the Gulf Stream, calm quiet water reflects
the late afternoon sun—and an approaching fog bank.

then it was evening. On our small scale chart of the southern coasts of Nova Scotia we could identify none of what we saw ahead of us, and finally with darkness and fog both lowering around us and the threat of all this becoming a lee shore before long, we went about again and with heavy hearts put out to sea. A careful reconstruction of the various bits and pieces of land sighted convinced me later that we'd been in the approaches to Sable River, but it is unsafe to navigate on educated hunches and it was then too late anyway.

Three more days of fog and cold had to be endured at sea. The grey blinding blanket was bad enough, forcing us to be especially wary of shipping, but the cold chilled us to the very marrow and even the thought of taking our watches in the cockpit was intolerable. Unlike the lube oil in the diesel our blood hadn't yet thickened up enough and we cowered under the hatch warming our hands over the stove and listening fearfully for the unwelcome sound of foghorns. The wind lashed at us and the chilling spray flew across the decks and into our oilskins whenever we looked out. There was no point in sailing anywhere. We lay hove-to having once won our sea room. The echo sounder helped reassure us that we were staying well clear of the coast.

Each day the faithful old brass sextant lay at the ready in its box on my bunk just in case the fog should lift. I felt a great affection for it. It had found nearly every bit of land we ever wanted it to, but it couldn't point our way through fog. I'd paid five pounds for it once to an American in England who had inherited two sextants with his newly acquired yacht. We were told later that it was an antique and I resolved to have it checked over at the National Maritime Museum in Greenwich that summer to determine its history. This I did and the museum staff established it as having been made in London in 1825. Presumably it must have served many years on square riggers. The staff took photographs of it and recorded its details in their own files. What surprised them was not that the sextant had still existed unknown to them but that instead of being in the hands of a collector of such things it was still doing service around the world under sail.

The dense wet pall around us persisted even after the wind eased and went into the southwest. Every ten minutes we put a head out to strain for a hint of fog horn or engine or breaking surf.

We hadn't cared for the strong onshore wind but at least we could move in it when we wanted to and when it fell away to a faint air I worried at our lack of decisive manoeuverability in the event of an imminent collision. The diesel would be needed then but it was hopelessly stiff as if lubricated with chewing gum and I had to keep the kettle filled with hot water to pour into the cooling jacket in case I might have to start it up. Boiling water would always do the trick. Several times I had to resort to this time-consuming procedure when ships could be heard approaching.

Seated on the starboard settee, Katie shows off a few of her collection of courtesy flags.

At journey's end, Katie offloads a quantity of carvings and artifacts from New Guinea onto the dock at the Royal Nova Scotia Yacht Squadron.

Two of these occasions were logged as "close calls." I never actually saw the ships; the fog took care of that. Even our bowsprit was dim enough. But they were both close enough for me to be able to hear voices clearly on the bridge and the clanging of the telegraph. Our reflector was hoisted of course. Perhaps they saw us on their radar. However that could never be anything better than a comforting possibility.

It was cold. We put on everything warm we could think of. Katie tore up a towel and fashioned it into pairs of warm socks. We warmed our hands on cups of tea and our insides with soup. We snuggled together in my bunk for warmth. Yet still we were cold. And we were scared. We were weary of the sea and we felt afraid that even yet we might not make it, here on the doorstep of our destination. Ships bellowed dismally in various undiscernible directions and as unobtrusively as possible so as not to betray my apprehensions to Katie I untied the lashings on the dinghy; the liferaft was underneath.

But on the fifth day of this awful fog the pale disc of the sun glowed at last through the clammy gloom bringing with it a promise to burn off what it could before sunset. One position line, I prayed to the disc, that's all I need. Just let me get one shot.

He who would learn to pray,
Let him go to sea.

By early afternoon enough of the fog had dissipated and enough of the water surface had appeared to view that I could make a reasonable guess at the exact level of the invisible horizon. This gave me a position line passing close through the shoals and ledges around Sambro Island in the approaches to Halifax. Sure enough, sailing in along the direction of this position line I at last spotted far ahead the dim grey silhouette of Sambro, its identity confirmed by the high lighthouse standing on top of it.

Nanook slowly closed the distance. The lower edges of the mainland gradually emerged underneath the lifting blanket. Buoys began appearing in all the right places clanging their bells or hooting their whistles at us in welcome and in the sunshine of late afternoon, with all the fog gone, *Nanook* came in to the piney freshness of Ketch Harbour just out of Halifax and lowered her anchor.

I know of no freedom so absolute as the freedom of the small-boat ocean sailor. Returning to a life among the Eskimos of the Arctic was a matter of mixed emotions. The sudden adjustment to living in a house and going to work as other landsmen do, even Arctic landsmen, at 8:30 every morning, Monday to Friday, and conforming to all the understood imperatives of a middle class consumerist society, these things took some adjusting to, and for Katie the adjustment was even more painful than it was for me. Worse was the wrenching sadness of having to part with *Nanook*. We had no thought of selling her but plainly she could not accompany us into the Arctic and we had no choice but to leave her on a mooring at the Royal Nova Scotia Yacht Squadron where, we knew, many new-found friends were keeping an eye on her.

It was all inescapable. By the time we flew out from Halifax bound for Baffin Island we were down to our last few hundred dollars, and we knew that if we were ever again to recapture that precious freedom it would have to come from another long stint in the Arctic.

So by November, *Nanook* had snow on her decks while Katie and I were engulfed again in the gloomy darkness of the long Arctic night far above the Arctic Circle, several worlds away, it seemed to us, from the days and years behind us when we were barefoot and carefree, when all the world was ours and every day was Saturday.

A World to the West is not a technical book and I do not intend to repair that deficiency by adding technical appendices to it. There is now a multitude of how-to-do-it books on the market for the would-be sailor, and most of these deal far more adequately than I could with the elements of sailing, seamanship and navigation. However, it occurs to me that there

There is a tradition that cruising yachts returning home from abroad fly the courtesy flags of all the countries they visited. With 47,000 miles behind her, *Nanook* lies here in Halifax with 35 flags hoisted.

may be many readers who are themselves interested in making long-distance voyages and who would be interested in examining *Nanook* a little more closely as one particular example of a long distance sailboat, and learning a little more than the text reveals about how her crew planned her voyages and carried them out. Ships are as different from each other as are sailors themselves, and comparative studies of different yachts, and the different techniques, ambitions and attitudes of those who dwell within them, can be as instructive to the novice as they are fascinating to the experienced voyager. With all of this in mind, I am offering these few additional pages of information for those who may wish to interest themselves in such detail.

APPENDICES

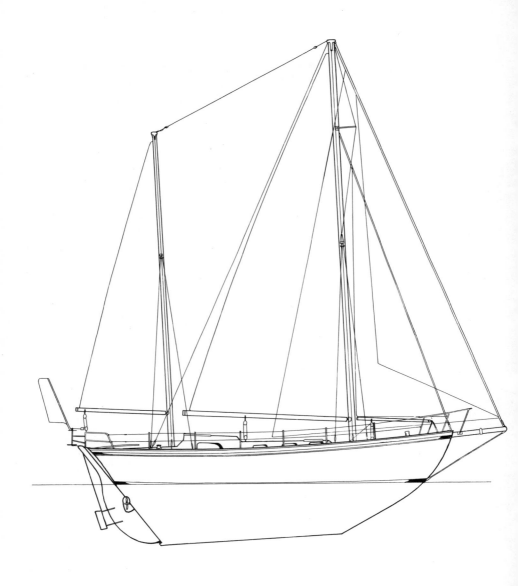

APPENDIX 1

A Description of Nanook

When Katie and I bought *Nanook*, we believed her to be fairly close to our ideal of a solid, competent and sea-kindly long-distance cruising yacht suited for two people, and our years aboard her have fully justified that original faith.

She is 34 ft. 2 in. overall on the deck, 28 ft. at her designed waterline, with a beam of 9 ft. 8 in. and a draft of 5 ft. 9 in. She is constructed largely of the dense Australian hardwood spotted gum, carvel planked and copper fastened. Spars and topside planks are of Douglas fir, and the decks are of Australian white beech which everyone mistakes for teak.

Interior joinery work is attractively done in contrasting light and dark woods, mostly mahogany and ash, all varnished. The deck and coachroof are supported and reinforced with heavy grown-oak knees. The cupboards and lockers in the saloon we found adequate for the purpose of carrying all the food, clothes, books and general supplies needed for lengthy passages.

Forty gallons of fresh water are carried in a fibreglass-sheathed plywood tank located under the stove and starboard quarter berth. This tank, together with ten gallons in jerry cans, was easily sufficient for all the long passages. A thirty gallon diesel fuel tank is fitted on the port side between the lazarette and the quarter berth, and this proved to be much larger than strictly necessary for a little engine that would run up to six hours on one gallon of fuel. A full tank could be expected to last us for nearly eighteen months. Kerosene was stored in plastic containers in the bilge, and had to be fed into the stove and lamps by means of a plastic hand pump.

The galley has a two-burner Primus stove pivoted for and aft in a stainless frame. A heavy lead bar bolted to the bottom of the frame provided adequate ballast, and it was quite unknown for kettle or pot to leap out of this stable gimballed platform. Behind the stove are cup hooks, plate racks and a deep saucepan bin where, with the help of a towel or two, pots and pans can be securely stowed without the annoying clinking that occurs when such things are free to move about in a seaway.

Alongside and forward of the stove is a 40-inch stainless counter with a sink set into it beneath the fresh-water pump. We have no pump for salt water. Cutlery and other odds and ends are stowed in three drawers underneath the counter, and more food lockers are provided beneath these drawers and behind the stainless counter.

In a seaway, the cook, like the navigator on the other side, is supported at her stern by a horizontal stainless bar. The whole arrangement of the galley is simple and adequate and Katie is in the habit of declaring that she has never seen a galley on any other boat that would suit her better. We both have a clear preference for kerosene as a fuel because of its safety, dependability and availability in remote places, but this preference seems to run counter to present-day trends. A small folding oven can be set over the Primus stove, but we found in practice that baking can be carried out well enough in a covered frying pan set over an asbestos sheet.

The navigator has a chart table across from the galley. This measures 29 by 40 in., large enough for Admiralty charts to be laid out open on it. A generous chart drawer lies underneath this, but we were in the habit of storing there only those charts that covered our immediate cruising area. All other charts were stored flat underneath the quarter berth mattresses. The short-wave radio receiver is located behind the table, and above that is a large cupboard with sliding doors where we keep the sextants, chronometer and sight reduction tables and other navigation volumes, as well as typewriter and correspondence files. A small electric light on a flexible arm is placed over the table, and the Sumlog dial which records distances sailed and speed in knots on a 1 to 10 scale, is located against the bulkhead abaft the table where it can be seen easily from the cockpit. I liked the navigator's arrangements as much as the cook liked hers, and the only problem in having such a generous table area was that in port it very quickly became littered with tools, food, flashlights, clothing, paintpots and a thousand other things unless we exercised iron self-discipline in replacing things back to their assigned places, a discipline that the sea itself imposes when on passage.

Apart from the forepeak where a toilet dwells behind a curtain between mainmast and chain locker, the accommodation is quite undivided. Visitors must share the open saloon with the crew, and two can be slept on the settee backs which hinge up to a horizontal position, Pullman style, above the settee seats and alongside the bookshelves. A mahogany table with two fold-down flaps stands between the settees, offset to one side to allow easy passage forward.

The open arrangement often gives visitors the impression of a boat considerably larger than a 34-footer.

Between the self-draining cockpit and the stern is a large space, the lazarette, accessible from either of the quarter berths or through a hatch in the deck. This is where we stowed bulky items like water containers, fenders, lumber, fishing gear and the like.

Nanook carried three anchors, two 35-pound plows which were in use regularly, and a small Danforth that was hardly ever used (not because of its design but because of its size). She has 35 fathoms of ⅜″ chain for the bower, and a four fathom length of chain and 35 fathoms of nylon rode for the other plow. Usually the bower was stowed on its roller against the bowsprit, and though we had no windlass we tended to use this anchor and its heavy chain rather than depend on rope, even when other boats around us used nylon rodes. Whenever a strong wind got up I would double the scope of the chain, and in really troublesome winds I would also get the second anchor down into the bottom, much sooner, usually, than the other yachts around us. While lying in this fashion in very strong winds, I often passed the slack nylon rode of the kedge around a sheet winch in the cockpit in such a way that if the bower should drag and the kedge warp take up the strain, it would cause the noisy winch to clatter and wake me up. Our habitual fretting at least meant that we almost never dragged, and even when the kedge wasn't strictly necessary, I found that I would sleep much better on stormy nights knowing that it was down there.

I have no prejudices in favour of a ketch rig over, say, a cutter, or bermudan over gaff sails, but I still am perfectly satisfied with what we have. Sail changes can be carried out easily with only one person on deck and having a possible total of four sails at any one time, and three of them capable of points reefing, means that I have a large variety of combinations to choose from. I found it easier to drop one sail in a rising wind than to mess about changing or reefing. The only jobs not much appreciated were putting reefs into the main in bad weather, or climbing out in those conditions onto the bowsprit to hand the headsail.

The auxiliary is a 4½ hp Yanmar dating from the mid-60's. It drives a two-bladed propellor on the centre line. It has no integral electrics, but a generator bolted to the hull runs off a belt from the fly wheel. It is really just a primitive workboat engine such as might be used by inshore fishermen in open boats, and as the reader will already have gathered, we regarded it as a bit inadequate. Yet it was incredibly dependable, and for all our frustration at its lack of authority, it always eventually got us where we wanted to go.

APPENDIX 2
Route Planning

Nobody likes working to windward in a sailboat for any length of time or lying idle in a protracted calm. Still less does anyone relish storms, especially those twisting monsters that breed in the torrid late-summer and autumn months in certain parts of the tropics. In planning a long ocean passage from any one island or port to any other it is quite essential to bear these truths in mind and to realize that there is an appropriate time of year to set out and an appropriate route to take. A general understanding of the world's wind systems, which every ocean sailor must have, didn't take any profound effort on our part. We remembered from our elementary schooling that the doldrums of the equatorial belt are flanked to north and south by the northeast and southeast trades, and that these in turn are separated from the westerlies of higher temperate latitudes by a belt of light variable winds. It needed only a little more research to discover that most tropical ocean areas either side of the equator have the nasty habit of breeding tropical revolving cyclones, but that these occur within fairly predictable seasons and areas. On the other hand we needed no reminder that lands lying in the paths of the westerlies, England and New Zealand for example, are apt to be stormy and unpleasant in the winter months. The obvious inference was that we must so time our passages that we would avoid being in any of these areas in the wrong season.

I sometimes feel that the world has been rather nicely arranged by its Creator with ocean cruising sailors specifically in mind, for it all works out rather nicely that one can go from one part of the world to another, using the appropriate wind in its allotted latitude, with time to spare to relax along the way, to repair and maintain the boat, eat of the lotus and admire the island girls.

Here was the drill: First we kept in mind that temperate lands and seas are best during the summer months when the air is warmer and the sea less given to gales, and that lands lucky enough to lie in the trade winds are best during the winter and spring months of their particular hemisphere when the air is less humid and cyclones (hopefully) do not occur. Then by laying off our likely routes, keeping those theoretically prevailing winds as much as possible abaft the beam, and by making allowance for about 100 miles of progress for every 24 hours at sea, we were able to estimate with fair accuracy how long the intervening passages would take and how much time would therefore be left of the season for visiting those lands that interested us and that lay reasonably close to our course. Consider for example the North Atlantic, *i.e.*, all of the Atlantic north of the equator. The lands that lie north of, say, 35° N are in the path of the westerlies, and the seas in these latitudes are far less stormy in summer than in other times of the year, and of course warmer. The best cruising months in those areas whether in eastern North America or western Europe are from about April to September. Less time further north, more time further south. In the trade wind areas, parts of the Caribbean and Gulf of Mexico are subject to hurricanes from July to about early November.

These limitations mean that cruising yachtsmen in the Caribbean at the approach of the cyclone or hurricane season have three choices: 1. Go north and enjoy, for example, the coasts of either the U.S. and Canada or of western Europe. 2. Stay put (or cruise very locally) in an area that offers, in the event of a hurricane, really adequate all-round shelter. Or, 3. Cross into the opposite hemisphere. (In this case go through Panama. Or you could go down to Brazil, but because of the trend of the Brazilian coast you would be close-hauled if not actually beating to get there.) These generally are the three choices one has when confronted with the approach of a cyclone season. On the other hand, the sailor who happens to be spending his summer and fall in, say, New England or the Maritimes, or in western Europe, has only two choices as autumn wears on. Either hole up for the cheerless winter, or go south to kinder latitudes.

Given the generally clockwise circulation of winds and currents in the North Atlantic, these seasonal imperatives result in a constant flow of yachts from western Europe, drifting southward towards the Canaries (or the Mediterranean) with the Portuguese trades from July to October, eastward with the northeast trade to the Caribbean October to February, through Caribbean and adjacent waters December to June, and north to North America and/or Bermuda and western Europe from April to August.

The same general principles can be applied to the other oceans, with two notable exceptions: First, the North Indian Ocean doesn't extend into temperate latitudes and, instead, the proximity of the Asian land mass northwards produces a wet onshore monsoon blowing from southwest in summer, replacing the northeast trade of other months. Second, the South

Atlantic for some strange reason does not breed tropical cyclones at all, so one could remain there all year without having to worry about them. It's also worth remembering that cyclones will practically never occur within 5 or 6 degrees of the equator.

When we first set out from England we carried with us the well-known old British Admiralty volume *Ocean Passages for the World*. This makes for some romantic reading on winter nights for it outlines in some detail the routes to be followed by ships, either power or sail, bound to and from every major port, strait, coast or canal in the world. But the book has big ships in mind, and it doesn't attempt to describe all the varied routes that small yachts would want to follow. Fascinating, perhaps, but rather useless unless one is in need of added ballast. What we found most useful—essential in fact for route planning—was a supply of the excellent Pilot Charts published by the U.S. Navy Hydrographic Office. These charts cover everything a sailor needs to know of the ocean in planning a voyage. Twelve such charts are published for the North Atlantic, one for each month of the year. Other ocean areas are also covered with similar series, either monthly or quarterly. The charts divide the oceans into five degree squares and indicate inside each square the average strength of winds and the percentage of winds from each of eight sectors of the compass. They show the percentage of gales and of calms, the direction and rate of currents, the percentage of fog, magnetic variation, average barometric pressure, major shipping routes, and even the tracks of a few representative storms experienced in that particular month.

By consulting these charts, we were able to establish the kinds of conditions we could expect to find along the way at various times of year, and like other long-distance yachtsmen we became, I think, much more knowledgeable about prevailing conditions, weather systems and seasonal changes in all the oceans than the big-ship navigators who reach for their copy of *Ocean Passages*. It is only by acquiring this understanding that the ocean sailor can properly plan the timing of his passages and the routes he should follow.

APPENDIX 3

Heavy Weather Handling

An excellent way to feel humble is to cling to your wildly tossing little bit of man-made hull, your straw, in the midst of a spectacular storm a thousand miles from land. An excellent way to feel grand and grateful is to survive it. But storm survival is a controversial subject that can inspire a great deal of heated argument amongst ocean sailors. I don't pretend to be an authority on heavy weather sailing, and given the lack of consensus amonst experienced people I cannot help asking, Who is? A wide variety of divergent and contradictory views are held regarding the type of boat best suited to surviving heavy weather more or less unscathed, and the best tactics to adopt to ensure such survival, and in the face of all this controversy the aspiring sailor can only hope to absorb as much as possible of other people's experiences and opinions and to judge what is best for himself when, at last, he is faced with a violent storm.

Some people claim to enjoy storms at sea, just as others (probably with more reason) claim to like celibacy, stewed tripe, Shostakovich or beds of nails. All I can say is that I do not. But if the mighty sea in its occasional moods of colossal rage has any one lesson to teach us it is that of humility, and I think I have learned just enough of that to disclaim that my own findings are the answer for anyone else, or even, ultimately, the best answer for *Nanook*. So it is only with the hope that my ideas, added to those of other people, will be of some help to the interested reader in working out his own salvation that I offer them here.

Sail long enough or far enough and the time comes when you will be caught at sea in severe weather. We found that as the wind freshened so the sails were reefed or dropped one by one. This wasn't ever so much my decision as the yacht's. Quite simply, she *told* us when it was time to get on deck and reduce sail. She did so in no uncertain terms, insisting by her increasingly violent motion, by the roaring of the waves along her sides, her exaggerated heel and tremendous fuss that it was time to do something. I often felt like ignoring it, especially on wild black nights when the very thought of going out and working on the wild wet deck was intolerable. But I could never ignore it for long, and I would eventually claw my way past Katie's concerned and sympathetic eyes and into the cockpit to prepare for the assault on those areas of Dacron cloth. Once the work was finished and I could grope my way below again, *Nanook* rewarded me with her easier motion and her competence and quieter untroubled progress. I could collapse again with an easier mind.

Reefing on *Nanook* is a matter of tying down her lines of reefing "points" on the main, mizzen or staysail with square or reef knots tied under the foot of the sail and finished with a slip knot or bow for easy release later. The only departure from normal practice here was that in the early stages I found it difficult to haul the reef cringles down to the boom with long tackles prior to tying the reefs. It was very much easier instead to lower the sail completely and rest the boom on its crutch before attempting the long wet business of tying down all those points. The only problem then was getting the reduced sail back up again, but with a struggle that could always be achieved.

All of this heavy weather work on deck, incidentally, I did by myself as if I were single-handed. We both much preferred this. Katie often insisted on turning out into the cockpit to haul sheets in or to guide the main boom into its crutch. But the tossing, pitching, slippery deck was no place for Katie and I would not have wanted the worry of her presence there at such times even if she could have been of any assistance. At night the one thing that kept me company was the spreader light. With it, I could manage everything alone, even if it did mean much crawling and groping to and fro along the deck.

I was normally mindful of the danger of going overboard, and always wore a harness over my clothes in bad weather. In the beginning I was in the habit of attaching myself to lifelines or shrouds as I moved about on deck, but I became increasingly troubled by stories of other people going overboard while changing the position of their harness shackle. So I bought a braided terylene line and at the beginning of long passages I tied one end of this to a stern bollard, laid it along the deck against the coachroof coaming to the pulpit, and back along the other deck to the other stern bollard. I was then able to snap myself onto the braided line before I was fully out of the companionway and to go all the way forward to the bowsprit or aft to the steering vane without having to worry about re-attaching myself anywhere. The harness line from my chest was just long enough to reach down to deck level with no extra slack in it, and with that worry off my mind I was able, when moving about, to devote both hands to the demanding business of hanging on. In retrospect, apart from a couple of times when I slipped slightly on the bowsprit, I cannot recall any time when I was actually close to going overboard, and this must be credited to good fortune plus the extra care that comes from being scared!

As conditions continue to deteriorate, the skipper will sooner or later abandon for the time being his first object of continuing on his route and concentrate instead on ensuring the safety of his vessel. With us it was usually sooner rather than later. Basically I had four choices before me:

1. *Heaving to*. This is generally carried out by sheeting the reefed main or trysail hard in amidships and sheeting the storm jib or other headsail to weather. Then with the helm lashed down, the yacht will generally lie quietly at about 50° to the wind, and make a "square drift," that is, slowly work herself across the seas at right angles to the weather. In *Nanook*'s case this generally amounted to about 1 knot of progress. After the torment of pressing on in rough gale conditions, the sudden transformation of life on board to the comfortable and quiet condition of being hove to seems almost miraculous. However I was not often in the habit of heaving to for several reasons. The bowsprit was a tricky place in a gale and I was never happy leaving the jib up in worsening weather knowing that, eventually, I would have to go out there and it would have to come down. On the other hand the staysail, which was more easily raised or handed, would not sheet to weather as it was on a boom sheeted to a traveller. I did sometimes haul the boom to weather and lash it there, and this worked well enough. But the best procedure I found was simply to use the main alone, double-reefed, and the boom hauled slightly to weather by a rope that I secured through the weather scuppers. This kept the sail "asleep" and the yacht in a comfortable state so long as the seas were not great enough to bury our lee decks or to hurl green water into the sail. If that situation develops (and it will if the gale blows long enough and hard enough) then the sails will need to come down for their own sakes if not for the safety of the yacht herself. The vessel may then lie ahull.

Given as I am to a pessimistic view of bad weather I usually felt inclined to anticipate this stage in the development of gales and, instead of heaving to, to go straight from passage-making under reduced sail directly to the second alternative:

2. *Lying ahull*. This simply involved lowering all sail, lashing the tiller "down" or to leeward, with a little elasticity in its lashing to allow some limited movement, and going below to let the wind blow its guts out while we turned in. *Nanook* would take up a comfortable position almost beam on (perhaps 80°) to the weather. If strong enough, the wind in the rigging would ensure that we did not roll to weather unduly on the backs of the waves, and there we would ride, rising and falling easily over the big seas, taking the occasional violent breaker on the beam and, perhaps, over the coachroof but never sustaining any damage from them.

With nothing but masts and rigging aloft, we did of course roll, especially in Mediterranean gales when the short steep seas of Aegean and other waters met us in quick succession. But the roll never bothered

Nanook and we found it easy enough to take. It was nothing like the infuriating ballet we would endure if such seas were combined with no wind, as sometimes we discovered. The long straight keel seemed always to take an authoritative grip on the water, and our lateral drift downwind was so slow as hardly to be noticed, apart from the whirlpools at the rudder and the bow, and the slick of smoother water upwind where an upwelling flow from under the keel disturbed the oncoming seas enough to take some of the sting out of them. This leeway or lateral drift with the resultant slick being left directly upwind was, I found, one advantage of lying ahull over being hove to when the sail would cause the yacht to forereach slowly across the wind and leave that protective slick behind.

3. *Running under bare poles*. If while lying ahull it is felt that the seas are becoming so dangerous that the vessel stands a good chance of being rolled right over by a sea of unusual size, the decision may be made to release the helm and turn her stern to the weather. The yacht will then gather way, and the pressure of wind and waves will drive the likes of *Nanook* along at something like 4 or 5 knots, and occasionally a lot more. In fact if the storm happens to be going your way (as was often our good fortune) why heave to or lie ahull at all when you could simply run under bare poles and maintain your course? (Assuming of course that no dangers lie downwind and that sailing that course will not bring the yacht closer to the projected track of the storm centre as could happen in a tropical cyclone.)

The one thing to avoid when running in this manner is a broach. This is caused by the stern being hurled bodily sideways by a big wave, throwing the yacht on her beam ends, causing her to lose way and leaving her to wallow beam on to the next big one. An alert helmsman will prevent this happening by keeping the seas either directly astern or a little out on one quarter. But on a short-handed cruising boat, round-the-clock alert helmsmen are not easily called up, and in our case I found that the steering vane could be engaged and left to steer us fairly competently downwind at times when we needed the rest that is essential in such times of stress. Occasionally, though, a broach would occur. As our vessel lost way, the steering vane would become ineffective and I would have to scramble to the cockpit and, with the tiller hard over, bring the stern around into the weather before the vane would again resume duty, for to work at all the trim tab on the rudder requires a flow of water past it. If I wasn't too tired, though, I preferred to steer manually myself if only because I preferred being on deck doing something than lying below worrying and listening to the orchestra.

4. *Using sea anchors*. If only a sailboat would lie with her bows into the weather, this might well be the best position of all in a big storm. But that is not so easily achieved. Even with a large sea anchor streamed from the bow, most yachts will tend always to fall off and lie beam on to the

weather. Instead, for generations, many sailors have made use of sea anchors of one kind or another streamed overboard from the stern. The effect is to hold the yacht stern to the seas but allowing her to drift slowly (depending on the size of the anchor and the weight of the storm) downwind. This is a practice much disputed nowadays, some maintaining that the yacht should be left to run unencumbered so as to maintain a sufficient speed to give the helmsman the opportunity to take each wave at the correct angle. I don't quite understand that one, because the use of a sea anchor is a *means* of steering the vessel downwind, not a hindrance to steering. Others assert that by running freely under bare poles (or with a modicum of canvas up) a yacht can be kept ahead of the towering, smashing monster-sea that could cause her otherwise to pitchpole. But that one is even harder to understand because if the yacht cannot sail as fast as the wave then it assuredly cannot move fast enough to stay ahead of breaking water.

It seems to me that pitchpoling, that ultimate horror when the bow digs in and the stern is lifted over and beyond it in a forward somersault, might best be insured against by towing something that offers strong resistance to the wall of water rising behind, and the tendency of the stern to be carried up unresisting. That means a sea anchor.

Nanook however never carried any sea anchors of the usual design. I did once try towing a car tire that served normally as a fender. This worked well enough but it could not be "tripped", *i.e.*, its grip on the water could not be released by a secondary line from on board, and having recovered the thing I never used it again. As the text indicates, my normal "anchor" was a massive manilla warp which resided in the forepeak and which I could carry out of there only with great difficulty. This dreadful thing was streamed in a loop with its ends secured to the two stern bollards, and the effect was to give the yacht an immediate feeling of steadiness and control. With this warp streamed astern, the steering vane could be left to attend to the steering in really violent conditions, with assurance that the warp would prevent broaching. It was a good arrangement and one that I would rely on again in such weather.

Whether the warp, or a series of them, would be enough to save us from pitchpoling in the kind of monster seas that one could encounter in, for example, high southern latitudes, I do not know. Perhaps a combination of warps, together with one or two conical sea anchors, and/or anything else, sails maybe, mattresses or a parachute that could, when dragged astern, serve to hold the stern firmly up to the advancing seas, perhaps this might be the answer. But if it is not, I don't know what is.

In all of the preceding, I have not considered the special problems that have to be confronted when dangers lie not too far distant downwind, but it should go without saying that one would not merrily run off downwind under bare poles when there lies a long lee shore or an intended landfall fifty or a hundred miles, say, to leeward. The storm could worsen, and it could last much longer than you think, so, come hell or high water (and you had better expect both) every mile of searoom must be conserved. My own reaction would be to lie ahull in the hopes of the wind going round into a different quarter, and, if and when it became unwise to persist at that, to raise sufficient sail to work across the wind one way or the other according to whichever direction promised to provide more searoom.

I am inclined to think that the idea of sailing to weather in much more than a Force 9 wind is a bit of a vanity. Thank goodness I have never had to do it.

I found it important, finally, to have an adequate understanding of the way fronts, depressions, cyclones and other weather systems work, how the winds in them circulate in each hemisphere, and how they normally move across the oceans. Armed with this understanding, one can tell fairly well from changes in barometer and wind direction what the low pressure centre is doing, what changes can be expected in the direction of the storm and what nearby shores might therefore become (or cease to be) lee shores.

APPENDIX 4

Provisioning and Finance

Stocking the galley for a lengthy voyage is a task that many first-timers seem to contemplate with bewildered uncertainty. In the Arctic, supply ships came to our remote settlements just once a year, so Katie was in the habit each spring up there of ordering a whole year's supply of food at one time. This experience, I suppose, made her task of stocking *Nanook*'s shelves and food lockers an easy one.

We knew in advance that some countries ahead of us had a reputation for being very expensive or for not having the wide variety of foods available that we might need, and we knew also that some other places, Malta for example, New Zealand, Australia, Christmas Island and South Africa, were said to be ideal places to reprovision as they offered food of good variety and quality at reasonable prices. So as much as possible we attempted to provision ship in such places with sufficient (or more than sufficient) tinned and dried food to carry us on to the next known point of reprovisioning. While in the Mediterranean for example we took sufficient stores aboard for the long haul out to New Zealand, as we believed the West Indies and Panama would be too expensive and the Galapagos and the island groups of the South Seas would be inadequate for our needs.

As an illustration, the following is a list of food taken aboard *Nanook* in Malta and Gibraltar, prior to our sailing down the Atlantic. This was intended for about a twelve months' voyage. In actual practice supplies listed were replenished or supplemented from time to time all along our routes so that the shelves were always well stocked and the variety of them always changing.

359

Tea	5 lbs.
Rice, long grain	14 lbs.
Curry and savoury rice	10 pcks.
Sugar	24 lbs.
Coffee, instant	12 × 2-oz. tins
Milk, "Long Life"	60 cartons
Milk, Nestle's Ideal Evaporated	18 small tins
Milk, Full cream powder	6 × 2-lb. tins
Cream, Nestle's tinned dairy cream	12 tins
Butter	10 x 1-lb. tins
Margarine	10 lbs.
Cheese, Parmesan	8 pcks
Cheddar, fresh	6 lbs.
processed	8 pcks
Soup, dried	19 pcks.
canned	12 tins
Vegetables, peas	35 tins
broad beans	20 tins
French beans	20 tins
tomatoes, whole	12 tins
mushrooms	10 tins
kidney beans	14 tins
beets	6 tins
carrots	6 tins
potato salad	24 tins
baked beans	18 tins
tomato paste	12 tins
Meat, bacon	12 tins
chicken chunks	20 tins
steak (various)	36 tins
minced beef	20 tins
corned beef	6 tins
canned whole chicken	2 tins
roast pork	10 tins
meat balls	8 tins
stuffed pork roll	4 tins
sausages	12 tins
roast lamb	8 tins
Fish, sardines	9 tins
tuna	10 tins
pilchards	3 tins
mackerel	4 tins
smoked kippers	6 tins

cockles	3 jars
mussels	2 jars
oysters, smoked	4 tins
clams	6 tins
Fruit, grapefruit	30 tins
apricots	10 tins
peaches	8 tins
mandarin oranges	20 tins
gooseberries	20 tins
fruit salad	6 tins
rhubarb	6 tins
plums	4 tins
raisins	6 lbs.
General: blackcurrant juice concentrate	4 bottles
peanuts, shelled	2 lbs.
creamed rice pudding	6 tins
marmalade	6 tins
apricot jam	3 tins
blackcurrant jam	4 jars
peanut butter	3 jars
Marmite	2 × ½ lb. jars
cookies, assorted	19 pcks.
crackers, cream	4 pcks.
cereals, various dry	13 boxes
rolled oats	1 tin
salad cream	2 bottles
pickles, assorted	7 jars
tomato ketchup	4 bottles
vinegar	3 bottles
Ovaltine	2 tins
cooking oil	2 gals.
cocoa powder	2 lbs.
salt	2 lbs.
baking powder	2 tins
flour, plain	10 lbs.
macaroni	8 lbs.
spaghetti	4 boxes
rum	16 bottles
gin	12 bottles
Brasso	1 tin
toilet tissue	24 rolls
face soap	6 bars
laundry powder	2 boxes

matches, wooden	12 boxes
methyl alcohol	3 qts.
kerosene	5 gals.

Fresh supplies:

potatoes	25 lbs.
eggs	4 dozen
tomatoes	2 lbs.
grapefruit	6
onions	10 lbs.
apples	3 lbs.
bread	4 loaves

The fresh supplies listed above were intended just for immediate use, and replacement whenever possible. We had no refrigeration or freezer, yet we enjoyed fresh food a great part of our time for we always stocked with whatever products we found available locally in the ports and islands along the way. It is probably true to say that a good variety of tinned and dried foods can now be expected in remote places where once one could hardly find much more on the shelves than bully beef and fish hooks.

From time to time we would discover tins in the lockers that were puffed out by pressure from bacterial action inside. These automatically went unopened to the bottom of the sea.

Preserving   We carried a number of preserving jars on board, and when we found ourselves with a plentiful supply of one kind of food, as for example when we caught a large tuna at sea, we were able to bottle this in preserving jars by processing in the pressure cooker. The food that we bottled ourselves tasted far better than the same food bought commercially in tins. One has to be scrupulous and thorough, though, in following instructions exactly, for improperly processed food can be hazardous. But if done properly it can be very satisfying and the possibilities of preserving food along the way are endless.

Medical supplies   These varied from time to time so an exact list is not possible, and may not be appropriate for others anyway. Generally speaking we enjoyed very good health and apart from the occasional band-aid and the routine malaria tablets that were needed in the western Pacific, we seldom had to use the kit. Generally, this is what it contained:

thermometers
aspirin
band-aids
cotton bandages (5 cm wide)
sterile dressings for treatment of burns
calamine lotion
sunburn lotion
laxative tablets

Kaolin for diarrhoea
antibiotic powder for topical treatment of skin and wound infections
malaria tablets (one taken per week)
penicillin tablets
ampicillin tablets for serious infections *(e.g., appendicitis, pneumonia)*
antibiotic eye ointment
anti-seasickness tablets
Dettol

Spare parts   The long-distance sailor has to be self-sufficient. On the
safe assumption that things would go wrong at the worst possible time, a
thousand miles from the nearest chandlery or competent help, I provided
myself with a fairly wide range of spare parts for the diesel auxiliary, the
stove, the toilet, the Sumlog and the electrical system, and gradually
taught myself how to use them. It would be pointless to list these many
things here, for few other boats would have the same equipment on board
as we had. In addition, we carried a generous variety of bronze and
stainless steel screws, bolts, nuts, hooks, hinges, nails, shackles and the
like. I also kept a few odd pieces of oak and mahogany for the occasional
repair, and some pieces of marine ply. For mending sails we carried two
sailmaker's palms, a wide variety of needles wrapped in an oily cloth,
several spools of synthetic thread of different thicknesses, a roll of dacron
sail cloth and a supply of brass grommets.

I should add that our voyage was entirely unsponsored, that we
financed it completely out of our own pockets, and that allowing for
inflation and changing exchange rates, we would expect at the present
time to need about $5,000 a year to sail and to live in the same style.

APPENDIX 5
Improvements

There's no such thing as a perfect or "ideal" boat, and *Nanook* has her shortcomings like the rest. Following are some improvements that we have either carried out already or are simply considering as a possibility for "next time round":

1. Folding spray hood ("dodger") over the companionway hatch. Such a thing would have saved us many a dollop of salt water on the bunks in bad weather, and would allow us to leave the hatch open during those humid tropical downpours.

2. Conversion of the forepeak to serve as an occasional darkroom. I intend in future to carry an enlarger.

3. Installation of a 10-gallon kerosene tank in an empty space behind the galley counter.

4. I have no trouble yet in hauling our anchor and chain up from eight fathoms by hand. But the time might come, and in anticipation of that I plan to bolt a small manual windlass on the bowsprit between the stem and the samson post.

5. We obviously need a new auxiliary, one rated at about 20 hp, but we have not yet decided whether we can afford such a thing.

6. I am working on (but have not yet perfected) a simple vane release system that can be operated by a person falling overboard. *Nanook* always carries weather helm to some degree, and if at any time the vane could be released, the yacht would tend always to turn round into the wind, spill the wind from her sails and stop. By trailing a long floating rope from each quarter while on passage, and connecting each to a system incorporating a loaded spring that would disconnect the vane from the trim-tab shaft, we could expect that anyone going overboard might manage to stop the yacht himself.

7. Finally, at the first mate's insistence ("I'm not going round the world again without one") I have altered the saloon table to a fold-down

arrangement so that, together with the settee seats on each side and mattresses borrowed from the quarter berths, it converts neatly to a double bed. This would only be used while at anchor. It is wide and spacious, and lies directly under the forward hatch where the trade wind can be caught and funneled below during those long hot tropical nights.

Double berths were once unheard of in the best traditional circles. Such a thing would have been regarded, I suppose, as an offensive and unseamanlike abomination. But a double berth after all is something that most cruising couples nowadays would expect to have installed aboard their yacht, and even the single-hander will, with any luck, before many islands are left behind, meet up with many compelling and attractive reasons for wanting to have one too.